First World War
and Army of Occupation
War Diary
France, Belgium and Germany

50 DIVISION
Headquarters, Branches and Services
Adjutant and Quarter-Master General
23 April 1915 - 30 November 1918

WO95/2813/1

The Naval & Military Press Ltd
www.nmarchive.com
Published in association with The National Archives

Published by

The Naval & Military Press Ltd

Unit 10 Ridgewood Industrial Park,

Uckfield, East Sussex,

TN22 5QE England

Tel: +44 (0) 1825 749494

www.naval-military-press.com

www.nmarchive.com

This diary has been reprinted in facsimile from the original. Any imperfections are inevitably reproduced and the quality may fall short of modern type and cartographic standards.

© **Crown Copyright**
Images reproduced by permission of The National Archives, London, England, 2015.

Contents

Document type	Place/Title	Date From	Date To
Heading	WO95/2813/1		
Heading	50th Division 'A' & 'Q' Branch Apr 1915-Dec 1918		
Heading	War Diary Of Northumbrian Division From 23rd April 1915-30.4.15 Volume I		
War Diary	Steenvoorde	23/04/1915	30/04/1915
War Diary	War Diary Of 50th (Northb'n) Division From 1st to 31st May 1915		
War Diary	Steenvorde	01/05/1915	09/05/1915
War Diary	Poperinghe	11/05/1915	20/05/1915
War Diary	Watou	21/05/1915	27/05/1915
War Diary	L13. Sheet 27	28/05/1915	31/05/1915
Heading	War Diary June 1915 50th Northumbrian Division Vol III		
War Diary	L 13 Sheet 27	01/06/1915	04/06/1915
War Diary	G 21 C Sheet 25	06/06/1915	24/06/1915
War Diary	St. Jans Cappel	24/06/1915	30/06/1915
Heading	War Diary Administrative Staff 50th (North) Division From 1st July 1915 To 31st July 1915 Vol IV		
War Diary	St Jans Cappel	01/07/1915	20/07/1915
War Diary	Armentieres	21/07/1915	31/07/1915
Heading	War Diary 50th Division August 1915 Vol V		
War Diary	Armentieres	01/08/1915	31/08/1915
Heading	War Diary 50th (Northumbrian) Division (A & Q) From 1st September 1915 To 30th September 1915 Vol VI		
War Diary	Armentieres	01/09/1915	30/09/1915
Heading	50th Division 50th (Nbn) Divn (A & Q) Oct 15 Vol VII		
Heading	50th (Northumbrian) Division Administrative War Diary From 1st October 1915 To 31st October 1915		
War Diary	Armentieres	01/10/1915	31/10/1915
Heading	War Diary 50th Division (A & Q) From 1st November 1915 To 30th November 1915 Vol VIII		
War Diary	Armentieres	01/11/1915	12/11/1915
War Diary	Merris	13/11/1915	30/11/1915
Heading	War Diary 50th (Northn) Division Administrative Staff From 1st December 1915 To 31st December 1915 Vol IX		
War Diary	Merris	01/12/1915	20/12/1915
War Diary	Hooggraaf	21/12/1915	31/12/1915
Heading	War Diary From 1st January 1916 To 31st January 1916 Vol X		
War Diary	Hoograaf	01/01/1916	31/01/1916
Heading	War Diary 50th (Northumbrian) Division From 1st February 1916 To 29th February 1916 Vol XI		
War Diary	Hoograaf	01/02/1916	29/02/1916
Heading	War Diary Of 50th (Northumbrian) Division From 1st March 1916 To 31st March 1916 Vol XII		
War Diary	Hoograaf	01/03/1916	31/03/1916
Heading	War Diary 50th (Northumbrian) Division From 1st April 1916 To 30th April 1916		
War Diary	Hoograaf	01/04/1916	12/04/1916

War Diary	Westoutre	12/04/1916	24/04/1916
War Diary	Fletre	25/04/1916	30/04/1916
Heading	50th (Northumbrian) Division Administrative Staff War Diary From 1st May 1916 To 31st May 1916 Vol 14		
War Diary	Fletre	01/05/1916	26/05/1916
War Diary	Westoutre	27/05/1916	31/05/1916
War Diary	Fletre	01/05/1918	26/05/1918
War Diary	Westoutre	27/05/1918	31/05/1918
Heading	50th (Northn) Division War Diary Administrative Staff From 1st June 1916 To 30th June 1916 Vol 15		
War Diary	Westoutre	01/06/1916	30/06/1916
Heading	Vol 16 50th Division Administrative Staff War Diary From 1st July 1916 To 31st July 1916 Vol 16		
War Diary	Westoutre	01/07/1916	31/07/1916
Heading	War Diary 50th (Northn) Division From 1st August 1916 To 31st August 1916 Volume XVI		
War Diary	Westoutre	01/08/1916	07/08/1916
War Diary	Fletre	08/08/1916	10/08/1916
War Diary	Bernaville	11/08/1916	14/08/1916
War Diary	Vignacourt	15/08/1916	15/08/1916
War Diary	Montigny	16/08/1916	31/08/1916
War Diary	Westoutre	01/08/1916	07/08/1916
War Diary	Fletre	08/08/1916	10/08/1916
War Diary	Bernaville	11/08/1916	14/08/1916
War Diary	Vignacourt	15/08/1916	15/08/1916
War Diary	Montigny	16/08/1916	31/08/1916
Heading	A. & Q. 50th. Division September 1916		
Heading	50th Division Administrative Staff War Diary From 01 September 1916 To 30th September 1916 Volume XVIII		
War Diary	Montigny	01/09/1916	17/09/1916
War Diary	Millencourt	18/09/1916	30/09/1916
Heading	Administrative Staff 50th Division War Diary From 1st October 1916 To 31st October 1916 Volume XVIII		
War Diary	Millencourt	01/10/1916	24/10/1916
War Diary	Fricourt Farm	25/10/1916	31/10/1916
War Diary	Millencourt	01/10/1916	24/10/1916
War Diary	Fricourt Farm	25/10/1916	31/10/1916
Heading	50th Division Administrative Staff War Diary From 1st November 1916 To 30th November 1916 Volume XIX		
War Diary	Fricourt Farm	01/11/1916	18/11/1916
War Diary	Albert	19/11/1916	30/11/1916
Heading	50th Division Administrative Staff War Diary December 1916 Volume XX		
War Diary	Baizieux	01/12/1916	31/12/1916
Heading	War Diary 50th (Northumbrian) Division From 1st January 1917 To 31st January 1917 Volume XXI		
War Diary	Fricourt Farm	01/01/1917	27/01/1917
War Diary	Ribemont	28/01/1917	30/01/1917
Heading	50th Division Administrative Staff War Diary From 1st February 1917 To 28th February 1917 Volume XXII		
War Diary	Ribemont	01/02/1917	12/02/1917
War Diary	P.C. Gabrielle	13/02/1917	28/02/1917
Heading	50th (Northumbrian) Division Administrative Staff War Diary From 1st March 1917 To 31st March 1917 Volume XXIII		

War Diary	P.C. Gabrielle	01/03/1917	08/03/1917
War Diary	Mericourt Sur-Somme	09/03/1917	30/03/1917
War Diary	Moillens Au Bois	31/03/1917	31/03/1917
Heading	50th Division Administrative Staff War Diary From 1st April 1917 To 30th April 1917 Volume XXIV		
War Diary	Molliens Au Bois	01/04/1917	01/04/1917
War Diary	Beauval	02/04/1917	02/04/1917
War Diary	Boquemaison	03/04/1917	03/04/1917
War Diary	Ramecourt	04/04/1917	06/04/1917
War Diary	Roellecourt	07/04/1917	07/04/1917
War Diary	Le Cauroy	08/04/1917	09/04/1917
War Diary	Berneville	10/04/1917	11/04/1917
War Diary	Arras	12/04/1917	25/04/1917
War Diary	La Couturelle	26/04/1917	30/04/1917
Heading	50th Division Administrative Staff War Diary From 1st May 1917 To 31st May 1917 Volume XXV		
War Diary	Couturelle	01/05/1917	01/05/1917
War Diary	Basseux	02/05/1917	03/05/1917
War Diary	Couturelle	04/05/1917	18/05/1917
War Diary	Beaumetz	19/05/1917	22/05/1917
War Diary	Couin	23/05/1917	31/05/1917
Heading	50th Division Administrative Staff War Diary From 1st June 1917 To 30th June 1917 Volume XXVI		
War Diary	Couin	01/06/1917	17/06/1917
War Diary	Camp S.17.a.8.4	18/06/1917	30/06/1917
Heading	50th Division Administrative Staff War Diary From 1st July 1917 To 31st July 1917 Volume XXVII		
War Diary	Camp S.17.a.8.4	01/07/1917	31/07/1917
Heading	50th Division Administrative Staff War Diary From 1st August 1917 To 31st August 1917 Volume XXVIII		
War Diary	Near Boisleux Au Mont S.17.a.8.4.	01/08/1917	31/08/1917
Heading	50th Division Administrative Staff War Diary From 1st September 1917 To 30th September 1917 Volume XXIX		
War Diary	Near Boisleux Au-Mont-S.17.a.84.	01/09/1917	30/09/1917
Heading	50th Division Administrative Staff War Diary From 1st October 1917 To 31st October 1917 Volume XXX		
War Diary	Boisleux-Au-Mont	01/10/1917	05/10/1917
War Diary	Achiet-Le-Petit	06/10/1917	17/10/1917
War Diary	Lederzeele	18/10/1917	19/10/1917
War Diary	Proven	20/10/1917	23/10/1917
War Diary	Elverdinghe	24/10/1917	31/10/1917
Heading	50th Division Administrative Staff War Diary From 1st November 1917 To 30th November 1917 Volume XXXI		
War Diary	Elverdinghe	01/11/1917	09/11/1917
War Diary	Eperlecques	10/11/1917	30/11/1917
Heading	50th Division Administrative Staff War Diary From 1st December 1917 To 31st December 1917 Volume XXXII		
War Diary	Eperlecques	01/12/1917	12/12/1917
War Diary	Brandhoek	13/12/1917	16/12/1917
War Diary	Ypres (Advcd H.Q.) Brandhoek (Rear H.Q.)	17/12/1917	22/12/1917
War Diary	Advd H.Q. Ypres. Rear H.Q. Brandhoek	23/12/1917	31/12/1917
Miscellaneous	Establishment Of Ammunition At Main Divisional Dump-Cambridge Dump		

Miscellaneous	Water Supply Arrangements		
Miscellaneous	Salvage Scheme		
Miscellaneous	Burial Scheme		
Miscellaneous	Baths And Clothing	11/12/1917	11/12/1917
Heading	50th Division Administrative Staff War Diary From 1st January 1918 To 31st January 1918 Volume XXXIII		
War Diary	Ypres (Advd D.H.Q.)	01/01/1918	01/01/1918
War Diary	Brandhoek (Rear D.H.Q.)	01/01/1918	05/01/1918
War Diary	Steenvoorde (Rue De Carnot)	06/01/1918	18/01/1918
War Diary	Wizernes	19/01/1918	29/01/1918
War Diary	Ramparts Ypres	30/01/1918	31/01/1918
Heading	50th (Northumbrian) Division Administrative Staff War Diary February 1918 Volume No. XXXIV		
War Diary	Advd D.H.Q. Ramparts Ypres	01/02/1918	02/02/1918
War Diary	Rear D.H.Q. Brandhoek	02/02/1918	22/02/1918
War Diary	Wizernes	23/02/1918	28/02/1918
Heading	50th Division Administration A & Q 50th (Northumbrian) Division March 1918		
Heading	50th Division Administrative Staff War Diary From 1st March 1918 To 31st March 1918 Volume XXXV		
War Diary	Wizernes	01/03/1918	09/03/1918
War Diary	Moreuil	10/03/1918	10/03/1918
War Diary	Harbonnieres	11/03/1918	20/03/1918
War Diary	Beaumetz	21/03/1918	21/03/1918
War Diary	Le Mesnil	22/03/1918	22/03/1918
War Diary	Villers Carbonnel	23/03/1918	23/03/1918
War Diary	Foucaucourt	23/03/1918	23/03/1918
War Diary	Valley St Martin	24/03/1918	25/03/1918
War Diary	Harbonnieres	25/03/1918	25/03/1918
War Diary	Marcelcave	26/03/1918	26/03/1918
War Diary	Villers Bretonneux	27/03/1918	27/03/1918
War Diary	Hangard Sourdon	28/03/1918	28/03/1918
War Diary	Sourdon	29/03/1918	29/03/1918
War Diary	Boves	29/03/1918	30/03/1918
War Diary	Douriez	31/03/1918	31/03/1918
Miscellaneous	50th (Northumbrian) Division		
Miscellaneous	50th Division Administrative Instructions No. 35	08/03/1918	08/03/1918
Miscellaneous	Starting Hours Of Trains		
Heading	A. & Q. 50th (Northumbrian) Division April 1918 Casualty Lists Attached		
War Diary	Douriez	01/04/1918	03/04/1918
War Diary	Robecq	04/04/1918	07/04/1918
War Diary	Merville	08/04/1918	11/04/1918
War Diary	La Motte Thiennes	12/04/1918	13/04/1918
War Diary	Advd. D.H.Q. Thiennes Rear D.H.Q. Wittes	14/04/1918	15/04/1918
War Diary	Roquetoire	16/04/1918	19/04/1918
War Diary	Aire Rue De St Omer	20/04/1918	27/04/1918
War Diary	Arcis Le Ponsart Under IX Corps	28/04/1918	30/04/1918
Miscellaneous	50th (Northumbrian) Division Casualty Return	09/04/1918	09/04/1918
Miscellaneous	50th (Northumbrian) Division Casualty Return	10/04/1918	10/04/1918
Miscellaneous	Names Of Officers		
Miscellaneous	50th (Northumbrian) Division Casualties Noon 10/4/18 to Noon 11/4/18	12/04/1918	12/04/1918
Miscellaneous	50th (Northumbrian) Division Casualties Noon 11/4/18 to Noon 12/4/18	11/04/1918	11/04/1918

Miscellaneous	50th (Northumbrian) Division Casualties Noon 12/4/18 to Noon 13/4/18	13/04/1918	13/04/1918
Miscellaneous	50th (Northumbrian) Division Casualties Noon 13/4/18 to Noon 14/4/18	13/04/1918	13/04/1918
Miscellaneous	50th (Northumbrian) Division Casualties Noon 14/4/18 to Noon 15/4/18	15/04/1918	15/04/1918
Miscellaneous	50th (Northumbrian) Division Casualties Noon 14/4/18 to Noon 15/4/18	16/04/1918	16/04/1918
Miscellaneous	Names Of Officers		
Miscellaneous	50th (Northumbrian) Division Casualties	17/04/1918	17/04/1918
Miscellaneous	50th (Northumbrian) Division Casualties	18/04/1918	18/04/1918
Heading	A & Q 50th Div May 1918		
Heading	50th Division Administrative Staff War Diary From 1st May 1918 To 31st May 1918 Volume XXXVIII		
War Diary	Arcis-Le-Ponsart	01/05/1918	04/05/1918
War Diary	Rear DHQ. Arcis-Le-Ponsart Adv. DHQ. Beaurieux	05/05/1918	05/05/1918
War Diary	Beaurieux	06/05/1918	26/05/1918
War Diary	Adv. DHQ. Beaurieux. Rear DHQ. Chateau Revillon	27/05/1918	27/05/1918
Heading	50th Division Administrative Staff War Diary From 1st May 1918 To 31st May 1918 Volume XXXVIII		
War Diary	Arcis-Le-Ponsart	01/05/1918	04/05/1918
War Diary	Rear DHQ. Arcis-Le-Ponsart Adv. DHQ. Beaurieux	05/05/1918	05/05/1918
War Diary	Beaurieux	06/05/1918	26/05/1918
War Diary	Adv. DHQ. Beaurieux Rear DHQ. Chateau Revillon	27/05/1918	27/05/1918
War Diary	Dravegny	28/05/1918	28/05/1918
War Diary	Lhery	28/05/1918	28/05/1918
War Diary	Lhery Cuiles Igny-le-Jard	29/05/1918	29/05/1918
War Diary	Igny-Le-Jard	30/05/1918	30/05/1918
War Diary	Breuil	30/05/1918	30/05/1918
War Diary	Vert-la Gravelle	31/05/1918	31/05/1918
Miscellaneous	50th (Northumbrian) Division Casualties		
Miscellaneous	50th (Northumbrian) Division Appendix I		
Miscellaneous	50th (Northumbrian) Division Casualties	30/05/1918	30/05/1918
Miscellaneous	50th (Northumbrian) Division Casualties From 27th May 1918 to date	27/05/1918	27/05/1918
Miscellaneous	50th (Northumbrian) Division Casualties From 27th May 1918 to Date	04/06/1918	04/06/1918
Miscellaneous	50th (Northumbrian) Division Casualties From 27th May 1918 to Date	08/06/1918	08/06/1918
Miscellaneous	50th (Northumbrian) Division Casualties From 27th May 1918 to Date	27/05/1918	27/05/1918
Miscellaneous	50th (Northumbrian) Division Casualties From 27th May 1918 to date Other Ranks	27/05/1918	27/05/1918
Miscellaneous	50th (Northumbrian) Division Casualties From 27th May 1918 to Date	27/05/1918	27/05/1918
Miscellaneous	50th (Northumbrian) Division Casualties From 27/5/18 To Date	07/06/1918	07/06/1918
Miscellaneous	50th (Northumbrian) Division Casualties List No. 6	08/06/1918	08/06/1918
Miscellaneous	50th (Northumbrian) Division Casualties List No. 8	09/06/1918	09/06/1918
Miscellaneous	50th (Northumbrian) Division Casualties From 27/5/18 To Date	27/05/1918	27/05/1918
Heading	50th Division Administrative Staff War Diary From 1st June 1918 To 30th June 1918 Volume XXXIX		
War Diary	Vert La Gravelle	01/06/1918	08/06/1918
War Diary	Chateau Montgivreux Mondemont	09/06/1918	16/06/1918
War Diary	Chateau La Noue	17/06/1918	30/06/1918

Heading	50th Division Administrative Staff War Diary From 1st July 1918 To 31st July 1918 Volume XL		
War Diary	La Noue Chateau	01/07/1918	03/07/1918
War Diary	Huppy	04/07/1918	11/07/1918
War Diary	Martin Eglise And Huppy	12/07/1918	15/07/1918
War Diary	Greges	16/07/1918	31/07/1918
Heading	50th Division Administrative Staff War Diary From 1st August 1918 To 31st August 1918 Vol XLI		
War Diary	Greges	01/08/1918	31/08/1918
Heading	50th Division Administrative Staff War Diary From 1st September 1918 To 30th September 1918 Volume XLII		
War Diary	Greges	01/08/1918	16/08/1918
War Diary	Lucheux	17/08/1918	25/08/1918
War Diary	Montigny	26/08/1918	28/08/1918
War Diary	Combles	29/08/1918	30/08/1918
Heading	50th Division Administrative Staff War Diary From 1st October 1918 To 31st October 1918 Volume XLIII		
War Diary	Lieramont	01/10/1918	04/10/1918
War Diary	Epehy	05/10/1918	09/10/1918
War Diary	Guisancourt Farm	10/10/1918	11/10/1918
War Diary	Le Trou Aux Soldats	11/10/1918	29/10/1918
War Diary	Le Cateau	30/10/1918	31/10/1918
Heading	50th Division Casualties (Officers) 1st Phase-1st/14th Oct. 1918 2nd Phase-Comm'g 15th Oct. 1918		
Miscellaneous	50th Divnl Hd Qrs		
Heading	50th Division Casualties (Officers) 1st Phase-1st/14th Oct 1918 2nd Phase-Commg 15th Oct 1918		
Miscellaneous	50th Divnl Hd Qrs		
Miscellaneous	50th Division Actual Casualties Reported For Phase 1st to 14th Octr 1918	14/10/1918	14/10/1918
Miscellaneous	Appendix "B" 50th Division.		
Miscellaneous	50th Division Appendix I	14/10/1918	14/10/1918
Miscellaneous	Prisoners Of War Captured		
Miscellaneous	50th Division "G"	10/03/1919	10/03/1919
Heading	50th Division Administrative Staff War Diary From 1st November 1918 To 30th November 1918		
War Diary	Le Cateau	01/11/1918	03/11/1918
War Diary	La Fayt Fme	04/11/1918	04/11/1918
War Diary	Lannoy	05/11/1918	05/11/1918
War Diary	Fontaine	06/11/1918	06/11/1918
War Diary	Noyelles	07/11/1918	07/11/1918
War Diary	Monceau	08/11/1918	10/11/1918
War Diary	Dourlers	11/11/1918	30/11/1918
Miscellaneous	Actual Casualties For Phase 1st to 11th Novr 1918	11/11/1918	11/11/1918
Miscellaneous	Actual Casualties For Phase 1st To 11th November 1918	11/11/1918	11/11/1918
Heading	50th Division 18 Fns V 15 Fns		
Miscellaneous	R.A 711/3	26/09/1915	26/09/1915
Miscellaneous	2nd Corps G.905	04/09/1915	04/09/1915
Miscellaneous	2nd Corps Headquarters	10/08/1915	10/08/1915
Miscellaneous	R.A 711/3/1	10/08/1915	10/08/1915
Miscellaneous	R.A 711/3/1	10/08/1914	10/08/1914
Miscellaneous	R.A 711/3/5	03/09/1915	03/09/1915
Miscellaneous	R.A 711/3	26/09/1915	26/09/1915
Miscellaneous	S.C /723	29/08/1915	29/08/1915
Miscellaneous	50th. Divn. G.X.388	29/08/1915	29/08/1915

Miscellaneous	2nd Corps G.773	30/08/1915	30/08/1915
Miscellaneous	2nd Corps Headquarters	27/09/1915	27/09/1915
Miscellaneous	2nd Corps Headquarters	03/09/1915	03/09/1915
Miscellaneous	50th Divn. G.X 388	29/08/1915	29/08/1915
Miscellaneous	50th Divn. Artillery S.C 723 G.X 388	29/08/1915	29/08/1915
Miscellaneous	Q.C 1683	15/11/1915	15/11/1915
Miscellaneous	C Form (Duplicate) Messages And Signals		
Miscellaneous	2nd Corps Headquarters	30/08/1915	30/08/1915
Miscellaneous	2nd Corps Headquarters	27/09/1915	27/09/1915
Miscellaneous	2nd Corps Headquarters	03/09/1915	03/09/1915
Heading	Head Qrs R.A. 50th Division Vol I 1.4-31.5.15		
Heading	50th Division Aug 1/15		
Miscellaneous	O/c 1st North Bde		
Miscellaneous	O/c 1st Northumbrian Bde R.F.A. (T)	30/07/1915	30/07/1915
Miscellaneous	58th Division	30/07/1915	30/07/1915
Diagram etc	Diagram		
Miscellaneous	Headquarters 2nd Corps	01/08/1915	01/08/1915
Miscellaneous	Headquarters 50th Division	31/07/1915	31/07/1915
Miscellaneous	Headquarters, 50th Division B.M 377	31/07/1915	31/07/1915
Miscellaneous	To O.C. 1st Northumbrian Brigade R.F.A.	30/07/1915	30/07/1915
Miscellaneous	To O.C. 1st Northumbrian Brigade R.F.A.T		
Miscellaneous	To O.C. 1st Northumbrian Brigade R.F.A.	30/07/1915	30/07/1915

WO 95/28131

50TH DIVISION

'A' & 'Q' BRANCH.

APR 1915 - DEC 1918

50

121/5207

Confidential

Administrative

War Diary.

of

Northumbrian Division

From 23rd April 1915 —   23 — 30. 4. 15.

To   30. 4. 15

Volume I

Army Form C. 2118.

WAR DIARY
or
INTELLIGENCE SUMMARY.
(Erase heading not required.)

Instructions regarding War Diaries and Intelligence Summaries are contained in F. S. Regs., Part II. and the Staff Manual respectively. Title pages will be prepared in manuscript.

Place	Date	Hour	Summary of Events and Information	Remarks and references to Appendices
STEENVOORDE	April 23rd		The Northumbrian Division completed concentration in the vicinity of STEENVOORDE. The Division was to attached to the 2nd Army —	
	24th		The three Infantry Brigades are attached to 5th Corps for operation in the vicinity of Ypres — Divisional Headquarters remain at STEENVOORDE and Divisional troops in that vicinity. The strength of the Division exclusive of lines of Communication units is 572 officers 18,850 other ranks. As the Division entered into operation, the Day of the concentration it was found a great inconvenience that Stores, Barrack clothing etc had only been issued to units a few days before leaving England — especially as men had to march in new boots — It is found necessary owing to the bad roads here that Mules be shod behind. Casualties to midday 5. O.R. Killed 1 Wounded 103 Missing 85	A A A A
	25th			
	26th			
	27th		Officers killed 28 wounded 45 Missing 14. O.R. Killed 332 Wounded 1143 Missing 1169	A
	28th		The first two days there was some difficulty in getting supplies into the trenches thus were due to O.C. Units not understanding that it was their duty to send back their Cooks Vehicles to the filling stations for drawing rations and also because Staff Captains had not had any previous experience as to their duties in this battle — Casualties to midday. Officers wounded 1— O.R. Killed 1 Wounded 16 —	A A

Army Form C. 2118.

WAR DIARY
or
INTELLIGENCE SUMMARY.
(Erase heading not required.)

Instructions regarding War Diaries and Intelligence Summaries are contained in F. S. Regs., Part II. and the Staff Manual respectively. Title pages will be prepared in manuscript.

Place	Date	Hour	Summary of Events and Information	Remarks and references to Appendices
STEE NWOORT	March 29th		Casualties to midday - Officers Wounded 5. O.R. Killed 8 Wounded 48. Missing 4.	aw
	30th		Casualties midday Officers Wounded 1. O.R. Wounded 3.	aw
			Total Casualties from 26th to 30th Officers Killed 26 Wounded 57 Missing 14 - O.R. Killed 342 - Wounded 1313 - Missing 1258 -	

1577 Wt. W16791/1773 500,000 1/15 D. D. & L. A.D.S.S./Forms/C. 2118.

Confidential.

War Diary

OF

50th (Northbn) Division

From 1st to 31st May, 1915.

Army Form C. 2118.

3

ADMINISTRATIVE WAR DIARY 50th Division
or
INTELLIGENCE SUMMARY.

(Erase heading not required.)

Place	Date	Hour	Summary of Events and Information	Remarks and references to Appendices
STEENVORDE	May 1st		Casualties - Officers wounded 2 - O.R. Killed 16 - Wounded 59 - Missing 3 -	(and)
	2nd		Casualties - Officers wounded 6 - O.R. Killed 6 - Wounded 314 - Missing 3 -	(and)
	3rd		Headquarters and the 2nd York & Durham Brigade return to STEENVORDE - The Durham Light Infy and Northumbd Brigade to POPERINGHE.	(and)
	4th		The Division concentrates in the vicinity of STEENVORDE and came under 2nd Army -	
			Casualties - 6.R. 1 Wounded 3 (who were not previously reported) -	(and)
	5th		Casualties - Officers Killed 1. Wounded 16 - O.R. Killed 80. Wounded 226 5th N:R: Border Regt. join the Division as is attached to Northumbd Brigade.	
			Reinforcements arrive - 7th N.F. 8 officers - 4th N.F. 5 officers	
	6th		Casualties - O.R. 10 who were reported missing, returned.	(and)
	7th		Reinforcements arrive - 6th D.L.I. 128 officers - 5th N.F. 2 officers - 7th D.L.I. 8 officers 9th D.L.I - 2 officers -	(and)
			Casualties. 1 officer reported killed rejoins - Stated previously wounded 1 reported not wounded -	
			Officers wounded 1 - O.R. Killed 17 wounded 145 missing 13 -	
	8th		Reinforcement arrive 6th D.L.I 8 officers - 7th D.L.I 2 officers - 8th D.L.I 19 officers	(and)

Army Form C. 2118.

WAR DIARY
or
INTELLIGENCE SUMMARY.
(Erase heading not required.)

Instructions regarding War Diaries and Intelligence Summaries are contained in F. S. Regs., Part II. and the Staff Manual respectively. Title pages will be prepared in manuscript.

Place	Date	Hour	Summary of Events and Information	Remarks and references to Appendices
STEENWOORDE	Nov 8th		Casualties:– O.R. Killed 12 – Wounded 63 –	
	9th		2 Officers reports missing now reported killed – 1 Officer reported Wounded now reported missing. O.R. 387 reported missing now reported. Casualties:– 1 Officer missing 1 – O.R. killed 1 – Wounded 9 missing 3 – The HdQrs Division move to POPERINGHE – The HdQrs Division move to POPERINGHE. The infantry Brigades – R.E. Coy to BRANDHOEK. Artillery to WATEU –	as
POPERINGHE	11th		Reinforcements:– Officers 6 for 4th E. Yorks – 5 for 4th Yorks –	
	12th		Reinforcements:– Officers 1 for 4th E. Yorks –	
			Casualties:– Officers Wounded and Died of Wounds 1 – Wounded 3 (2 slightly). O.R. Killed 4 – Died of Wounds 1 – Wounded 19 (including 8 slightly) –	as
	15th		Reinforcements:– Officers 6 for 6th D.L.I – 1 for 8th D.L.I – 4th Northumberland Fusiliers 2 – 5th Northumberland Fusiliers 1 – 7th Northumberland Fusiliers 3 – Casualties – Officers wounded 1 – O.R. Killed 3 – Wounded 30 –	as
	16th		Casualties:– Officers killed 1 – Wounded 1 – O.R. Killed 8 Died of Wounds 2 – Wounded 22 – 2 men previously reported missing now reports wounded. 149 Infantry Brigade attached to 7th Division – 150th Infantry Brigade to 27th Division – 151st Infantry Brigade to Cavalry Corps.	as

WAR DIARY
INTELLIGENCE SUMMARY.
(Erase heading not required.)

Army Form C. 2118.

5

Place	Date	Hour	Summary of Events and Information	Remarks and references to Appendices
POPERINGHE	May 17th		Casualties Officers killed 1 — Wounded 1 — accidentally wounded 1 — O.R. Killed 13 Wounded 26.	
	18th		Casualties O.R. Killed 2 — Wounded 11	
	19th		O.R. Killed 2 — Wounded 19 — missing 1	
	20		Officers Killed 1 — Wounded slightly at duty 1 — O.R. Wounded 12 — missing 2	
			reported missing now reported killed 10	
WATOU	21st		"A" & "Q" Branch of Divisional Headquarters move to WATOU	
			Casualties Officers wounded 1 — O.R. Killed 3 wounded 13	
	22nd		Casualties Officers wounded 1 — O.R. Killed 1 wounded 4 —	
	23rd		Casualties — Officers wounded 1 — O.R. Killed 8 (between 18th & 22nd) wounded 9 —	
			wounded (between 18th & 22nd) 22.	
			Reinforcements 27 men for the Border Regiment (attached to the Division) —	
	24th		Casualties — O.R. Killed 1 — Died of wounds 2 — Wounded 13 — gassed 4 missing 1	
			Reinforcements — 4th N.F. O.R. 16 — 5th N.F. O.R. 10 — 6th N.F. O.R. 19 — 7th N.F. O.R. 17	
			5th D.L.I. O.R. 7 — 6th D.L.I. O.R. 12 — 7th D.L.I. O.R. 2 — 8th D.L.I. O.R. 18	
			4th Yorks Officers 2 O.R. 2 — 5th Yorks O.R. 6 — 4th E. Yorks O.R. 11	
			G.O.C. and General Staff move to WATOU —	

WAR DIARY
or
INTELLIGENCE SUMMARY

Army Form C. 2118.

Instructions regarding War Diaries and Intelligence Summaries are contained in F. S. Regs., Part II. and the Staff Manual respectively. Title pages will be prepared in manuscript.

Place	Date	Hour	Summary of Events and Information	Remarks and references to Appendices
WATOU	May 25th		Casualties — Officers Wounded 10 (includes 2 shykk — 1 S. Doig'Dak — 4 gassed) — Missing 1 — O.R. Killed 15 — Wounded 121 (includes 64 gassed) — Missing 9 —	(ii)
	26th		Casualties — (including some not already reported) — Officers Killed 3 — Wounded 14 — Missing 4 — O.R. Killed 26 — Wounded 208 — Missing 129	(ii)
	27th		Casualties — Officers — Killed 3 — Wounded 13 — Missing 7 — O.R. Killed 49 — Wounded 196 — Missing 257	(ii)
L13. Sheet 27	28th		Casualties — Officers. Killed 2 — Wounded 4 — O.R. — Killed 42 — Wounded 274 — Missing 89 —	(ii)
	29th		Casualties — Officers — Wounded 1 — (no reports missing and reported wounded) — O.R. Killed 4 — Wounded 30 — 11 reported Missing now reported —	(ii)
	30th		Casualties — Officers — Wounded 1 — O.R. Killed 3 — Wounded 11 — Missing 120	(ii)
	31st		Casualties — Officers — Wounded 1 — O.R. Killed 1 — Wounded 9 —	(ii)

50th Division

"Confidential"   121/5921

Administrative Staff   A+Q

War Diary

June 1915

50th Northumbrian Division

Vol. III

Army Form C. 2118.

WAR DIARY
Armentières
INTELLIGENCE SUMMARY.
(Erase heading not required.)

Instructions regarding War Diaries and Intelligence Summaries are contained in F. S. Regs., Part II. and the Staff Manual respectively. Title pages will be prepared in manuscript.

Place	Date 1915	Hour	Summary of Events and Information	Remarks and references to Appendices
L 13 Sheet 27	June 1		Casualties — Officers died of wounds 1 — Wounded 1 — O.R. Killed 5. Wounded 6 — 8 Missing reported	app
	2		Casualties — O.R. Killed 16 — Wounded 37 — Missing 2 —	app
	3		Casualties — Officers slightly wounded at duty 1 — O.R. Killed 5 — Wounded 5 — 4 Missing reported.	app
	4		Casualties — O.R. Killed 1 — Wounded 9 — 10 Missing reported	app
			Divisional Headquarters moved to G.21.c Sheet 28 — The Division moved into the Lethely area occupied by 2nd Division	app
			The Division forms part of 5th Corps —	
G.21.C Sheet 20	6		Casualties — O.R. Killed 1 — Wounded 12 — 11 Missing reported	app
	7		Casualties — O.R. Wounded 2	app
	8		Casualties — O.R. Killed 1 — Wounded 8 — 34 previously reported Missing have returned to Camp.	app
	9		Casualties — O.R. Wounded 2 — Missing 2 —	app
	10th		Casualties — O.R. Wounded 11 —	app
	11th		Casualties — Officers Wounded 1 — O.R. Wounded 5 — reports many casualties killed —	app
	12th		5th Bn Loyal North Lancs joined the Division & was transferred to 151st Brigade — Neuve — 29 Officers and 961 other Ranks —	app
	12th		Casualties O.R. Killed 8 Wounded 11 — 2 previously reported Missing now Wounded —	app

Army Form C. 2118.

ADMINISTRATIVE
WAR DIARY
or
INTELLIGENCE SUMMARY.
(Erase heading not required.)

Instructions regarding War Diaries and Intelligence Summaries are contained in F. S. Regs., Part II. and the Staff Manual respectively. Title pages will be prepared in manuscript.

Place	Date	Hour	Summary of Events and Information	Remarks and references to Appendices
	June			
G21c Sh.28	13th		Casualties - Officers Killed 1 - Wounded 2 (include one accidental) - O.R. Killed 4 - Wounded 24	a.v
	14th		Casualties - Officers Wounded 1 - O.R. Killed 3 - Wounded 20	a.v
	15th		Casualties - O.R. Killed 2 - Wounded 21 - Missing 1	a.v
	16th		Casualties - Officers Killed 2 - Wounded 5 - O.R. Killed 15 - Wounded 51	a.v
	17th		Casualties - O.R. Killed 12 - Wounded 50 - Missing 1	a.v
	18th		Casualties - Officers Wounded 2 - O.R. Killed 5 - Wounded 52 - Missing 29 -	a.v
	19th		Casualties - Officers Wounded 2 - O.R. Killed 2 - Wounded 35	a.v
	20th		Casualties - O.R. Killed 3 - Wounded 15	a.v
	21st		Casualties - O.R. Killed 1 - Wounded 4 - One (receiving injuries from reports one ges)	a.v
	22nd		Casualties - Officers Wounded one slightly - O.R. Killed 4 - Wounded 24 - 9 Missing one accidental.	a.v
	23rd		Casualties - Officers Wounded one - O.R. Killed 3 - W. 17 -	a.v
	24		Casualties - Officers K. 2 - W. 2 - O.R. Killed 3 - W 19 -	
St Jans Cappel			During Headquarters moves to St Jans Cappel - Divisional troops moved to billets in that vicinity and relieved 46th North Midland Division - Infantry Brigades had relieved 46th Division on the previous days - Headquarters 149th Brigade Nieuwe Eglise - 150th Brigade DRANOUTRE - 151st Brigade KEMMEL	a.v

Army Form C. 2118.

53rd Divn

ADMINISTRATIVE
WAR DIARY
or
INTELLIGENCE SUMMARY.
(Erase heading not required.)

No. 9

Instructions regarding War Diaries and Intelligence
Summaries are contained in F. S. Regs., Part II.
and the Staff Manual respectively. Title pages
will be prepared in manuscript.

Place	Date	Hour	Summary of Events and Information	Remarks and references to Appendices
ST JEANS CAPPEL	June 25		Casualties - O.R. K 5 - W.6	aw
	26		Casualties - O.R. W. 10 - 1 previous wound died afterwards	
			Difficulty has been experienced by this Division since it came to the country in obtaining sufficient Trench Stores —	aw
			Casualties Officers W. 2. — O.R. K 1 - W 2.	aw
	27		Casualties Officers Wounded 1 — O.R. Killed 2 Wounded 8	aw
	28		Casualties Officers Wounded 1 — O.R. Killed 5 Wounded 13	aw
	29		Casualties - O.R. Killed 2. Wounded 7	aw
	30		The total Casualties of this Division since arrival in the country up to the end of June are —	aw
			Officers Killed 50 - Wounded 152 — Missing 23 —	aw
			O.R.s Killed 682 — Wounded 3608 — Missing 1511 ____	aw
			The strength of the Divn is 462 officers 11814 other ranks which is 5044 less than when we arrived in the country. This does not include the 5 Border Regiment and 5th North Lancs which total 44 officers and 1452 men — which were sent to replace Cavalry	
			To day reinforcements arrived — 7th D.L.I 170 9th D.L.I 50	
			There are as yet no reinforcements from home for the Divisions arrived — except for officers —	aw

50th Division

Confidential   121/6308

War Diary

Administrative Staff.
50th (North'n.) Division.

From 1st July, 1915.
to 31st July, 1915.

Vol IV

50TH DIVISION.

Army Form C. 2118.

10.

ADMINISTRATIVE
WAR DIARY

INTELLIGENCE SUMMARY.
(Erase heading not required.)

JULY, 1915.

Instructions regarding War Diaries and Intelligence Summaries are contained in F. S. Regs., Part II. and the Staff Manual respectively. Title pages will be prepared in manuscript.

Place	Date	Hour	Summary of Events and Information	Remarks and references to Appendices
ST JANS CAPPEL.	JULY. 1st.		Casualties - Other ranks, Killed 1, Wounded 5.	(a)
	2nd.		Casualties - Other ranks, Killed 1, Wounded 1.	(a)
	3rd.		Reinforcements arrived, 7th North'd Fusiliers, Other Ranks 106; 4th East Yorks Regt, Other R. 95.	
			Casualties - Officers, Wounded 2, Other Ranks, Killed 4, Wounded 15.	(a)
	4th.		Casualties - Officers, Wounded 1, Other Ranks, Killed 3, Wounded 12.	(a)
	5th.		Casualties - Other Ranks, Killed 3, Wounded 7.	(a)
	6th.		Casualties - Officers, Wounded 1, Other Ranks, Killed 6, Wounded 14.	(a)
			2/1st Northumbrian Field Coy, R.E. arrived and were billeted ST JANS CAPPEL.	
	7th.		Casualties - Other Ranks, Killed 2, Wounded 6.	(a)
			2nd Corps asked for name of Battalion recommended for Pioneer Battalion. 8th Durham Light Infantry were selected as Pioneer Battalion for the Division.	
	8th.		Casualties - Officers, Wounded 1, Other Ranks, Killed 2, Wounded 9.	(a)
	9th.		Casualties - Officers, Killed 1, Other Ranks, Killed 2, Wounded 15.	(a)
			Orders were received for 2/1st Northumbrian Field Coy, R.E. to be transferred to 28th Division.	
	10th.		Casualties - Other Ranks, Killed 4, Wounded 9.	(a)
			Reinforcements arrived - 9th Durham Light Infantry, Other Ranks 184; 7th Durham Light I. O.R.18.	

Army Form C. 2118.

50TH DIVISION.

ADMINISTRATIVE WAR DIARY
INTELLIGENCE SUMMARY.

(Erase heading not required.)

JULY, 1915.

Instructions regarding War Diaries and Intelligence Summaries are contained in F.S. Regs., Part II. and the Staff Manual respectively. Title pages will be prepared in manuscript.

Place	Date	Hour	Summary of Events and Information	Remarks and references to Appendices
ST JANS CAPPEL.	JULY 11th.		Casualties - Other Ranks, Killed 3, Wounded 12.	(a)
	12th.		Casualties - Other Ranks, Killed 6, Wounded 31. Reinforcements - 12 Officers arrived for 5th Bn. Border Regt. Orders received, 2nd Corps to consist of 12th, 28th and 50th Divisions.	(a)
	13th.		Casualties - Other Ranks, Killed 5, Wounded 20.	(a)
	14th.		Casualties - Officers, Wounded 1, Other Ranks, Killed 2, Wounded 8. Reinforcements - 4th North'd Fus. 2 Offrs, 5th North'd Fus. 5 Offrs, 7th North's Fus. 3 Offrs.	(b)
	15th.		Casualties - Other Ranks, Killed 8, Wounded 21. The 151st Infantry Brigade was relieved by 28th Div. on night 15/16th, and moved to billets and trenches in ARMENTIERES.	(a)
	16th.		Casualties - Officers, Wounded 1, Other Ranks, Killed 1, Wounded 14. The 150th Infantry Brigade was relieved by 28th Div. on night 16/17th, and moved to billets and trenches in ARMENTIERES.	(a)
	17th.		Orders having been received for the Division to take up part of the line near ARMENTIERES, the 149th Infantry Brigade moved to new area on night of 16/17th, having been relieved by the Canadian Division.	(a)
	18th.		Casualties - Other Ranks, Killed 2, Wounded 2. Casualties - Other Ranks, Killed 2, Wounded 2.	(a)

1577 Wt.W10791/1773 500,000 1/15 D.D.&L. A.D.S.S./Forms/C.2118.

50TH DIVISION.

Instructions regarding War Diaries and Intelligence Summaries are contained in F. S. Regs., Part II. and the Staff Manual respectively. Title pages will be prepared in manuscript.

ADMINISTRATIVE.
WAR DIARY
INTELLIGENCE SUMMARY.

(Erase heading not required.)

Army Form C. 2118.

JULY, 1915.

Place	Date	Hour	Summary of Events and Information	Remarks and references to Appendices
ST JANS CAPPEL.	JULY. 18th.		150th Infantry Brigade having been relieved, moved to billets at PONT DE NIEPPE.	(a)
	19th.		Casualties - Nil.	(a)
	20th.		Casualties - Officers, Killed 1, Other Ranks, Killed 3, Wounded 7.	(a)
ARMENTIERES.	21st.		Casualties - Officers, Wounded 1, Other Ranks, Killed 1, Wounded 7.	(a)
			The Headquarters of Division moved from ST JANS CAPPEL to the Ecole Nationale, ARMENTIERES.	
	22nd.		Casualties - Officers, Killed 1, Wounded 1, Other Ranks, Killed 3, Wounded 6.	(a)
	23rd.		Casualties - Other Ranks, Killed 1, Wounded 4.	(a)
	24th.		Casualties - Other Ranks, Killed 1, Wounded 4.	(a)
			42nd Fortress Coy, R.E. attached to 50th Division from this date.	
	25th.		Casualties - Other Ranks, Wounded 4.	(a)
	26th.		Casualties - Other Ranks, Wounded 3.	(a)
	27th.		Casualties - Other Ranks, Killed 7, Wounded 9.	(a)
	28th.		Casualties - Officers, Killed 2, Other Ranks, Wounded 3.	(a)
	29th.		Casualties - Other Ranks, Killed 3, Wounded 3.	(a)
	30th.		Casualties - Officers, Wounded 1, Other Ranks, Killed 5, Wounded 5.	(a)
	31st.		Casualties - Officers, Wounded 2, Other Ranks, Wounded 1.	(a)

50th Division

Confidential

121/6754

War Diary of

50th Division (A & Q)

August 1915.

Vol V

Army Form C. 2118.

50TH DIVISION.

Instructions regarding War Diaries and Intelligence Summaries are contained in F. S. Regs., Part II. and the Staff Manual respectively. Title pages will be prepared in manuscript.

ADMINISTRATIVE
WAR DIARY
or
INTELLIGENCE SUMMARY.
(Erase heading not required.)

AUGUST, 1915.

Place	Date	Hour	Summary of Events and Information	Remarks and references to Appendices
ARMENTIERES.	AUG. 1st.		Casualties - Other Ranks, Killed 4, Wounded 4. Orders received for the reversion to the original formation of 6th & 8th Durham Light Infantry to be carried out.	
	2nd.		Casualties - Officers, Wounded 1, Other Ranks, Wounded 2.	
	3rd.		Casualties - Nil. Drafts arrived - 6th Durham Light Infantry, 2 Officers, Other Ranks 112. 8th Durham Light Infantry, Other Ranks 188.	
	4th.		Casualties - Wounded, Other Ranks 5. Reinforcements, 5th North'd Fusrs. Other Ranks 19. Major-General P.S.Wilkinson, C.B.,C.M.G.,arrived from England to take command of 50th Division.	
	5th.		Casualties - Other Ranks, Killed 3, Wounded 2. Major-General Lord Cavan having handed over Command of Division to Major-General Wilkinson, proceeded to England to report to War Office.	
	6th.		Casualties - Officers, Wounded 1, Other Ranks, Killed 1, Wounded 5. 6 Shrapnel proof helmets of French Design issued to this Division for trial and report.	
	7th.		Casualties - Officers, Wounded 1, Other Ranks, Killed 3, Wounded 4.	
	8th.		Casualties - Other Ranks, Killed 1, Wounded 6.	

Army Form C. 2118.

50TH DIVISION.

ADMINISTRATIVE WAR DIARY or INTELLIGENCE SUMMARY.

(Erase heading not required.)

AUGUST, 1915.

Instructions regarding War Diaries and Intelligence Summaries are contained in F.S. Regs., Part II. and the Staff Manual respectively. Title pages will be prepared in manuscript.

Place	Date	Hour	Summary of Events and Information	Remarks and references to Appendices
ARMENTIERES.	AUGT. 9th.		Casualties, – Other Ranks, Wounded 11.	
	10th.		2 Composite Battalions, 111th Brigade, arrived at ARMENTIERES for Defence Work, they are attached to the Division for Administration. Casualties – Other Ranks, Killed 2, Wounded 1. Major O.C.Borrett,D.S.O. arrived, appointed to command 6th Bn.Durham Light Infantry.	
	11th.		Casualties – Other Ranks, Killed 2.	
	12th.		Casualties – Other Ranks, Wounded 7.	
	13th.		Casualties – Other Ranks, Killed 2, Wounded 15. 700 men 3rd Cavalry Division arrived for defence work and are attached to the Division.	
	14th.		Casualties – Other Ranks, Killed 3, Wounded 8. Captain A.W.B.Wallace, D.A.A.& Q.M.G. admitted to hospital. 200 men 3rd Cavalry Division arrived for defence work and are attached to the Division.	
	15th.		Casualties – Other Ranks, Wounded 3. Major O.C.Borrett, D.S.O. to command 5th Shropshire Light Infantry. Captain J.W.Jeffreys to command 6th Durham Light Infantry.	

1577 Wt. W10791/1773 500,000 1/15 D. D. & L. A.D.S.S./Forms/C. 2118.

ADMINISTRATIVE WAR DIARY or INTELLIGENCE SUMMARY.

(Erase heading not required.)

Army Form C. 2118.

50TH DIVISION.

AUGUST, 1915.

Instructions regarding War Diaries and Intelligence Summaries are contained in F. S. Regs., Part II. and the Staff Manual respectively. Title pages will be prepared in manuscript.

Place	Date	Hour	Summary of Events and Information	Remarks and references to Appendices
ARMENTIERES.	AUGT. 16th		Casualties - 1st Field Co,R.E. 2nd Lt.H.E.Case, Killed; 9th Durham L.I. 2nd Lt.R.T.Hardy, Wounded; Other Ranks, Wounded 6; 10th Royal Hussars attached, Other Ranks, Wounded 3.	
	17th		Casualties, Other Ranks, Wounded 6.	
	18th		Casualties - Other Ranks, Killed 1, Wounded 3.	
	19th		Casualties - Other Ranks, Killed 2, Wounded 5. Captain Henderson Scott, Q.W.R. assumed duties of Assistant Provost Marshal. Captain Earl of Clanwilliam left to join Guards Division.	
	20th		Casualties - Other Ranks, Wounded 11; 9th Leicester Regt attached, Other Ranks, Wounded 3.	
	21st		Casualties - Other Ranks, Wounded 2; Attached, 8th Leicester Regt, Other Ranks, Wounded 1, 9th Leicester Regt, Other Ranks, Wounded 1, 2nd Life Guards, Other Ranks, Wounded 4.	
	22nd		Casualties - Other Ranks, Killed 2, Wounded 3; Attached 7th Field Coy,R.E. Other Ranks, Wounded 1. Lt.R.St.B.Gregorie,A.D.C. and Lt.Col.Barclay, Town Major, arrived.	
	23rd		Casualties - Other Ranks, Killed 2, Wounded 2. Major H.W.Grubb, D.A.A. & Q.M.G. joined. Brig.General Fitton,C.B.,D.S.O.,A.D.C. attached for instruction with 10 Commanding Officers from England.	
	24th		Casualties - Other Ranks, Wounded 2.	

Army Form C. 2118.

50TH DIVISION.

ADMINISTRATIVE.

WAR DIARY or INTELLIGENCE SUMMARY.

(Erase heading not required.)

AUGUST, 1915.

Instructions regarding War Diaries and Intelligence Summaries are contained in F. S. Regs., Part II. and the Staff Manual respectively. Title pages will be prepared in manuscript.

Place	Date	Hour	Summary of Events and Information	Remarks and references to Appendices
ARMENTIERES.	AUGT. 25th.		Casualties – Other Ranks, Killed 1, Wounded 8.	
	26th.		Casualties – 2nd Lt.W.Winkworth, 5th N.F. Wounded, Other Ranks, Killed 1, Wounded 4. Brig.General Fitton and 10 Officers left.	
	27th.		Casualties – Other Ranks, Wounded 6. Major lord Montgomerie, Ayrshire Yeomanry, A.D.C. joined.	
	28th.		Casualties – Other Ranks, Killed 1, Wounded 1. Army Commander inspected 150th Brigade.	
	29th.		Casualties – Other Ranks, Killed 3, Wounded 3.	
	30th.		Casualties – Other Ranks, Killed 1, Wounded 3.	
	31st.		Casualties – Capt. J.Errington,7th Durham Light Infantry,Killed; Other Ranks, Wounded 2.	

50th Division

Confidential

121/7016

War Diary.

50th (Northumbrian) Division
(A & Q)

From
1st September, 1915.
To
30th September 1915.

Vol VI

Army Form C. 2118.

ADMINISTRATIVE
WAR DIARY
or
INTELLIGENCE SUMMARY.
(Erase heading not required.)

50TH DIVISION.   SEPTR, 1915.

Instructions regarding War Diaries and Intelligence Summaries are contained in F. S. Regs., Part II. and the Staff Manual respectively. Title pages will be prepared in manuscript.

Place	Date	Hour	Summary of Events and Information	Remarks and references to Appendices
ARMENTIERES.	SEPTR. 1st.		Casualties - Other Ranks, Killed 2, Wounded 3. Lt.Winkworth,5th North'd Fusiliers,wounded 25th August, reported died of wounds 27th August.	
	2nd.		Casualties - Other ranks, Killed 2, Wounded 6.	
	3rd.		Casualties - Other Ranks, Killed 1, Wounded 7.	
	4th.		Casualties - 2nd Lt.W.A.Dent,6th D.L.I. wounded, Other Ranks, Killed 1.	
	5th.		Casualties - Other ranks, Killed 2, Wounded 6. Major Buttye arrived as G.S.O.3.	
	6th.		Casualties - Other Ranks, Killed 1, Wounded 2.	
	7th.		Casualties - Killed 1. 2nd Army Commander inspected 151st Infantry Brigade.	
	8th.		Casualties - Other Ranks, Wounded 4. Lieut.C.Sproxton, 4th East Yorkshire Regt, granted Military Cross, 2nd Acting Sergt.Major. A.Mackay, Distinguished Conduct Medal.	
	9th.		Casualties - Other Ranks, Wounded 2.	
	10th.		Casualties - Other Ranks, Killed 2, Wounded 4.	
	11th.		Casualties - Other Ranks, Wounded 24,including 1 accidentally. Soldiers' Club opened.	
	12th.		Casualties - Other Ranks, Wounded 5. Reinforcements, 4th Yorks Regt, Other Ranks 100.	
	13th.		Casualties - Other Ranks, Wounded 3.	
			10 Officers from England attached to 149th Infantry Brigade,and 10 to 151st Infantry Brigade, for 24 hours in trenches.	

Army Form C. 21

50th DIVISION.

ADMINISTRATIVE.
WAR DIARY
or
INTELLIGENCE SUMMARY.
(Erase heading not required.)

SEPTR, 1915.

Instructions regarding War Diaries and Intelligence Summaries are contained in F. S. Regs., Part II. and the Staff Manual respectively. Title pages will be prepared in manuscript.

Place	Date	Hour	Summary of Events and Information	Remarks and references to Appendices
ARMENTIERES	SEPTR 14th.		Casualties, - Other Ranks,Wounded 1; 3 French Artillery Officers from 2nd Army Headquarters, visited Division.	
	15th.		Casualties - Other Ranks,Wounded 1; Capt.G.E.Hunter,6th Bn.Northumberland Fusiliers reported missing 26.4.15, now reported killed.	
	16th.		Casualties - Lt.A.T.Price, 7th Bn.Durham L.I. Wounded, Other Ranks,Killed 1, Wounded 11. Lieut.Colonel Stewart, A Branch,attached this Division. General Officer Commanding inspected 4th Yorks Regt and 5th Bn.Durham L.I. and Transport of 150th Infantry Brigade.	
	17th.		Casualties - Other Ranks previously reported Wounded,now reported Died of Wounds.1; Wounded 1. General Officer Commanding inspected 4th East Yorks and 5th Yorks. Reinforcements for Cyclist Co,Officers 2.	
	18th.		Casualties - Other Ranks Killed 1, Wounded 5.	
	19th.		Casualties - Lt.Boys Stones, 9th Durham L.I. Wounded, Other Ranks,Wounded 9. Reinforcements Officers 2, Other Ranks 210.	
	20th.		Casualties - Other Ranks Killed 2, Wounded 3.	
	21st.		Casualties - 2nd Lt.Ernest Blackburn,5th Loyal North Lancs,Wounded; Other Ranks Killed 2, Wounded 3.	

Army Form C. 21

50TH DIVISION.

ADMINISTRATIVE
WAR DIARY
or
INTELLIGENCE SUMMARY.
(Erase heading not required.)

SEPTR, 1915.

Instructions regarding War Diaries and Intelligence Summaries are contained in F. S. Regs., Part II. and the Staff Manual respectively. Title pages will be prepared in manuscript.

Place	Date	Hour	Summary of Events and Information	Remarks and references to Appendices
ARMENTIERES	Septr. 22nd.		Casualties - Other Ranks, Killed 1, Wounded 11, also 14th Anti-Aircraft Section, Other Ranks, Wounded 4.	
	23rd.		Casualties - Other Ranks, Wounded 5; Lt.Kleist, Belgian Liaison Officer and 10 Belgian Interpreters left; replaced by 10 French Interpreters.	
	24th.		Casualties - Other Ranks, Killed 1, Wounded 10. Reinforcements, 5th D.L.I. Other Ranks 40.	
	25th.		Casualties - Other Ranks, Killed 1, Wounded 4.	
	26th.		Casualties - Wounded, 2/Lt.E.Fisher, 8th D.L.I., Lt.E.S.Wilson, 5th Border Regt. Other Ranks, Killed 2, Wounded 22.	
	27th.		Casualties - Wounded, 2nd Lt.R.C.Dunford; Other Ranks Killed 2, Wounded 15. Reinforcements Officers 6, Other Ranks 5.	
	28th.		Casualties - Other Ranks, Killed 3, Wounded 7. 2 Battalions, 74th Brigade attached for billets and instruction.	
	29th.		Casualties - Other Ranks, Killed 1, Wounded 13. Captain Darley gave demonstration in Salvus Breathing apparatus. 2 Battalions, 74th Brigade, attached for billets and instruction.	
	30th.		Casualties - Captain I.N.Tweedy, 5th North'd Fusiliers, Wounded, Other Ranks, Wounded 6.	

50th Kirwin

D/7449

50th (N-ten) Divn. (A+Q)

Dec 15

Vol VII

Confidential

50th (Northumbrian) Division

Administrative
War Diary

From 1st October, 1915.

To 31st October, 1915.

Army Form C. 2118.

50TH DIVISION.

Instructions regarding War Diaries and Intelligence Summaries are contained in F. S. Regs., Part II. and the Staff Manual respectively. Title pages will be prepared in manuscript.

ADMINISTRATIVE WAR DIARY or INTELLIGENCE SUMMARY.

OCTOBER, 1915.

(*Erase heading not required.*)

Place	Date	Hour	Summary of Events and Information	Remarks and references to Appendices
ARMENTIERES	OCT. 1.		Casualties – Lt.M.T.Morrison, 5th D.L.I. Wounded,slightly at duty; Other Ranks,Killed 1,Wounded 7. Reinforcements, 4th North'd Fus. 70 other ranks, 5th North'd Fus, 1 Off.19 Other Ranks, 6th North'd Fus, 28 Other Ranks, 5th Borders 40 Other ranks, 4th Yorks.Regt, 1 Officer, 53 Other Ranks, 5th D.L.I. 29 Other Ranks, 6th D.L.I. 10 Other Ranks.	
	2.		Casualties – Other Ranks,Killed 3, Wounded 1. Col.J.V.W.Rutherford,A.D.of M.S., evacuated sick. Lt.Col.Thurston, D.S.O. Acting A.D.of M.S.	
	3.		Casualties – 2nd Lt.G.T.E.Polge, 5th D.L.I. Wounded; Lt.R.K.Dibb, 4th East Yorks, Wounded slightly at duty. Other Ranks, Killed 3, Wounded 9.	
	4.		Casualties – Other Ranks, Killed 4, Wounded 7.	
	5.		Casualties – 2nd Lt.Callender, 9th D.L.I. Killed accidentally; Lt.R.Boys Stones and 2nd Lieut. J.H.Edgar, wounded accidentally. Other ranks, Killed 3, Wounded 5. Wounded accidentally 14.	
	6.		Casualties – Other Ranks, Killed 2, Wounded 5. Wounded addidentally at duty 4. Reinforcements Divnl Ammunition Column, Other Ranks 40; 5th Border Regt, 3 Officers; 4th Yorks Regt, Other Ranks 116; 5th Yorks Regt, Other Ranks 39; 8th D.L.I. 1 Officer. 3 Sections R.F.A. to La Kreule V.16.b.5.5. Sheet 27, on relief by 21st Division.	
	7.		Casualties – Other Ranks, Killed 2, Wounded 9, Missing 3. Reinforcements, 5th North'd Fus.	

Army Form C. 2118.

50TH DIVISION.

ADMINISTRATIVE.
WAR DIARY
or
INTELLIGENCE SUMMARY.

(Erase heading not required.)

OCTOBER, 1915.

Instructions regarding War Diaries and Intelligence Summaries are contained in F. S. Regs., Part II. and the Staff Manual respectively. Title pages will be prepared in manuscript.

Place	Date	Hour	Summary of Events and Information	Remarks and references to Appendices
ARMENTIERES	OCT. 7.		1 Officer,44 Other Ranks; 4th East Yorks Regt,10 Other Ranks; 5th Yorks Regt,11 Other Ranks, 5th D.L.I. 26 Other Ranks; 7th D.L.I. 22 Other Ranks, 8th D.L.I. 22 Other Ranks. 1 Brigade Ammn.Col. to La Kreule,V.16.b.5.5. Sheet 27,onrelief by 21st Division.	
	8.		Casualties - Other Ranks,Killed 4, Wounded 4. Reinforcements, 4th North'd Fus. 1 Officer, 30 Other Ranks,; 7th North'd Fus.38 Other Ranks; 4th Yorks.Regt. 9 Other Ranks, 5th Yorks. Regt, 23 Other Ranks; 6th D.L.I. 40 Other Ranks; Divnl.Cyclist Co, 1 Other Rank. 3 Sections,R.F.A. to La Kreule on relief by 21st Division. 2 Battns,62nd Brigade, 21st Division attached for instruction.	
	9.		Casualties - Lt.Dymond, 5th Yorks.Regt, Wounded, Other Ranks,Wounded 3, Missing 5. Reinforcements, 5th North'd Fus. 1 Officer; 6th North'd Fus. 3 Officers,45 Other Ranks, 7th North'd Fus. 1 Officer, 4th Yorks Regt, 2 Officers, 5th Yorks.Regt,23 Other Ranks, 5th D.L.I. 3 Other Ranks. 2 Field Cos,21st Divn arrived. 1 Pioneer Bn. 21st Divn.arr.	
	10.		Casualties - Other Ranks, Killed 1, Wounded 4.	
	11.		Casualties - Other Ranks, Killed 4, Wounded 7, includes 1 slightly at duty.	
	12.		Casualties - Other Ranks, Wounded 4. Reinforcements, R.F.A. 1 Off, 6th North'd Fus. 1 Off, 7th North'd Fus. 2 Officers, 4th Yorks Regt, 1 Off.	

Army Form C. 2118.

50TH DIVISION.

ADMINISTRATIVE.
WAR DIARY
or
INTELLIGENCE SUMMARY.
(Erase heading not required.)

OCTOBER, 1915.

Instructions regarding War Diaries and Intelligence Summaries are contained in F.S. Regs., Part II. and the Staff Manual respectively. Title pages will be prepared in manuscript.

Place	Date	Hour	Summary of Events and Information	Remarks and references to Appendices
ARMENTIERES	Oct. 13.		Casualties - Other Ranks, Killed 1, Died of wounds 1, Wounded 5.	
	14.		Casualties - Other Ranks, Killed 5, Wounded 21, includes 1 slightly at duty. 2 Bns. 62nd Bde left. 4 Bns. and Bde H.Q. 64th Bde, 21st Div. attached for instruction.	
	15.		Casualties - Other Ranks, Killed 3, Wounded 12.	
	16.		Casualties - Capt.E.Dales, 4th E.Yorks Regt,Wounded, Other Ranks, Wounded 9. Reinforcements, 2 M.G.,R.G.A., 2 Officers; Divnl Ammn.Col. Other Ranks 6; 5th North'd Fus. 18 Other Ranks; 6th North'd Fus. 1 Off, 37 Other Ranks; 4th East Yorks. 20 Other Ranks; 5th Yorks Regt. 17 Other Ranks; 5th D.L.I. 14 Other Ranks; 8th D.L.I. 3 Other Ranks.	
	17.		Casualties - Other Ranks, Killed 2, Wounded 3.	
	18.		Casualties - 2nd Lt.Vaus, 5th Yorks Regt, Wounded, Other Ranks Killed 5, Wounded 19. Reinforcements, 8th Durham L.I. Other Ranks 12. Major Franklin, A.D.of V.S. arrived.	
	19.		Casualties - Capt.H.A.Ryott, 6th North'd Fus: Wounded; Other Ranks Killed 1, Wounded 11. Reinforcements, 1st Field Co, Other Ranks 1, 2nd Field Co. Other Ranks 1.	
	20.		Casualties - Lt.D.McLaren, 4th Yorks Regt, Wounded; Other Ranks Wounded 7. Major Fail, A.D. of V.S., to England.	
	21.		Casualties - Other Ranks, Wounded 6.	

1577 Wt.W10791/1773 500,000 1/15 D. D. & L. A.D.S.S./Forms/C. 2118.

Army Form C. 2118.

ADMINISTRATIVE
WAR DIARY
or
INTELLIGENCE SUMMARY.
(Erase heading not required.)

50TH DIVISION. OCTOBER, 1915.

Instructions regarding War Diaries and Intelligence Summaries are contained in F. S. Regs., Part II. and the Staff Manual respectively. Title pages will be prepared in manuscript.

Place	Date	Hour	Summary of Events and Information	Remarks and references to Appendices
ARMENTIERES	Oct. 22.		Casualties - Lieut.A.Wilkinson, 5th D.L.I.,Wounded;O.R.Killed 1, Wounded 4. Divisional	
	23.		Artillery started to move to HONDEGHEM area.	
	24.		Casualties - Killed Other Ranks 3, Wounded Other Ranks 12.	
	25.		Casualties - Other Ranks, Killed 2, Wounded 4.	
	26.		Casualties - Other Ranks, Wounded 2. 149th Infantry Brigade to Strazeele area.	
	27.		Casualties - Other Ranks, Killed 1, Wounded 1.	
	28.		Casualties - Other Ranks, Killed 3, Wounded 3. H.M.The King inspected "representative" Composite Battalion formed from troops of the Division.	
	29.		**Casualties - Other Ranks, Wounded 1.**	
	30.		**Casualties - Other Ranks, Wounded 1.**	
	31.		**Casualties - Other Ranks, Killed 4, Wounded 4.**	
			Casualties - Other Ranks, Wounded 5.	

Confidential

War Diary

30th Division (A & Q)

From 1st November 1915
To 30th November 1915

Vol VIII

Army Form C. 2118

50TH DIVISION.

ADMINISTRATIVE.

WAR DIARY
or
INTELLIGENCE SUMMARY.

25TH NOVEMBER, 1915.

(Erase heading not required.)

Instructions regarding War Diaries and Intelligence Summaries are contained in F. S. Regs., Part II. and the Staff Manual respectively. Title pages will be prepared in manuscript.

Place	Date	Hour	Summary of Events and Information	Remarks and references to Appendices
ARMENTIERES	Nov. 1		Casualties, Other ranks killed 1, wounded 4.	
	2			
	3			
	4		Lieut. H.M. McNair wounded accidentally.	
	5		Casualties, Other ranks killed 1, wounded 6.	
	6		Casualties, Other ranks wounded 4, includes 1 slightly, at duty.	
	7		Casualties, Other ranks wounded 3.	
	8		Casualties, Other ranks wounded 5.	
	9		Casualties, other ranks killed 1, wounded 4. 1 Section No. 4 Coy. Divisional Train to OUTTERSTEENE, 1 Section No 2 Field Ambulance to STRAZEELE.	
	10		Casualties, Other ranks wounded 7, includes 5 accidentally at 2nd Army Bombing School, 5th November, 1915. 1 Battalion 150th Infantry Brigade to OUTTERSTEENE No.1 area. 2 Battalion 151st Brigade to LA CRECHE area, 1 Section No.3 Coy.Div'nl Train to LA CRECHE area.	
	11		Casualties, Other ranks killed 1, wounded.5.No. 4 Coy. Div'nl Train less 1 Section to OUTTERSTEENE, No. 2 Coy. Field Ambulance less 1 Section to PRADELLES. No 3 Coy. Field Ambulance less 1 Section to LA CRECHE.	

50TH DIVISION.

ADMINISTRATIVE.
WAR DIARY or INTELLIGENCE SUMMARY.

25TH NOVEMBER, 1915.

Army Form C. 2118.

Instructions regarding War Diaries and Intelligence Summaries are contained in F. S. Regs., Part II. and the Staff Manual respectively. Title pages will be prepared in manuscript.

(Erase heading not required.)

Place	Date	Hour	Summary of Events and Information	Remarks and references to Appendices
ARMENTIERES	Nov. 12		Casualties, Other ranks wounded 1. Mobile Veterinary Section and Field Ambulance Workshop Unit to MERRIS, Divisional Headquarters and Divisional Cyclist Coy. to MERRIS. 3 Battalions 150th Brigade to OUTTERSTEENE No. 1 area. No.3 Coy. Div'nl Train less 1 Section to LA CRECHE.	
MERRIS	13		Casualties, Other ranks killed 10, wounded 35 includes 10 slightly at duty, 7th Field Coy. R.E. ARMENTIERES. 3 Battalions 151st Brigade to LA CRECHE area. Left in ARMENTIERES No 1 and 2 Co panies Northumbrian R.E. 7th Field Coy. R.E. and 42nd Army Troops Coy. R.E.	
	14		Casualties, wounded 6, not previously reported.	
	15		Casualties, Other ranks, wounded 3 not previously reported.	
	16		Casualties, Other ranks wounded 3 ARMENTIERES.	
	17		Casualties, Other ranks wounded 2 ARMENTIERES.	
	18			
	19		2nd Army Commander inspected 149th Infantry Brigade.	
	20			
	21			
	22		2nd Army Commander inspected 151st Infantry Brigade.	
	23		Gas demonstration 151st Infantry Brigade. 2nd Army Commander inspected 150th Brigade. 18-pdrs arrive.	

Army Form C. 2118

50TH DIVISION.

ADMINISTRATIVE.
WAR DIARY
or
INTELLIGENCE SUMMARY.
(Erase heading not required.)

Instructions regarding War Diaries and Intelligence Summaries are contained in F. S. Regs., Part II. and the Staff Manual respectively. Title pages will be prepared in manuscript.

Place	Date	Hour	Summary of Events and Information	Remarks and references to Appendices
MERRIS.	Nov 24			
	25		Gas demonstration 149th Infantry Brigade. 18-pdr guns arrive.	
	26			
	27			
	28			
	29			
	30		2nd Army Commander inspected all Artillery (3 Brigades 18-pdr, 1 Brigade 5" Howitzer).	

Confidential

War Diary.

50th (North'n) Division

Administrative Staff.

From 1st December. 1915.
To 31st December. 1915.

Vol IX

Army Form C. 2118.

ADMINISTRATIVE
WAR DIARY
or
INTELLIGENCE SUMMARY.
(*Erase heading not required.*)

50TH DIVISION.   DECEMBER, 1915.

Instructions regarding War Diaries and Intelligence Summaries are contained in F. S. Regs., Part II. and the Staff Manual respectively. Title pages will be prepared in manuscript.

Place	Date	Hour	Summary of Events and Information	Remarks and references to Appendices
MORRIS.	Decr. 1.			
	2.		Major W.R.Dodds, Div.Signal Co, to England. Capt.Dale, R.E. to command Signal Co.	
	3.			
	4.			
	5.		Casualties - Other ranks, Killed 1 (accidentally) wounded 1 (acc.) 2nd Army Bomb School.	
	6.		Divisional Artillery to Practice Camp, WATTEN.	
	7.		1st, 2nd and 7th Field Cos, R.E., from ARMENTIERES to Divnl Area. 1st and 2nd Cos. CAESTRE, 7th Co. NOOTBOOM.	
	8.		Major Withy, A.S.C. from 63rd Division, for training in 'Q' Branch.	
	9.			
	10.			
	11.		Floods in LA CRECHE Area.	
	12.			
	13.		1st, 2nd and 7th Field Cos R.E. to H.21.b. Sheet 28 - New Area. Details to 5th Corps H.Qrs.	
	14.			
	15.		Advance Party to new area 5th Corps.	

Army Form C. 2118.

ADMINISTRATIVE
WAR DIARY
or
INTELLIGENCE SUMMARY.
(Erase heading not required.)

50TH DIVISION.

DECEMBER, 1915.

Instructions regarding War Diaries and Intelligence Summaries are contained in F. S. Regs., Part II. and the Staff Manual respectively. Title pages will be prepared in manuscript.

Place	Date	Hour	Summary of Events and Information	Remarks and references to Appendices
MERRIS.	Decr. 16.		Mounted Troops and Cyclists to New Area.	
	17.		1 Bn. 149th, 150th and 151st Brigades by rail to POPERINGHE, also H.Qrs and 1 Co, 7th D.L.I. Pioneers.	
	18.		1 Bn. 149th, 150th and 151st Brigades by rail to POPERINGHE, also 1 Coy, 7th D.L.I. Pioneers.	
	19.		Casualties - Capt.J.E.Brydon, R.A.M.C. Wounded, Hon.Lt.& Qr.Mr.F.W.Cook,4th East Yorks Wounded, Other Ranks, Wounded 2. 1 Bn. 149th, 150th and 151st Brigades by rail to POPERINGHE, also 1 Coy, 7th D.L.I. Pioneers. Advanced Section Royal Artillery to New Area.	
	20.		Casualties - Major C.B.O.Symons,7th Field Co,R.E. Wounded, 2nd Lt.J.B.Glubb, Wounded,slightly at duty, Lt-Col.J.W.Jeffreys, 6th Bn.Durham L.I. Wounded, Other Ranks Killed 2, Wounded 15. Remainder Royal Artillery to New Area.	
HOOGGRAAF.	21.		Casualties - Lt. H.Y.Bell, 5th North'd Fus; Wounded, Lt. J.E.Stafford, 9th Durham L.I. Wounded slightly at duty, Other Ranks Killed 6, Wounded 17. 50th Division took over New Line 10 a.m. On our right 3rd Division, on our left 17th Division. All 3 Brigades in Line.	
	22.		Casualties - Other Ranks Killed 2, Wounded 26.	
	23.		Casualties - 2nd Lt.L.H.Pobery, 6th Durham L.I. Killed, Other Ranks, Killed 3, Wounded 6.	
	24.		Casualties - Other Ranks Wounded 14.	
	25.		Casualties - Lt.S.T.Dopkin, 7th Nb'd Fus, Capt.G.J.Scott, 5th Yorks Regt, Killed, 2nd Lt.C.H. Dell, 5th Yorks Regt, Lt.T.P.Fry, 5th Durham L.I. Wounded, Capt.J.A.B.Thomson, 5th Yorks Regt.	

Army Form C. 2118.

50TH DIVISION.

DECEMBER, 1915.

ADMINISTRATIVE

WAR DIARY

OF

INTELLIGENCE SUMMARY.

(Erase heading not required.)

Instructions regarding War Diaries and Intelligence Summaries are contained in F. S. Regs., Part II. and the Staff Manual respectively. Title pages will be prepared in manuscript.

Place	Date	Hour	Summary of Events and Information	Remarks and references to Appendices
HOOGGRAAF.	Decr. 25.		- Wounded slightly at duty, Other Ranks Killed 4, Wounded 8.	
	26.		Casualties - Killed 3, Wounded 4 (includes 1 self-inflicted) Other Ranks. Brigadier-General Henshaw, C.R.A. left for 15th Corps. Brigadier-General W.A.Robinson, C.R.A.	
	27.		Casualties - Other Ranks Killed 1, Wounded 3.	
	28.		Casualties - Other Ranks Killed 1, Wounded 7.	
	29.		Casualties - Lieut.H.Miley, 1st North'bn Bde,R.F.A. Wounded; Lieut.W.V.Varvill, 1st North'bn Field Co,R.E. Wounded, Lieut-Colonel V.T.Wilkinson, D.S.O., 4th East Yor'ks Regt, Wounded slightly at duty. Other Ranks Wounded 8.	
	30.		Casualties - Other Ranks Killed 5, Wounded 12.	
	31.		Lieut.J.S.Bainbridge,4th Yorks Regt,Wounded;Lieut.G.A.Birnie,R.A.M.C.,attd 5th N.F., Wounded, Other Ranks Killed 1, Wounded 11. Major Bonham Carter to G.S.O.1, 7th Division.	
			Note: Importance of every man having 1 pair Gum Boots,Thigh,in trenches, warm food and drink.	

Confidential

50th Division.

Administrative Staff

War Diary

From 1st January 1916.

To 31st January 1916.

Vol X

Army Form C. 2118.

50TH DIVISION.
ADMINISTRATIVE
WAR DIARY
or
INTELLIGENCE SUMMARY.

(Erase heading not required.)

JANUARY, 1916.

Instructions regarding War Diaries and Intelligence Summaries are contained in F. S. Regs., Part II. and the Staff Manual respectively. Title pages will be prepared in manuscript.

Place	Date	Hour	Summary of Events and Information	Remarks and references to Appendices
HOOGRAAF.	JANY. 1.		Casualties – Other Ranks, Killed 2, Wounded 15, includes 1 accidental.	
	2.		Casualties – Other Ranks, Wounded 13. Major A.G. Stewart, G.S.O. 2, arrived. Major C. Bonham Carter to 7th Division. Major E.R. Clayton, Brigade Major, 151st Infantry Brigade to 11th Corps as G.S.O. 2.	
	3.		Casualties – 2nd Lt. A.C. Clapham, 4th East Yorks Regt. Killed. Other Ranks Killed 1, Wounded 6. Major-General Forster, Brigadier-General Gilbert, and 14 Officers 57th Division, attached for instruction.	
	4.		Casualties – 2nd Lieut. R.G. Smith, 4th North'bn (How) Brigade, Wounded slightly, at duty. Capt. H.K. Woodhead, 18th Res. Inf. Bde. Wounded. Other ranks Killed 2, Wounded 8, including 1 slightly at duty, 1 self-inflicted.	
	5.		Casualties – Major S.B. Quibell, 4th East Yorks. Wounded. Other Ranks 2 Killed, 17 Wounded.	
	6.		Casualties – 2nd Lieutenants W.H. Collinson, E.R.B. White, Killed. Capt. E. Temperley. 2nd Lieut. C. Cooke, wounded. 6th Bn. Northumberland Fusiliers. Other ranks 2 killed including 1 accidentally, wounded 7 including 1 accidentally. Officers attached for instruction left.	
	7.		Casualties – Capt. W. Southern and Lieut. A.O. Dyer, 1st North'bn Brigade, R.F.A. 2nd Lieut. T.W. Greenwell, 6th Northumberland Fusiliers, wounded. Other ranks Killed 1, wounded 9.	
	8.		Casualties – Capt. G.V. Grinnell, 4th East Yorks, wounded. Other ranks Killed 2, Wounded 10.	

1577 Wt.W10791/1773 500,000 1/15 D.D.&L. A.D.S.S./Forms/C. 2118.

Army Form C. 2118.

50TH DIVISION.

ADMINISTRATIVE.

WAR DIARY
or
INTELLIGENCE SUMMARY.

(Erase heading not required.)

Instructions regarding War Diaries and Intelligence Summaries are contained in F.S. Regs., Part II. and the Staff Manual respectively. Title pages will be prepared in manuscript.

JANUARY, 1916.

Place	Date	Hour	Summary of Events and Information	Remarks and references to Appendices
HOOGRAAF.	JANY. 9.		Casualties – Major T.P. Guthe, and Lieut. E.R. Bushell, 3rd Northumbrian Brigade, R.F.A.	
	10.		2nd Lieut. W.D. Hubbard, 4th Yorkshire Regiment, wounded. Other ranks killed 2, wounded 5.	
			Casualties – Major F.P. Paynter, 4th North'bn Brigade, R.F.A. Killed. Capt. G.F. Bell, 4th Northumberland Fusiliers, wounded slightly at duty. Other ranks killed 7, wounded 9.	
	11.		Casualties – 2nd Lieut. H.S. Lambert, 5th Yorkshire Regiment, killed. Other ranks killed 9, wounded 14.	
	12.		Casualties – Killed 1. Wounded 4. Other ranks.	
	13.		Casualties – Killed 1, Wounded 8. Other ranks.	
	14.		Casualties – Capt. H. Cheesmond, 4th Northumberland Fusiliers, wounded. Other ranks wounded 2.	
	15.		Casualties – Other ranks wounded 11.	
	16.		Casualties – 2nd Lieut. J.C. Corringham, 8th Durham Light Infantry, wounded. Other ranks killed 1, wounded 4.	
	17.		Casualties – Capt. G.E. Gardew, Devon: Regt: (attached 6th Durham Light Infantry) Lieut. G.E. Atkinson, 8th Durham Light Infantry wounded. Other ranks killed 2, wounded 4.	
	18.		Casualties – Capt. H.F. Wilkin, R.A.M.C. (attcd. 5th Durham Light Infantry) wounded, Major A.L. Raines and Major H. Ensor, 5th Durham Light Infantry wounded, slightly at duty. Other ranks killed 1, wounded 17.	

Army Form C. 2118.

50th Division.

JANUARY, 1916.

ADMINISTRATIVE WAR DIARY or INTELLIGENCE SUMMARY.

(Erase heading not required.)

Instructions regarding War Diaries and Intelligence Summaries are contained in F. S. Regs., Part II and the Staff Manual respectively. Title pages will be prepared in manuscript.

Place	Date	Hour	Summary of Events and Information	Remarks and references to Appendices
HOOGRAAF	JANY 19.		Casualties - Other ranks Killed 2, Wounded 16.	
	20.		Casualties - Other ranks Killed 2. Wounded 8.	
	21.		Casualties - 2/Lieut. C. Barnard, 7th Northumberland Fusiliers, wounded. Other ranks wounded 4.	
	22.		Casualties - Captain R.W. Nicholson, 6th Northumberland Fusiliers, wounded. Other ranks Killed 2, wounded 13.	
	23.		Casualties - Major S.B. Quibell, 4th East Yorks. Regt. Wounded. Other ranks wounded 8.	
	24.		Casualties - Lieut. J.S.C. Herald, 5th Durham Light Infantry, Killed, Other ranks wounded 8.	
	25.		Casualties - Major G.C. Pollard, R.E. 2nd Lieut. C.A. Collingwood, 2nd Lieut.W.R. Allen, 4th Northumberland Fusiliers, Wounded. Other ranks Killed 2, Wounded 19.	
	26.		Casualties - Capt. D.H. Walker, 5th Yorkshire Regiment, Wounded. Other ranks Killed 4, Wounded 4.	
	27.		Casualties - Capt. D.H. Walker, 5th Yorkshire Regiment, died of wounds, 2/Lieut T. Mack, 9th Durham Light Infantry, killed. Lieut. S.W. Milburn, 3rd Mbn. Brigade R.F.A. Wounded slightly, at duty. Other ranks killed 2, Wounded 11. 1 Naval Officer & 10 men R.N. arrived.	
	28.		Casualties - Other ranks wounded 6. (29^{d}) Lt. Col. G.V. Hordern, G.S.O. 1 left for B.G.G.S. 1st Corps.	

Army Form C. 2118.

ADMINISTRATIVE.
WAR DIARY
or
INTELLIGENCE SUMMARY.
(Erase heading not required.)

Instructions regarding War Diaries and Intelligence Summaries are contained in F. S. Regs., Part II. and the Staff Manual respectively. Title pages will be prepared in manuscript.

Place	Date	Hour	Summary of Events and Information	Remarks and references to Appendices
HOOGRAAF	JANY. 29.		Casualties - Other ranks Killed 3, Wounded 16.	
	30.		Casualties - C.H.D. Seymour, 5th Northumberland Fusiliers, Wounded. Other ranks Killed 4, Wounded 15. 1 Naval Officer, 10 men R.N. left. Lieut. Wilkinson, A.D.C. arrived. Major Thorpe. G.S.O. 2. arrived from 9th Division.	
	31.		Casualties - Other ranks Killed 2. Wounded 15.	

1577 Wt.W10791/1773 500,000 1/15 D. D. & L. A.D.S.S./Forms/C. 2118.

Confidential

Administrative Staff.
War Diary.

50th (Northumbrian) Division

From 1st February 1916.

To 29th February 1916.

Vol XI

Army Form C. 2118.

50TH DIVISION.

FEBRUARY, 1916.

ADMINISTRATIVE
WAR DIARY
or
INTELLIGENCE SUMMARY.
(Erase heading not required.)

Instructions regarding War Diaries and Intelligence Summaries are contained in F. S. Regs., Part II. and the Staff Manual respectively. Title pages will be prepared in manuscript.

Place	Date	Hour	Summary of Events and Information	Remarks and references to Appendices
HOOGRAAF.	FEB. 1.		Casualties – Other Ranks Killed 2, Wounded 5.	
	2.		Casualties – Killed 2/Lt.J.B.Roberts, 4th North'd Fusiliers; O.R. Killed 2, Wounded 9.	
	3.		Casualties – Wounded 2/Lt.C.Stephenson, 4th North'd Fusiliers, O.R. Killed 3, Wounded 6.	
	4.		Casualties – Other Ranks Killed 2, Wounded 6, incl: 1 slightly at duty. Major H.W.Grubb, D.A.A.& Q.M.G., left to take up duty as A.A.& Q.M.G., 56th Division.	
	5.		Casualties – Wounded 2/Lt.C.G.Sharp, 4th North'd Fusiliers, O.R. Killed 5, Wounded 11.	
	6.		Casualties – Killed,Capt P.D.Forrett, 2/Lt.F.C.Phillips, 5th North'd Fusiliers, Wounded 2/Lt. H.W.Gill, 5th North'd Fusiliers; O.R. Killed 3, Wounded 10.	
	7.		Casualties – Died of Wounds,2/Lt.C.G.Sharp, 4th North'd Fusiliers; Wounded Lt.E.Doherty, 3rd North'bn Field Amblce; O.R. Killed 6, Wounded 30 incl: 1 slightly at duty. Major B.C.Battye, left to take up duty as Brigade Major,141st Brigade. Captain W.Anderson, 6th North'd Fusiliers, assumed duty as G.S.O.3.	
	8.		Casualties – Wounded 2/Lt.G.Palmer,9th D.L.I.; Wounded slightly at duty 2/Lt.H.G.Weller, 175th Tunnelling Co,R.E.; O.R. Killed 9, Wounded 24,incl: 3 slightly at duty.	
	9.		Casualties – Wounded Lt.W.Golding, R.F.A.,2/Lt.G.R.Angus, 6th D.L.I., Major J.A.S.Ritson,8th D.L.I.; Lt.E.H.Motum, 8th D.L.I; O.R. Killed 5, Wounded 40, incl: 5 slightly at duty.	

ADMINISTRATIVE

50TH DIVISION. FEBRUARY, 1916. WAR DIARY

or

INTELLIGENCE SUMMARY.

(Erase heading not required.)

Army Form C. 2118.

Instructions regarding War Diaries and Intelligence
Summaries are contained in F. S. Regs., Part II.
and the Staff Manual respectively. Title pages
will be prepared in manuscript.

Place	Date	Hour	Summary of Events and Information	Remarks and references to Appendices
HOOGRAAF.	FEBY. 9.		Captain A.E.G.Palmer, Yorks Regt assumed duty as D.A.A.& Q.M.G.,	
	10.		Casualties - O.R. Killed 2, Wounded 31.	
	11.		Casualties - O.R. Killed 6, Wounded 8.	
	12.		Casualties - Wounded Lt.R.N.Nickels, 2nd North'bn Bde,R.F.A. O.R. Killed 2, Wounded 10.	
	13.		Casualties - Other Ranks Killed 6, Wounded 25.	
	14.		Casualties - Other Ranks Wounded 7,incl: 1 accidentally.	
	15.		Casualties - Killed 2/Lt.J.W.Daglish,4th Yorks Regt; Wounded 2/Lt.R.G.Harrowing, 4th Yorks Regt, Lt.N.H.Joy, 4th E.Yorks, Wounded slightly at duty Capt.H.Boyd Cunningham,R.A.M.C.,3rd North'bn Brigade,R.F.A.; O.R. Killed 38, Wounded 119.	
	16.		Casualties - Wounded, Lt.A.R.Welsh,4th Yorks Regt, Lt.E.A.Fawcus,6th North'd Fusiliers, O.R. Killed 7, Wounded 27.	
	17.		Casualties - Killed Capt.J.Maughan,4th Yorks Regt, Wounded slightly at duty Capt.N.W.Stead, 4th Yorks Regt, O.R. Killed 1, Wounded 9. Major F.H.Moore,D.S.O., Brigade Major,149th Infantry Brigade,left for duty as G.S.O.2,23rd Division.	
	18.		Casualties - Wounded Capt.R.K.Dibb, 4th E.Yorks Regt, O.R.Wounded 9,incl: 1 slightly at duty.	
	19.		Casualties - O.R. Killed 7, Wounded 11.	

Army. Form C. 2118.

Instructions regarding War Diaries and Intelligence Summaries are contained in F. S. Regs., Part II, and the Staff Manual respectively. Title Pages will be prepared in manuscript.

50TH DIVISION.

ADMINISTRATIVE
WAR DIARY
or
INTELLIGENCE SUMMARY

(*Erase heading not required*).

FEBRUARY 1916.

Place	Date	Hour	Summary of Events and Information	Remarks and references to Appendices
HOOGRAAF.	FEBY. 20.		Casualties - Killed,Lt.R.E.Atkinson,9th D.L.I., Wounded Capt.W.P.Gill,6th D.L.I., O.R. Wounded 5.	
	21.		Casualties - Wounded, Capt.J.Welch,7th North'd Fusiliers, Wounded slightly at duty,Capt. H.Shield, R.A.M.C. attd 4th Yorks Regt; O.R.Killed 2, Wounded 6.	
			Capt.E.Withy,A.S.C. (attached) left for England.	
	22.		Casualties - O.R. Killed 2, Wounded 8.	
	23.		Casualties - O.R. Killed 1, Wounded 14.	
	24.		Casualties - Died of Wounds Lt.J.H.Edgar, 9th D.L.I; Killed,Lt.L.Ewbank,5th Border Regt; O.R. Killed 2, Wounded 13.	
	25.		Casualties - Other Ranks,Killed 6, Wounded 32.	
	26.		Casualties - Other Ranks,Wounded 5.	
	27.		Casualties - Killed Lt.E.M.Thompson, 5th Yorks Regt. O.R. Killed 16, Wounded 28. 8th D.L.I.	
	28.		Casualties - Killed,Lt.R.E.Harrison; Wounded 2/Lt.J.H.Scarth,4th Yorks Regt; O.R. Killed 3, Wounded 18.	
			4th Northumberland Fusiliers evacuated Scottish Lines and went to Dickebusch Huts.	
	29.		Casualties - Other Ranks,Killed 5, Wounded 17.	

BSD B ME31 22/1 12/15 5000.

HQ A+Q 50 Div / Vol XII

Confidential

War Diary

of

50th (Northumbrian) Division

From 1st March 1916.

To 31st March 1916.

Army Form C. 2118.

ADMINISTRATIVE
WAR DIARY
or
INTELLIGENCE SUMMARY.
(Erase heading not required.)

50TH (NORTHUMBRIAN) DIVISION.   MARCH, 1916.

Instructions regarding War Diaries and Intelligence Summaries are contained in F. S. Regs., Part II. and the Staff Manual respectively. Title pages will be prepared in manuscript.

Place	Date	Hour	Summary of Events and Information	Remarks and references to Appendices
HOOGRAAF.	March 1st.		Casualties - O.R. Killed 8, Wounded 22, includes 1 slightly at duty. 8th Yorks Regt (3rd Div.) occupied Scottish Lines.	
	2nd.		Casualties - Killed, 4th Yorks Regt, Lt.G.H.Hutchinson, 5th Yorks Regt, Lieut.E.R.Spofforth, wounded 2nd Lt.H.Barron,R.G.A.,Trench Mortars; 2nd Lt. F.S.Steenberg, 149th Bde Machine Gun Coy; Capt.J.A.R.Thompson and Lieut.E.H.Weighell, 5th Yorks Regt; 2nd Lt.G.Atkinson, 8th D.L.I. O.R. Killed 30, Wounded 97, includes 1 slightly at duty, Missing,believed killed 1.	
	3rd.		Casualties - Wounded Lt.W.H.Bainbridge,6th North'd Fusiliers; 2nd Lt.A.Colter, 8th Durham L.I. Capt.E.A.Abraham, & Lt.J.D.Rickaby, 9th Durham L.I., O.R. Killed 16, Wounded 73, Missing 10. Captain Bayford,attached to 150th Infantry Brigade for one week.	
	4th.		Casualties - O.R. Killed 8, Wounded 28, Missing 1. 8 missing rejoined.	
	5th.		Casualties - Wounded,Lt.F.W.Webb, 47th Siege Battery,R.G.A. O.R. Killed 4,Wounded 11.	
	6th.		Casualties - Wounded 2nd Lt. W.E.Hewatt, 4th East Yorks Regt. O.R. Killed 2, Wounded 5.	
	7th.		Casualties - O.R. Killed 8, Missing 2,reported wounded, 1 missing rejoined.	
	8th.		Casualties - O.R. Wounded 6.	
	9th.		Casualties - O.R. Killed 6, wounded 5.	
	10th.		Casualties - O.R. Killed 4, Wounded 5.	

T2134. Wt. W708—776. 500000. 4/15. Sir J. C. & S.

Army Form C. 2118.

50TH (NORTHUMBRIAN) DIVISION.

ADMINISTRATIVE WAR DIARY or INTELLIGENCE SUMMARY.

MARCH, 1916.

(Erase heading not required.)

Instructions regarding War Diaries and Intelligence Summaries are contained in F.S. Regs., Part II. and the Staff Manual respectively. Title pages will be prepared in manuscript.

Place	Date	Hour	Summary of Events and Information	Remarks and references to Appendices
HOOGRAAF.	10th.		150th Brigade, 1 Bn.at "D" Campn G.30.a. 3 Bns at POPERINGHE. 151st Brigade at DICKEBUSCH and CANADA HUTS. 149th Brigade in line.	
	11th.		Casualties - Wounded slightly at duty, Capt.G.F.Bell, 6th Bn.North'd Fusiliers, O.R.Killed 2, Wounded 12.	
	12th.		Casualties - Wounded 2nd Lt.A.H.Topham, 5th North'd Fusiliers; O.R. Killed 5, Wounded 19.	
	13th.		Casualties - O.R. Killed 3, Wounded 13,includes 2 slightly at duty	
	14th.		Casualties - O.R. Killed 1, Wounded 5,includes 1 slightly at duty.	
	15th.		Casualties - O.R. Killed 4, Wounded 10.	
	16th.		Casualties - Wounded,2nd Lt.H.Blackman,6th D.L.I. O.R. Killed 3, Wounded 8.	
	17th.		Casualties - Killed,Major L.A.Barrett,4th Yorks Regt, Wounded Lieut.R.Ferraby,4th East Yorks, Lt.-Colonel J.R.Hedley, 5th Border Regt,Wounded slightly at duty; O.R.Killed 3,Wounded 11. includes 1 slightly at duty.	
	18th.		Casualties - O.R. Killed 2, Wounded 7, includes 1 slightly at duty.	
	19th.		Casualties - O.R. Wounded 9; Captain Bayford,D.S.O. 18th Hussars,to V. Corps.	
	20th.		Casualties - Wounded, Lieut.P.E.Grant, D61 Battery,R.F.A; O.R. Killed 8, Wounded 21, includes 1 at duty.	

T2134. Wt. W708—776. 500000. 4/15. Sir J.C. & S.

Army Form C. 2118.

50TH (NORTHUMBRIAN) DIVISION.

ADMINISTRATIVE
WAR DIARY
or
INTELLIGENCE SUMMARY.
(Erase heading not required.)

MARCH, 1916.

Instructions regarding War Diaries and Intelligence Summaries are contained in F. S. Regs., Part II. and the Staff Manual respectively. Title pages will be prepared in manuscript.

Place	Date	Hour	Summary of Events and Information	Remarks and references to Appendices
HOOGRAAF.	21st.		Casualties - O.R. Killed 3, Wounded 8, includes 3 at duty.	
	22nd.		Casualties -(Capt. R.Condy, R.A.M.C. attd 4th Yorks Regt; Killed 2, Wounded 16, includes 3 at duty. (Wounded slightly at duty.)	
	23rd.		Casualties - O.R. Killed 1.	
	24th.		Casualties - O.R. Killed 5, Wounded 2.	
	25th.		Casualties - Wounded, 2nd Lt.H.G.Robson, 5th North'd Fusiliers, 2nd Lt.J.H.C.Swinney, 7th North'd Fusiliers; O.R. Killed 2, Wounded 18, includes 2 at duty.	
	26th.		Casualties - Wounded Capt.N.A.Mackinnon, 7th Durham L.I., Lt.R.Ellis, 5th North'd Fusiliers, O.R. Killed 1, Wounded 2.	
	27th.		Casualties - Killed 2nd Lt.R.F.Burt,7th North'd Fusiliers; 2nd Lt.W.Lawson, 8th Durham L.I. Wounded 2nd Lt.F.Merivale, 7th North'd Fusiliers, Capt.R.A.Howe, 2nd Lt.K.B.Stuart, 6th Durham I.I., O.R.Killed 9, Wounded 29, includes 3 at duty. (Killed 1(Lieut.J.R.Platt, 3rd Northumbrian Brigade, R.F.A.	
	28th.		Casualties -(O.R. Killed 5, Wounded 14. 150th Brigade and No.4 Coy Divnl Train to Canadian Rest Area II.	
	29th.		Casualties - Wounded O.R. 12, includes 1 accidental.	
	30th.		Casualties - Killed O.R.1, Wounded 5, includes 1 at duty. 2 Bns 150th Brigade from Canadian Rest Area II to LOCRE.	

T2134. Wt. W708-776. 500000. 4/15. Sir J. C. & S.

50TH (NORTHUMBRIAN) DIVISION.

ADMINISTRATIVE WAR DIARY or **INTELLIGENCE SUMMARY.**

(Erase heading not required.)

Army Form C. 2118.

MARCH, 1916.

Instructions regarding War Diaries and Intelligence Summaries are contained in F. S. Regs., Part II. and the Staff Manual respectively. Title pages will be prepared in manuscript.

Place	Date	Hour	Summary of Events and Information	Remarks and references to Appendices
HOOGRAAF.	31st.		Casualties - Wounded, O.R.5. Mounted Troops to WESTOUTRE. Headquarters and 2 Battalions 150th Brigade to LOCRE.	

HQ A+Q / Vol XIII

Confidential

Administrative Staff.

War Diary.

50th (Northumbrian) Division.

From 1st April 1916

to 30th April 1916.

Army Form C. 2118.

ADMINISTRATIVE
WAR DIARY
or
INTELLIGENCE SUMMARY

(Erase heading not required.)

50TH DIVISION. **APRIL, 1916.**

Instructions regarding War Diaries and Intelligence Summaries are contained in F.S. Regs., Part II. and the Staff Manual respectively. Title Pages will be prepared in manuscript.

Place	Date	Hour	Summary of Events and Information	Remarks and references to Appendices
HOOGRAAF.	APRIL 1.		Casualties - O.R. Killed 2, Wounded 3. 2 Battns, 149th Inf.Bde to Canadian Rest Area I.	
	2.		Casualties - Wounded, Captain J.G.HARTER, D.L.I. Brigade Major, 151st Inf.Bde. Wounded O.R. 1. 2 Battns 149th Brigade to LOCRE.	
	3.		Casualties - Died of Wounds, Captain J.G.Harter. Killed O.R.6, Wounded 44, Missing 4. 2 Battns 151st Brigade to LA CLYTTE. Division took over new line 3 p.m. Headquarters, WESTOUTRE.	
	4.		Casualties - Wounded at duty, Capt.A.L.CURRY, 4th Nbn.Bde, R.F.A., O.R.15, including 3 at duty. 2 Battns 151st Inf.Bde to RIDGEWOOD.	
	5.		Casualties - Killed 2nd Lieut. P.C.BURTON, 4th East Yorks Regt; O.R. Killed 5, Wounded 17, including 3 at duty.	
	6.		Casualties - Wounded 2nd Lieut.A.E.ELLIOT, 7th Bn.North'd Fusiliers; Lieut.J.N.FRANKS,5th Border Regt; Lt.H.C.MACNAMARA, Trench Mortar Battery; Wounded at duty Lt.J.COUTTS,R.A.M.C. 3rd North'bn Field Ambloe; Capt.G.F.BELL, 6th Bn.North'd Fusrs; O.R. Killed 2, Wounded 29, including 1 at duty.	
	7.		Casualties - O.R. Killed 1, Wounded 8, including 1 at duty.	
	8.		Casualties - Wounded 2nd Lt.H.N.LAING, 4th Yorks Regt; O.R. Killed 4, Wounded 26,incl:4 at duty.	
	9.		Casualties - O.R. Killed 4, Wounded 25, including 1 at duty.	
	10.		Casualties - Wounded R.H.WHARRIER, 8th Bn.D.L.I. O.R.Killed 3, Wounded 41. 2nd Lt/	
	11.		Casualties - Wounded 2nd Lt.F.O.OUTHWAITE, 7th Bn.North'd Fusrs; Capt.W.MARLEY, 5th Bn.D.L.I. O.R. Killed 4, Wounded 27, including 2 at duty, 1 self-inflicted.	
	12.		Casualties - Killed, 2nd Lt.H.L.BENSON, 6th Bn.North'd Fusrs; Wounded Lt.S.R.C.PLIMSOLL, 2nd Northumbrian Brigade, R.F.A. Capt.R.W.NICHOLSON, 2nd Lt.E.L.BELL, 6th Bn.North'd Fusrs.	

Army Form C. 2118.

ADMINISTRATIVE
WAR DIARY
or
INTELLIGENCE SUMMARY

(Erase heading not required.)

50TH DIVISION.
APRIL, 1916.

Instructions regarding War Diaries and Intelligence Summaries are contained in F. S. Regs., Part II. and the Staff Manual respectively. Title Pages will be prepared in manuscript.

Place	Date	Hour	Summary of Events and Information	Remarks and references to Appendices
WESTOUTRE.	APRIL 12.		Casualties - Wounded Major A.L.RAIMES, 5th Bn.D.L.I.; O.R. Killed 5, Wounded 41, incl:1 at duty.	
	13.		Casualties - Killed O.R. 10, Wounded 32.	
	14.		Casualties - Wounded Capt.V.F.GLOAG, 5th Bn.D.L.I. O.R. Killed 4, Wounded 16.	
	15.		Casualties - O.R. Killed 4, Wounded 12, including 1 self-inflicted. Capt.Hon.FRAZER,Gordon Highlanders, joined as Brigade Major, 151st Infantry Brigade.	
	16.		Casualties - Killed,Lt.P.W.MACLAGAN, 5th Border Regt; O.R. Killed 4, Wounded 11.	
	17.		Casualties - O.R. Killed 4, Wounded 12.	
	18.		Casualties - Killed Capt.N.H.BETTISON,9th Bn.D.L.I. O.R. Killed 1, Wounded 5. Major R.G. Thomson, Brigade Major, R.A. left to take up duties 153rd Brigade,R.F.A. Major FERGUSSON, joined for duty as Brigade Major, R.F.A.	
	19.		Casualties - O.R. Killed 2, Wounded 14.	
	20.		Casualties - Wounded Lt.H.E.JACKSON, 4th Bn.East Yorks Regt; O.R. Killed 3, Wounded 19.	
	21.		Casualties - O.R. Killed 2, Wounded 17.	
	22.		Casualties - Wounded, Lt.W.P.BENNETT, Trench Mortar Battery, 5th Border Regt: O.R. Killed 4, Wounded 23.	
	23.		Casualties - O.R. Killed 4, Wounded 13. Headquarters,151st Inf.Bde to Rest Area, S. of MONT DE CATS.	
	24.		Casualties - Wounded 2nd Lt.R.W.GODLEY, R.G.A. Trench Mortar Bde; 2nd Lt.R.K.TEASDALE, 7th Bn. North'd Fusrs; 2nd Lt.C.W.READ, 8th Bn.D.L.I. O.R. Killed 2, Wounded 10.	

Army Form C. 2118.

ADMINISTRATIVE
WAR DIARY
or
INTELLIGENCE SUMMARY

(Erase heading not required.)

50TH DIVISION.   APRIL, 1916.

Instructions regarding War Diaries and Intelligence Summaries are contained in F. S. Regs., Part II. and the Staff Manual respectively. Title Pages will be prepared in manuscript.

Place	Date	Hour	Summary of Events and Information	Remarks and references to Appendices
FLETRE.	APRIL 25th.		Casualties - Wounded Lt.C.M.JOICEY, 4th Bn.North'd Fusrs; O.R. Killed 1, Wounded 17. Divisional H.Q. to Fletre. 149th Inf.Bde H.Q. from BRULOOZE to LOCRE.	
	26th.		Casualties - Killed O.R. 1, Wounded 5, incl.2 at duty.	
	27th.		Casualties - Wounded 2nd Lt.E.M.ROBSON, 5th Bn.Yorks Regt; O.R. Killed 2, Wounded 11. Headquarters 150th Inf.Bde from LOCRE to THIESOUK.	
	28th.		Casualties - O.R. Wounded 4.	
	29th.		Casualties - Wounded at duty 2nd Lt.L.G.,CARPENTER., 5th Bn.D.L.I. Commander-in-Chief inspected 151st Infantry Brigade.	
	30th.		Casualties - Wounded, O.R. 3.	

2449 Wt. W14957/M90 750,000 1/16 J.B.C. & A. Forms/C.2118/12.

50th (NORTHUMBRIAN) DIVISION.

ADMINISTRATIVE STAFF

WAR DIARY.

F R O M :- 1st May. 1916.
T O   :- 31st May. 1916.

ORIGINAL Army Form C. 2118.

50TH DIVISION.

ADMINISTRATIVE
WAR DIARY
or
INTELLIGENCE SUMMARY
(Erase heading not required.)

MAY, 1916.

Place	Date	Hour	Summary of Events and Information	Remarks and references to Appendices
FLETRE	MAY 1		Headquarters, Divisional Artillery, Westoutre – moved to EECKE.	
	2		Casualties – O.R. wounded 2. General Officer Commanding visit to Base, HAVRE.	
	3		Casualties – ------	
	4		Casualties – ------	
	5		Casualties – ------ General Officer Commanding returned from HAVRE.	
	6		Casualties – ------	
	7		Casualties – ------	
	8		Casualties – ------	
	9		Casualties – ------	
	10		Casualties – ------	
	11		Casualties – ------	
	12		Casualties – ------	
	13		Casualties – ------	
	14		Casualties – ------	
	15		Casualties – ------	
	16		Brig.-Gen. J.S.M.SHEA, C.B., D.S.O., to command 30th Division.	
	17		Brig.-Gen. P.T.WESTMORLAND, C.M.G., D.S.O., to command 151st Inf. Bgde. Brig.-Gen. SHEA left to take up new command.	

2449 Wt. W14957/M90 750,000 1/16 J.R.C. & A. Forms/C.2118/12.

Army Form C. 2118.

ADMINISTRATIVE
WAR DIARY
or
INTELLIGENCE SUMMARY
(Erase heading not required.)

50TH DIVISION.   MAY, 1916.

Instructions regarding War Diaries and Intelligence Summaries are contained in F. S. Regs., Part II. and the Staff Manual respectively. Title Pages will be prepared in manuscript.

Place	Date	Hour	Summary of Events and Information	Remarks and references to Appendices
FLETRE	MAY 18		Casualties ---	
	19		Casualties ---	
	20		Casualties ---	
	21		Casualties - 250th Bgde, RFA, wounded accidentally by tampering with a German fuze, O.R. 6. V Corps Cyclists and Mounted Troops (less Headquarters) to KEMMEL DEFENCES.	
	22		Casualties - 2/Lieut. A.G.HESLOP, 9th Bn. Durham L.I. accidentally wounded; wounded O.R. 2, includes one accidentally.	
	23		2 Battalions 149th Inf. Brigade to LOCRE. Second Army Commander presented Distinguished Conduct and Military Medals to Division.	
	24		Casualties ---	
	25		Casualties - 151st Inf. Bgde Bombing accident, casualties - 2/Lieut.'s Mackay and Bennett, 5th Border Regt., and 2/Lieut. Stooken, Middlesex Regt., att'd 5th Border Regt wounded; O.R. killed 3, wounded 13. 2 Battalions 149th Inf. Bgde to LOCRE.	
	26		Casualties - Wounded 2/Lieut.'s Adams, Robson, Watson, Rendell and Magee, 5th North'd Fus. O.R. killed 9, wounded 60, includes 1 at duty. 2 Battalions 150th Bgde to LOCRE. 2 Battalions 151st Inf. Bgde to LA CLYTTE.	
WESTOUTRE	27		Casualties - O.R. killed 3, wounded 17. 2nd Nbn Field Co. RE. to LOCRE. 7th Field Co. RE. to M.12.d.2.4. Divisional Headquarters moved to WESTOUTRE. Took over line from 3rd Division.	

Army Form C. 2118.

ORIGINAL

ADMINISTRATIVE
WAR DIARY
or
INTELLIGENCE SUMMARY

(Erase heading not required.)

50TH DIVISION.   MAY, 1916.

Instructions regarding War Diaries and Intelligence Summaries are contained in F. S. Regs., Part II. and the Staff Manual respectively. Title Pages will be prepared in manuscript.

Place	Date	Hour	Summary of Events and Information	Remarks and references to Appendices
WESTOUTRE	MAY 28		Casualties - O.R. killed 2, wounded 14 (included 1 self-inflicted, 5th North'd Fuslrs). 2 Battalions 150th Inf. Bgde to LOCRE. 2 Battalions 151st Inf. Bgde to LA CLYTTE.	
	29		Casualties - O.R. killed 2, wounded 14 (included 1 at duty).	
	30		Casualties - O.R. killed 3, wounded 12.	
	31		Casualties - O.R. killed 8, wounded 32 (included 6 at duty).	

Army Form C. 2118.

50TH DIVISION.

Instructions regarding War Diaries and Intelligence Summaries are contained in F. S. Regs., Part II. and the Staff Manual respectively. Title Pages will be prepared in manuscript.

WAR DIARY DUPLICATE
or
INTELLIGENCE SUMMARY

MAY, 1916.

(Erase heading not required.)

Place	Date	Hour	Summary of Events and Information	Remarks and references to Appendices
FLETRE	MAY 1		Headquarters, Divisional Artillery, Westoutre - moved to EECKE.	
	2		Casualties - O.R. wounded 2. General Officer Commanding visit to Base, HAVRE.	
	3		Casualties -	
	4		Casualties -	
	5		Casualties - General Officer Commanding returned from HAVRE.	
	6		Casualties -	
	7		Casualties -	
	8		Casualties -	
	9		Casualties -	
	10		Casualties -	
	11		Casualties -	
	12		Casualties -	
	13		Casualties -	
	14		Casualties -	
	15		Casualties -	
	16		Brig.-Gen. J.S.M.SHEA, C.B., D.S.O., to command 30th Division.	
	17		Brig.-Gen. P.T.WESTMORLAND, C.M.G., D.S.O., to command 151st Inf. Bgde. Brig.-Gen. SHEA left to take up new command.	

Army Form C. 2118.

50TH DIVISION.

Instructions regarding War Diaries and Intelligence Summaries are contained in F.S. Regs., Part II. and the Staff Manual respectively. Title Pages will be prepared in manuscript.

ADMINISTRATIVE WAR DIARY or INTELLIGENCE SUMMARY

MAY, 1916.

(Erase heading not required.)

Place	Date	Hour	Summary of Events and Information	Remarks and references to Appendices
FLETRE	MAY 18		Casualties ---	
	19		Casualties ---	
	20		Casualties ---	
	21		Casualties - 250th Bgde, RFA, wounded accidentally by tampering with a German fuze, O.R. 6. V Corps Cyclists and Mounted Troops (less Headquarters) to KEMMEL DEFENCES.	
	22		Casualties - 2/Lieut. A.G. HESLOP, 9th Bn. Durham L.I. accidentally wounded; wounded O.R. 2, includes one accidentally.	
	23		2 Battalions 149th Inf. Brigade to LOCRE. Second Army Commander presented Distinguished Conduct and Military Medals to Division.	
	24		Casualties ---	
	25		Casualties - 151st Inf. Bgde Bombing accident, casualties - 2/Lieut.'s Mackay and Bennett, 5th Border Regt., and 2/Lieut. Stocken, Middlesex Regt., att'd 5th Border Regt wounded; O.R. killed 3, wounded 13. 2 Battalions 149th Inf. Bgde to LOCRE.	
	26		Casualties - Wounded 2/Lieut.'s Adams, Robson, Watson, Rendell and Magee, 5th North'd Fus. O.R. killed 9, wounded 60, includes 1 at duty. 2 Battalions 150th Bgde to LOCRE. 2 Battalions 151st Inf. Bgde to LA CLYTTE.	
WESTOUTRE	27		Casualties - O.R. killed 3, wounded 17. 2nd Nbn Field Co. RE. to LOCRE. 7th Field Co. RE. to M.12.d.2.4. Divisional Headquarters moved to WESTOUTRE. Took over line from 3rd Division.	

50TH DIVISION.

ADMINISTRATIVE

DUPLICATE

MAY, 1916.

WESTOUTRE	MAY 28	Casualties - O.R. killed 2, wounded 14 (included 1 self-inflicted, 5th North'd Fuslrs). 2 Battalions 150th Inf. Bgde to LOCRE. 2 Battalions 151st Inf. Bgde to LA CLYTTE.
	29	Casualties - O.R. killed 2, wounded 14 (included 1 at duty).
	30	Casualties - O.R. killed 3, wounded 12.
	31	Casualties - O.R. killed 8, wounded 32 (included 6 at duty).

Confidential

50th (North'n) Division

War Diary.

Administrative Staff.

From 1st June 1916.
To 30th June 1916.

Army Form C. 2118.

ADMINISTRATIVE WAR DIARY or INTELLIGENCE SUMMARY

50TH DIVISION. **JUNE, 1916.**

(Erase heading not required.)

Instructions regarding War Diaries and Intelligence Summaries are contained in F.S. Regs., Part II. and the Staff Manual respectively. Title Pages will be prepared in manuscript.

Place	Date	Hour	Summary of Events and Information	Remarks and references to Appendices
WESTOUTRE.	1916. JUNE 1		Casualties – Killed Capt.L.RAIMES, 5th Bn.Durham L.I., 2nd Lieut.N.B.STEPHENS, 150th Brigade Machine Gun Coy, Wounded 2nd Lieut.F.C.ROE,149th Brigade Machine Gun Coy, 2nd Lieut.E.C. PALMER, 9th Bn.Durham L.I., 2nd Lieut.E.J.PURSGLOVE, 5th Border Regt, Other Ranks Killed 2, Wounded 13.	
	2.		Casualties – Wounded 2nd Lieut.L.S.P.SCAIFE (Shell shock) 4th Bn.North'd Fusiliers, 2nd Lieut. H.J.SPENCER, 9th Bn.Durham L.I. Other Ranks,Wounded 8,includes 1 at duty.	
	3.		Casualties – Other Ranks, Killed 3, Wounded 13.	
	4.		Casualties – Killed Lt.-Col. A.G.STUART, G.S.O. 1, 50th Division, Other Ranks Killed 3,Wounded 24, includes 3 at duty.	
	5.		Casualties – Wounded 2nd Lieut.N.G.TURNBULL, 149th Brigade M.G.Coy, Other Ranks, Killed 1, Wounded 8, includes 1 self-inflicted, 2 at duty.	
	6.		Casualties – Killed, Other Ranks 2, Wounded 15.	
	7.		Casualties – Wounded Capt.N.B.M.GOOD, 4th North'd Fusiliers, 2nd Lt. W. .WOODWARD, Other Ranks Killed 2, Wounded 18.	
	8.		Casualties – Other Ranks, Killed 1, Wounded 7, includes 1 acc: at duty.	
	9.		Casualties – Other Ranks, Killed 1, Wounded 9.	
	10.		Casualties – Other Ranks, Wounded 5.	
	11.		Casualties – Killed, 2nd Lieut.L.MEYER, 6th Bn.Durham L.I. Other Ranks Killed 2, Wounded 17.	
	12.		Casualties – Other Ranks, Wounded 5, including 1 at duty. Lieut.-Colonel D.Foster, R.E. joined for duty as G.S.O. 1. 2nd Suffolks and 8th K.Lanc.Regt, left. 1st North'd Fus. and 4th Royal Fus. arrived at LOCRE.	

Army Form C. 2118.

ADMINISTRATIVE WAR DIARY or INTELLIGENCE SUMMARY

(Erase heading not required.)

50TH DIVISION.

JUNE, 1916.

Instructions regarding War Diaries and Intelligence Summaries are contained in F.S. Regs., Part II. and the Staff Manual respectively. Title Pages will be prepared in manuscript.

Place	Date	Hour	Summary of Events and Information	Remarks and references to Appendices
WESTOUTRE.	JUNE 13.		Memorial Service for LORD KITCHENER.	
	14.		Casualties - Other Ranks, Killed 2, Wounded 10.	
	15.		Casualties - Other Ranks, Wounded 1.	
	16.		Casualties - Other Ranks, Killed 2, Wounded 8, includes 1 at duty.	
	17.		Casualties - Other Ranks, Killed 2, Wounded 7, includes 1 at duty.	
	18.		Casualties - Killed, 2nd Lieut.F.P.LEES, 4th North'd Fusrs: 2nd Lieut.F.W.CARLTON, 4th East Yorks: Wounded, Capt.C.SPROXTON, Major B.H.CHARLTON (at duty) 2nd Lieut.A.D.SCOTT (at duty) 4th Yorks.Regt: Lieut.R.GREEN, 5th Yorks Regt: 2nd Lieut.C.A.H.SUTTON, 2nd Lieut.G.Gresham, 2nd Lieut.W.R.BROWN, 4th Bn.East Yorks Regt: Lieut.J.A.GARNELLY, R.E. 250th Tunnelling Coy. Other Ranks, Killed 25, Wounded 113, Missing 1.	
	19.		Casualties - Wounded Lieut-Colonel D.FOSTER, G.S.O. 1, R.E., 2nd Lieut.S.MARSHALL, 4th East Yorks, 2nd Lieut.C.J.ROBERTS, 250th Tunnelling Co. Other Ranks, Killed 4, Wounded 28, includes 1 at duty.	
	20.		Casualties - Died of Wounds Lieut.J.A.GARNELLY, 2nd Lieut.C.J.ROBERTS, 250th Tunnelling Co.R.E. Killed, 2nd Lieut.O.WILLIS, 5th North'd Fusrs. Wounded 2nd Lieut.P.J.BARTHOLOMEW, 1st Entrenching Battalion: Other Ranks, Killed 1, Wounded 23, Missing 1.	
	21.		Casualties - Wounded 2nd Lieut.C.H.STRACHAN, 2nd Lieut.H.HALL, 9th Durham L.I., Other Ranks Killed 1, Wounded 12, includes 3 accidentally.	
	22.		Casualties - Other Ranks, Killed 1, Wounded 7, includes 2 at duty.	
	23.		Casualties - Other Ranks, Killed 1, Wounded 13.	
	24.		Casualties - Killed, 2nd Lieut.H.V.CHARLTON, 7th North'd Fusrs: Other Ranks, Killed 2, Wounded 15, includes 1 at duty.	

Army Form C. 2118.

50TH DIVISION.

ADMINISTRATIVE WAR DIARY or INTELLIGENCE SUMMARY

JUNE, 1916.

(Erase heading not required.)

Instructions regarding War Diaries and Intelligence Summaries are contained in F. S. Regs., Part II. and the Staff Manual respectively. Title Pages will be prepared in manuscript.

Place	Date	Hour	Summary of Events and Information	Remarks and references to Appendices
WESTOUTRE.	JUNE 25.		Casualties - Wounded 2nd Lieut.A.E.BRAUND, 2nd Lieut.A.K.SMITH, 7th Bn.North'd Fusrs: Other Ranks Killed 2, Wounded 23, includes 1 at duty.	
	26.		Casualties - Died of Wounds, 2nd Lieut.J.F.G.ASHWORTH, 9th Durham L.I., Wounded 2nd Lieut. J.G.GARRARD, 5th Bn.North'd Fusrs: Other Ranks Killed 2, Wounded 37, includes 1 at duty.	
	27.		Casualties - Killed, 2nd Lieut.C.HAWDON, 4th Yorks Regt., Other Ranks Killed 4, Wounded 37, includes 1 at duty, missing 1. Major H.KARSLAKE, C.M.G., D.S.O., joined for duty as G.S.O. 1.	
	28.		Casualties - Killed 2nd Lieut.G.S.H.JACQUES, 6th Bn.North'd Fusrs: Wounded 2nd Lieut.H.BROWNE, Trench Mortar Brigade, Other Ranks Killed 5, Wounded 17, includes 1 self-inflicted. Hd.Qrs, 150th Inf.Bde moved from LOCRE to farm N. of MONT ROUGE.	
	29.		Casualties - Wounded 2nd Lieut.R.E.TURNBULL, 6th Bn.North'd Fusrs. Other Ranks Killed 3, Wounded 24. 1 missing on 27th now reported wounded.	
	30.		Casualties - Other Ranks, Killed 2, Wounded 20, includes 3 at duty, 1 accidental. Capt.L.D.DALY, D.S.O., Leinster Regt, joined for duty as Brigade Major, 151st Brigade.	

DUPLICATE A.F. C.2118.

ADMINISTRATIVE
WAR DIARY
or
INTELLIGENCE SUMMARY.

50TH DIVISION.

JUNE, 1916.

	1916.	
WESTOUTRE.	JUNE 1	Casualties – Killed Capt.L.RAIMES, 5th Bn.Durham L.I., 2nd Lieut.N.B.STEPHENS, 150th Brigade Machine Gun Coy. Wounded 2nd Lieut.F.C.ROE,149th Brigade Machine Gun Coy, 2nd Lieut.E.C. PALMER, 9th Bn.Durham L.I., 2nd Lieut.E.J.PURSGLOVE, 5th Border Regt, Other Ranks Killed 2, Wounded 13.
	2.	Casualties – Wounded 2nd Lieut.L.S.P.SCAIFE (Shell shock) 4th Bn.North'd Fusiliers, 2nd Lieut. H.J.SPENCER, 9th Bn.Durham L.I. Other Ranks,Wounded 8,includes 1 at duty.
	3.	Casualties – Other Ranks, Killed 3, Wounded 13.
	4.	Casualties – Killed Lt.-Col. A.G.STUART, G.S.O.1, 50th Division, Other Ranks Killed 3,Wounded 24, includes 3 at duty.
	5.	Casualties – Wounded 2nd Lieut.N.G.TURNBULL, 149th Brigade M.G.Coy, Other Ranks, Killed 1, Wounded 8, includes 1 self-inflicted, 2 at duty.
	6.	Casualties – Killed, Other Ranks 2, Wounded 15.
	7.	Casualties – Wounded Capt.N.B.N.GOOD, 4th North'd Fusiliers, 2nd Lt. W. .WOODWARD, Other Ranks Killed 2, Wounded 18.
	8.	Casualties – Other Ranks, Killed 1, Wounded 7, includes 1 acc: at duty.
	9.	Casualties – Other Ranks, Killed 1, Wounded 9.
	10.	Casualties – Other Ranks, Wounded 5.
	11.	Casualties – Killed, 2nd Lieut.L.MEYER, 6th Bn.Durham L.I. Other Ranks Killed 2, Wounded 17.
	12.	Casualties – Other Ranks, Wounded 5, including 1 at duty. Lieut.-Colonel D.Foster, R.E. joined for duty as G.S.O.1. 2nd Suffolks and 8th K.Lanc.Regt. left. 1st North'd Fus. and 4th Royal Fus. arrived at LOCRE.

A.F. C.2118.

ADMINISTRATIVE
WAR DIARY
or
INTELLIGENCE SUMMARY.

50TH DIVISION.

JUNE, 1916.

WESTOUTRE. JUNE 13.		Memorial Service for LORD KITCHENER.
14.	Casualties - Other Ranks, Killed 2, Wounded 10.	
15.	Casualties - Other Ranks, Wounded 1.	
16.	Casualties - Other Ranks, Killed 2, Wounded 8, includes 1 at duty.	
17.	Casualties - Other Ranks, Killed 2, Wounded 7, includes 1 at duty.	
	Casualties - Killed, 2nd Lieut.F.P.LEES, 4th North'd Fusrs: 2nd Lieut.F.W.CARLTON, 4th East Yorks: Wounded, Capt.C.SPROXTON, Major B.H.CHARLTON (at duty) 2nd Lieut.A.D.SCOTT (at duty) 4th Yorks.Regt: Lieut.R.GREEN, 5th Yorks Regt. 2nd Lieut.C.A.H.SUTTON, 2nd Lieut.G.Gresham, 2nd Lieut.W.R.BROWN, 4th Bn.East Yorks Regt: Lieut.J.A.CARNELLY, R.E. 250th Tunnelling Coy. Other Ranks, Killed 25, Wounded 113, Missing 1.	
18.	Casualties - Wounded Lieut-Colonel D.FOSTER, G.S.O. 1, R.E., 2nd Lieut.S.MARSHALL, 4th East Yorks, 2nd Lieut.C.J.ROBERTS, 250th Tunnelling Co. Other Ranks, Killed 4, Wounded 28, includes 1 at duty.	
19.	Casualties - Died of Wounds Lieut.J.A.CARNELLY, 2nd Lieut.C.J.ROBERTS, 250th Tunnelling Co.R.E. on 18th. Killed,	
20.	Casualties - 2nd Lieut.O.WILLIS, 5th North'd Fusrs. Wounded 2nd Lieut.P.J.BARTHOLOMEW, 1st Entrenching Battalion. Other Ranks, Killed 1, Wounded 23, Missing 1.	
21.	Casualties - Wounded 2nd Lieut.C.H.STRACHAN, 2nd Lieut.H.HALL, 9th Durham L.I., Other Ranks Killed 1, Wounded 12, includes 3 accidentally.	
22.	Casualties - Other Ranks, Killed 1, Wounded 7, includes 2 at duty.	
23.	Casualties - Other Ranks, Killed 1, Wounded 13.	
24.	Casualties - Killed, 2nd Lieut.H.V.CHARLTON, 7th North'd Fusrs: Other Ranks, Killed 2, Wounded 15, includes 1 at duty.	

ADMINISTRATIVE
WAR DIARY
or
INTELLIGENCE SUMMARY.

A.F. C.2118.

50TH DIVISION.

JUNE, 1916.

WESTOUTRE.	JUNE 25.	Casualties – Wounded 2nd Lieut.A.E.BRAUND, 2nd Lieut.A.K.SMITH, 7th Bn.North'd Fusrs; Other Ranks Killed 2, Wounded 23, includes 1 at duty.
	26.	Casualties – Died of Wounds, 2nd Lieut.J.F.G.ASHWORTH, 9th Durham L.I., Wounded 2nd Lieut. J.G.GARRARD, 5th Bn.North'd Fusrs; Other Ranks Killed 2, Wounded 37, includes 1 at duty.
	27.	Casualties – Killed, 2nd Lieut.C.HAWDON, 4th Yorks Regt., Other Ranks Killed 4, Wounded 37, includes 1 at duty, missing 1. Major H.KARSLAKE, C.M.G., D.S.O., joined for duty as G.S.O. 1.
	28.	Casualties – Killed 2nd Lieut.G.S.H.JACQUES, 6th Bn.North'd Fusrs: Wounded 2nd Lieut.H.BROWNE, Trench Mortar Brigade, Other Ranks Killed 5, Wounded 17, includes 1 self-inflicted. Hd.Qrs, 150th Inf.Bde moved from LOCRE to farm N. of MONT ROUGE.
	29.	Casualties – Wounded 2nd Lieut.R.E.TURNBULL, 6th Bn.North'd Fusrs. Other Ranks Killed 3, Wounded 24. 1 missing on 27th now reported wounded.
	30.	Casualties – Other Ranks, Killed 2, Wounded 20, includes 3 at duty, 1 accidental. Capt.L.D.DALY, D.S.O., Leinster Regt, joined for duty as Brigade Major, 151st Brigade.

Confidential

50th Division

Administrative Staff

War Diary

From 1st July 1915
to 31st July 1916

Volume XV

Army Form C. 2118.

ADMINISTRATIVE WAR DIARY or INTELLIGENCE SUMMARY

(Erase heading not required.)

50TH DIVISION.

Instructions regarding War Diaries and Intelligence Summaries are contained in F. S. Regs., Part II. and the Staff Manual respectively. Title Pages will be prepared in manuscript.

Place	Date	Hour	Summary of Events and Information	Remarks and references to Appendices
WESTOUTRE.	1916. JULY 1.		Casualties - Killed, Lieut.W.J.DAVIS, 2nd Lieut.G.A.BURNETT, 7th Bn.North'd Fusrs. Other Ranks Killed 3, Wounded 25.	
	2.		Casualties - Killed, 2nd Lieut.A.W.DALE (on 1st) 7th Bn. North'd Fusrs. Wounded, 2nd Lieut. M.W.LAWSON (Shell shock) 5th Bn.North'd Fusrs. Other Ranks, Killed , Wounded 14.	
	3.		Casualties - Wounded, 2nd Lieut.A.E.MOORHOUSE, 5th Bn.North'd Fusrs; 2nd Lieut.P.L.DOBINSON, 6th Bn.Durham L.I.; Other Ranks, Killed 1, Wounded 15, includes 1 at duty.	
	4.		Casualties - Other Ranks, Killed , Wounded 3.	
	5.		Casualties - Other Ranks, Killed 1, Wounded 8, includes 1 at duty.	
	6.		Casualties - Other Ranks, Killed 6, Wounded 19.	
	7.		Casualties - Wounded, 2nd Lieut.C.S.JOHNSON, 4th Bn.East Yorks.Regt; Other Ranks, Killed 5, Wounded 9, includes 2 at duty.	
	8.		Casualties - Other Ranks, Killed 2, Wounded 9.	
	9.		Casualties - Other Ranks, Killed 4, Wounded 7.	
	10.		Casualties - Wounded, 2nd Lieut.W.F.BALDWIN, 7th Field Coy.R.E.; Capt.B.BUNNISON, 6th Bn.Durham L.I.; Capt.H.BROWN, D.S.O.,5th Bn.Yorks.Regt, at duty; 2nd Lieut.H.P.BAGGE, 5th Bn.Yorks Regt, at duty; Other Ranks, Killed 1, Wounded 23, includes 4 at duty.	
	11.		Casualties - Wounded, 2nd Lieut.G.E.W.SPRAGG, 4th Bn.East Yorks Regt; Other Ranks, Killed 4, Wounded 7.	
	12.		Casualties - Killed, 2nd Lieut.H.RUSSELL, 7th Field Coy.R.E.; Wounded 2nd Lieut.L.G.DAWE, 5th Bn.Durham L.I.; Other Ranks, Killed 1, Wounded 14.	

2449 Wt. W14957/M90 750,000 1/16 J.B.C. & A. Forms/C.2118/12.

Army Form C. 2118.

50TH DIVISION.

Instructions regarding War Diaries and Intelligence Summaries are contained in F. S. Regs., Part II. and the Staff Manual respectively. Title Pages will be prepared in manuscript.

ADMINISTRATIVE WAR DIARY or INTELLIGENCE SUMMARY

(Erase heading not required.)

JULY, 1916.

Place	Date	Hour	Summary of Events and Information	Remarks and references to Appendices
WESTOUTRE.	1916. JULY 13.		Casualties - Other Ranks, Killed 4, Wounded 11 (includes 1 at duty and 1 self-inflicted); Major P.S.Rowan, DSO., Brigade Major, 149th Infantry Bgde, to G.S.O.2, 32nd Division.	
	14.		Casualties - Other Ranks, Killed 2, Wounded 15 (includes 4 at duty and 1 self-inflicted); Major R.F.Guy, D.S.O., Brigade Major, 150th Infantry Bgde, to G.S.O.2, 11th Division.	
	15.		Casualties - Other Ranks, Killed 7, Wounded 12.	
	16.		Casualties - Wounded, 2nd Lieut.P.RAMSDEN, 8th Bn.Durham L.I., Other Ranks,Killed 4, Wounded 29, including 1 at duty.	
	17.		Casualties - Killed, 2nd Lieut.V.A.TURNBULL, Wounded Lieut.P.ROBINSON, 251st Brigade,R.F.A. Other Ranks Killed 3, Wounded 15, includes 2 at duty.	
	18.		Casualties - Wounded,2nd Lieut.S.W.MATTHEWS, 5th Bn.North'd Fusrs; 2nd Lieut.H.S.WEBSTER, 2nd Lieut.G.VIVIAN,4th Bn.East Yorks Regt; 2nd Lieut.G.H.SMITH, 2nd Lieut.H.A.FaCAM, 5th Bn. Yorks Regt; Other Ranks, Killed 8, Wounded 32, includes 2 at duty, 1 accidentally.	
			Captain W.Anderson, 6th Bn.North'd Fusrs, G.S.O.3,50th Division, appointed Brigade Major, 149th Infantry Brigade. Captain E.J.de C.Boys, 17th Infantry Brigade, appointed Brigade Major, 150th Infantry Brigade.	
	19.		Casualties - Other Ranks, Killed 4, Wounded 19. 151st Brigade Hd.Qrs. moved to DRANOUTRE. Captain N.R.Crockatt, Adj; 5th Bn.Yorks Regt, appointed G.S.O.3,50th Division.	
	20.		Casualties - Killed, Captain G.C.BAGSHAWE, 5th Bn.Yorks Regt; Wounded 2nd Lieut.J.JACOBS, 5th Bn.Yorks Regt; Other Ranks, Killed 2, Wounded 21, Missing 1.	
	21.		Casualties - Died of Wounds, 2nd Lt. P.M.L.McINNES, 5th Bn.Yorks.Regt; Killed Captain R.C.R. BLAIR,D.S.O.,5th Bn.Border Regt; Wounded, 2nd Lieut. FURLEY, 4th Bn.East Yorks.Regt,at duty; Other Ranks, Killed 1, Wounded 18, includes 2 at duty.	

Army Form C. 2118.

50TH DIVISION.

ADMINISTRATIVE WAR DIARY or INTELLIGENCE SUMMARY

(Erase heading not required.)

JULY, 1916.

Instructions regarding War Diaries and Intelligence Summaries are contained in F. S. Regs., Part II. and the Staff Manual respectively. Title Pages will be prepared in manuscript.

Place	Date	Hour	Summary of Events and Information	Remarks and references to Appendices
WESTOUTRE.	1916. JULY 22.		Casualties :- Wounded, Captain W.H.CHARLEWOOD, 6th Bn.North'd Fusrs; Other Ranks, Killed 2, Wounded 31. 149th Brigade moved from LA CLYTTE to S. of NEUVE EGLISE.	
	23.		Casualties :- Missing, 2nd Lieut.E.W.BRODRICK, 5th Bn.Yorks Regt; 2nd Lieut.D.A.BROWN, 9th Bn. Durham L.I.; Other Ranks, Killed 5, Wounded 14, including 1 at duty, Missing 2, rejoined 1.	
	24.		Casualties :- Killed, 2nd Lieut.R.PYEBUS, 8th Bn.Durham L.I.; Other Ranks, Killed 2, Wounded 19, including 3 at duty; Missing 1.	
	25.		Casualties :- Wounded, Lieut.A.H.LEATHART, 250th Brigade, R.F.A.; 2nd Lieut.G.E.W.BRIDGE, 2nd Lieut.W.D.B.THOMPSON, 9th Bn.Durham L.I.; Other Ranks, Killed 2, Wounded 6. 6th H.L.I. attd.	
	26.		Casualties :- Wounded, 2nd Lieut.A.MUIR, 4th Bn.North'd Fusrs; 2nd Lieut.R.M.SHEPHERD (accidental) Captain A.ROSS, 1st Entrenching Battalion,at duty; Other Ranks Killed 4, Wounded 28,including 2 at duty, 1 self-inflicted.	
	27.		Casualties :- Wounded, Captain D.T.TURNER, 4th Bn.North'd Fusrs; 2nd Lieut.R.P.BAXTER, 5th Bn. Border Regt; Other Ranks,Killed 5, Wounded 17,included 1 self-inflicted.	
	28.		Casualties :- Killed,2nd Lieut.G.R.WOLLEY,5th Bn.Durham L.I.; Wounded,2nd Lieut.H.C.MARSH, 1st Entrenching Battalion,at duty; Other Ranks,Killed 7, Wounded 13.	
	29.		Casualties :- Wounded,Captain H.MCNAIR,6th Bn.Durham L.I.;shell shock; Other Ranks,Killed 3, Wounded 14, includes 2 at duty, 1 self-inflicted. 151st Brigade moved to LITTLE KEMMEL. 149th Brigade moved to DRANOUTRE. 150th Brigade moved to BRULOOZE.	
	30.		Casualties :- Wounded,2nd Lieut.K.H.SAUNDERS,5th Bn.Durham L.I. Other Ranks,Killed 3,Wounded 13.	
	31.		Casualties :- Wounded,2nd Lieut.F.E.JONES,4th Bn.Yorks.Regt; 2nd Lieut.O.M.SADLER,5th Bn.Durham L.I.; Other Ranks,Killed 1, Wounded 11, including 1 self-inflicted.	

Army Form C. 2118.

50TH DIVISION.

Instructions regarding War Diaries and Intelligence Summaries are contained in F.S. Regs., Part II. and the Staff Manual respectively. Title Pages will be prepared in manuscript.

WAR DIARY or INTELLIGENCE SUMMARY

JULY, 1916.

(Erase heading not required.)

Place	Date	Hour	Summary of Events and Information	Remarks and references to Appendices
WESTOUTRE.	1916. JULY 1.		Casualties – Killed, Lieut.W.J.DAVIS, 2nd Lieut.G.A.BURNETT, 7th Bn.North'd Fusrs. Other Ranks killed 5, Wounded 25.	
	2.		Casualties – Killed, 2nd Lieut.A.W.DALE (on 1st) 7th Bn. North'd Fusrs. Wounded, 2nd Lieut. M.W.LAWSON (Shell shock) 5th Bn.North'd Fusrs. Other Ranks, Killed , Wounded 14.	
	3.		Casualties – Wounded, 2nd Lieut.A.E.MOORHOUSE, 5th Bn.North'd Fusrs; 2nd Lieut.P.L.DOBINSON, 6th Bn.Durham L.I.; Other Ranks, Killed 1, Wounded 15, includes 1 at duty.	
	4.		Casualties – Other Ranks, Killed , Wounded 3.	
	5.		Casualties – Other Ranks, Killed 1, Wounded 8, includes 1 at duty.	
	6.		Casualties – Other Ranks, Killed 6, Wounded 19.	
	7.		Casualties – Wounded, 2nd Lieut.C.S.JOHNSON, 4th Bn.East Yorks.Regt; Other Ranks, killed 5, Wounded 9, includes 2 at duty.	
	8.		Casualties – Other Ranks, Killed 2, Wounded 9.	
	9.		Casualties – Other Ranks, Killed 4, Wounded 7.	
	10.		Casualties – Wounded, 2nd Lieut.W.F.BALDWIN, 7th Field Coy.R.E.; Capt.B.BENNISON, 6th Bn.Durham L.I.; Capt.H.BROWN, D.S.O.,5th Bn.Yorks.Regt, at duty; 2nd Lieut.H.P.BAGGE, 5th Bn.Yorks Regt, at duty; Other Ranks, Killed 1, Wounded 25, includes 4 at duty.	
	11.		Casualties – Wounded, 2nd Lieut.G.E.W.SPRAGG, 4th Bn.East Yorks Regt; Other Ranks, Killed 4, Wounded 7.	
	12.		Casualties – Killed, 2nd Lieut.H.RUSSELL, 7th Field Coy.R.E.; Wounded 2nd Lieut.L.G.DAWE, 5th Bn.Durham L.I.; Other Ranks, Killed 1, Wounded 14.	

Army Form C. 2118.

50TH DIVISION.

Instructions regarding War Diaries and Intelligence Summaries are contained in F.S. Regs., Part II. and the Staff Manual respectively. Title Pages will be prepared in manuscript.

ADMINISTRATIVE WAR DIARY
or
INTELLIGENCE SUMMARY
JULY, 1916.

(Erase heading not required.)

Place	Date	Hour	Summary of Events and Information	Remarks and references to Appendices
WESTOUTRE.	1916. JULY 13.		Casualties – Other Ranks, Killed 4, Wounded 11 (includes 1 at duty and 1 self-inflicted); Major P.S. Rowan, DSO., Brigade Major, 149th Infantry Bgde, to G.S.O.2, 32nd Division.	
	14.		Casualties – Other Ranks, Killed 2, Wounded 15 (includes 4 at duty and 1 self-inflicted); Major R.F. Guy, D.S.O., Brigade Major, 150th Infantry Bgde, to G.S.O.2, 11th Division.	
	15.		Casualties – Other Ranks, Killed 7, Wounded 12.	
	16.		Casualties – Wounded, 2nd Lieut. P. RAMSDEN, 8th Bn. Durham L.I., Other Ranks, Killed 4, Wounded 29, including 1 at duty.	
	17.		Casualties – Killed, 2nd Lieut. W.A. TURNBULL, Wounded Lieut. P. ROBINSON, 251st Brigade, R.F.A. Other Ranks Killed 3, Wounded 15, includes 2 at duty.	
	18.		Casualties – Wounded, 2nd Lieut. S.W. MATTHEWS, 5th Bn. North'd Fusrs; 2nd Lieut. H.S. WEBSTER, 2nd Lieut. G. VIVIAN, 4th Bn. East Yorks Regt; 2nd Lieut. G.R. SMITH, 2nd Lieut. H.A. FAGAN, 5th Bn. Yorks Regt; Other Ranks, Killed 8, Wounded 32, includes 2 at duty, 1 accidentally. Captain W. Anderson, 6th Bn. North'd Fusrs, G.S.O.3, 50th Division, appointed Brigade Major, 149th Infantry Brigade. Captain E.J. de C. Boys, 17th Infantry Brigade, appointed Brigade Major, 150th Infantry Brigade.	
	19.		Casualties – Other Ranks, Killed 4, Wounded 19. 151st Brigade Hd.Qrs, moved to DRANOUTRE. Captain N.R. Crockatt, Adj: 5th Bn. Yorks Regt, appointed G.S.O.3, 50th Division.	
	20.		Casualties – Killed, Captain G.C. BAGSHAWE, 5th Bn. Yorks Regt; Wounded 2nd Lieut. J. JACOBS, 5th Bn. Yorks Regt; Other Ranks, Killed 2, Wounded 21, Missing 1.	
	21.		Casualties – Died of Wounds, 2nd Lt. P.M.L. McINNES, 5th Bn. Yorks. Regt; Killed Captain R.C.R. BLAIR, D.S.O., 5th Bn. Border Regt; Wounded, 2nd Lieut. FURLEY, 4th Bn. East Yorks. Regt, at duty; Other Ranks, Killed 1, Wounded 18, includes 2 at duty.	

Army Form C. 2118.

50TH DIVISION.

Instructions regarding War Diaries and Intelligence Summaries are contained in F. S. Regs., Part II. and the Staff Manual respectively. Title Pages will be prepared in manuscript.

ADMINISTRATIVE WAR DIARY or INTELLIGENCE SUMMARY

JULY, 1916.

(Erase heading not required.)

Place	Date	Hour	Summary of Events and Information	Remarks and references to Appendices
WESTOUTRE.	1916. JULY 22.		Casualties - Wounded, Captain W.H.CHARLEWOOD, 6th Bn.North'd Fusrs; Other Ranks, Killed 2, Wounded 21. 149th Brigade moved from LA CLYTTE to S. of NEUVE EGLISE.	
	23.		Casualties - Missing, 2nd Lieut.E.W.BRODRICK, 5th Bn.Yorks Regt; 2nd Lieut.D.A.BROWN, 9th Bn. Durham L.I.; Other Ranks, Killed 5, Wounded 14, including 1 at duty, Missing 2, rejoined 1.	
	24.		Casualties - Killed, 2nd Lieut.R.PYBUS, 8th Bn.Durham L.I.; Other Ranks, Killed 2, Wounded 19, including 5 at duty; Missing 1.	
	25.		Casualties - Wounded, Lieut.A.H.LEATHART, 250th Brigade,R.F.A.; 2nd Lieut.G.E.W.BRIDGE, 2nd Lieut.W.D.B.THOMPSON, 9th Bn.Durham L.I.; Other Ranks, Killed 2, Wounded 6.	
	26.		Casualties - Wounded, 2nd Lieut.A.MUIR, 4th Bn.North'd Fusrs; 2nd Lieut.R.M.SHEPHERD (accidental) 6th H.L.I. attd. Captain A.ROSS, 1st Entrenching Battalion, at duty; Other Ranks Killed 4, Wounded 28, including 2 at duty, 1 self-inflicted.	
	27.		Casualties - Wounded, Captain D.T.TURNER, 4th Bn.North'd Fusrs; 2nd Lieut.R.P.BAXTER, 5th Bn. Border Regt; Other Ranks, Killed 5, Wounded 17, included 1 self-inflicted.	
	28.		Casualties - Killed, 2nd Lieut.C.R.WOLLEY, 5th Bn.Durham L.I.; Wounded, 2nd Lieut.H.C.MARSH, 1st Entrenching Battalion, at duty; Other Ranks, Killed 7, Wounded 15.	
	29.		Casualties - Wounded, Captain H.McNAIR, 6th Bn.Durham L.I.; shell shock; Other Ranks, Killed 5, Wounded 14, includes 2 at duty, 1 self-inflicted. 149th Brigade moved to DRANOUTRE. 151st Brigade moved to LITTLE KEMMEL. 150th Brigade moved to BRULOOZE.	
	30.		Casualties - Wounded, 2nd Lieut.K.H.SAUNDERS, 5th Bn.Durham L.I. Other Ranks, Killed 3, Wounded 13.	
	31.		Casualties - Wounded, 2nd Lieut.E.E.JONES, 4th Bn.Yorks.Regt; 2nd Lieut.C.M.SADLER, 5th Bn.Durham L.I.; Other Ranks, Killed 1, Wounded 11, including 1 self-inflicted.	

Vol 17

Confidential

Administrative
War Diary

50th (North'n) Division

From 1st August 1916.
To 31st August 1916.

Volume XVI

Army Form C. 2118.

ADMINISTRATIVE WAR DIARY or INTELLIGENCE SUMMARY

(Erase heading not required.)

50TH DIVISION. **AUGUST 1916.**

Instructions regarding War Diaries and Intelligence Summaries are contained in F. S. Regs., Part II. and the Staff Manual respectively. Title Pages will be prepared in manuscript.

Place	Date	Hour	Summary of Events and Information	Remarks and references to Appendices
WESTOUTRE.	AUGT. 1		Casualties – Other Ranks, Killed 2, Wounded 4 including 1 accidental.	
	2.		Casualties – Lieut. E.E.Jones, 4th Bn.Yorks Regt, Wounded 51st July – died of wounds. Killed, Other Ranks 1. Wounded Major P.P.Phillips, 5th Bn.North'd Fuslrs, Other Ranks 14, including 1 at duty.	
	3.		Casualties – Other Ranks, Killed 2, Wounded 25, includes 7 at duty, 1 accidental, 1 self-inflicted.	
	4.		Casualties – Other Ranks, Killed 1, Wounded 16.	
	5.		Casualties – Killed, Other Ranks 1. Wounded 2nd Lieut.R.L.Lumsden, 9th Bn.D.L.I. Wounded at duty, Captain W.S.Ridley, 9th Bn.D.L.I. Wounded Other Ranks 14, including 1 at duty.	
	6.		Casualties – Killed, Other Ranks 2. Wounded 2nd Lt.L.C.Barnes, 7th Bn.North'd Fuslrs, Other Ranks 11. 7th Bn.North'd Fuslrs to Rest Area.	
	7.		Casualties – Wounded 2nd Lt. H.Potts, 9th Bn.D.L.I. Other Ranks 3. 149th Brigade Hd.Qrs and 150th Brigade Hd.Qrs to FLETRE Rest Area.	
FLETRE.	8.		Casualties – Wounded, Other Ranks 1. Divisional Hd.Qrs to FLETRE.	
	9.		Casualties – Other Ranks, Killed 2, Wounded 9, including 3 at duty. Royal Artillery Hd.Qrs to EECKE.	
	10.	9.28 p.m.	Division commences entraining for Reserve Army.	
BERNAVILLE	11.		Divisional Hd.Qrs to BERNAVILLE, Fifth Army, IX Corps.	
	12.		Division finishes detraining, DOULENS N, DOULENS S. and FIENVILLERS CANDAS.	
	13.			
	14.			

Army Form C. 2118.

50TH DIVISION.

ADMINSITRATIVE WAR DIARY or INTELLIGENCE SUMMARY

(Erase heading not required.)

AUGUST 1916.

Instructions regarding War Diaries and Intelligence Summaries are contained in F. S. Regs., Part II. and the Staff Manual respectively. Title Pages will be prepared in manuscript.

Place	Date	Hour	Summary of Events and Information	Remarks and references to Appendices
VIGNACOURT.	AUGT. 15		Divisional Hd.Qrs to VIGNACOURT.	
MONTIGNY.	16.		Divisional Hd.Qrs to MONTIGNY, III Corps, Fourth Army.	
	17.		Distribution - 149th Brigade HEMENCOURT WOOD, 150th Brigade MILLENCOURT, 151st Brigade BAIZEUX WOOD, 7th (Pioneer) Bn. Durham L.I. BAIZEUX Village, R.F.A. BAVELINCOURT, 1st Field Coy RE. MILLENCOURT, 2nd Field Coy RE., BAIZEUX Village, 7th Field Coy RE., FRANVILLERS, 1st Field Ambce., BAIZEUX, 2nd Field Ambce FRANVILLERS, 3rd Field Ambce 2,000 yards East of BRESLE on Albert-Amiens Road.	
	18.		R.A. begin to move into the Line (2 Brigades and Hd.Qrs.).	
	19.		2 Brigades R.F.A. remain in BEHENCOURT Area.	
	20.			
	21.		Casualties - Wounded acc: 2/Lt. H.L.DUNCAN, 4th E.Yorks, O.R.1, 4th Yorks - wounded acc: at duty O.R. 1.	
	22.		Casualties - 252nd Bgde RFA. Wounded acc: O.R. 1, 5th North'd Fus. Wounded acc: O.R. 1.	
	23.		Casualties - 7th North'd Fuslrs. Wounded acc:(at duty) O.R. 1.	
	24.		Casualties - 252nd Bgde RFA. Wounded O.R.2; 4th E.Yorks Wounded acc: O.R. 1.	
	25.		Casualties - 250th Bgde RFA. O.R. Killed 3, Wounded 4; 252nd Bgde RFA Wounded O.R. 3, includes 1 accidentally.	
	26.		Casualties - 250th Bgde RFA. O.R. Killed 2, Wounded 5.	

Army Form C. 2118.

ADMINISTRATIVE WAR DIARY or INTELLIGENCE SUMMARY

(Erase heading not required.)

50TH DIVISION.   **AUGUST 1916.**

Instructions regarding War Diaries and Intelligence Summaries are contained in F. S. Regs., Part II. and the Staff Manual respectively. Title Pages will be prepared in manuscript.

Place	Date	Hour	Summary of Events and Information	Remarks and references to Appendices
MONTIGNY.	August 27.		Casualties – Wounded O.R.2, includes 1 at duty; Major B. Jackson, Staff Capt. 150th Bgde, appointed Brigade Major, 142nd Infantry Brigade.	
	28.		Casualties – Killed O.R.2, Wounded O.R.2. III Corps Commander presents Medals to Division, 3.30 p.m.	
	29.		Casualties – Wounded O.R.6, includes one accidentally.	
	30.		Casualties – NIL.	
	31.		Casualties – NIL.	

Army Form C. 2118.

ADMINISTRATIVE WAR DIARY or INTELLIGENCE SUMMARY

50TH DIVISION.   AUGUST 1916.

(Erase heading not required.)

Instructions regarding War Diaries and Intelligence Summaries are contained in F.S. Regs., Part II. and the Staff Manual respectively. Title Pages will be prepared in manuscript.

Place	Date	Hour	Summary of Events and Information	Remarks and references to Appendices
WESTOUTRE.	AUGT. 1		Casualties - Other Ranks, Killed 2, Wounded 4 including 1 accidental.	
	2.		Casualties - Lieut.E.E.Jones, 4th Bn.Yorks Regt, Wounded 31st July - died of wounds. Killed, Other Ranks 1. Wounded Major P.P.Phillips, 5th Bn.North'd Fuslrs, Other Ranks 14, including 1 at duty.	
	3.		Casualties - Other Ranks, Killed 2, Wounded 25, includes 7 at duty, 1 accidental, 1 self-inflicted.	
	4.		Casualties - Other Ranks, Killed 1, Wounded 16.	
	5.		Casualties - Killed, Other Ranks 1. Wounded 2nd Lieut.R.L.Lumsden, 9th Bn.D.L.I. Wounded at duty, Captain W.S.Ridley, 9th Bn.D.L.I. Wounded Other Ranks 14, including 1 at duty.	
	6.		Casualties - Killed, Other Ranks 2. Wounded 2nd Lt.L.C.Barnes, 7th Bn.North'd Fuslrs, Other Ranks 11. 7th Bn.North'd Fuslrs to Rest Area.	
	7.		Casualties - Wounded 2nd Lt. H.Potts, 9th Bn.D.L.I. Other Ranks 5. 149th Brigade Hd.Qrs and 150th Brigade Hd.Qrs to FLETRE Rest Area.	
FLETRE.	8.		Casualties - Wounded, Other Ranks 1. Divisional Hd.Qrs to FLETRE.	
	9.		Casualties - Other Ranks, Killed 2, Wounded 9, including 3 at duty. Royal Artillery Hd.Qrs to EECKE.	
	10.	9.28 p.m.	Division commences entraining for Reserve Army.	
BERNAVILLE	11.		Divisional Hd.Qrs to BERNAVILLE, Fifth Army, IX Corps.	
	12.		Division finishes detraining, DOULENS N, DOULENS S. and FIENVILLERS CANDAS.	
	13.			
	14.			

Army Form C. 2118.

ADMINSTRATIVE WAR DIARY or INTELLIGENCE SUMMARY

(Erase heading not required.)

50TH DIVISION.

AUGUST 1916.

Instructions regarding War Diaries and Intelligence Summaries are contained in F.S. Regs, Part II. and the Staff Manual respectively. Title Pages will be prepared in manuscript.

Place	Date	Hour	Summary of Events and Information	Remarks and references to Appendices
VIGNACOURT.	AUGT. 15		Divisional Hd.Qrs to VIGNACOURT.	
MONTIGNY.	16.		Divisional Hd.Qrs to MONTIGNY, III Corps, Fourth Army.	
	17.		Distribution - 149th Brigade HENENCOURT WOOD, 150th Brigade MILLENCOURT, 151st Brigade BAIZEUX WOOD, 7th (Pioneer) Bn. Durham L.I. BAIZEUX Village, R.F.A. BAVELINCOURT, 1st Field Coy RE. MILLENCOURT, 2nd Field Coy RE., BAIZEUX Village, 7th Field Coy RE., FRANVILLERS, 1st Field Ambce., BAIZEUX, 2nd Field Ambce FRANVILLERS, 3rd Field Ambce 2,000 yards East of BRESLE on Albert-Amiens Road.	
	18.		R.A. begin to move into the line (2 Brigades and Hd.Qrs.).	
	19.		2 Brigades R.F.A. remain in BEHENCOURT Area.	
	20.			
	21.		Casualties - Wounded acc: 2/Lt. H.L.DUNCAN, 4th E.Yorks, O.R.1, 4th Yorks - wounded acc: at duty O.R. 1.	
	22.		Casualties - 252nd Bgde RFA. Wounded acc: O.R. 1, 5th North'd Fus. Wounded acc: O.R. 1.	
	23.		Casualties - 7th North'd Fuslrs. Wounded acc:(at duty) O.R. 1.	
	24.		Casualties - 252nd Bgde RFA. Wounded O.R.2; 4th E.Yorks Wounded acc: O.R. 1.	
	25.		Casualties - 250th Bgde RFA. O.R. Killed 3, Wounded 4; 252nd Bgde RFA Wounded O.R. 3, includes 1 accidentally.	
	26.		Casualties - 250th Bgde RFA. O.R. Killed 2, Wounded 5.	

Army Form C. 2118.

50TH DIVISION.   AUGUST 1916.

ADMINISTRATIVE WAR DIARY
or
INTELLIGENCE SUMMARY

(Erase heading not required.)

Instructions regarding War Diaries and Intelligence Summaries are contained in F. S. Regs., Part II. and the Staff Manual respectively. Title Pages will be prepared in manuscript.

Place	Date	Hour	Summary of Events and Information	Remarks and references to Appendices
MONTIGNY.	AUGst 27.		Casualties - Wounded O.R.2, includes 1 at duty; Major B. Jackson, Staff Capt. 150th Bgde, appointed Brigade Major, 142nd Infantry Brigade.	
	28.		Casualties - Killed O.R.2, Wounded O.R.2. III Corps Commander presents Medals to Division, 3.30 p.m.	
	29.		Casualties - Wounded O.R.6, includes one accidentally.	
	30.		Casualties - NIL.	
	31.		Casualties - NIL.	

50th. DIVISION

A. & Q.

50th. DIVISION

SEPTEMBER 1916.

Vol 15

Confidential

50th Division

Administrative Staff

War Diary

From 1st September 1916

To 30th September 1916

Volume XVII

Army Form C. 2118.

ADMINISTRATIVE
WAR DIARY
or
INTELLIGENCE SUMMARY

(Erase heading not required.)

50TH DIVISION.   **SEPTEMBER 1916.**

Instructions regarding War Diaries and Intelligence Summaries are contained in F. S. Regs., Part II. and the Staff Manual respectively. Title Pages will be prepared in manuscript.

Place	Date	Hour	Summary of Events and Information	Remarks and references to Appendices
MONTIGNY	Septr. 1		Div. Hd.Qrs., MONTIGNY; Casualties - Killed O.R. 1, Wounded O.R. 3 R.F.A. in action.	
	2		Casualties - Killed O.R.1, Wounded O.R.5.	
	3		Casualties - Wounded O.R.2, 1 at duty.	
	4			
	5			
	6		Casualties - Wounded O.R.4, 2 accidental.	
	7		Casualties - Wounded O.R.7.	
	8		149th and 150th Brigades to Line. Casualties - Wounded Lt.H.Stewart 7th Durham L.I., O.R. 4.	
	9		Div. Hd.Qrs. to Camp D.6.b.5.3., East of MILLENCOURT from MONTIGNY. Casualties - Wounded 2nd Lt. A.H.Raine, 1st Field Coy RE., O.R. Killed 2, Wounded 16.	
	10		Casualties - Wounded 2nd Lt.V.G.McCallum and 2nd Lt. J.C.Lynn 250th Bde RFA, both at duty, Capt.P.W.Ransom RAMC attd 5th N.F.; O.R. killed 1, wounded 13. 151st Infy Bde from BAIZIEUX to BECOURT WOOD. General Officer Commanding took over Line 12 Noon.	
	11		Casualties - Killed Br.-Gen.H.F.H.Clifford 149th Inf.Bde; Ounded 2/Lt.R.W.Colley, T.W.Bde, 2nd Lt.T.F.KELSTING 4th East Yorks; Killed O.R.21, wounded 93.Lt.Col.Turner 5th N.F. commands 149th Inf.Bde temporarily.	
	12		Casualties - Killed Capt. H.R.Wilson 5th Durham L.I.- Wounded 2nd Lt.V.Hills 5th Durham L.I.; 2nd Lt. W.J.Smith 2nd Field Coy RE, 2nd Lt. R.B.Wade 7th Field Coy RE (Gas), 2nd Lt. J.L.Challoner No.149 L.Gun Coy, Capt. N.H.North, 2nd Lt. J.C.Sinclair 5th N.F., 2nd Lt. C.L.Young 4th E.Yorks; Killed O.R.12, Wounded O.R.76, Missing O.R.3.	

Army Form C. 2118.

50TH DIVISION.   SEPTEMBER 1916.

ADMINISTRATIVE WAR DIARY or INTELLIGENCE SUMMARY.

(Erase heading not required.)

Instructions regarding War Diaries and Intelligence Summaries are contained in F.S. Regs., Part II. and the Staff Manual respectively. Title Pages will be prepared in manuscript.

Place	Date	Hour	Summary of Events and Information	Remarks and references to Appendices
	Septr 13		Casualties - Wounded 2nd Lt.R.Skelton 150th T.M.Bty (gas) at duty; Killed O.R.6, Wounded O.R.41 including 9 gas.	
	14		Casualties - Killed Capt.W.Featherstone 5th Yorks, Wounded 2nd Lt.A.B.Pearcy (gas) 5th Yorks, 2nd Lt.I.Bewley 7th Durham L.I. attd 6th N.F.; O.R. Killed 7, Wounded 45, Missing 1. General Officer Commanding to advanced Div.Hd.Qrs. Brig.-Gen.Ovens to command 149th Inf.Bde.	
	15		Attack commenced 6.50 a.m. Casualties - 250th Bde RFA 2nd Lt.J.C.Lynn (died of wounds), O.R. wounded 9 (2 died of wounds), O.R. killed 5 wounded 15 (includes 2 S.I.W.); Wounded 2nd Lt. C.S.Palethorpe 50th Div. T.Ms; Died of wounds 2nd Lt. C.Ryan 250th Bde. Lt.A.R.Westrop 252nd Bde. 149th Brigade - Capt.B.C.Orme, 5th K.O.Y.L.I. attd 149th T.M.Battery, 2nd Lt.W.F.Horsley No.149 M.Gun Coy, 2nd Lt.V.Taylor 7th Nun.Fus. attd 149th M.Gun Coy. Killed 4th N.Fus. Officers killed 2nd Lt.G.J.Balfour 6th H.L.I. attd, Capt.J.T.Henderson, 2nd Lt.H.H.Bell, 2nd Lt.H.T.Melville; wounded Capt.J.M.Mitchell RAMC attd.; Capt.L.D.Plummer, Capt.J.A.Bagnall, Capt.H.A.Long (believed killed) Capt.H.Cheesmond, 2nd Lt.G.P.Welton, 2nd Lt.E.McIver, 2nd Lt.H.Tully, 2nd Lt.A.S.Waite, 2nd Lt.A.J.McKenzie 6th H.L.I. attd. 5th N.Fus. Officers wounded - 2nd Lt.J.O.Robson, 2nd Lt.H.L.Daglish, Capt.G.W.Dodds, Capt.R.E.Turnbull. 6th N.Fus. Officers killed - Capt.T.C.Tweedy; wounded 2nd Lts G.E.Towers, G.L.Young, C.M.Bramah 6th H.L.I. attd and S.T.Paton 6th H.L.I. attd, Capt.R.C.Dunford and Capt.C.Cooke. 7th N.Fus. Officers killed - Lt.A.Stroud 4th N.F. attd, Capt.J.W.Morivale, 2nd Lt.J.I.Grey, wounded - 2nd Lt.E.R.Brain, Capt.G.F.Ball, Lt.B.Brooke Booth, Lt.F.Buckley (died of wounds), 2nd Lt.A.P.Campbell, 2nd Lt. A.N.Smith. 150th Brigade - 4th E.Yorks Officers killed - 2nd Lt.J.H.Grainger, 2nd Lt.H.Oughtred (died of wounds); wounded - 2nd Lt.W.W.Harrison, 2nd Lt. G.H.Lofthouse, Capt.K.A.Wilson Barkworth, 2nd Lt.B.V.Hillyard, 2nd Lt.F.E.Furley, and 2nd Lt.C.S.Johnson. 4th Yorks Officers killed - Capt.T.S.Rowlandson, 2nd Lt.R.B.Abrahams, Lt.J.Miller (died of wounds) wounded - Capt.W.W.Constantine, 2nd Lts V.A.Bell, R.S.Ormand, O.J.Minister, A.S.Brentnall, R.M.Howes. 5th Yorks Officers killed - Lt.-Col.J.Mortimer CMG., Capt.F.Woodcock; Wounded - 2nd Lt. L.B.Walker.	

Army Form C. 2118.

50TH DIVISION.

ADMINISTRATIVE WAR DIARY or INTELLIGENCE SUMMARY

(Erase heading not required.)

SEPTEMBER 1916.

Instructions regarding War Diaries and Intelligence Summaries are contained in F. S. Regs., Part II. and the Staff Manual respectively. Title Pages will be prepared in manuscript.

Place	Date	Hour	Summary of Events and Information	Remarks and references to Appendices
	Septr 15		5th Durham L.I. - Officers Killed - 2nd Lt.E.Robinson; Wounded Capt.P.Wood DSO, Lt.F.D.Brown, 2nd Lieuts. H.W.Froud, E.C.Whitmore, R.W.H.Empson, O.J.Williams, S.Chadwick. 151st Inf.Brigade. 9th Durham L.I. - Officers Killed - Capt.R.Rutherford.	
	16		Casualties - 250th Brigade R.F.A. Officers Killed Lt.J.G.Browell; O.R. Wounded 2. 251st Brigade R.F.A. O.R. Killed 2, wounded 4. 252nd Brigade R.F.A. O.R. Killed 1, wounded 1. 253rd Brigade R.F.A. O.R. died of wounds 1. 149th Inf.Brde - 4th N.F. - Officers killed - 2nd Lt.H.T.Melville, O.R. Killed 13, Wounded 200, Missing 385. 5th N.F. - Wounded 2nd Lt.H.E.Merritt; O.R. killed 4, wounded 50. 6th N.F. - Wounded 2nd Lt.W.K.Duncanson 6th H.L.I. attd; O.R. killed 120, Wounded 150. 7th N.F. - O.R. Killed 50, wounded 300. 150th Inf.Brde - 4th E.Yks - Officers Killed - 2nd Lt.H.K.Gibson (died of wounds); Wounded - 2nd Lieuts G.Lishman, H.Rollett, W.H.S.Phillips and W.Joy. 4th Yorks- Officers Killed - 2nd Lieuts.H.M.Laing and W.B.Hayton, Wounded - 2nd Lt.T.C.Thornton (shell shock); O.R. Killed 35, wounded 100. 5th Yorks- O.R. Killed 40, wounded 95. 5th D.L.I. O.R. Killed 30, wounded 150. 151st Inf.Brde - 6th D.L.I. Officers killed - 2nd Lt.H.C.Annett; wounded Capt.W.F.E.Badcock, 2nd Lts E.J.Harveyn V.R.Tattersall, C.Ramsey, W.F.Charlton. 9th D.L.I. Officers wounded- Capt.J.O.Innes, 2nd Lts J.H.Tytler and E.S.Gibson. 5th Borders- Officers killed - Lt.G.E.Dawes; Wounded - Capt.W.F.Spedding, 2nd Lts F.J.Lain, J.Pattinson, J.E.A.Combes.	

Army Form C. 2118.

50TH DIVISION.
SEPTEMBER 1916.

ADMINISTRATIVE
WAR DIARY
or
INTELLIGENCE SUMMARY
(Erase heading not required.)

Instructions regarding War Diaries and Intelligence Summaries are contained in F. S. Regs., Part II. and the Staff Manual respectively. Title Pages will be prepared in manuscript.

Place	Date	Hour	Summary of Events and Information	Remarks and references to Appendices
	Septr. 17		Casualties - 251st Bde RFA Officers wounded - Lt.P.Robinson, O.R.2. 252nd Bde RFA Woun ded O.R.2.	
			149th Bde - Machine Gun Coy - Killed O.R.1, Wounded O.R.7, Missing O.R.1. T.Mortar Batty - Wounded O.R.1. 4th Northd Fus: - Officers wounded - 2nd Lt.J.A.J.McKenzie 8th H.L.I. attd; O.R. Killed 22, wounded 3. 132 of the 585 reported missing on 16th accounted for. 5th Northd Fus: - Officers killed - 2nd Lt.C.V.Adler (died of wounds); O.R. Killed 4, wounded 3, Missing 18. 6th Northd Fus: - O.R. wounded 30, Missing 40. Of the 120 O.R. reported killed on the 16th 70 have now been accounted for. 7th Northd Fus: - Wounded - Capt.E.C.Fenwicke Clennel, 2nd Lt.J.Unsworth; O.R. missing 68. Of those previously reported killed deduct 15 and of those wounded deduct 70 which have since been accounted for.	
			150th Bde - Machine Gun Coy - Wounded - 2nd Lt.E.P.Spooner; O.R. Killed 2, wounded 9. T.Mortar Batty - O.R. Killed 3, wounded 10. 4th Yorks Regt. - Killed - 2nd Lt.R.F.William RAMC (died of wounds); Wounded - 2nd Lts H.L.Harrison, J.Robson, R.Forrest. 4th E.Yorks. - O.R. Killed 15, wounded 40. 5th Yorks Regt. - Killed - 2nd Lts W.R.Lawson, G.S.Phillips- Wounded - 2nd Lts G.H.Dell, P.H.Sykes; Missing - 2nd Lt.N.H.Fell; O.R. Killed 35, wounded 105.	
			5th D.L.I. - Killed - 2nd Lt.H.Green (died of wounds); Wounded - 2nd Lt.L.J.Wilmot, 2nd Lt.J.N.M.Hessler, 2nd Lt. F.E.S.Townsend; O.R. Killed 30, wounded 90.	
			151st Bde - 6th D.L.I. - O.R. Killed 8, wounded 34, Missing 402. 9th D.L.I. - Officers wounded - 2nd Lt.H.Whiteley, H.Burrell, S.Wilson, J.G.Steel; Missing (believed killed) 2nd Lt.H.A.Walton and 2nd Lt.A.Lawson. 5th Borders. - Officers wounded - Capt.N.P.Inglis, RAMC, 2nd Lt.J.E.H.Coombes, O.R. Killed 57, wounded 96, Missing 37. T.M.Battery. - Officers Killed - 2nd Lt.J.W.Lauderdale.	

Army Form C. 2118.

WAR DIARY or INTELLIGENCE SUMMARY

(Erase heading not required.)

Instructions regarding War Diaries and Intelligence Summaries are contained in F. S. Regs., Part II. and the Staff Manual respectively. Title Pages will be prepared in manuscript.

Place	Date	Hour	Summary of Events and Information	Remarks and references to Appendices
MILLENCOURT	Sept. 18.		Casualties :- 150th Bde. 4th East Yorks Regt. O.R. Wounded 32, Missing 13. Of 40 O.R. reported killed on 16th, 26 have been accounted for, total Killed 14. Pereyra 151st Bde. 5th Durham L.I. Officer Wounded, 2nd Lt. A.E.W. Pereyra. 6th Durham L.I. Officers, Killed, 2/Lts H.J.Harris and W.F.Charlton; Wounded Captain J.W.Cook. O.R. Wounded 13, Missing 17. 8th Durham L.I. Officers, Wounded, Capt.A.Oswell, 2/Lt.G.D.Dolds. O.R. Killed 17, Wounded 43, Missing 49. 9th Durham L.I. Officers, Wounded, 2/Lt.J.Slater; O.R. Killed 53, Wounded 94, Missing 280. 5th Border Regt. Officers, Killed, Capt.D.W.Glass, 2/Lt.A.Feetham; Wounded, Lt. H.P.Smith; O.R. Killed 10, Wounded 20, Missing 35. Trench Mortar Battery. O.R. Missing 1.	
	19.		Casualties :- 251st Bde, R.F.A. Officers, Wounded, Capt.A.B.Law; O.R. Wounded 2. 150th Bde. 4th East Yorks Regt. O.R. Wounded 2, Missing rejoined 4. 5th Yorks Regt. Officers (Shell Shock) 2/Lt.J.S.Purvis. 5th Durham L.I. O.R. 14 previously reported killed, now accounted for; Wounded 44, Missing 54. 151st Bde. 9th Durham L.I. Officers, Wounded, Lt.J.M.Herring; O.R. Wounded 2. 5th Border Regt. Officer, Wounded, 2/Lt. S.Hall. No. 151 M.G.Coy. Officer, Killed, Capt.H.C.Webb, 5th Border Regt. O.R.Wounded 2. (M'Gauy?)	
	20.			
	21.		Casualties :- 251st Bde, R.F.A. O.R. Wounded 1. 150th Brigade. 5th Yorks Regt. O.R. Deduct, Killed 2; Wounded 59, Missing 17, wounded, returned to duty, and rejoined.	

Army Form C. 2118.

ADMINISTRATIVE
WAR DIARY
or
INTELLIGENCE SUMMARY

(Erase heading not required.)

Instructions regarding War Diaries and Intelligence Summaries are contained in F. S. Regs., Part II. and the Staff Manual respectively. Title Pages will be prepared in manuscript.

50TH DIVISION.   SEPTEMBER 1916.

Place	Date	Hour	Summary of Events and Information	Remarks and references to Appendices
	Septr 22		Casualties -	
			250th Bde RFA - Officers wounded, Lt.H.C.Earle; O.R. wounded 1.	
			251st Bde RFA - O.R. killed 2 (1 died of wounds).	
			252nd Bde RFA - O.R. wounded 2.	
			253rd Bde RFA - O.R. wounded 2.	
			149th Inf.Bde - 4th N.Fus. O.R. Killed 1 wounded 1.; 5th N.Fus. O.R. Killed 1, wounded 12.	
			6th N.Fus. O.R. Wounded 2; 7th N.Fus. O.R. Wounded 2.	
			150th Inf.Bde - 4th E.Yorks. O.R. Wounded 1; 4th Yorks O.R. wounded 1; 5th Yorks Wounded) 2/Lt.W.H.Game.)	
			151st Inf.Bde - 8th D.L.I. O.R. Killed 2, wounded 3; 5th Border Regt. O.R. deduct Killed 40 wounded 28, missing 52. Now wounded, returned to duty and rejoined.	
	23		Casualties -	
			250th Bde RFA - O.R. wounded 3; 252nd Bde RFA - O.R. wounded 2.	
			149th Inf.Bde -	
			attd Revd H.Wooldridge wounded.	
			4th N.Fus. - Officers wounded 2/Lt.C.Stephenson (shell shock, at duty); O.R. killed 1, wounded 9, missing 1.	
			5th N.Fus. - O.R. Killed 1, wounded 5, missing 5.	
			6th N.Fus. - O.R. Killed 2, wounded 4, missing 3.	
			150th Inf.Bde -	
			4th E.Yorks - O.R. killed 4 (2 died of wounds), wounded 7.	
			4th Yorks. - O.R. wounded 2 accidentally.	
			151st Inf.Bde -	
			6th D.L.I. - O.R. killed 16, wounded 51, reported missing since rejoined 347.	
			8th D.L.I. - O.R. killed 2, wounded 52, reported missing since rejoined 27.	
			9th D.L.I. - O.R. wounded 92, 39 rept killed now wounded, 209 reptd missing now rejoined.	
			5th Borders - O.R. killed 4, wounded 21, missing 4.	

Army Form C. 2118.

50TH DIVISION.
SEPTEMBER 1916.

Instructions regarding War Diaries and Intelligence Summaries are contained in F. S. Regs., Part II. and the Staff Manual respectively. Title Pages will be prepared in manuscript.

ADMINISTRATIVE WAR DIARY or INTELLIGENCE SUMMARY
(Erase heading not required.)

Place	Date	Hour	Summary of Events and Information	Remarks and references to Appendices
	Septr. 24		Casualties - 250th Bde RFA - O.R. wounded 6 ; 253rd Bde RFA - O.R. wounded 2 ; D.A.C. - O.R. wounded 1. 149th Inf.Bde - 5th N.Fus.- O.R. wounded 7, reptd missing now rejd 3. 6th N.Fus.- O.R. wounded 3. ; 7th N.Fus.- O.R. killed 1, wounded 5. 150th Inf.Bde - 4th E.Yorks.- Killed 1, wounded 2 O.R. ; 4th Yorks.- O.R. killed 1. 5th Yorks. - O.R. killed 5, wounded 12 (1 accidentally). 5th D.L.I. - O.R. killed 1, wounded 3. 151st Inf.Bde - 4th D.L.I. - O.R. wounded 1.	
	25		Casualties - 151st Inf.Bde - 5th Border Regt. - wounded Capt.S.Rigg.	
	26		Casualties - 250th Bde RFA - O.R. wounded 1. ; 251st Bde RFA - O.R. wounded 1 ; 253rd Bde RFA - O.R. w 5. D.A.C. - O.R. wounded 1 ; 4th E.Yorks - Killed O.R. 1 (died of wounds), wounded 8. 4th Yorks Regt - O.R. wounded 1 ; 5th Yorks Regt - O.R. killed 1, wounded 1. 5th D.L.I. - O.R. killed 1, wounded 2 ; 8th D.L.I. O.R. wounded 3. 5th Border Regt - O.R. killed 1, wounded 6.	
	27		Casualties - 250th Bde RFA - O.R. wounded 1 (shell shock, at duty). 251st Bde RFA - O.R. killed 1, w 2. 253rd Bde RFA - O.R. wounded 1. 4th E.Yorks. - O.R. killed 2, wounded 5, missing 1. 4th Yorks. - Officers killed - 2/Lt.E.L.Perris, wounded - 2/Lt.Prior Wandesforde, W.L.Batty, G.A.Tugwell, E.Richardson, F.E.A.Postill, D.P.Hirsch; O.R. killed 1, wounded 23, missing 55. 5th Yorks. - Officers wounded - 2/Lts J.A.Sleightholme, A.J.L.Ramm, E.A.M.Lester- O.R. killed 4, wounded 16, missing 30. 5th D.L.I. - O.R. killed 1, wounded 20 ; 6th D.L.I. - O.R. killed 2, wounded 11. 5th Borders. - O.R. wounded 4.	

Army Form C. 2118.

WAR DIARY or INTELLIGENCE SUMMARY

(Erase heading not required.)

Instructions regarding War Diaries and Intelligence Summaries are contained in F. S. Regs., Part II. and the Staff Manual respectively. Title Pages will be prepared in manuscript.

Place	Date	Hour	Summary of Events and Information	Remarks and references to Appendices
	Sept. 28		Casualties - 250th Bde RFA - O.R. wounded 1. 251st Bde RFA - O.R. wounded 1. 252nd Bde RFA - O.R. w 1. 149th Inf.Bde - 4th N.Fus. O.R. killed 1. 6th N.Fus. O.R. wounded 3. 7th N.Fus. O.R. wounded 1. 150th Inf.Bde - 4th E.Yorks. O.R. wounded 2, prev. reptd missing now rejd 1. 4th Yorks.-Wounded 2/Lt.M.W.Macnay. 5th Yorks.-O.R. killed 2, wounded 9, previously reported missing now rejoined 30. 151st Inf.Bde - 5th D.L.I.- O.R. killed 3, missing 6. 150th M.G.Coy.- O.R. wounded 1. 6th D.L.I.- O.R. wounded 12. 8th D.L.I.- O.R. wounded 2. 9th D.L.I.- 2nd Lt.W.J.Harris and Capt.W.S.Ridley wounded; 2/Lt.W.E.C.Scott missing. 5th Border Regt.- O.R. wounded 2. 151st M.G.Coy.- Wounded 2nd Lt.P.H.Jenrick.	
	29		Casualties - 252nd Bde R.F.A. - O.R. wounded 1. 6th N.Fus. - wounded 2/Lt.H.P.Brookes. 151st Inf.Bde. - 6th D.L.I.- O.R. wounded 3. 8th D.L.I. Officers killed 2/Lts W.G.Russell, W.T.Roan, H.M.Berwick; Wounded - 2/Lts R.H.Guest Williams, G.R.Russell, J.Frost, R.Wallace; O.R. wounded 2. 9th D.L.I. - O.R. killed 6, wounded 10. 5th Border Regt.- O.R. wounded 4.	
	30		Casualties - 250th Bde RFA - Wounded 2/Lt.E.Darling; O.R. wounded 2. 251st Bde RFA - O.R. wounded 2 (includes 1 at duty). 253rd Bde RFA - O.R. wounded 1. 50th D.A.C. - O.R. killed 1. T.M.Bde.(H.&H.)- O.R. wounded 2. 149th Inf.Bde. - 4th N.Fus. O.R. wounded 1. 5th N.Fus. O.R. wounded 1. 6th N.Fus. O.R. wounded 3 (includes 2 shell shock). 150th Inf.Bde.- 4th Yorks. O.R. wounded acc. 1. 4th Yorks. O.R. wounded 2. 5th Yorks. O.R. wounded 3 (includes 1, at duty). 5th D.L.I. - O.R. wounded 1 accidentally. 151st Inf.Bde.- 6th D.L.I. - O.R. killed 1. 9th D.L.I.- O.R. wounded 7 (includes 1 at duty). 5th Borders- O.R. wounded 3.	

CONFIDENTIAL

Administrative Staff

50th Division

War Diary

From 1st October 1918

To 31st October 1918

Volume XVIII

Army Form C. 2118.

WAR DIARY or INTELLIGENCE SUMMARY

(Erase heading not required.)

50TH DIVISION.   OCTOBER 1916.

Instructions regarding War Diaries and Intelligence Summaries are contained in F.S. Regs., Part II. and the Staff Manual respectively. Title Pages will be prepared in manuscript.

Place	Date	Hour	Summary of Events and Information	Remarks and references to Appendices
MILLENCOURT.	OCT. 1		Casualties - Royal Artillery - 250th Bde OR killed 1; 251st Bde OR wounded 3 (inc. 1 at duty); 253rd Bde OR wounded 1. 149th Inf.Bgde. - 4th N.Fus. OR killed 2, wounded 5, missing 1. 5th N.Fus. Officers wounded 2/Lt.A.P.LETTS, 2/Lt.P.F.BEATON; OR wounded 26. 6th N.Fus. Officers wounded 2/Lt.H.S.FOTHERBY; OR killed 6, wounded 30 (inc. 12 shell shock) missing 5. 150th Inf.Bgde. - 4th E.Yorks. OR killed 1, prev. reptd missing, now reptd. killed. 4th Yorks. OR wounded 1. 151st Inf.Bgde. - 6th Durham L.I. Officers wounded Lt. & Adjt. A.EBSWORTH and 2/Lt.A.APPLEBY (at duty), Lt.R.PEBERDY and 2/Lt.E.P.BARNETT; OR killed 9 wounded 61. 8th Durham L.I. Officers wounded 2/Lts G.C.RUSCOE, A.V.McLARE, J.HUTCHINSON, R.A.WORSWICK, A.H.TWIGG;; OR killed 3, wounded 106, missing 142. 9th Durham L.I. Officers wounded 2/Lt.H.R.HESLOP; OR wounded 6. 5th Border Regt. Officers killed 2/Lt.A.G.CONDI, wounded 2/Lt.P.B.C.HOLDSWORTH; OR killed 6, wounded 30. No:151 M.Gun Coy. Officers wounded 2/Lt.J.W.BRADDELL.	
	2		Casualties - Royal Artillery - 251st Bde OR wounded 1 (shell shock). 252nd Bde OR wounded 1. Trench Mortar Bgde OR killed 1, wounded 1. 149th Inf.Bgde. - 4th N.Fus. OR wounded 8. 5th N.Fus. OR killed 5, wounded 73, missing 6. 150th Inf.Bgde. - 4th N.Fus. OR killed 3, wounded 10, missing 1. 4th Yorks. OR wounded 1. 151st Inf.Bgde. - 6th Durham L.I. OR killed 1, wounded 2, missing 1 (believed killed). 9th Durham L.I. OR wounded 37.	
	3		Withdrawal of Division from front line. 149th Inf.Bgde moves to MAMETZ WOOD. 150th Inf.Bgde moves to ALBERT en route for BAIZIEUX. 151st Inf.Bgde moves into BECOURT as Brigade in Reserve. Casualties - 149th Inf.Bgde. - 4th N.Fus. OR killed 2, wounded 8. 5th N.Fus. Officers killed CAPT.C.A. PATTERSON, wounded 2/Lt.J.B.WILSON (at duty), CAPT.W.H.LEETH. OR Correction Killed 19, wounded 4, prev. reptd missing 3, now accounted for. 6th N.Fus. Officers wounded 2/Lt.R.C.PENKETH. 7th N.Fus. Officers killed 2/Lt.A.G.STRAKER, wounded 2/LT.G.H.MOUATT†	

Army Form C. 2118.

ADMINISTRATIVE WAR DIARY or INTELLIGENCE SUMMARY

(Erase heading not required.)

50TH DIVISION. **OCTOBER 1916.**

Instructions regarding War Diaries and Intelligence Summaries are contained in F. S. Regs., Part II. and the Staff Manual respectively. Title Pages will be prepared in manuscript.

Place	Date	Hour	Summary of Events and Information	Remarks and references to Appendices
	OCTR. 3		Casualties - 7th N.Fus. OR killed 1, wounded 5, missing 2. M.Gun Coy. Officers killed 2/Lt.J.G.WOOD. Trench Mortar Battery OR killed 1, wounded 2. 4th Yorks. OR correction Killed 31, wounded 6, prev. rept. missing now accounted for 51. 5th Yorks. OR correction Killed 7, prev. reptd wounded now reported unwounded 36, prev. reptd missing now accounted for 19. 5th Durham L.I. OR correction Killed 18, wounded 30, prev. reptd missing now accounted for 40.	
			150th Inf.Bgde. - 9th Durham L.I. OR wounded 37. 5th Border Regt Officers wounded 2/Lt.J.N.FRANKS; correction OR prev. reptd killed 3, missing 4, wounded 8 151st Inf.Bgde now accounted for.	
	4		150th Inf.Bgde at BAIZIEUX. 149th Inf.Bgde moves to MILLENCOURT via ALBERT. 151st Inf.Bgde moved from BECOURT to HENENCOURT WOOD. Casualties.- 149th Inf.Bgde. - 5th N.Fus. Died of wounds 2/Lt.D.ARMSTRONG. 6th N.Fus. OR killed 2, wounded 12 (includes six shell shk) missing 1. 150th Inf.Bgde. - 4th E.Yorks. OR wounded 2.	
	5		149th Inf.Bgde at MILLENCOURT. Casualties - Royal Artillery.- 252nd Bde wounded OR 1 (at duty). Div.Amm.Col. wounded OR 1 at duty.	
	6		Casualties.- Royal Artillery.- 252nd Bde OR wounded 1. 253rd Bde OR wounded 2 (inc. 1 at duty). Trench Mortar Bde OR wounded 2 accidentally. D.A.C. OR wounded 2 149th Inf.Bgde. - 6th N.Fus. Correction OR killed 26, wounded 52, prev. reptd missing now accounted for 38. 151st Inf.Bgde. - 6th Durham L.I. OR killed 20, wounded 71, missing 38. 9th Durham L.I. OR killed 8, prev. reptd wounded now unwounded 14, missing 2. 5th Border Regt. OR killed 7, wounded 24, missing 8.	
	7		Casualties.- Royal Artillery - 250th Bde Officers killed Lt.H.WEDDELL, OR wounded 6.	

2449 Wt. W14957/M90 750,000 1/16 J.B.C. & A. Forms/C.2118/12.

Army Form C. 2118.

ADMINISTRATIVE WAR DIARY or INTELLIGENCE SUMMARY

(Erase heading not required.)

50TH DIVISION.   OCTOBER 1916.

Instructions regarding War Diaries and Intelligence Summaries are contained in F. S. Regs., Part II. and the Staff Manual respectively. Title Pages will be prepared in manuscript.

Place	Date	Hour	Summary of Events and Information	Remarks and references to Appendices
	OCTR. 8		Casualties - Royal Artillery - 250th Bde OR wounded 6.	
	9		Casualties - 149th Inf.Bgde + 4th N.Fus. Officers killed CAPT.L.D.PLUMMER, 2/Lt.J.A.BAGNALL, 2/LT.H.A.LONG, 2/Lt.J.FLEMING, 2/Lt.A.S.WAITE.	
	10		Casualties - 7th Durham L.I. (Pioneers) OR wounded 7.	
	11		Casualties - Royal Artillery - 250th Bde OR killed 1, wounded 6 (inc. 1 at duty). 252nd Bde OR wounded 2. Div'nl Amm.Col. OR wounded 1.	
			7th Durham L.I. (Pioneers) - OR wounded 7.	
	12		Casualties - NIL.	
	13		Casualties - 7th Field Co.RE. wounded OR 2. 250th (Nbn) Bde RFA OR wounded 1.	
			7th Durham L.I.(Pioneers) OR wounded 2.	
	14		Casualties - NIL.	
	15		Casualties - NIL.	
	16		Casualties - NIL.	
	17		Casualties - Royal Artillery - 250th Bde OR killed 2. 252nd Bde OR wounded 1.	
			7th Durham L.I.(Pioneers) wounded OR 1.	
	18		Casualties - 252nd Bde RFA OR wounded 2; 253rd Bde RFA OR killed 1.	
	19		Casualties - 250th Bde RFA OR wounded 1. 252nd Bde RFA OR wounded 2.	

Army Form C. 2118.

50th DIVISION A&Q October 1916

50TH DIVISION.

ADMINISTRATIVE WAR DIARY or INTELLIGENCE SUMMARY

OCTOBER 1916.

(Erase heading not required.)

Instructions regarding War Diaries and Intelligence Summaries are contained in F. S. Regs., Part II. and the Staff Manual respectively. Title Pages will be prepared in manuscript.

Place	Date	Hour	Summary of Events and Information	Remarks and references to Appendices
	OCTR.			
	20		Casualties - 250th Bde RFA OR wounded 1.	
	21		Casualties - 253rd Bde RFA OR killed 2, wounded 1.	
	22		Casualties - 250th Bde RFA OR wounded 2.	
	23		Casualties - NIL.	
	24		Division goes into front line. 149th Infy Bgde relieved 26th Infantry Brigade in the Line. 150th Infy Bgde relieved 26th Infantry Brigade in the Line. Casualties - 50th D.A.Col. OR wounded 1 (acc). 4th E.Yorks OR wounded 3.	459-
FRICOURT FARM.	25		151st Infy Bgde relieved 27th Infantry Brigade in reserve in MAMETZ WOOD. Divisional Headquarters moved to FRICOURT FARM. Casualties - 50th D.A.Col. OR wounded 1 (acc). 4th N.Fus. OR wounded 1. 6th N.Fus. Officers killed 2/Lt.J.H.MACKILLAR; OR killed 1, wounded 3 (6th H.L.I. attd). 7th N.Fus. OR wounded 2. 4th Yorks.- Officers killed 2/Lts W.L.BATTY and J.B.HUDSON; OR killed 2, wounded 4. 5th Yorks OR killed 1, wounded 7. No.150 M.Gun Coy OR wounded 2.	
	26		Casualties - 4th N.Fus OR killed 1, wounded 4, missing 1. 6th N.Fus wounded Lt.E.G.PROCTOR; OR killed 3, wounded 5, missing 10. 7th N.Fus OR wounded 2 (shell shock, at duty). No.149 M.Gun Coy OR wounded 1. 4th Yorks OR wounded 7. 5th Yorks Officers wounded 2/Lt.F.LEWIN; OR killed 5, wounded 6, missing 1. 6th Durham L.I. OR killed 1, wounded 1 (both accidentally).	
	27		Casualties - 6th N.Fus. wounded Capt.J.H.MACKENZIE RAMC attd. 7th N.Fus OR wounded 1. No.149 M.Gun Coy OR wounded 4. 4th E.Yorks OR killed 1 wounded 7. 4th Yorks killed 2/Lt.A.COATES ; OR wounded 3. 5th Yorks OR killed 3, wounded 11, missing 1. 5th Durham L.I. OR killed 1 wounded 4. No.150 M.Gun Coy OR wounded 1. 150th Trench M.Bty OR wounded 5. 7th Durham L.I.(Pioneers) OR killed 1, wounded 3.	

Army Form C. 2118.

50TH DIVISION.
ADMINISTRATIVE WAR DIARY or INTELLIGENCE SUMMARY
(Erase heading not required.)

OCTOBER 1916.

460-

Place	Date	Hour	Summary of Events and Information	Remarks and references to Appendices
	OCTR. 28		Casualties - 253rd Bde RFA OR wounded 2. 4th N.Fus OR killed 3, wounded 4, missing 1. 5th N.Fus OR wounded 1. 6th N.Fus OR killed 4, wounded 12. 7th N.Fus OR wounded 2. No.149 M.Gun Coy OR wounded 1. 4th E.Yorks OR killed 2, wounded 3. 4th Yorks OR wounded 5. 5th Yorks OR wounded 6, missing 1. No.150 M.Gun Coy OR 1 prev. reptd wounded now killed. 7th Durham L.I. (Pioneers) OR wounded 1. 2nd Fd Coy RE wounded 2/Lt.E.W.MATHER. 2nd Nbn Fd Amb2c Capt.H.B.LOW wounded at duty; OR killed 2 wounded 2.	
	29		Casualties - 4th N.Fus OR killed 1 wounded 2. 6th N.Fus OR killed 1 wounded 6. 7th N.Fus OR wounded 2. No.149 M.Gun Coy OR missing 1. 4th E.Yorks OR wounded 4 missing 1. 4th E.Yorks OR wounded 4. 5th Yorks OR wounded 3. 5th Durham L.I. OR wounded 4. No.150 M.Gun Coy OR killed 1, wounded 1 at duty. 5th Border Regt OR wounded 2.	
	30		Casualties - 4th N.Fus Officers 2/Lt.W.C.CLEMITSON wounded at duty; OR killed 8, wounded 12. 5th N.Fus OR wounded 1. 6th N.Fus OR wounded 1. 7th N.Fus OR wounded 1 at duty. No.149 T.Mortar Btty OR wounded 1. 4th E.Yorks OR wounded 1. 5th Yorks - prev. reptd missing now rejoined OR 1. 5th Durham L.I. OR wounded 3. No.150 Trench Mortar Btty OR wounded 1. 7th Dur.L.I.(Pioneers) OR killed 1, wounded 2.	
	31		Casualties - 4th N.Fus. OR killed 1, wounded 3, missing 1. 5th N.Fus Officers - 2/Lt.C.JONES wounded; OR killed 2, wounded 9, missing 2. 6th N.Fus OR wounded 1 at duty. prev. reptd missing now rejoined 10. 4th E.Yorks OR killed 1 wounded 2. 4th Yorks OR missing 1. 5th Durham L.I. OR wounded 1.	

50TH DIVISION.

ADMINISTRATIVE

OCTOBER 1916.

MILLENCOURT. **OCT. 1**

Casualties -
- Royal Artillery — 250th Bde OR killed 1; 251st Bde OR wounded 3 (inc. 1 at duty); 253rd Bde OR wounded 1.
- 149th Inf.Bgde. — 4th N.Fus. OR killed 2, wounded 5, missing 1. 5th N.Fus. officers wounded 2/Lt.A.P.LETTS, 2/Lt.P.F.BEATON; OR wounded 25. 6th N.Fus. officers wounded 2/Lt.H.S.FOTHERBY; OR killed 6, wounded 30 (inc. 12 shell shock) missing 5.
- 150th Inf.Bgde. — 4th E.Yorks. OR killed 1, prev. reptd missing, now reptd. killed. 4th Yorks. OR wounded 1.
- 151st Inf.Bgde. — 6th Durham L.I. officers wounded Lt. & Adjt.A.EBSWORTH and 2/Lt.A.APPLEBY (at duty), Lt.R.PEBERDY and 2/Lt.E.P.BARNETT; OR killed 9 wounded 61. 8th Durham L.I. officers wounded 2/Lts G.C.RUSCOE, A.V.McLARE, J.HUTCHINSON, R.A.WORSWICK, A.H.TWIGG; OR killed 3, wounded 106, missing 142. 9th Durham L.I. officers wounded 2/Lt.H.R.HESLOP; OR wounded 6. 5th Border Regt. officers killed 2/Lt.A.G.CONDI, wounded 2/Lt.P.B.C.HOLDSWORTH; OR killed 6, wounded 30.
  No:151 M.Gun Coy. officers wounded 2/Lt.J.W.BRADDELL.

2

Casualties -
- Royal Artillery — 251st Bde OR wounded 1 (shell shock). 252nd Bde OR wounded 1. Trench Mortar Bgde OR killed 1, wounded 1.
- 149th Inf.Bgde. — 4th N.Fus. OR wounded 6. 5th N.Fus. OR killed 5, wounded 73, missing 6.
- 150th Inf.Bgde. — 4th E.Yorks. OR killed 3, wounded 10, missing 1. 4th Yorks. OR wounded 1.
- 151st Inf.Bgde. — 6th Durham L.I. OR killed 1, wounded 2, missing 1 (believed killed). 9th Durham L.I. OR wounded 57.

3 Withdrawal of Division from front line. 149th Inf.Bgde moves to MAMETZ WOOD. 150th Inf.Bgde moves to ALBERT en route for BAIZIEUX. 151st Inf.Bgde moves into BECOURT as Brigade in Reserve.

Casualties -
- 149th Inf.Bgde. — 4th N.Fus. OR killed 2, wounded 8. 5th N.Fus. Officers killed CAPT.C.A.PATTERSON, wounded 2/Lt.J.B.WILSON (at duty), CAPT.W.H.LEETE. OR Correction Killed 19, wounded 4, prev. reptd missing 3, now accounted for.
- 6th N.Fus. Officers wounded 2/Lt.R.C.PENKETH.
- 7th N.Fus. Officers killed 2/Lt.A.G.STRAKER, wounded 2/Lt.G.H.MOUATT;

ADMINISTRATIVE

50TH DIVISION.   OCTOBER 1916.

OCTR.

3 Casualties -   7th N.Fus. OR killed 1, wounded 5, missing 2. M.Gun Coy. Officers killed 2/Lt.J.G.WOOD. Trench Mortar Battery OR killed 1, wounded 2.
  150th Inf.Bgde. -   4th Yorks. OR correction Killed 31, wounded 6, prev. rept. missing now accounted for 51. 5th Yorks. OR correction killed 7, prev. reptd wounded now reported unwounded 36, prev. reptd missing now accounted for 19. 5th Durham L.I. OR correction Killed 18, wounded 30, prev. reptd missing now accounted for 40.
  151st Inf.Bgde. -   9th Durham L.I. OR wounded 37. 5th Border Regt Officers wounded 2/Lt.J.M.FRANKS; correction OR prev. reptd killed 3, missing 2, wounded 8 now accounted for.

4 150th Inf.Bgde at BAIZIEUX. 149th Inf.Bgde moves to MILLENCOURT via ALBERT. 151st Inf.Bgde moved from BECOURT to HENENCOURT WOOD.
  Casualties -
  149th Inf.Bgde. -   5th N.Fus. Died of wounds 2/Lt.D.ARMSTRONG. 6th N.Fus. OR killed 2, wounded 12 (includes 6 shell shock missing 1.
  150th Inf.Bgde. -   4th E.Yorks. OR wounded 2.

5 149th Inf.Bgde at MILLENCOURT.
  Casualties.
  Royal Artillery.-   252nd Bde wounded OR 1 (at duty). Div.Amm.Col. wounded OR 1 at duty.

6 Casualties. -
  Royal Artillery.-   252nd Bde OR wounded 1. 253rd Bde OR wounded 2 (inc. 1 at duty). Trench Mortar Bde OR wounded 2 accidentally. D.A.C. OR wounded 2
  149th Inf.Bgde. -   6th N.Fus. Correction OR killed 26, wounded 52, prev. reptd missing now accounted for 58.
  151st Inf.Bgde. -   6th Durham L.I. OR killed 20, wounded 71, missing 38. 9th Durham L.I. OR killed 8, prev. reptd wounded now unwounded 14, missing 2. 5th Border Regt. OR killed 7, wounded 24, missing 8.

7 Casualties. -
  Royal Artillery   - 250th Bde Officers killed Lt.H.WEDDELL, OR wounded 6.

50TH DIVISION.   ADMINISTRATIVE

                            OCTOBER 1916.

OCTR.
8   Casualties –
    Royal Artillery – 250th Bde OR wounded 6.

9   Casualties –
    149th Inf.Bgde – 4th N.Fus. Officers killed CAPT.L.D.PLUMMER, 2/Lt.J.A.BAGNALL, 2/Lt.H.A.LONG,
                      2/Lt.J.FLEMING, 2/Lt.A.S.WAITE.

10 Casualties –
    7th Durham L.I. (Pioneers) OR wounded 7.

11 Casualties –
    Royal Artillery – 250th Bde OR killed 1, wounded 6 (inc. 1 at duty). 252nd Bde OR wounded 2.
                       Div'nl Amn.Col. OR wounded 1.
    7th Durham L.I. (Pioneers) – OR wounded 7.

12 Casualties – NIL.

13 Casualties – 7th Field Co.RE. wounded OR 2. 250th (Mbn) Bde RFA OR wounded 1.
                  7th Durham L.I.(Pioneers) OR wounded 2.

14 Casualties – NIL.

15 Casualties – NIL.

16 Casualties – NIL.

17 Casualties –
    Royal Artillery – 250th Bde OR killed 2. 252nd Bde OR wounded 1.
                       7th Durham L.I.(Pioneers) wounded OR 1.

18 Casualties – 252nd Bde RFA OR wounded 2; 253rd Bde RFA OR killed 1.

19 Casualties – 250th Bde RFA OR wounded 1. 252nd Bde RFA OR wounded 2.

50TH DIVISION.   ADMINISTRATIVE

OCTOBER 1916.

OCTR. 20	Casualties –	250th Bde RFA OR wounded 1.
21	Casualties –	253rd Bde RFA OR killed 2, wounded 1.
22	Casualties –	250th Bde RFA OR wounded 2.
23	Casualties –	NIL.
24	Division goes into front line.	
	149th Infy Bgde relieved 26th Infantry Brigade in the Line.	
	150th Infy Bgde relieved 26th Infantry Brigade in the Line.	
	Casualties –	50th D.A.Col. OR wounded 1 (acc). 4th E.Yorks OR wounded 3.

FRICOURT FARM.

25 151st Infy Bgde relieved 27th Infantry Brigade in reserve in MAMETZ WOOD.
    Divisional Headquarters moved to FRICOURT FARM.
    Casualties – 50th D.A.Col. OR wounded 1 (acc). 4th N.Fus. OR wounded 1. 6th N.Fus. officers killed 2/Lt.J.H.MACKILLAR; OR killed 1 wounded 3 (6th H.L.I. attd). 7th M.Fus. OR wounded 2. 4th Yorks.– Officers killed 2/Lts W.L.BATTY and J.B.HUDSON; OR killed 2, wounded 4. 5th Yorks OR killed 1, wounded 7. No.150 M.Gun Coy OR wounded 2.

26 Casualties – 4th N.Fus OR killed 1, wounded 4, missing 1. 6th N.Fus wounded Lt.E.G.PROCTOR; OR killed 3, wounded 5, missing 10. 7th N.Fus OR wounded 2 (shell shock, at duty). No.149 M.Gun Coy OR wounded 1. 4th Yorks OR wounded 7. 5th Yorks Officers wounded 2/Lt.F.LEWIN; OR killed 3, wounded 6, missing 1. 6th Durham L.I. OR killed 1, wounded 1 (both accidentally).

27 Casualties – 6th N.Fus. wounded Capt.J.H.MACKENZIE RAMC attd. 7th N.Fus OR wounded 1. No.149 M.Gun Coy OR wounded 4. 4th E.Yorks OR killed 1 wounded 7. 4th Yorks killed 2/Lt.A.COATES ; OR wounded 3. 5th Yorks OR killed 3, wounded 11, missing 1. 5th Durham L.I. OR killed 1 wounded 4. No.150 M.Gun Coy OR wounded 1. 150th Trench M.Bty OR wounded 5. 7th Durham L.I.(Pioneers) OR killed 1 wounded 3.

50TH DIVISION.

ADMINISTRATIVE

OCTOBER 1918.

Duplicate

OCTR.
28 Casualties – 253rd Bde RFA OR wounded 2. 4th N.Fus OR killed 3, wounded 4, missing 1. 5th N.Fus OR wounded 1. 6th N.Fus OR killed 4, wounded 12. 7th N.Fus OR wounded 2. No.149 M.Gun Coy OR wounded 1. 4th E.Yorks OR killed 2, wounded 3. 4th Yorks OR wounded 5. 5th Yorks OR wounded 6, missing 1. No.150 M.Gun Coy OR 1 prev. reptd wounded now killed. 7th Durham L.I.(Pioneers) OR wounded 1 at 2nd Fd Coy NF wounded 2/Lt.E.V.KATHER. 2nd Hm Rd Ambce Capt.H.B.LOW wounded at duty; OR killed 2 wounded 2.

29 Casualties – 4th N.Fus OR killed 1 wounded 2. 6th N.Fus OR killed 1 wounded 6. 7th N.Fus OR wounded 2. No.149 M.Gun Coy OR missing 1. 4th E.Yorks OR wounded 4 missing 1. 4th Yorks OR wounded 4. 5th Yorks OR killed 1, wounded 1 at duty. 5th Durham L.I. OR wounded 2. No.150 M.Gun Coy OR killed 1 at duty. 5th Border Regt OR wounded 2.

30 Casualties – 4th N.Fus officers 2/Lt.W.C.CLEMITSON wounded at duty; OR killed 8, wounded 12. 5th N.Fus OR wounded 1. 6th N.Fus OR wounded 1. 7th N.Fus OR wounded 1 at duty. No.149 T.Mortar Btty OR wounded 1. 4th E.Yorks OR wounded 1. 5th Yorks – prev. reptd missing now rejoined OR 1. 5th Durham L.I. OR wounded 5. No.150 Trench Mortar Btty OR wounded 1. 7th Dur.L.I.(Pioneers) OR killed 1, wounded 2.

31 Casualties – 4th N.Fus. OR killed 1, wounded 5, missing 1. 5th N.Fus officers – 2/Lt.C.JONES wounded; OR killed 2, wounded 9, missing 2. 6th N.Fus OR wounded 1 at duty, prev. reptd missing now rejoined 10. 4th E.Yorks OR killed 1 wounded 2. 4th Yorks OR missing 1. 5th Durham L.I. OR wounded 1.

ORIGINAL.

463-
LB

Confidential.

50th Division

Administrative Staff.

War

Diary

1st November 1916

30th November 1916

Army Form C. 2118.

50th DIVISION.

ADMINISTRATIVE WAR DIARY or INTELLIGENCE SUMMARY

NOVEMBER 1916.

(Erase heading not required.)

Instructions regarding War Diaries and Intelligence Summaries are contained in F.S. Regs., Part II. and the Staff Manual respectively. Title Pages will be prepared in manuscript.

464

Place	Date	Hour	Summary of Events and Information	Remarks and references to Appendices
FRICOURT FARM.	NOVR. 1		Casualties – 250th Bde RFA O.Rs wounded 1 (acc.); 253rd Bde RFA O.Rs wounded 1; Div.A.C. O.Rs Killed 1 wounded 10 (inc. 1 at duty). 30th October – Trench Mortars–wounded Captain W.C.Hand, R.G.A. 149th Inf.Bde – 4th N.F. O.Rs wounded 1; 5th N.F. O.Rs wounded 9; 6th N.F. Officers killed 2/Lieut.T.Lant; 7th N.F. O.Rs Killed 1, wounded 5 (at duty); 149th T.M.Battery O.Rs wounded 1. 150th Inf.Bde. – 4th E.Yorks O.Rs missing 1; 5th Yorks O.Rs Killed 1, wounded 1; 5th Durham L.I. O.Rs killed 3, wounded 10.	
	2		Casualties – 149th Inf.Bde – 5th N.F. O.Rs wounded 3; 7th N.F. O.Rs killed 1; 149th Machine Gun Coy O.Rs wounded 1. 150th Inf.Bde. – 4th E.Yorks O.Rs killed 1, wounded 5; 4th Yorkshire Regt Officers wounded 2/Lt.F.E.A.Posthill, O.Rs wounded 3; 5th Yorkshire Regt O.Rs wounded 3; 5th Durham L.I. O.Rs killed 1, wounded 2; No:150 M.G.Coy O.Rs wounded 1. 2nd (Nbn) Field Coy RE. wounded (at duty) O.Rs 1.	
	3		Casualties – 149th Inf.Bde. – 5th N.F. killed 2/Lt.S.Stones, O.Rs wounded 13; 7th N.F. O.Rs wounded 1 (self-inflicted). 150th Inf.Bde. – 4th Yorkshire Regt O.Rs killed 2, wounded 2; 5th Yorkshire Regt O.Rs killed 1, wounded 1, missing 2. 151st Inf.Bde. – 8th Durh.L.I. O.Rs wounded 2, missing 1; 9th Durh.L.I. O.Rs wounded 2. R. A. M. C. – 1st (Nbn) Fd. Ambce O.Rs wounded 2.	
	4		Casualties = 250th Bde RFA O.Rs wounded 1 (shell shock). 149th Inf.Bde.– 6th N.F. Officers wounded Lt.A.C.Wilson, RAMC attd; O.Rs wounded 1, missing 1. 150th Inf.Bde.– 5th Yorkshire Regt. O.Rs wounded 1, 2 prev. rep. "M" now rejoined; 5th Durh.L.I. O.Rs killed 2, wounded 1; No:150 M.G.Coy O.Rs killed 2. 151st Inf.Bde.– 6th D.L.I. O.Rs killed 1, wounded 3; 8th D.L.I. O.Rs killed 1, wounded 2, prev. rep. "M" now rejoined 1. 5th Border Regt wounded O.Rs 1. 7th Durh.L.I.(Pioneers) Officers killed Lt.N.R.Shepherd, wounded 2/Lt.J.McLeman, Capt.A.R. Williamson, 2/Lt.A.H.Polge ; O.Rs killed 3, wounded 8. 2nd (Nbn) Fd Co RE. O.Rs wounded at duty 1.	

2449 Wt. W14957/Mgo 750,000 1/16 J.B.C. & A. Forms/C.2118/12.

50th DIVISION.

ADMINISTRATIVE WAR DIARY or INTELLIGENCE SUMMARY

NOVEMBER 1916

Army Form C. 2118.

Place	Date	Hour	Summary of Events and Information	Remarks and references to Appendices
	5		Casualties - 250th Bde RFA O.Rs wounded 1. 149th Inf.Bde.- 5th N.F. O.Rs Missing 1; 6th N.F. O.Rs wounded 1; 7th N.F. O.Rs wounded 1. 151st Inf.Bde.- 6th D.L.I. Officers killed 2/Lts A.S.Robson, G.W.Robson 8th D.L.I. attd, K.B.Stuart., Wounded 2/Lts C.L.Tyreman, R.H.Stewart, T.W.Burton, J.H.F.Ludgate, G.Corbett 7th D.L.I. attd, Missing 2/Lts H.Fell, A.S.Ritson 5th D.L.I. attd, T.F.Applegarth; O.Rs killed 34, wounded 114, missing 111.; 8th D.L.I. Officers killed 2/Lt.W.Boyd, 2/Lt.M.H.Kay, wounded Capt.A.N.Clark, 2/Lt.H.H.Beck 6th D.L.I. attd, 2/Lt.J.Barnett 6th D.L.I. attd, 2/Lt.C.L.G.Hill 5th D.L.I. attd, 2/Lt.M.C.Tozer 5th D.L.I.W attd; Missing 2/Lts B.C.Banks, H.J.T.Bennehr; O.Rs killed 37, wounded 100, missing 83. 9th Durham L.I. Officers killed 2/Lt.G.E.Higginbotham, 2/Lt.F.A.Blackett, wounded Lt# W.E.Meikle, Captains J.D.Rickaby, T.Harker, 2/Lt.H.V.Chisholm, 2/Lt#S.T.Paxton, W.Walton, W.Kelly, R.W.G.Potts, S.V.Plaskett 5th D.L.I. attd, L.A.Howe, J.Belfitt 7th D.L.I. attd, J.F.Green 7th D.L.I. attd, F.W.Manners 6th D.L.I. attd, G.Burn (shell shock), Missing 2/Lt.T.E.Coulson. 5th Border Regt Officers wounded 2/Lt.J.Hamilton 4th Borders attd, O.Rs wounded 10. No:151 MMG.Coy Officers wounded 2/Lt.G.V.Cox, O.Rs killed 3, wounded 19, missing 8. R.A.M.C.- 2/2nd (Nbn) Fd. Ambce O.Rs wounded 1.	1165
	6		Casualties - 250th Bde RFA O.Rs wounded 2 (inc. 1 at duty). 149th Inf.Bde.- 4th N.F. O.Rs wounded 1, Missing 2. 5th N.F. O.Rs wounded 7. 7th N.F. O.Rs wounded 1. No:149 M.G.Coy O.Rs killed 1, wounded 11. 6th N.F. O.Rs wounded 1. 151st Inf.Bde.- 9th D.L.I. O.Rs killed 30, wounded 250, missing 140. 5th Borders Regt. O.Rs killed 4, wounded 22 7th Durham L.I.- O.Rs killed 8, wounded 23 (inc. 8 at duty). R.A.M.C.- 2/2nd Fd. Ambce. O.Rs wounded 1 at duty. 3rd Fd.Ambce. O.Rs wounded 4, inc; 2 shell shock.	
	7		Casualties - 149th Inf.Bde.- 4th N.F. O.Rs wounded 1. 6th N.F. O.Rs killed 2, wounded 16. 7th N.Fus. O.Rs killed 1, wounded 4. No:149 M.G.Coy O.Rs wounded 1. 150th Inf.Bde.- 4th E.Yorks officers wounded 2/Lt.T.G.Hollis, O.Rs killed 1, wounded 5, 4th Yorkshire Regt O.Rs wounded 1 (self-inflicted). 5th Yorkshire Regt O.Rs killed 1. 5th D.L.I. Officers killed Lieut.G.J.H.Ashwin, wounded 2/Lt.A.M.McDougall, O.Rs killed 6 wounded 21. (9th DLI attd) R.A.M.C.- 3rd Fd.Ambce O.Rs wounded 2, inc. 1 at duty.	

Army Form C. 2118.

50th DIVISION.
NOVEMBER, 1916.

ADMINISTRATIVE WAR DIARY or **INTELLIGENCE SUMMARY**
(Erase heading not required.)

Instructions regarding War Diaries and Intelligence Summaries are contained in F.S. Regs., Part II. and the Staff Manual respectively. Title Pages will be prepared in manuscript.

4/66.

Place	Date	Hour	Summary of Events and Information	Remarks and references to Appendices
	8		Casualties :- 149th Inf.Bde. - 4th N.F. Killed O.Rs 1. 7th N.F. O.Rs killed 1, wounded 3. 150th Inf.Bde. - 4th E.Yorks O.Rs killed 2, wounded 6. 5th D.L.I. O.Rs wounded 2. No:150 M.G.Coy O.Rs wounded 1, missing 1. 150th T.M.Battery O.Rs wounded 4. 151st Inf.Bde. - 5th Border Regt O.Rs killed 3, wounded 1. 7th Durh.L.I. - O.Rs killed 3, wounded 4.	
	9		Casualties :- 149th Inf.Bde. - 5th N.F. O.Rs wounded 1. 6th N.F. O.Rs wounded 7. 7th N.F. O.Rs wounded 1. 150th Inf.Bde. - 4th Yorkshire Regt O.Rs killed 1, wounded 9, missing 1. 5th Yorkshire Regt O.Rs killed 1, wounded 1. 5th D.L.I. O.Rs wounded 16. No:150 M.G.Coy O.Rs killed 2, wounded 2. 150th T.M.Battery O.Rs wounded 3.	
	10		Casualties :- R.A. - 250th Bde RFA O.Rs killed 1, wounded 6 (inc.1 at duty) 149th Inf.Bde. - 4th N.F. O.Rs wounded 2. 6th N.F. O.Rs wounded 1, missing 2. 7th N.F. O.Rs killed 1. 150th Inf.Bde. - 4th E.Yorks O.Rs killed 4, wounded 15. 4th Yorkshire Regt O.Rs wounded 4. 5th Yorkshire Regt O.Rs killed 1, wounded 6, Missing 1. 5th D.L.I. O.Rs killed 1, wounded 6.	
	11			
	12		Casualties :- 149th Inf.Bde.- 4th N.F. O.Rs killed 3, wounded 21 (inc. 5 shell shock). 5th N.F. O.Rs wounded 1. 6th N.F. Officers wounded 2/Lt.S.Morpeth. 7th N.F. Officers wounded Lieut.E.Nixon, 2/Lt.R.A.Brown. O.Rs wounded 1. 150th Inf.Bde.- 4th E.Yorks O.Rs killed 1. 4th Yorkshire Regt O.Rs killed 2, wounded 5. 5th Yorkshire Regt O.Rs killed 3, wounded 12, prev. rep. "M" now rejoined 1. No:150 M.G.Coy O.Rs wounded 1. No:151 M.G.Coy O.Rs wounded 1. 7th D.L.I. (Pioneers). O.Rs wounded 1. 151st Inf.Bde.- 2nd Field Co.RE. O.Rs wounded 1. 2nd (Nbn) Fd. Ambce O.Rs wounded 1.	

50th DIVISION.   **NOVEMBER 1916.**

Army Form C. 2118.

ADMINISTRATIVE WAR DIARY or INTELLIGENCE SUMMARY

(Erase heading not required.)

467-

Date	Hour	Summary of Events and Information
13		Casualties - 149th Inf.Bde.- 5th N.F. O.rs killed 3, wounded 4. 6th N.F. Officers wounded 2/Lt.G.H. Stevenson, 6th H.L.I. attd, O.R. killed 5, wounded 11. 7th N.F. O.Rs wounded 14. No:149 M.Gun Coy O.Rs wounded 2, missing 2. 149th T.M.Battery O.Rs wounded 1, missing 1. 4th N.F. killed 8, wounded 5, prev. rep. Missing now accounted for O.Rs 8. 150th Inf.Bde.- 5th Yorkshire Regt. O.Rs killed 1, wounded 4.
14		Casualties - 149th Inf.Bde.- 4th N.F. Officers killed Capt.J.W.Robinson, 2/Lt.F.J.Larken (7th N.F. attd), 2/Lt.A.E.Moorhouse (5th N.F. attd); wounded 2/Lieut.C.A.Balden, 2/Lt.T.Bonner at duty, Lt.-Col.B.D.Gibson and Captain R.W.Cranage; Missing 2/Lt.A.J.Derrick (7th N.F. attd), O.Rs killed 2, wounded 21. 5th N.F.- Officers wounded 2/Lt.B.Head, Capt.H.W.Gill, 2/Lts L.Surfleet, R.Boulton, A.B.Park; Missing believed killed 2/Lt.T.N.Melrose, 2/Lt.H.Armstrong, 2/Lt. N.W.Lawson. 6th N.F.- Officers killed 2/Lts A.Smith and W.R.Clepham. 7th N.F. - Officers killed 2/Lt.L.H.F.Woods, D.R.D.O'Daly; wounded 2/Lts J.W.Young, B.C.Donaldson (5th N.F. attd), E.G.Lawson, J.P.Sowerby, R.A.Prescott, H.J.Clarke, Missing N.S.Robson. O.Rs killed 15, wounded 50. No:149 M.Gun Coy.- O.Rs wounded 8. 149th T.M.Battery.- Officers missing 2/Lt.R.Wilson. 150th Inf.Bde.- 5th Yorks.- Officers wounded (gas shell) 2/Lt.D.Norbury (7th W.Rid.R.attd), O.Rs wounded 2, missing 1. No:150 M.Gun Coy.- O.Rs wounded 1. 7th Durh.L.I.(Pioneers).- Officers wounded 2/Lt.V.A.Grayston, O.Rs killed 3, wounded 7.
15		Casualties - 149th Inf.Bde.- 4th N.F. O.Rs killed 3, wounded 2 missing 2. 5th N.F. O.Rs killed 33, wounded 144, missing 85. 6th N.F. Officers wounded 2/Lt.A.Palmer, O.Rs killed 9, wounded 112, missing 1. 7th N.F. Officers 2/Lt.G.D.Gleddon wounded, O.Rs killed 4, wounded 45, missing 104. No:149 M.Gun Coy.- officers killed 2/Lt.J.A.Wilson (15th N.F. attd), O.Rs killed 1, wounded 5, missing 9. 149th T.M.Battery.- O.Rs wounded 2. 150th Inf.Bde.- 5th Yorkshire Regt.- O.Rs killed 2, wounded 1. No:150 M.Gun Coy.- O.Rs wounded 2. 151st Inf.Bde.- 6th D.L.I. officers wounded 2/Lt.J.Philips, O.Rs wounded 1. 8th D.L.I. O.Rs wounded 2, missing 1. 7th Durh.L.I.(Pioneers).- O.Rs wounded 2. 2nd Fd.Ambce.- O.Rs wounded 2 (inc.1 at duty). 3rd Fd. Ambce.- wounded O.Rs 1 at duty.

Army Form C. 2118.

WAR DIARY
or
INTELLIGENCE SUMMARY

(Erase heading not required.)

50th DIVISION.

NOVEMBER 1916.

Instructions regarding War Diaries and Intelligence Summaries are contained in F. S. Regs., Part II. and the Staff Manual respectively. Title Pages will be prepared in manuscript.

468

Place	Date	Hour	Summary of Events and Information	Remarks and references to Appendices
	16		Casualties — 149th Inf.Bde. — 4th N.F. O.Rs killed 18, wounded 56, missing 10. 150th Inf.Bde. — 4th E.Yorks O.Rs wounded 13. 4th Yorkshire Regt. O.Rs killed 3, wounded 5. 7th Durh.L.I.(Pioneers).- O.Rs wounded 1. Hd.Qrs., 150th Inf.Bde moved to BECOURT. 151st Inf.Bde H.Q., 9th Durh.L.I. and T.M.Battery moved to MILLENCOURT. 6th and 8th Durh.L.I. and 5th Border Regt remained at BECOURT for work on roads.	
	17		4th E.Yorks and 4th Yorkshire Regt moved to S.E. HIGH WOOD. 150 M.G.Coy and T.M.Battery moved to BAZENTIN-le-GRAND. Casualties — 150th Inf.Bde.- 4th E.Yorks Officers 2/Lt.T.G.Hollis wounded. O.Rs wounded 24, missing 27. 4th Yorkshire Regt Officers wounded Lt.-Col.F.F.Deakin at duty, 2/Lt.J.R.James, O.Rs killed 2, wounded 12. 1st (Nbn) Fd. Ambce O.Rs wounded 1. 3rd (Nbn) Fd. Ambce O.Rs wounded 1.	
	18		4th, 5th and 7th N.Fus moved to ALBERT. 4th Yorkshire Regt and 4th E.Yorks moved to BECOURT from HIGH WOOD.	
ALBERT.	19		149th Inf.Bde H.Qrs. and units at ALBERT. 150th Inf.Bde H.Qrs. and units at BECOURT. 151st Inf.Bde H.Qrs. and units at MILLENCOURT. Divisional Hd. Qrs. moved from FRICOURT FARM and established at Villa Rochers, ALBERT.	
	20			
	21			
	22			
	23			
	24			
	25			

Army Form C. 2118.

WAR DIARY or INTELLIGENCE SUMMARY

(Erase heading not required.)

50th DIVISION.   **NOVEMBER 1916.**

Instructions regarding War Diaries and Intelligence Summaries are contained in F. S. Regs., Part II. and the Staff Manual respectively. Title Pages will be prepared in manuscript.

H.69-
EB

Place	Date	Hour	Summary of Events and Information	Remarks and references to Appendices
	26		Casualties - 7th Field Co RE. O.Rs killed 1, wounded 2.	
	27			
	28		Casualties - 251st (Nbn) Bde RFA O.Rs wounded 2. 4th E.Yorks O.Rs killed 2, wounded 2, both accidentally. 7th (Nbn) Field Co. RE. O.Rs killed 1, wounded 2.	
	29		Casualties - 252nd (Nbn) Bde RFA O.Rs wounded 1.	
	30		4th E.Yorks and 4th Yorkshire Regt (150th Inf.Bde) moved from BECOURT to CONTAY. 5th Durh.L.I. moved from BECOURT to BAIZIEUX. No:150 M.Gun Coy to VADENCOURT. T.M.Battery to CONTAY. 5th Border Regt and 6th and 8th Durh.L.I. (151st Inf.Bde) moved from MAMETZ WOOD to BECOURT.	

Confidential

50ᵗʰ Division

Administrative Staff

War Diary

December 1916

Volume XX.

Army Form C. 2118.

ORIGINAL VOL XX

50th DIVISION.

ADMINISTRATIVE
WAR DIARY
or
INTELLIGENCE SUMMARY

(*Erase heading not required.*)

Instructions regarding War Diaries and Intelligence Summaries are contained in F. S. Regs., Part II. and the Staff Manual respectively. Title Pages will be prepared in manuscript.

DECEMBER 1916.

Place	Date	Hour	Summary of Events and Information	Remarks and references to Appendices
BAIZIEUX.	DECR. 1		Completion of move of Division to rest. Hd. Qrs. of Division at Baizieux Chateau. 149th Inf. Bde and Units at BRESLE. 150th Inf. Bde H.Q., 4th E.Yorks and 4th Yorks., and T.M.Battery at CONTAY. 5th Yorks and 5th D.L.I. at BAIZIEUX and Machine Gun Coy at VADENCOURT. H.Q., 151 Inf. Bde U.24.d.6.4. Units at WARIOY. Hd. Qrs., Divisional Artillery BAVLINCOURT. Two Batteries (251st and 252nd) in action, remainder at BEHENCOURT. Hd.Qrs., R.E. at FRICOURT FARM. 50th Div'nl Signal Coy RE BAIZIEUX Chateau, remainder in forward area. 7th Durham L.I. (Pioneers) remains in forward area. Divisional Train BAIZIEUX also No:23 Div'l Supp.Col. 2nd (Nbn) Fd. Ambce VADENCOURT, remainder at LAVIEVILLE. Veterinary Section BAIZIEUX.	
	2			
	3		Casualties - 5th Yorks Rert O.R. wounded (accidentally) 1.	
	4		Conference at Div'nl Hd. Qrs. of Staff Captains, Qr.Mrs and Transport officers.	
	5		*Casualties - 251st Bde RFA O.R. wounded slightly at duty 1.	
	6			
	7		General officer Commanding returns from leave and resumes command of Division. Casualties - R.F.A. D/250 Bde wounded O.R.1; 251 Bde wounded O.R.1 (accidentally).	
	8		Accident at Fourth Army Trench Mortar School - 149th T.Mortar Battery in which the following casualties occurred :- Officers killed 2/Lt. A.LITTLEWOOD, 6th North'd Fus. attd., wounded Capt. J.L.G.Thomas, 4th N.Fus attd and 2/Lt.J.R.C.ROGERS 6th N.F. attd. O.R. Killed 4th N.F. 1, 5th N.F. 2 (attd to 149th T.M.Battery), wounded O.R. 4th N.F. 2, 5th N.F. 1, 6th N.F. 1, 7th N.F. 1 (attd to 149th T.M.Battery). Casualties - Shell fire 252nd Bde RFA wounded O.R. 1.	
	9			
	10			

ADMINISTRATIVE WAR DIARY or INTELLIGENCE SUMMARY

50th DIVISION.   **DECEMBER 1916**

Army Form C. 2118.

Place	Date	Hour	Summary of Events and Information	Remarks and references to Appendices
	11		Casualties - 252nd Bde RFA wounded O.R. 1.	
	12		Conference at Div'nl Hd. Qrs., of Staff Captains, Qr. Mrs and Transport Officers.	
	13		Casualties - 250th Bde RFA wounded O.R. 1. 251st Bde RFA wounded O.R. 1, 252nd Bde RFA O.R. killed 1, wounded 1.	
	14		Casualties - 4th North'd Fus wounded acc. O.R. 1.	
	15			
	16			
	17		Casualties - 8th Durh.L.I. killed 1 O.R. (S.I.)	
	18			
	19		Casualties - 7th Field Coy RE wounded O.R. 2 (gas).	
	20		Casualties - 50th Div. T.M.Batteries, killed acc. at Fourth Army T.Mortar School O.R. 1 (coal gas poisoning).	
	21		Casualties - 1st Field Coy RE - wounded O.R. 1 at duty.	
	22		Casualties - 250th Bde RFA wounded O.R. 1 (at duty).	
	23		Casualties - 50th D.A.C. wounded, shell shock, since died 22/12/16 1/Lt. G.T. POLAK. 250th Bde RFA killed O.R. 2. 251st Bde RFA wounded O.R. 1.	
	24		Casualties - 7th Durh.L.I. (Pioneers) wounded O.R. 1.	

Army Form C. 2118.

ADMINISTRATIVE WAR DIARY or INTELLIGENCE SUMMARY

(Erase heading not required.)

50th DIVISION.
DECEMBER 1916.

Instructions regarding War Diaries and Intelligence Summaries are contained in F.S. Regs., Part II. and the Staff Manual respectively. Title Pages will be prepared in manuscript.

Place	Date	Hour	Summary of Events and Information	Remarks and references to Appendices
	25		Casualties - 250th Bde RFA wounded O.R. 1 (at duty). 7th Field Coy RE wounded O.R. 1 (at duty).	
	26		Conference at Div'nl Hd. Qrs., of Staff Captains, Qr.Mrs. and Transport Officers.	
	27		Casualties - 250th Bde RFA wounded O.R. 1.	
	28		Major R.C.GWYNN, DSO, South Wales Borderers, (attached H.Q. 50th Division) proceeded to H.Q. III Corps for temporary duty. Division commences move to forward area - 149th Inf. Bde: from BRESLE to BECOURT and relieves 145th Inf. Bde. 151st Inf. Bde. from VARLOY to ALBERT and relieves three Bns 143rd Inf. Bde and one Bn. 144th Inf. Bde.	
	29		Colonel C.M.Cartwright C.B., A.A. & Q.M.G., 50th Division, proceeded to hospital. Casualties - 7th Field Coy RE wounded O.R. 1 (accidental). 149th Inf. Bde moves from BECOURT to BAZENTIN and HIGH WOOD in relief of two Bns 1st Inf. Bde and 2 Bns 3rd Inf. Bde. H.Q. and Nos: 1, 2 and 3 Companies 50th Divisional Train move to Camp E.5.d.3.3., Sheet 57c. 1/1st (Wsn) Mob. Vet. Section move to Camp D.6.b.5.4., Combined Sheet ALBERT.	
	30		151st Inf. Bde (less two Bns) moves from ALBERT to BAZENTIN in relief of 2nd Inf. Bde. 150th Inf. Bde (less two Bns) moves from GONTAY to BECOURT and relieves 144th Inf. Bde. One Bn. 150th Inf. Bde moves from BAIZIEUX to ALBERT and one to MILLENCOURT in relief of one Bn 151st Inf. Bde and one Bn 144th Inf. Bde. No:4 Company, 50th Divisional Train, A.S.C. moves to Camp E.5.d.3.3., Sheet 57c. Colonel C.M.Cartwright C.B., A.A. & Q.M.G., 50th Division, evacuated sick to C.C.S. Northern end of Camp site 2, BAZENTIN, occupied by 9th Bn. Durham L.Infy shelled by the enemy - casualties O.R. killed 1, wounded 5.	

Army Form C. 2118.

50th DIVISION.
DECEMBER, 1916.

ADMINISTRATIVE
WAR DIARY
or
INTELLIGENCE SUMMARY

(Erase heading not required.)

Instructions regarding War Diaries and Intelligence Summaries are contained in F. S. Regs., Part II. and the Staff Manual respectively. Title Pages will be prepared in manuscript.

Place	Date	Hour	Summary of Events and Information	Remarks and references to Appendices
	DECR. 31st		On right of 30th/31st December 149th Inf. Bde moved from BAZENTIN and HIGH WOOD into Front System Trenches and support in relief of two Bns 1st Inf. Bde and two Bns of 3rd Inf. Bde. 2 Bns 151st Inf. Bde moved from ALBERT to BAZENTIN and relieved two Bns of 1st Inf. Bde. Casualties - 5th N.F.us wounded O.R.1; 6th N.F. wounded O.R.2; 7th N.F. killed O.R.1; 149th Trench Mortar Battery missing O.R.2; 9th Durham L.I. killed O.R.1, wounded O.R.5.	

2449 Wt. W14957/M90 750,000 1/16 J.B.C. & A. Forms/C.2118/12.

Original.   Confidential.

Administrative Staff
    War Diary.

50th (Northumbrian) Division.

From 1st January 1917
to 31st January 1917.

Volume XXI.

Army Form C. 2118.

50th DIVISION.

WAR DIARY or INTELLIGENCE SUMMARY

JANUARY, 1917.

(Erase heading not required.)

Instructions regarding War Diaries and Intelligence Summaries are contained in F. S. Regs., Part II. and the Staff Manual respectively. Title Pages will be prepared in manuscript.

Place	Date	Hour	Summary of Events and Information	Remarks and references to Appendices
FRICOURT FARM.	JANY: 1		Divisional Hd. Qrs. move to FRICOURT FARM; Hd. Qrs., 50th Divisional Artillery to FRICOURT FARM; 1/1st (Nbn) Field Ambulance to BAZENTIN-le-PETIT; D.A.D.O.S. to ALBERT and Salvage Company to BAZENTIN.	
			Casualties – 4th N.Fus. Killed O.R.2. 149th T.M.Battery Wounded O.R.1 (accidental), -2 missing prev. rep."M" 31/12/16 now reported not missing. 7th Durham L.I. killed 2/Lieut.(T/Capt.) W.R.GOODRICK, wounded 2/Lieut. J.H.KEIRL.	
	2		Casualties – 251st (Nbn) Bde RFA wounded O.R.1, 5th N.Fus O.R. killed 2, wounded 2, 9th Durham L.I. O.R. wounded 1.	
	3		Casualties – 7th Field Coy R.E. O.R. wounded 1; 5th N.F. O.R. killed 1; 5th Border Regt O.R. wounded 1; 9th Durham L.I. O.R. killed 1, wounded 1.	
	4		Casualties – 4th N.F. O.R. killed 1, wounded 2; 7th N.Fus wounded 2/Lt.J.H.C.Swinney (3/1/17), O.R. 1; 4th Yorkshire Regt O.R. killed 1; 5th Border Regt O.R. wounded 3; 8th Durham L.I. O.R. wounded 1; 9th Durham L.I. O.R. wounded 2 (S.I.W.).	
	5		Casualties – 5th N.Fus O.R. killed 1, wounded 1, missing 1; 4th East Yorkshire Regt O.R. wounded 2, 4th Yorkshire Regt O.R. killed 1.	
	6		Casualties – 1st (Nbn) Fd Co RE O.R. wounded 1; 50th Divl Signal Co RE O.R. killed 1; 4th N.Fus O.R. wounded 2; 5th N.Fus O.R. wounded 1; 7th N.Fus O.R. missing 1; 4th East Yorkshire Regt O.R. wounded 1; 5th Yorkshire Regt O.R. wounded 1; 8th Durham L.I. O.R. wounded 1; 7th Durham L.I. O.R. wounded 3.	
	7		Casualties – 4th N.Fus O.R. wounded 1; 5th N.Fus O.R. wounded 1; 7th N.Fus O.R. wounded 1; Attached Unit – 12th (Lab) Bn. West Riding Regt O.R. wounded 1.	
	8		Casualties – 4th N.Fus O.R. wounded 2; 5th N.Fus O.R. wounded 2; 4th East Yorkshire Regt O.R. wounded 2, 5th Yorkshire Regt O.R. wounded 1; 5th Durham L.I. O.R. wounded 1, 7th Durham L.I.(Pioneers) killed 2/Lt. C.S.DALZIEL, O.R. wounded 2.	

Army Form C. 2118.

WAR DIARY or INTELLIGENCE SUMMARY

(Erase heading not required.)

50th DIVISION.

JANUARY 1917.

Instructions regarding War Diaries and Intelligence Summaries are contained in F.S. Regs., Part II. and the Staff Manual respectively. Title Pages will be prepared in manuscript.

564

Place	Date	Hour	Summary of Events and Information	Remarks and references to Appendices
FRICOURT FARM.	JANY: 9		Casualties - 252nd (Nbn) Bde RFA O.R. wounded 5; 5th Yorkshire Regt O.R. wounded 1, 5th Durham L.I. O.R. wounded 1.	
	10		Casualties - 5th N.Fus O.R. wounded 1; 9th Durham L.I. O.R. killed 1 wounded 3 (inc.1 acc.); No:151 M.Gun Coy O.R. wounded 1.	
	11		Casualties - 4th Yorkshire Regt O.R. wounded 5; 5th Yorkshire Regt O.R. killed 1, wounded 4; 9th Durham L.I. O.R. killed 3, wounded 7.	
	12		Casualties - 4th Yorkshire Regt O.R. killed 1, wounded 3; 5th Yorkshire Regt O.R. killed 1, wounded 1; 5th Durham L.I. O.R. wounded 1, 5th Border Regt O.R. wounded 1, missing 1.	
	13		Casualties - 4th East Yorkshire Regt O.R. wounded 1; 4th Yorkshire Regt O.R. 1 rep. killed in error 5/1/17, wounded O.R.3 (inc. 2 acc.); 5th Yorkshire Regt O.R. killed 1, wounded 1; 5th Border Regt O.R. missing 3; 8th Durham L.I. O.R. wounded 2; 9th Durham L.I. O.R. killed 1.	
	14		Casualties - 4th N.Fus O.R. wounded 1; 6th N.Fus O.R. wounded 1 (acc.); 4th Yorkshire Regt O.R. wounded 3; 5th Border Regt O.R. killed 1 prev. rep. "M" 13/1/17, 2 O.R. rejoined prev. rep. "M" 14/1/17; 6th Durham L.I. O.R. wounded 2; 8th Durham L.I. wounded O.R. 1.	
	15		Casualties - 7th N.Fus. O.R. wounded 1; 4th Yorkshire Regt O.R. wounded 3 (inc. 1 acc.); attached Units - 25th Bde RFA O.R. wounded 2.	
	16		Casualties - 7th N.Fus O.R. killed 4, wounded 2; No.149 M.G.Coy O.R. wounded 1; 4th East Yorkshire Regt O.R. killed 1, wounded 1; 6th Durham L.I. O.R. wounded 9; 8th Durham L.I. O.R. killed 1, wounded 1; 9th Durham L.I. O.R. killed 8, wounded 21 (inc.5 "W", at duty); 151st T.M.Battery O.R. wounded 1.	
	17		Casualties - 6th Durh.L.I. O.R. killed 1 (prev. rep. "W" now rep. "D of W"); 8th Durh.L.I. wounded 2/Lt E.FISHER;8th D.L.I. (9th D.L.I. att) 2/Lt W.M.HIND, O.R.1; 9th Durh.L.I. wounded 2/Lt. F.HALL, O.R. killed 1, wounded 5.	

2449 Wt. W14957/Mg0 750,000 1/16 J.B.C. & A. Forms/C.2118/12.

Army Form C. 2118.

57+

50th DIVISION.

WAR DIARY or INTELLIGENCE SUMMARY

JANUARY 1917.

(Erase heading not required.)

Instructions regarding War Diaries and Intelligence Summaries are contained in F. S. Regs., Part II. and the Staff Manual respectively. Title Pages will be prepared in manuscript.

Place	Date	Hour	Summary of Events and Information	Remarks and references to Appendices
FRICOURT FARM.	JANY: 18		Casualties – 4th N.Fus O.R. wounded 2; 5th Border Regt O.R. killed 2, wounded 2; 8th Durh.L.I. wounded O.R.1; 151st T.M.Battery O.R. killed 1, wounded 1.	
	19		Casualties – 4th N.Fus O.R. wounded 1; 5th N.Fus O.R. wounded 2; 8th Durh.L.I. O.R. wounded 4; 9th Durh.L.I. O.R. killed 1, wounded 1; 25th Bde RFA (attached unit) O.R. wounded 1.	
	20		Casualties – 4th East Yorkshire Regt O.R. killed 1; 4th Yorkshire Regt O.R. wounded 2 (inc. 1 at duty); 7th Durh.L.I. (Pioneers) O.R. killed 1, wounded 3; 2nd (Nbn) Fd Co RE O.R. killed 1, wounded 1.	
	21		Casualties – 4th N.Fus O.R. killed 1, wounded 1, wounded 3; 5th N.Fus O.R. wounded 4; 8th Durh.L.I. O.R. wounded 1; 9th Durh.L.I. wounded 2/Lt D.STEPHENSON; 113th Bty RFA (attached unit) wounded Major F.SASSOON RFA.	
	22		Casualties – 7th N.Fus O.R. wounded 1; 8th Durh.L.I. O.R. wounded 1.	
	23		Casualties – 4th N.Fus O.R. wounded 2; 5th N.Fus O.R. wounded 1; 6th N.Fus O.R. killed 3, wounded 4; 7th N.Fus O.R. killed 1, wounded 3.	
	24		Casualties – 4th East Yorkshire Regt O.R. wounded 1; 4th Yorkshire Regt O.R. wounded 2; 5th Yorkshire Regt O.R. wounded 1; 150th T.M.Battery O.R. wounded 1 (slightly, at duty); 6th Durh.L.I. O.R. killed 5, wounded 4; 8th Durh.L.I. O.R. killed 3, wounded 4; 7th Durh.L.I. (Pioneers) O.R. killed 2, wounded 1 (acc); 250th Bde RFA O.R. killed 1, wounded 5.	
	25		149th Infantry Brigade move to ALBERT. Casualties – 5th Yorkshire Regt O.R. wounded 1; 5th Durh.L.I. O.R. wounded 2; 5th Border Regt wounded 2/Lt.(T/Capt.) H.BELL; 250th (Nbn) Bde RFA O.R. wounded 1, 50th Divl Signal Coy RE O.R. wounded 1.	
	26		Casualties – 4th N.F. O.R. wounded 6, missing 1; 4th East Yorkshire Regt O.R. wounded 4; 4th Yorkshire Regt O.R. wounded 2 (inc. 1 at duty). 151st Inf. Bde Hd. Qrs. to S.13.b.4.3., Sh.57c; 5th Border Regt to S.8.c.8.6.; 6th & 8th Durh.L.I. to BECOURT; 9th Durh.L.I. to S.8.a.8.8.	

Army Form C. 2118.

WAR DIARY or INTELLIGENCE SUMMARY

(Erase heading not required.)

50th DIVISION.

JANUARY 1917.

Instructions regarding War Diaries and Intelligence Summaries are contained in F. S. Regs., Part II. and the Staff Manual respectively. Title Pages will be prepared in manuscript.

58+
1B

Place	Date	Hour	Summary of Events and Information	Remarks and references to Appendices
FRICOURT FARM.	JANY: 27		151st Inf. Bde. Hd. Qrs., 5th Border Regt and 9th Durh.L.I. to BECOURT. 150th Inf. Bde Hd. Qrs., to SABOT COPSE, 4th E.Yorkshire R. to S.8.a.8.6., 4th Yorks.R. to S.8.c.8.6., 5th Yorkshire R. to MAMETZ HUTS, 5th Durh.L.I. to S.8.d.2.4. Casualties - 4th Yorkshire R. O.R. wounded 1; 5th Durh.L.I. O.R. killed 1, wounded 1; 5th Border Regt. O.R. wounded 1, 7th Durh.L.I. O.R. killed 1, wounded 1. 50th Divl. Signal Coy RE Killed Lieut. C.J.CADMAN MC. (Special Res. R.E. attd)	
RIBEMONT.	28		Divisional Headquarters to RIBEMONT. 4th E.Yorks., 4th Yorks., and 5th Durh.L.I. to FRICOURT CAMPS.	
	29		149th Inf. Bde to DERNANCOURT. 151st Inf. Bde to RIBEMONT. Casualties - 4th N.Fus prev. rep. missing 28th Jan.1917 now rep. killed 28th January 1917 O.R. 1.	
	30		150th Infantry Brigade to BUIRE. Casualties - 7th Field Coy RE O.R. killed 1; 50th Divisional Train ASC O.R. killed 2, wounded 1.	
			Casualties - 7th Field Coy R.E. wounded.	

Confidential

Vol 23

56th Division.

Administrative Staff
War Diary.

From 1st February 1917.
to 28th February 1917.

Volume XXII

ORIGINAL

Army Form C. 2118.

50th DIVISION.

ADMINISTRATIVE WAR DIARY or **INTELLIGENCE SUMMARY**

FEBRUARY 1917.

(Erase heading not required.)

Instructions regarding War Diaries and Intelligence Summaries are contained in F. S. Regs., Part II. and the Staff Manual respectively. Title Pages will be prepared in manuscript.

Place	Date	Hour	Summary of Events and Information	Remarks and references to Appendices
RIBEMONT.	Feby. 1.		⎫	
	2.		⎪	
	3.		⎪ REST AREA.	
	4.		⎬	
	5.		⎪	
	6.		⎪	
	7.		⎭	
	8.		149th Infantry Brigade to MERICOURT Sur SOMME.	
	9.		150th Infantry Brigade to MORCOURT.	
	10.		151st Infantry Bde to HAMEL. 5th Border Regt (151st Bde) to MORCOURT. 149th Inf.Bde H.Q. FONTAINE le CAPPY, 4th N.F. BOIS TOUFFU, 5th N.F. CAMP de LAPIN, 6th N.F. BOIS TRIANGULAIRE, 7th N.F. FONTAINE LE CAPPY. 150th Inf.Bde H.Q. P.C.MOULIN FOUCAUCOURT, 4th E.Yorks, 5th Yorks and 5th D.L.I. BOIS ST. MARTIN.	
	11.		4th N.F. to BELLOY, 4th E.Yorks and 5th Yorks in Line.	
	12.		149th Inf.Bde H.Q. N.19.a.9.2., Sheet 62c., 5th N.F. N.28.c.0.5., 7th N.F. N.28.c.7.5., Sheet 62C. 150th Inf.Bde H.Q. N.25.d.8.5., 5th Yorks N.32.d.9.0., Sheet 62C. & 9th 151st Inf.Bde H.Q. PROYART, 5th Border Regt BOIS ST. MARTIN, 6th D.L.I. PROYART, 8th/D.L.I. FOUCAUCOURT.	

2449 Wt. W14957/M90 750,000 1/16 J.B.C. & A. Forms/C.2118/12.

Army Form C. 2118.

50th DIVISION.

ADMINISTRATIVE
WAR DIARY
or
INTELLIGENCE SUMMARY

(Erase heading not required.)

FEBRUARY 1917.

Instructions regarding War Diaries and Intelligence
Summaries are contained in F. S. Regs., Part II.
and the Staff Manual respectively. Title Pages
will be prepared in manuscript.

Place	Date	Hour	Summary of Events and Information	Remarks and references to Appendices
P.C.GABRIELLE	Feby. 13		Casualties – 149th Inf.Bde – 5th N.F. wounded O.R.1. 150th Inf.Bde – 4th E.Yorks Officers wounded 2/Lt. C.V.Mayfield, Killed O.R.1, wounded O.R.3. 151st Inf.Bde H.Q. M.31.b.3.2. Divisional Hd. Qrs. to P.C.GABRIELLE M.20.d.central, Sh.62c.	
	14		Casualties – 150th Inf.Bde – 4th E.Yorks wounded O.R.3, 4th Yorks killed O.R. 1, wounded O.R.1.	
	15		Casualties – 149th Inf.Bde – 7th N.F. wounded O.R.1. 150th Inf.Bde – 4th E.Yorks killed O.R. 1, wounded O.R.2, 4th Yorks killed O.R.3, wounded O.R.1, No:150 M.G.Coy wounded O.R.1.	
	16		Casualties – 149th Inf.Bde – 4th M.F. O.R. killed 1, wounded 6 (inc. 1 at duty), 5th N.F. O.R. wounded 1, 6th N.F. O.R. killed 1, wounded 1, 7th N.F. O.R. killed 1. 150th Inf.Bde – 4th E.Yorks O.R. killed 1, wounded 6, 4th Yorks O.R. wounded 1, 5th D.L.I. O.R. killed 1, wounded 7 (inc. 4 gassed shell), No:150 M.G.Coy. O.R. wounded 7 (slightly gassed shell). 251st (Nbm) Bde RFA O.R. killed 1. 447th (Nbm) Fld Coy RE O.R. wounded 3.	
	17		Casualties – 149th Inf.Bde – 4th N.F. O.R. wounded 1. 150th Inf.Bde – 4th.E.Yorks O.R. wounded 1 (acc.), 5th Yorks O.R. wounded 4. 250th Bde RFA 2/Lt. R.B.Clegg killed. 446th (Nbm) Fld Co RE O.R. wounded 1.	
	18		Casualties – 149th Inf.Bde – 4th N.F. O.R. wounded 2, 5th N.F. O.R. killed 1 (gas shell). 150th Inf.Bde – 5th Yorks O.R. wounded 1, 5th D.L.I. O.R. wounded 1. 7th D.L.I.(Pioneers) O.R. killed 1, wounded 5. 251st Bde RFA O.R. wounded 1.	
	19		Casualties – 149th Inf.Bde 7th N.F. O.R. killed 1, 150th Inf.Bde – O.R. wounded 1 5th D.L.I.	
	20		Casualties – 149th Inf.Bde – 5th N.F. O.R. missing 1, 6th N.F. O.R. wounded 1 acc., 7th N.F. O.R. killed 1. 150th Inf.Bde – 4th E.Yorks O.R. wounded 1. 251st Bde RFA O.R. wounded 1 slightly at duty.	

Army Form C. 2118.

"50th DIVISION.   ADMINISTRATIVE
FEBRUARY 1917.   WAR DIARY
or
INTELLIGENCE SUMMARY

(Erase heading not required.)

Instructions regarding War Diaries and Intelligence Summaries are contained in F.S. Regs., Part II. and the Staff Manual respectively. Title Pages will be prepared in manuscript.

Place	Date	Hour	Summary of Events and Information	Remarks and references to Appendices
P.C.GABRIELLE	Feby. 21		Casualties - 149th Inf.Bde - 5th N.F. O.R. wounded 1. 150th Inf.Bde - 2/5th Sherwood For: attd 5th D.L.I. O.R. killed 1. 7th Durh.L.I.(Pion's) O.R. wounded 2.	
	22		Casualties - 151st Inf.Bde - 6th D.L.I. O.R. killed 2, 9th D.L.I. 2/Lt.A.W.Bell wounded.	
	23		Casualties - 150th Inf.Bde - 5th D.L.I. 2/Lt.P.H.Quickfall wounded. 151st Inf.Bde - 8th D.L.I. O.R. wounded 2. 250th Bde RFA O.R. wounded 1. 251st Bde RFA O.R. wounded 1.	
	24		Casualties - 149th Inf.Bde 4th N.F. O.R. killed 1, wounded O.R.2, 5th N.F. Missing O.R.1, 6th N.F. O.R. wounded 1. 151st Inf.Bde - 6th D.L.I. O.R. killed 5, wounded O.R.11, 9th D.L.I. O.R. killed 2, O.R. wounded 1, No:151 M.G.Coy 4th Sea.H. attd 2/Lt.G.S.Hervey wounded.	
	25		Casualties - 149th Inf.Bde - 4th N.F. O.R. 1 wounded (acc), 5th N.F. O.R.1 prev. rep. "M" now rejoined. 151st Inf.Bde - 8th D.L.I. O.R. wounded 1, 9th D.L.I. O.R. wounded 4 (inc.1 acc.)	
	26		Casualties - 151st Inf.Bde - 5th Border Regt O.R. wounded 1, 9th D.L.I. O.R. wounded 1.	
	27		Casualties - 150th Inf.Bde - 4th E.Yorks O.R. killed 1, wounded 1. 151st Inf.Bde - 5th Border Regt O.R. wounded 1, 9th D.L.I. 2/Lt.J.H.Herring wounded, O.R. wounded 4 (inc. 1 at duty).	
	28		Casualties - 150th Inf.Bde - 4th E.Yorks O.R. killed 1, 5th Yorks O.R. wounded 6, 151st Inf.Bde - 5th Border Regt O.R. killed 1, 9th D.L.I. O.R. wounded 1, 7th D.L.I.(Pion's) O.R. wounded 1.	

CONFIDENTIAL

ORIGINAL

Vol 24

50th (Northumbrian) Division

Administrative Staff War Diary.

From 1st March 1917.

To 31st March 1917.

Volume. XXIII

Army Form C. 2118.

50th Division. **MARCH 1917.**

ADMINISTRATIVE WAR DIARY or INTELLIGENCE SUMMARY

(Erase heading not required.)

Instructions regarding War Diaries and Intelligence Summaries are contained in F.S. Regs., Part II. and the Staff Manual respectively. Title Pages will be prepared in manuscript.

Place	Date	Hour	Summary of Events and Information	Remarks and references to Appendices
P.C. GABRIELLE	MCH. 1.		Casualties - 149th Bde 4th N.Fus. O.R. wounded 1, 6th N.Fus 2/Lt.W.R.Clephan wounded, O.R. wounded 1, 149th T.M.Battery O.R. killed 1. 150th Infy Bde - 4th E.Yorks R. O.R. wounded 3, 4th Yorks R. O.R. wounded 3 (inc. 1 at duty). 151st Infy Bde 5th Border Regt. O.R. killed 2, 6th Durh.L.I. O.R. wounded 1, 8th D.L.I. O.R. killed 1, O.R. wounded 5.	
	2.		Casualties - 150th Infy Bde - 4th E.Yorks R. O.R. wounded 1, 5th D.L.I. O.R. wounded 1.	
	3.		Casualties - 150th Infy Bde - 4th E.Yorks killed O.R.1, wounded O.R.1, 4th Yorks W. O.R.1 acc. 5th Yorks wounded O.R.4. 7th D.L.I. (Pioneers) wounded O.R.1.	
	4.		Casualties - 150th Infy Bde - 5th Yorks wounded O.R. 2. 151st Infy Bde - 5th Border R. wounded O.R.3, 8th D.L.I. wounded O.R.2.	
	5.		Casualties - 150th Infy Bde - 5th Yorks killed O.R.1, wounded Lt.G.Goodman 2/5th Lincolns attd 5th D.L.I. 151st Infy Bde - 9th D.L.I. wounded O.R.3. 4th N.Fus to BAYONVILLERS, 7th N.Fus. to MORCOURT.	
	6.		Casualties - 150th Infy Bde - 5th Yorks O.R. killed 1, wounded 1. 151st Infy Bde - 6th D.L.I. O.R. killed 1. 250th Bde RFA O.R. wounded 1. 7th Field Coy RE to MORCOURT. 4th E.Yorks to BAYONVILLERS. 8th D.L.I. to MORCOURT.	
	7.		Casualties - 149th Infy Bde - 5th N.F. O.R. missing 1. 151st Infy Bde - 6th D.L.I. O.R. wounded 1, 8th D.L.I. O.R. killed 1 (gas shell). D.A.C. attd 250th Bde RFA 2/Lt. W. McLellan wounded. 9th D.L.I. to MERICOURT-sur-SOMME. 5th Yorks to BAYONVILLERS.	
	8.		5th D.L.I. to BAYONVILLERS. 5th Border Regt to MERICOURT-sur-SOMME. 446th (Nbn) Field Coy RE to BAYONVILLERS. 1/1st Fld Amb. to WARFUSEE. 2/2nd Fld Amb. to MORCOURT. 1/3rd Fld Amb. to BAYONVILLERS.	
MERICOURT sur-SOMME.	9.		Casualties - 5th N.F. O.R.1 reported "M" 7th, now rejoined. Div. H.Q. at MERICOURT-sur-SOMME. 149th Infy Bde at WARFUSEE. 150th Infy Bde BAYONVILLERS. 151st Infy Bde at MORCOURT. 7th D.L.I. to MORCOURT. 447th Fld Coy RE to WARFUSEE.	

2449 Wt. W14957/M90 750,000 1/16 J.B.C. & A. Forms/C.2118/12.

Army Form C. 2118.

ADMINISTRATIVE.
WAR DIARY
or
INTELLIGENCE SUMMARY

(Erase heading not required.)

Instructions regarding War Diaries and Intelligence Summaries are contained in F. S. Regs., Part II. and the Staff Manual respectively. Title Pages will be prepared in manuscript.

Place	Date	Hour	Summary of Events and Information	Remarks and references to Appendices
MERICOURT l'ABBE - Somme	MCH 10			
	11		Casualties - 6th N.Fus O.R.1 missing.	
	12		Casualties - 440th Fld Coy RE O.R. wounded 1 acc.	
	13			
	14			
	15		Capt.W.McCracken, 7th Argyll & Southern Highrs, joined and took up duties as D.A.Q.M.G. Division, vice Major A.E.Holbrook, DSO., A.S.C. appointed A.A. & Q.M.G., 1st Division.	
	16		Casualties - 251st Bde RFA O.R. wounded 1.	
	17		Major A.E.Holbrook, DSO., A.S.C. to 1st Division as A.A. & Q.M.G.	
	18			
	19			
	20			
	21		250th Bde RFA to R.23.d., Sheet 62D.	
	22		250th Bde RFA to FOUILLOY, T.M.Batteries to HAMELET.	
	23		251st Bde RFA to NAIRE. D.A.Col. to VAIRE.	
	24			
	25			

2449 Wt. W14957/M90 750,000 1/16 J.B.C. & A. Forms/C.2118/12.

Army Form C. 2118.

ADMINISTRATIVE WAR DIARY or INTELLIGENCE SUMMARY

(Erase heading not required.)

Instructions regarding War Diaries and Intelligence Summaries are contained in F.S. Regs., Part II. and the Staff Manual respectively. Title Pages will be prepared in manuscript.

Place	Date	Hour	Summary of Events and Information	Remarks and references to Appendices
	MCH 26		250th and 251st Bde RFA to FLESSELLES, D.A.Col to HAVERNAS.	
	27		Casualties - 5th Yorks O.R. killed 1, wounded 2 (acc.).	
	28		250th Bde RFA to HEM. 251st Bde RFA to OUTREBOIS. D.A.C. to BOIS BERGUES. T.M.Battery to OUTREBOIS.	
	29		Artillery - COURTREILLE AREA.	
	30		149th Infy Bde H.Q. GAGNY. 4th N.F. BOUTILLERIE. 5th N.F. CAMON. 6th & 7th N.F. RIVERY. 150th Infy Bde H.Q. BUSSY. 4th E.Yorks BLANGY TRONVILLE. 4th Yorks to BONNAY. 5th Yorks and 5th D.L.I. LA NEUVILLE. 151st Infy Bde H.Q. ST. GRATIEN (Mounted Portions only).	
MOILLENS AU BOIS.	31		H.Q. Division to MOILLENS AU BOIS. 149th Infy Bde VILLERS BOCAGE. 4th N.F. COISY. 5th N.F. BERTANGLES. 6th & 7th N.F. VILLERS BOCAGE. 150th Infy Bde MIRVAUX. 4th E.Yorks RAINNEVILLE. 4th Yorks MOLLIENS. 5th Yorks MIRVAUX. 5th D.L.I. PIERREGOT. 151st Infy Bde TALMAS. 5th Border Regt TALMAS. 6th D.L.I. HAVERNAS. 8th & 9th D.L.I. NAOURS.	by bus.

Confidential

50th Division

Administrative Staff

War Diary

From 1st April 1917

To 30th April 1917

Volume XXIV

Original

Army Form C. 2118.

50TH DIVISION.

ADMINISTRATIVE WAR DIARY or INTELLIGENCE SUMMARY

APRIL 1917.

(Erase heading not required.)

Instructions regarding War Diaries and Intelligence Summaries are contained in F. S. Regs., Part II. and the Staff Manual respectively. Title Pages will be prepared in manuscript.

Place	Date	Hour	Summary of Events and Information	Remarks and references to Appendices
MOLLIENS AU BOIS.	APL 1		Div.H.Q. moved to MOLLIENS AU BOIS; 149th Infy Bde to WILLERS BOCAGE; 150th Infy Bde to MIRVAUX; 151st Infy Bde to TALMAS; R.E. to MOLLIENS AU BOIS.	
BEAUVAL.	2		Div.H.Q. moved to BEAUVAL; 149th Infy Bde to BEAUVAL; 150th Infy Bde to TALMAS; 151st Infy Bde to GEZAINCOURT; R.E. to GEZAINCOURT.	
BOQUEMAISON.	3		Div.H.Q. moved to BOQUEMAISON; 149th Infy Bde to BONNIERES; 150th Infy Bde to GEZAINCOURT; 151st Infy Bde to REBREUVE; R.E. to BOQUEMAISON.	
RAMECOURT.	4		Div.H.Q. moved to RAMECOURT; 149th Infy Bde to NUNCQ; 150th Infy Bde to BONNIERES; 151st Infy Bde to BLANGERVAL and BLANGERMONT.	
	5			
	6			
ROELLECOURT.	7		Div.H.Q. moved to ROELLECOURT; 149th Infy Bde to BUNEVILLE; 150th Infy Bde to HOUVIN - MOUVIGNEUIL; 151st Infy Bde tp FOUFFLIN - RICAMETZ.	
LE CAUROY.	8		Div.H.Q. moved to LE CAUROY; 149th Infy Bde to MANIN; 150th Infy Bde to LIGNEREUIL; 151st Infy Bde to AMBRINES.	
	9			
BERNEVILLE.	10		Div.H.Q. moved to BERNEVILLE; 149th Infy Bde to WANQUENTIN; 150th Infy Bde to HARBARCQ; 151st Infy Bde to MONTENESCOURT.	

Army Form C. 2118.

50TH DIVISION.

ADMINISTRATIVE WAR DIARY or INTELLIGENCE SUMMARY

APRIL 1917.

(Erase heading not required.)

Instructions regarding War Diaries and Intelligence Summaries are contained in F. S. Regs, Part II. and the Staff Manual respectively. Title Pages will be prepared in manuscript.

Place	Date	Hour	Summary of Events and Information	Remarks and references to Appendices
BERNEVILLE.	APL. 11.		149th Infy Bde into Line - trenches S. of TILLOY; 151st Infy Bde to CAVES, FAUB-RONVILLE, ARRAS.	
ARRAS.	12.		Div.H.Q. at ARRAS. Casualties - 7th D.L.I. Pnrs Officers wounded Capt & Adjt W.F.Laing and 2/Lt A.E.Mullis; O.R. killed 1, wounded 19.	
	13.		Divisional Artillery rejoined Division at ARRAS.	
	14.		Casualties - Div.H.Q. Maj-Gen.P.S.Wilkinson, CB. CMG. wounded (at duty). 151st Infy Bde - 5th Border Regt O.R. killed 5, wounded 7. 9th Durham L.I. - Officers 2/Lt.J.T.Bailes 6th D.L.I. attd wounded; O.R. killed 1, wounded 2.	
	15.		Casualties - 8th D.L.I. Officers 2/Lt. S.Probert 7th D.L.I. attd, 2/Lt. A.Ranson and 2/Lt. A.Elliot; O.R. killed 10, wounded 37. 9th D.L.I. Officers killed 2/Lts R.Greenland, R.N.Bell; Wounded Lt.W.G.Wylie, 2/Lt.W.R.S.Catchaside (shell shock, returned to duty) 5th D.L.I. attd, 2/Lt. W.F.Cawthorn. O.R. killed 12, wounded 45, missing 5. 251st (Nbn) Bde RFA - Officers killed - Capt.H.W.O.Hillerns, 2/Lt. H.S.T.Bullen; Wounded Major C.W.Brims, 2/Lt. C.O.Frank.	
	16.		Casualties - 149th Infy Bde. - 6th N.Fus. Officers killed Lt. W.J.Bunbury 4th N.F. attd, Wounded Captain R.C.Penketh, 2/Lts E.D.Brown and S.W.Robinson. 5th N.F. - O.R. wounded 3. 151st Infy Bde. - 6th D.L.I. Officers killed Capt.A.L.Brock, 2/Lts W.L.Newton, H.Greener, J.W.Payne and W.H.Richardson. Wounded - 2/Lts E.R.Appleton, F.C.D.Scott (shell shock), D.F.Charlton, H.H.Nicholson 5th D.L.I. attd,Capt.R.S. Johnson, 2/Lt. R.B.Ainsworth 9th D.L.I. attd,2/Lt. C.Reed. O.R. - 6th D.L.I. killed 14, wounded 92, missing 66. 8th D.L.I. 5 prev. rep. killed now rep. missing. 9th D.L.I. killed 4, wounded,2, 1 prev. rep. missing now rep. killed. No:151 M.G.Coy - wounded 20 inc. 2 O.R. 5th Border R. and 1 O.R. 8th D.L.I. attd. 250th Bde R.F.A. O.R. wounded 4 inc. 2 at duty. 7th Field Coy RE. O.R. wounded 3.	

2449 Wt. W14957/M90 750,000 1/16 J.B.C. & A. Forms/C.2118/12.

Army Form C. 2118.

50TH DIVISION.

Instructions regarding War Diaries and Intelligence Summaries are contained in F. S. Regs., Part II. and the Staff Manual respectively. Title Pages will be prepared in manuscript.

ADMINISTRATIVE WAR DIARY or INTELLIGENCE SUMMARY

(Erase heading not required.)

APRIL 1917.

Place	Date	Hour	Summary of Events and Information	Remarks and references to Appendices
ARRAS.	APL. 16 (Contd)		Casualties - Divl Sig. Co. RE - O.R. wounded 1. Divl Train - O.R. wounded 1 at duty, attd 251 Bde RFA.	

	17		Casualties -
			                                                                            wounded
			 149th Infy Bde.- 5th N.F. O.R. wounded 2. 6th N.F. Officers/2/Lt.W.A.C.Darlington 7th N.F.
			                 attd. 7th N.F. O.R. killed 1, wounded 7, missing 1, Officers - 2/Lt.
			                 W.E.Harris wounded acc.
			 151st Infy Bde.- 5th Border R. - O.R. killed 1, wounded 4. 6th D.L.I. Officers wounded
			                 2/Lt.G.D.Roberts. 9th D.L.I. wounded at duty O.R. 1.	

	18		Casualties -
			 149th Infy Bde.- 5th N.F. O.R. wounded 7, missing 1. 6th N.F. O.R. killed 20, wounded 152.
			                 7th N.F. Officers killed 2/Lt.J.A.M.Miller; Wounded a/Capt.F.O.Outhwaite,
			                 2/Lt. G.H.Whitehouse; Missing a/Capt.J.H.C.Swinney. O.R. killed 3,
			                 wounded 45, missing 3.
			 151st Infy Bde.- M.G.Coy Missing now rep. killed O.R.1, prev. rep. wounded now missing O.R.1.
			 7th D.L.I. Pnrs- Killed O.R.1.
			 251st Bde RFA. - 2/Lt. W.S.Metcalfe wounded at duty.	

	19		Casualties -
			 149th Infy Bde.- 4th N.F. O.R. killed 1, wounded 5. 5th N.F. O.R. killed 2, wounded 8,
			                 missing 1. 6th N.F. 2/Lt. W.H.Sampson wounded. 7th N.F. O.R. killed 5,
			                 wounded 6, missing 3. M.G.Coy. O.R. killed 1, wounded 2.
			 7th D.L.I. Pnrs= O.R. wounded 4 inc. 2 at duty.
			 250th Bde RFA. = O.R. wounded 4.
			 251st Bde RFA. = 2/Lt. H.H.Dryland wounded.	

	20		wounded
			 Casualties -
			 149th Infy Bde.- 4th N.F. O.R. wounded 1. 5th N.F. Officers/2/Lts H.Brand, W.Howard,
			                 C.B.Marshall; O.R. killed 2, wounded 7. 7th N.F. O.R. killed 1, wounded 4.
			                 M.G.Coy O.R. killed 2, wounded 1.
			 150th Infy Bde.- 5th Yorks O.R. killed 2, wounded 11. 5th D.L.I. O.R. wounded 2.	

Army Form C. 2118.

50TH DIVISION.

ADMINISTRATIVE WAR DIARY or INTELLIGENCE SUMMARY

APRIL 1917.

(Erase heading not required.)

Instructions regarding War Diaries and Intelligence Summaries are contained in F. S. Regs., Part II. and the Staff Manual respectively. Title Pages will be prepared in manuscript.

Place	Date	Hour	Summary of Events and Information	Remarks and references to Appendices
ARRAS.	APL. 20 (Contd)		Casualties – 250th Bde RFA O.R. wounded 1. 251st Bde RFA O.R. killed 1, wounded 5. 7th Field Coy R.E. O.R. wounded 4. 447th Field Coy R.E. O.R. wounded 1.	
	21		Casualties – 4th E.Yorks O.R. wounded 5. 5th Yorks O.R. wounded 1. 5th D.L.I. O.R. wounded 2.	
	22		Casualties – 149th Infy Bde – 4th N.F. O.R. killed 1, wounded 1. 5th N.F./killed 4, wounded 11, missing 5. 7th N.F. O.R. killed 2, wounded 2. M.G.Coy. O.R. killed 1. O.R. 150th Infy Bde – 4th E.Yorks Officers wounded Capt.K.A.Wilson-Barkworth MC, 2/Lt.T.Gregory. 4th Yorks O.R. killed 9, wounded 14. 5th Yorks Officers killed 2/Lt.E.C. Welbourne, O.R. killed 3, wounded 13 (inc. 3 shell shock). 5th D.L.I. Officers wounded 2/Lt R.J.Stockdale slightly at duty, O.R. killed 7, wounded 12, M.G.Coy wounded O.R.1. 151st Infy Bde – 8th D.L.I. O.R. wounded 1 acc. 7th D.L.I.Pnrs – Officers killed 2/Lt.P.Macdonald, O.R. killed 2, wounded 2. 250th Bde RFA – Officers wounded Major C.L.Wilkinson DSO, Major F.G.D.Johnston DSO, 2/Lt.W.G.McCallum MC. O.R. killed 1, wounded 2. 251st Bde RFA – O.R. killed 5, wounded 2 inc. 1 at duty. 50th Divl Train – O.R. wounded 1.	
	23		Casualties – 150th Infy Bde – 4th E.Yorks O.R. killed 1, wounded 15 inc. 7 shell shock. 4th Yorks Officers wounded Capt.R.Theakston and 2/Lt C.J.Minister, O.R. wounded 7. 5th Yorks O.R. wounded 9 inc. 1 shell shock. 5th D.L.I. O.R. wounded 4. M.Gun Coy Lieut. V.A.Tylor wounded. 151st Infy Bde – Officers killed 8th D.L.I. attd 6th 2/Lt.D.D.R.Lewis. 5th Border Regt O.R. killed 45, wounded 71, missing 23. 9th D.L.I. O.R. killed 15, wounded 38, missing 3, Officers wounded Capt.E.S.Gibson, Lt.F.D.Brown, 2/Lt.U. Wheatley.	

2449 Wt. W14957/M90 750,000 1/16 J.B.C. & A. Forms/C.2118/12.

Army Form C. 2118.

50TH DIVISION.
ADMINISTRATIVE.
WAR DIARY
or
INTELLIGENCE SUMMARY
(Erase heading not required.)

APRIL 1917.

Instructions regarding War Diaries and Intelligence
Summaries are contained in F. S. Regs., Part II.
and the Staff Manual respectively. Title Pages
will be prepared in manuscript.

Place	Date	Hour	Summary of Events and Information	Remarks and references to Appendices
ARRAS.	APL. 23.(Contd)		Casualties.— 7th Fld Co RE — killed 2/Lt R.E.E.Chaplin, O.R. wounded 3. 7th D.L.I.Pnrs— wounded 2/Lt H.Walton, O.R. killed 1, wounded 9. 250th Bde RFA — O.R. wounded 3. 251st Bde RFA — O.R. wounded 11.	
	24.		Casualties — 149th Infy Bde — 7th N.F. O.R. wounded 1. M.G.Coy wounded 2/Lt W.R.Potter E.Surrey R. attd, O.R. killed 2, wounded 1. 150th Infy Bde — 4th E.Yorks killed Capt.C.Easton MC, 2/Lt C.C.Boyle, 2/Lt.H.Oughtred, wounded Lt.H.E.Jackson, Lt (T/Capt) N.W.Ingleby, 2/Lt.G.N.Waite, 2/Lt.W.W.Harrison, 2/Lt.F.Stevenson, 2/Lt.J.Frost, 2/Lt.T.W.Aitken, Missing 2/Lts B.V.Hildyard, G.H.Lofthouse, N.W.Green, W.C.Walgate, E.F.Peer, W.A.Earle, J.D.Cowl, W.C.F.Dixon. 4th Yorks 2/Lt.J.Robson. 151st Infy Bde — 5th Border Regt killed Capt.H.Pride 10th Middlesex R. attd, O.R. wounded 1 acc. 8th D.L.I. O.R. killed 12, wounded 49, missing 10. Capt.R.H.Guest-Williams killed. M.G.Coy O.R. killed 7, wounded 16. T.M.Btty O.R. wounded 1. 250th Bde RFA — wounded Capt.G.Chapman, O.R. 6, killed O.R. 1. 251st Bde RFA — O.R. killed 4, wounded 8. Divl R.E. HQ. — Capt.K.P.Mackenzie RAMC attd, wounded. Signal Coy RE — O.R. killed 1, wounded 1. 1/1st (Nbn) Fd Ambce. — O.R. wounded 4.	
	25		Casualties — 149th Infy Bde — 4th N.F. O.R. wounded 2. 150th Infy Bde — 4th E.Yorks O.R. killed 30, wounded 100, missing 15. 4th Yorks O.R. killed 25, wounded 80, officers killed a/Capt.G.A.Tugwell and a/Capt.A.R.Cawood. a/Capt. D.P.Hirsch, wounded a/Capt.A.R.Cawood. 5th Yorks O.R. killed 20, wounded 80, missing 10. officers killed Capt.W. Vause MC, wounded Bt.Major Brown DSO MC, 2/Lts W.Rennison, S.H.Collins and G.F.G.Rees. 5th D.L.I. O.R. killed 20, wounded 90, missing 18. Officers killed Capt.W.Marley, 2/Lts H.R.Herring, F.W.Heap, wounded Lt.W.E.Coulson-Mayne. 150 M.G.Coy O.R. wounded 14 and 2/Lt.W.J.S.Ranken.	

Army Form C. 2118.

50TH DIVISION.
APRIL. 1917.

ADMINISTRATIVE WAR DIARY or INTELLIGENCE SUMMARY
(Erase heading not required.)

Instructions regarding War Diaries and Intelligence Summaries are contained in F. S. Regs., Part II. and the Staff Manual respectively. Title Pages will be prepared in manuscript.

Place	Date	Hour	Summary of Events and Information	Remarks and references to Appendices
ARRAS.	APL. 25.	(Contd)	Casualties - 151st Infy Bde - 5th Border Regt O.R. wounded 50, officers wounded 2/Lts H.P.Rhind, C.E.Rendhaw, S.A.Robinson, J.P.Forster. 8th D.L.I. O.R. wounded 7. 9th D.L.I. O.R. wounded 46. 151 M.G.Coy 2/Lt.R.C.Hill wounded. 6th D.L.I. O.R. wounded 3. 250th Bde RFA = O.R. killed 3, wounded 6. 251st Bde RFA = wounded Lt.H.C.Macnamara. 7th Fld Co RE = O.R. wounded 6. 1/1st (Nbn) Fd. Ambce O.R. wounded 4. 447th " " = O.R. wounded 3. 2/2nd " " " O.R. wounded 1.	
LA COUTURELLE.	26.		Casualties (22nd and 23rd Continued) - 150th Infy Bde - 4th Yorks O.R. wounded 1. 5th Yorks Officers killed 2/Lts E.G.Herbert and A.S.Brentnall, wounded 2/Lt. G.E.Henderson, O.R. wounded 1. 5th D.L.I. O.R. wounded 3, officers wounded 2/Lts C.D.Marley, E.W.Weeks, A.B.L.Crosby. 151st Infy Bde - 5th Border Regt Officers killed 2/Lt.J.W.Buchan, Cameronians attd., 2/Lts F.Storey, H.S.James, J.Mackay, R.D.Wills. M.G.Coy Officers wounded 2/Lt. H.Lewis. 7th D.L.I.Pnrs - Officers wounded 2/Lt.J.Belfitt attd 9th D.L.I. Division moved to Rest Area. 149th Infy Bde to POMMERA MONDICOURT area. 150th Infy Bde to Div.H.Q. to LA COUTURELLE. 151st Inf'y Bde to HUMBERCOURT. Divnl Artillery remains at ARRAS. GRENAS.	
	27.		Casualties (23-24th reported 27th).— 4th E.Yorks O.R. wounded 19, missing 199. 4th Yorks Killed 25, wounded 95, missing 124 officers wounded 2/Lt.H.E.Aust, missing 2/Lt.J.H.Scarth. 5th Yorks officers killed 2/Lt.W.H.Game, missing 2/Lts G.F.Rogers and F.B.Whitehead, O.R. wounded 26, missing 62. 5th D.L.I. O.R. killed 3, wounded 47, missing 81. 150 M.G.Coy O.R. killed 10, wounded 10. 150 T.M.Btty officers wounded 2/Lt.W.Luckhurst 4th Yks attd. 7th D.L.I. wounded 2/Lt.J.H.R.Massey. Casualties (25th reported 27th).— 4th N.F. O.R. killed 5, wounded 18, missing 3. Officers killed 2/Lt.R.Johnson. 7th D.L.I.Pnrs O.R. wounded 3.	

Army Form C. 2118.

50TH DIVISION.   **APRIL, 1917.**

ADMINISTRATIVE WAR DIARY or INTELLIGENCE SUMMARY

(Erase heading not required.)

Instructions regarding War Diaries and Intelligence Summaries are contained in F. S. Regs., Part II and the Staff Manual respectively. Title Pages will be prepared in manuscript.

Place	Date	Hour	Summary of Events and Information	Remarks and references to Appendices
LA COUTURELLE.	APL. 27.	(Cond)	Casualties (26th reported 27th).— 5th N.F. wounded 2/Lt. L.P.Garbett. 4th N.F. O.R. 1 killed, wounded 15, missing 1. Officers wounded 2/Lt.A.Finlayson 6th H.L.I. attd 4th N.F., 2/Lt.W.Anderson 5th Royal Scots attd 4th N.F., 2/Lt.J.Herdman. 5th Yorks 2/Lt.H.J.Bath. 5th D.L.I. 2/Lt.J.Pauling. No:150 M.Gun Coy 2/Lt.S.A.Russell. 5th Border Regt. 2/Lt. S.V.Campbell.	
	28.			
	29.			
	30.		Casualties – 7th D.L.I. Pnrs Officers wounded 2/Lt.J.W.Shield, O.R. wounded 1.	

CASUALTIES.

PHASE I – 9/21-4-17.
```
           Officers.           O.Ranks.
         "K"  "W"  "M"      "K"   "W"   "M"
Actual:- 13   36    1       125   507    94
             =50                 =726
Est'd :-    .. 17              ..... 670
```

PHASE II – 22/25-4-17.
```
           Officers.           O.Ranks.
         "K"  "W"  "M"      "K"   "W"   "M"
Actual :- 15   47   11      239  1011   549
             =73                 =1799
Est'd :-    .... 63            ..... 1720
```

T O T A L.
```
             OFFICERS.              OTHER RANKS.
           "K"  "W"  "M"          "K"   "W"    "M"
PHASE I.-   13   36    1          125   507     94
PHASE II.-  15   47   11          239  1011    549
           ---------------       -------------------
TOTAL ACTUAL ......  28  83  12 = 123   464  1518  643 = 2625.
TOTAL ESTIMATED .......... = 80     ........... = 2390.
```

2449 Wt. W14957/M90 750,000 1/16 J.B.C. & A. Forms/C.2118/12.

CONFIDENTIAL

Vol 26

50th Division

Administrative Staff.

War Diary

From

1st May. 1917.

To

31st May. 1917.

Volume XXV

— ORIGINAL —

Army Form C. 2118.

50TH DIVISION.   MAY, 1917.

ADMINISTRATIVE WAR DIARY or INTELLIGENCE SUMMARY

(Erase heading not required.)

Instructions regarding War Diaries and Intelligence Summaries are contained in F. S. Regs., Part II. and the Staff Manual respectively. Title Pages will be prepared in manuscript.

Place	Date	Hour	Summary of Events and Information	Remarks and references to Appendices
COUTURELLE.	MAY 1.			
BASSEUX.	2.		Divl H.Q. BASSEUX, Advanced Divl H.Q. NEUVILLE VITASSE; 149th Infy Bde MERCATEL; 150th Infy Bde BLAIRVILLE; 151st Infy Bde BAILLEULVAL. Casualties - 5th Yorkshire R. wounded 2/Lt J.S.ROBSON; 5th Durham L.I. Missing 2/Lt A.E.W. PEREIRA; No:150 M.Gun Coy wounded 2/Lt M.A.HALL, missing 2/Lt A.E.CUMMINS; Divl T.Mortars wounded O.R. 1.	
	3.			
COUTURELLE.	4.		Divl H.Q. COUTURELLE; 149th Infy Bde SOUASTRE; 150th Infy Bde BAYENCOURT; 151st Infy Bde HUMBERCOURT.	
	5.		149th Infy Bde POMMIERA; 150th Infy Bde GRENAS; 151st Infy Bde HUMBERCOURT. Casualties - 149th Infy Bde - 4th North'd Fuslrs wounded Lt. H.H.CARRICK.	
	6.		Casualties - 149th Infy Bde - 5th North'd Fuslrs wounded O.R. 1.	
	7.			
	8.			
	9.			
	10.			
	11.			
	12.			
	13.		Casualties - 50th Divl Amm Colum - wounded O.R. 1.	

2449 Wt. W14957/M90 750,000 1/16 J.B.C. & A. Forms/C.2118/12.

Army Form C. 2118.

50TH DIVISION.

ADMINISTRATIVE.
WAR DIARY or INTELLIGENCE SUMMARY

MAY, 1917.

(Erase heading not required.)

Instructions regarding War Diaries and Intelligence Summaries are contained in F. S. Regs., Part II. and the Staff Manual respectively. Title Pages will be prepared in manuscript.

Place	Date	Hour	Summary of Events and Information	Remarks and references to Appendices
COUTURELLE.	14.			
	15.			
	16.			
	17.		149th Infy Bde from POMMERA to SOUASTRE; 150th Infy Bde BAYENCOURT; 151st Infy Bde HUMBERCOURT.	
	18.		149th Infy Bde BOIRY ST MARTIN; 150th Infy Bde DOUCHY LES AYETTE; 151st Infy Bde MONCHY AU BOIS. Casualties - 251st Bde RFA O.R. wounded 1.	
BEAUMETZ.	19.		Divl H.Q. to BEAUMETZ. Casualties - 251st Bde RFA O.R. killed 2, wounded 6.	
	20.		149th Infy Bde in line V" ST LEGER; 150th Infy Bde DOUCHY LES AYETTE; 151st Infy Bde MONCHY AU (BOIS).	
	21.			
	22.			
OJUIN.	23.		Divl H.Q. to OJUIN; 150th Infy Bde to BAYENCOURT; 151st Infy Bde to SAULTY. Casualties - 4th N.Fus O.R. killed 1, wounded 1; 5th N.F. wounded 2/Lt P.E.COX (4th N.F. attd) O.R.8; 6th N.F. O.R. killed 1, wounded 3; 149th T.Mortar Battery wounded O.R.1.	
	24.		151st Infy Bde to SOUASTRE. Casualties - 4th N.F. O.R. wounded 2; 5th N.F. O.R. wounded 6; 6th N.F. O.R. wounded 2; 7th N.F. O.R. killed 2, wounded 1.	
	25.		Casualties - 4th N.F. O.R. wounded 1; 5th N.F. O.R. killed 1, wounded 3; 6th N.F. O.R. killed 2, wounded 4, missing 2; 7th N.F. O.R. wounded 4.	
	26.		Casualties - 5th N.F. O.R. killed 1, wounded 3; 6th N.F. O.R. killed 3, wounded 2; 7th N.F. O.R. wounded 1; No:149 H.Gun Coy wounded O.R. 1.	

2449 Wt. W14957/M90 750,000 1/16 J.B.C. & A. Forms/C.2118/12.

Army Form C. 2118.

ADMINISTRATIVE
WAR DIARY
or
INTELLIGENCE SUMMARY

(Erase heading not required.)

50TH DIVISION.   MAY, 1917.

Instructions regarding War Diaries and Intelligence Summaries are contained in F. S. Regs., Part II. and the Staff Manual respectively. Title Pages will be prepared in manuscript.

Place	Date	Hour	Summary of Events and Information	Remarks and references to Appendices
COUIN.	MAY 27.		Casualties - 251st Bde RFA wounded O.R.1.	
	28.			
	29.		Casualties - 251st Bde RFA O.R. wounded 1.	
	30.		7th Durham L.I. Pars to FONQUEVILLERS.	
	31.		7th Durham L.I. Pars to BOYELLES.	

2449 Wt. W14957/M90 750,000 1/16 J.B.C. & A. Forms/C.2118/12.

CONFIDENTIAL

50th Division

Administrative Staff

War Diary

From 1st June 1917.
To 30th June 1917.

Volume XXVI

ORIGINAL.

Army Form C. 2118.

50th Division.

JUNE 1917.

ADMINISTRATIVE WAR DIARY or INTELLIGENCE SUMMARY

(Erase heading not required.)

Instructions regarding War Diaries and Intelligence Summaries are contained in F.S. Regs., Part II. and the Staff Manual respectively. Title Pages will be prepared in manuscript.

Place	Date	Hour	Summary of Events and Information	Remarks and references to Appendices
OUIN.	JUNE 1			
	2			
	3		Casualties - 250 Bde RFA wounded O.R.2 (1 acc, 1 acc gas).	
	4			
	5		Casualties - 251 Bde RFA wounded O.R.1 (slightly, at duty).	
	6			
	7		Casualties - 251 Bde RFA wounded O.R.1.	
	8			
	9			
	10			
	11			
	12			
	13		Casualties - 9th Durh.L.I. wounded acc. O.R.1.	
	14		Casualties - 251 Bde RFA wounded O.R.1, Y/50 T.Mortars wounded O.R.2 acc by shell explosion. 9th D.L.I. wounded 2/Lt.J.E.Smales, wounded O.R.7 inc. 1 at duty, all acc. (premature burst of bomb).	

2449 Wt. W14957/M90 750,000 1/16 J.B.C. & A. Forms/C.2118/12.

Army Form C. 2118.

50th Division.　　**JUNE 1917.**

WAR DIARY or INTELLIGENCE SUMMARY

(Erase heading not required.)

Instructions regarding War Diaries and Intelligence Summaries are contained in F.S. Regs., Part II. and the Staff Manual respectively. Title Pages will be prepared in manuscript.

Place	Date	Hour	Summary of Events and Information	Remarks and references to Appendices
OOUIN.	JUNE 15		Division commences move to Forward Area, 150th Inf'y Bde to Reserve Area S.17. B. H.Q. 150th Inf'y Bde, 4th and 5th Yorkshire Regt to Support Area N.25.c., N.26.c., N.31.a., N.32.b & c. Casualties – 7th D.L.I. 1mrs wounded O.R.1, 250th Bde RFA wounded O.R.	
	16		4th East Yorkshire Regt to N.34.a.8.0. and 4th Yorkshire Regt to N.35.c.0.9. 151st Inf'y Bde H.Q. to M.22.d.5.1. 5th Border Regt to Support Area. 9th D.L.I. to Support Area. (6th D.L.I. to N.30.b.6.2. (in line). 8th D.L.I. to N.30.a.2.5. (in support). 150th Inf'y Bde H.Q. to N.35.c.4.1, 5th Yorkshire Regt to T.5.b.3.7., 5th D.L.I. to N.36.b.3.1 (in line), 7th Durh.L.I. to N.35.b.9.4.	
	17		Casualties – 6th D.L.I. wounded O.R.1, 250th Bde RFA wounded O.R.1, 251st Bde RFA wounded O.R.1.	
Camp – S.17.a.8.4.	18		Div'l H.Q. moves to Camp S.17.a.8.4. and 149th Inf'y Bde H.Q. moves to Camp at S.17.	
	19		Casualties – 446th (Nbn) Fd. Coy wounded O.R.3 inc 1(shell shock?). 6th D.L.I. O.R. killed 1, wounded 5, missing 2. 7th D.L.I. wounded O.R.1.	
	20.		Casualties – 4th Yorkshire Regt O.R. 1 wounded at duty, 5th Yorkshire Regt wounded O.R.1. 9th D.L.I. wounded O.R.1.	
	21			
	22		Casualties – 4th E.Yorkshire R. killed O.R.2. 5th Yorkshire R. wounded Capt.L.B.Walker and 2/Lt.J.D.Brydon. 8th D.L.I. killed O.R.2, wounded O.R.8. 151st T.M.Bt'y wounded O.R.1.	
	23		Casualties – 4th E.Yorkshire R. wounded O.R.3 (shell shock NYD). 5th Yorkshire R. wounded O.R. 1 (shell shock NYD). 6th D.L.I. killed O.R.1, wounded O.R.1. 9th D.L.I. killed 2/Lt.O.J. Dixon, O.R.1, wounded O.R.2. 7th D.L.I. wounded O.R.1.	

Army Form C. 2118.

50th Division.

ADMINISTRATIVE
WAR DIARY
or
INTELLIGENCE SUMMARY
(Erase heading not required.)

JUNE 1917.

Instructions regarding War Diaries and Intelligence Summaries are contained in F. S. Regs., Part II. and the Staff Manual respectively. Title Pages will be prepared in manuscript.

Place	Date	Hour	Summary of Events and Information	Remarks and references to Appendices
Camp - S. 17 a.3.4.	JUNE 24		Casualties - 4th E.Yorkshire R. wounded O.R.5 (includes 2 shell shock NYD). 4th Yorkshire R. wounded, at duty O.R.1. 6th D.L.I. wounded O.R.1. 8th D.L.I. O.R. killed 1, wounded 15. 2/2nd (Nbn) Fld Ambce wounded O.R.2.	
	25		Casualties - 6th N.F. wounded O.R.1 acc. No:150 M.G.Co. wounded O.R.2 (inc. 1 at duty). 250 Bde RFA wounded, at duty Major F.G.D.Johnston, DSO. Attack on Fontaine Wood completely successful. 30 prisoners and a Machine Gun captured.	
	26		Casualties - 4th Yorkshire R. 3 O.R. wounded inc. 1 at duty. 5th D.L.I. 2/Lt.R.V.Heron wounded slightly, at duty, O.R. killed 4, wounded 5. 5th Yorkshire Regt O.R. killed 2, wounded 10. No:150 M.G.Coy O.R. wounded 1 at duty. 5th N.F. wounded O.R.2. 6th N.F. wounded O.R.1. No:151 M.G.Co. wounded Lt.J.G.R.Twetchley (M.G.Corps). 7th D.L.I. wounded 2/Lts C.S.Richardson and R.V.Iles, O.R. killed 3, wounded 8, missing 1.	
	27		Casualties - 50th D.A.C. killed O.R.2, wounded O.R.1. 149th Bde - 5/M.F. wounded O.R.1. 7th N.F. wounded O.R.1. No:149 M.G.Coy O.R. killed 1, wounded 2. 150th Bde - 4/E.Yorks O.R. killed 1, wounded 1(shell shock). 4th Yorks Officers killed Capt. J.E.Brydon RAMC attd, wounded Lt.C.B.Prior Wandesford, 2/Lt J.S.Bainbridge, 2/Lt.W.E.Pacey, 2/Lt.C.J.Perkins (gassed), O.R. killed 1, wounded 11 inc. 9 gas 1 acc. 5th Yorks officers missing 2/Lt.E.G.Stuart Corry, O.R. killed 2, wounded 1. 5th D.L.I. O.R. killed 11, wounded 27, missing 1. No:151 M.G.Coy killed 1 O.R., wounded O.R.2.	
	R.A.M.C.		2/2nd (Nbn) Fld Ambce O.R. killed 2 inc.1 gas, wounded O.R.5 inc. 2 gas. 1/3rd (Nbn) Fld Ambce O.R. wounded 4 gas.	
	R.E.		50th Divnl signal Coy O.R. wounded 1. All gas cases due to gas drum exploded by enemy fire.	

Army Form C. 2118.

WAR DIARY
or
INTELLIGENCE SUMMARY

ADMINISTRATIVE.

50th Division.

JUNE 1917.

(Erase heading not required.)

Instructions regarding War Diaries and Intelligence Summaries are contained in F. S. Regs., Part II. and the Staff Manual respectively. Title Pages will be prepared in manuscript.

Place	Date	Hour	Summary of Events and Information	Remarks and references to Appendices
Camp S.17. a.8.4.	JUNE 28		Casualties — 446th Field Coy RE wounded O.R.2.	
			149th Bde — 5th N.F. killed O.R.1, wounded O.R.1.	
			150th Bde — 4/Yorks O.R. killed 1, wounded 11 (inc.4 gas and 2 at duty). 5/Yorks Killed O.R.1, Missing
			believed killed O.R.1, wounded O.R.8 (inc. 4 gas). 5th D.L.I. killed O.R.2,	
			wounded O.R.10 (inc.5 gas), O.R.1 rep. "M" 27th now rep. wounded. 4/E.Yorks	
			wounded 2/Lt.H.T.Stephens attd from 1st Bn. on 27th. No:150 M.G.Coy killed O.R.4.	
			missing O.R.1, wounded O.R.5 (inc. 2 N.Y.D.N. shell shock).	
			R.A.M.C. — 2/2nd Fld Ambce wounded O.R.2 (gas). 1/3rd Fld Ambce wounded O.R.1 (gas).	
	29		Casualties	
			149th Bde — 5/N.F. wounded O.R.4.	
			150th Bde — 4/Yorks wounded 2/Lt.R.S.Wray, O.R. wounded 5 (inc. 3 gas). 5th D.L.I. wounded	
			O.R.1. 4/E.Yorks officers missing Capt.T.J.Morrill, 2/Lt.F.Linsley, 2/Lt.R.	
			Duggleby, O.R. killed 7, wounded 43 (23 NYDN), missing 60. No:150 T.M.Battery	
			wounded O.R.2.	
			7th D.L.I. Engrs wounded O.R.1.	
	30		Casualties — 4/N.F. killed O.R.2, wounded O.R.2. 6/N.F. killed O.R.1.	
			149th Bde — 4/E.Yorks wounded O.R.1 NYDN. 4/Yorks O.R. killed 1, wounded 1. 5th D.L.I.	
			150th Bde — O.R. killed 2, wounded 1. No:150 M.G.Coy O.R. killed 1, wounded 1.	
			151st Bde — No:151 M.Gun Coy O.R. wounded 1.	

CONFIDENTIAL

50th Division

Administrative Staff

War Diary

From :- 1st July 1917

To :- 31st July 1917

Volume XXVII

ORIGINAL

Army Form C. 2118.

50TH DIVISION.

Instructions regarding War Diaries and Intelligence Summaries are contained in F.S. Regs., Part II. and the Staff Manual respectively. Title Pages will be prepared in manuscript.

ADMINISTRATIVE WAR DIARY or INTELLIGENCE SUMMARY

(Erase heading not required.)

JULY 1917.

Place	Date	Hour	Summary of Events and Information	Remarks and references to Appendices
Camp - C.17 a.3.4.	JULY 1		Casualties - No.149 M.G.Coy wounded O.R.1. 150th Bde - 4th E.Yorks wounded O.R.1 (acc), 4th Yorks. wounded O.R.2, 5th Yorks. wounded O.R.1, 5th Durh.L.I. wounded O.R.1. Orders received for Division to take over portion of front now held by 56th Division. 5th Border Regt and 6th Durh.L.I. move to HUMIN Area.	
		2	Casualties - 7th N.F. wounded O.R.1, No.149 M.G.Coy killed O.R.2, 5th Durh.L.I. wounded O.R.1, 8th Durh.L.I. wounded O.R.1. 6th and 9th Durh.L.I. move to HUMIN Area. 150th Bde to Camp C.17.d. 151st Bde and H.Q. move to HUMIN.	
		3	Casualties - 50th Div.T.M.Btty wounded O.R.5, 446th Fld Coy RE wounded O.R.1 (S.I.W.). 149th Bde - 4th N.F. wounded O.R.1, 5th N.F. wounded O.R.5, 7th N.F. killed O.R.1, wounded 2/Lt.G.H.Colquhon, O.R.5. 151st Bde - 5th Borders killed O.R.2, wounded O.R.13, 6th D.L.I. wounded O.R.1 attd 151st T.M.Battery, R.A.M.C. wounded O.R.1 attd 5th D.L.I. 151st Bde H.Q. to N.10.d.2.5. 5th Borders in line. 8th D.L.I. in support.	
		4	9th Durh.L.I. Front line, 6th Durh.L.I. Support. Move complete and 151st Bde in command of portion of line vacated by 56th Division. Casualties - 250th Bde RFA wounded O.R.1, at duty. 149th Bde - 4th N.F. wounded O.R.4, 7th N.F. wounded O.R.2 died of wounds,O.R.1 wounded on 3rd. 150th Bde - No.150 M.G.Coy O.R.1 rep. Missing 28/6/17 now rep. wounded. 151st Bde - 5th Borders wounded O.R.2 N.Y.D.N., 6th D.L.I. wounded O.R.1 at duty.	
		5	8th D.L.I. in Reserve. 150th Bde to Reserve Area M.13.d.0.3. Casualties - 250th Bde RFA wounded O.R.1, 50th Divl T.Ms wounded O.R.1. 149th Bde - 4th N.F. wounded O.R.2, 5th N.F. killed O.R.1. 151st Bde - 5th Borders killed O.R.2, wounded O.R.2, 6th D.L.I.M. wounded O.R.2, 9th D.L.I. wounded O.R.1, No.151 M.G.Coy wounded O.R.2. 1/2nd (Nbn) Fld Ambce - wounded O.R.1. 1/3rd (Nbn) Fld Ambce wounded O.R.1.	

Army Form C. 2118.

ADMINISTRATIVE WAR DIARY or INTELLIGENCE SUMMARY

(Erase heading not required.)

50TH DIVISION.  **JULY 1917.**

Instructions regarding War Diaries and Intelligence Summaries are contained in F. S. Regs., Part II. and the Staff Manual respectively. Title Pages will be prepared in manuscript.

Place	Date	Hour	Summary of Events and Information	Remarks and references to Appendices
	JULY			
	6		Casualties – 6th N.F. wounded Lt.E.J.Proctor, O.R.6, Missing 2/Lt.F.P.Aldrich, O.R.1. 7th N.F. wounded 2/Lt.W.H.Fisher, at duty.	
	7		Casualties – 446th Fld Coy RE wounded O.R.1 at duty. 149th Bde – 6th N.F. wounded O.R.1, 7th N.F. wounded O.R.1. 151st Bde – 9th D.L.I. killed O.R.1, wounded O.R.1.	
	8		Casualties – 149th Bde – 5th N.F. wounded O.R.4, 6th N.F. wounded O.R.2, Missing 2/Lt.W.R. Clephan, O.R.1 (went on patrol and did not return). 151st Bde – 9th D.L.I. killed O.R.1, wounded O.R.1, 8th D.L.I. wounded O.R.1.	
	9		Casualties – 149th Bde – 5th N.F. 2/Lt.J.W.Moulden wounded (gas), O.R.5 (inc. 2 at duty). 6th N.F. killed O.R.1, 7th N.F. killed O.R.1, wounded O.R.2. 151st Bde – 8th D.L.I. killed O.R.2, wounded O.R.2, 9th D.L.I. wounded O.R.3.	
	10		Casualties – 50th T.M.B. killed O.R.2, wounded O.R.2 at duty. 149th Bde – 5th N.F. wounded O.R.3 (gas), 7th N.F. killed O.R.1. 150th Bde – 5th Yorks. wounded Lt-Col.C.H.Pearce. 151st Bde – 6th D.L.I. wounded O.R.4, 8th D.L.I. wounded O.R.1, 9th D.L.I. wounded O.R.1.	
	11		Casualties – 7th Fld Coy RE killed 2/Lt.C.W.S.Littlewood. 250th Bde RFA wounded O.R.8 inc. 2 at duty. 149th Bde – 7th N.F. wounded O.R.1. 150th Bde – 4th Yorks wounded O.R.1, 5th Yorks. wounded O.R.5. 151st Bde – 5th Borders wounded acc. discharge of rifle O.R.2, 6th D.L.I. killed O.R.1, wounded O.R.1, 9th D.L.I. wounded at duty 2/Lt.G.A.Marshall, 8th D.L.I. attd. No. 151 M.G.Coy killed O.R.1, wounded O.R.1. 2/2nd (Nrthn) Fld Amlce Wounded O.R.1 at duty.	

50TH DIVISION.

WAR DIARY or INTELLIGENCE SUMMARY

Army Form C. 2118.

JULY 1917.

Place	Date	Hour	Summary of Events and Information	Remarks and references to Appendices
	JULY	12	Investiture by His Majesty at ALBERT. Following were invested with Insignia and Decoration stated :- Major General P.S.WILKINSON, CB., CMG with K.C.M.G. Brig.-General B.G.PRICE, DSO., with C.M.G. Colonel C.H.CARTWRIGHT with C.B. Lieut. A.PEGLE, French Mission attd H.Q., 50th Divn with M.C.	
		13	Casualties - 250th Bde RFA wounded O.R.1. 7th Field Co RE wounded O.R.1. 150th Bde - 5th Yorks wounded O.R.1, 5th D.L.I. wounded O.R.1. 151st Bde - 5th Borders wounded O.R.1, No.151 L.G.Coy wounded Lt.G.Morton.	
		14	Casualties - 5th D.L.I. O.R. killed 1, wounded 2. 4th East Yor.s O.R. killed 1. No.150 M.G.Coy O.R. wounded 1.	
		15	Casualties - 150th Bde - 4th E.Yorks wounded O.R.3 (inc. 2 gas and 1 acc), 4th Yorks. killed O.R.4, wounded O.R.3 (inc. 1 M.Y.D.M.), 5th Yorks. killed O.R.2, wounded 2/Lt. C.H.Robis, O.R.2. 5th Duch.L.I. killed O.R.2, wounded O.R.1. 151st Bde - 9th D.L.I. killed O.R.1, wounded O.R.2. Casualties - 447th Fld Coy RE killed O.R.1, wounded O.R.1. 150th Bde - 4th E.Yorks wounded O.R.1 (gas), 4th Yorks. wounded O.R.2, inc. 1 at duty, 5th Yorks O.R. killed 1, wounded 2. 5th D.L.I. O.R. killed 1, wounded 5, wounded at duty 2/1tR.W.Wilkinson. 2/2nd (Wm) Fld Ambce wounded at duty Capt.G.D.Eccles RAMC and 1st Lieut. L.J. Gonella, United States Med. Corps attached. 9th D.L.I. - wounded O.R.1, 5th Borders lt-Col.J.R.Hedley, DSO., died suddenly.	
		16	Casualties - 50th divl T.Ms wounded O.R.1 at duty. 150th Bde - 4th E.Yorks wounded O.R.1, 4th Yorks killed O.R.1, wounded O.R.6. inc. 1 M.Y.D.M. 5th Yorks killed O.R.1, 5th D.L.I. wounded O.R.2, No.150 M.G.Coy wounded O.R.2, 150th T.M.Btty wounded O.R.1. 151st Bde - 5th Borders wounded O.R.3.	

50th DIVISION.

WAR DIARY
ADMINISTRATIVE.
or
INTELLIGENCE SUMMARY

(Erase heading not required.)

Army Form C. 2118.

JULY 1917.

Instructions regarding War Diaries and Intelligence Summaries are contained in F. S. Regs., Part II. and the Staff Manual respectively. Title Pages will be prepared in manuscript.

Place	Date	Hour	Summary of Events and Information	Remarks and references to Appendices
	JULY	17	Casualties - 447th Fld Coy RE wounded O.R.1 at duty. 50th Div.T.M.B. wounded O.R.2. 150th Bde - 4th E.Yorks wounded O.R.2, 4th Yorks wounded O.R.2 inc. 1 M.Y.D.M., 5th Yorks wounded O.R.1. 151st Bde - 5th Borders wounded O.R.1, 5th D.L.I. Killed O.R.1, wounded 10 inc. 1 &OC., 9th D.L.I. wounded O.R.1, No.151 M.G.Coy wounded O.R.1.	
		18	Casualties - 251st Bde RFA wounded O.R.1. 150th Bde - 4th E.Yorks wounded O.R.1, 5th Yorks killed O.R.1, wounded O.R.3, 5th D.L.I. wounded O.R.1 at duty. 151st Bde - 5th Borders wounded O.R.2, 8th D.L.I. killed O.R.1, wounded O.R.3. 7th Durh.L.I. (Pnrs) wounded O.R.1.	
		19	Casualties - 150th Bde - 4th E.Yorks killed O.R.3, wounded 2/Lt.E.W.Allchorn 1st Bn attd, O.R.8. 4th Yorks killed Capt.C.Sproxton, MC., O.R.5, wounded Capt.J.Dunbar, R.A.M.C. attd, at duty, O.R.6 inc. 1 M.Y.D.N. 5th Yorks killed O.R.15, wounded O.R.18, No.150 M.G.Coy wounded O.R.2. 151st Bde - 6th D.L.I. killed O.R.7, wounded O.R.3. 7th Durh.L.I. (Pnrs) wounded O.R.1. German attack on trenches held by 150th Bde which was repulsed.	
		20	Casualties - 149th Bde - 4th N.F. wounded 2/Lt.R.Main, O.R.1, 5th N.F. wounded O.R.1, 149 T.M.Btty wounded O.R.1. 150th Bde - 4th E.Yorks wounded O.R.1, 4th Yorks 2/Lts G.R.Cole and P.L.Leigh-Breeze M.Y.D.N., killed O.R.1. 250th Bde RFA wounded 2/Lt.W.Fairley, O.R.1.	
		21	Casualties - 149th Bde - 4th N.F. wounded O.R.3, 5th N.F. wounded O.R.1. 150th Bde - 4th Yorks wounded O.R.1, 5th D.L.I. wounded O.R.1.	
		22	Casualties - 149th Bde - 4th N.F. killed O.R.1, wounded O.R.1, 7th N.F. wounded O.R.1. 150th Bde - 4th E.Yorks wounded O.R.1, 5th Yorks wounded O.R.2, 5th D.L.I. wounded O.R.2. 7th Durh.L.I. (Pnrs) wounded O.R.2.	
		23	Casualties - 149th Bde - 4th N.F. killed O.R.1, wounded O.R.2, 150th Bde - 4th Yorks wounded O.R.2 inc. 1 at duty. 5th D.L.I. wounded O.R.6. 7th D.L.I. Pnrs wounded O.R.2.	

Army Form C. 2118.

50th DIVISION. **JULY 1917.**

ADMINISTRATIVE WAR DIARY or INTELLIGENCE SUMMARY

(Erase heading not required.)

Instructions regarding War Diaries and Intelligence Summaries are contained in F. S. Regs., Part II. and the Staff Manual respectively. Title Pages will be prepared in manuscript.

Place	Date	Hour	Summary of Events and Information	Remarks and references to Appendices
	JULY			
	24		Casualties – 149th Bde – 4th N.F. O.R. killed 1, wounded 1, 5th N.F. O.R. killed 2, wounded 2. 150th Bde – 4th Yorks wounded O.R.2 (gas), 5th Yorks wounded O.R.1. 7th Durham L.I. Pnrs wounded O.R.1.	
	25		Casualties – 149th Bde – 5th N.F. wounded 2/Lt.T.Gracie, O.R.1. 150th Bde – 4th E.Yorks wounded Capt.H.M.Seed, MC., 4th Yorks wounded O.R.1 at duty. 5th D.L.I. wounded O.R.1, No.150 M.G.Coy wounded O.R. 151st Bde – 8th D.L.I. wounded 2/Lt.T.U.Nicholson and O.R.3 acc. at duty (premature burst of rifle grenade). 7th Durh.L.T. Pnrs wounded 2/Lt.U.Haley.	
	26		Casualties – 250th Bde RFA – wounded Lt.A.F.Bourdas at duty 25/7/17. 251st Bde RFA wounded O.R.1. 149th Bde – 5th N.F. wounded O.R.2, 6th N.F. killed O.R.1, 7th N.F. wounded O.R.4 acc. explosion T.M.Fuse. 150th Bde – 4th E.Yorks killed O.R.1, wounded O.R.2. 4th Yorks wounded 2/Lt.D.J.E. Lamb 5th Yorks attd 26/7/17, O.R.2 inc. 1 gas. 5th Yorks wounded 2/Lt.J.H.E. Winston at duty 25/7/17. 5th D.L.I. wounded 2/Lt.R.W.Wilkinson-gas-26/7/17.	
	27		Casualties – 250th Bde RFA wounded O.R.3. 149th Bde – 7th N.F. killed O.R.1, wounded 2/Lt.R.H.Peckston 26/7/17, O.R.2. 150th Bde – 5th D.L.I. wounded 2/Lt.H.V.Proud 27/7/17, O.R.10. No.150 M.G.Coy O.R.1 gas.	
	28		Casualties – 250th Bde RFA wounded O.R.1. 149th Bde – 4th N.F. wounded O.R.3 (gas). 5th N.F. wounded O.R.1. 151st Bde – 8th D.L.I. wounded O.R.1. 9th D.L.I. wounded O.R.6 inc. 5 gas. No.151 M.G.Coy wounded O.R.1 gas.	
	29		Casualties – 4th N.F. killed O.R.1, wounded O.R.5 inc. 1 gas. 7th N.F. wounded O.R.1. 5th Borders wounded O.R.8, missing believed killed O.R.1. 9th D.L.I. wounded 2/Lt.C.B.Jameson at duty, No.151 M.G.Coy wounded O.R.1. 7th Durh.L.I. (Pnrs) wounded O.R.14 (gas).	
	30		Casualties – 5th N.F. wounded 2/Lt.F.Nesbit gun suspected. 5th Borders killed O.R.3, wounded O.R.3. 9th D.L.I. killed O.R.1. 7th Durh.L.I. Pnrs wounded O.R.3 gas shell.	

Army Form C. 2118.

50TH DIVISION.

ADMINISTRATIVE WAR DIARY or INTELLIGENCE SUMMARY

(Erase heading not required.)

JULY 1917.

Instructions regarding War Diaries and Intelligence Summaries are contained in F. S. Regs., Part II. and the Staff Manual respectively. Title Pages will be prepared in manuscript.

Place	Date	Hour	Summary of Events and Information	Remarks and references to Appendices
	JULY 30 (Contd)		Casualties - 4th E.Yorks wounded O.R.1 (S.I.W.). 5th Durh.L.I. missing O.R.2.	
	31		Casualties - 446th Fld Coy RE wounded O.R.1. 5th N.F. wounded O.R.1. 9th Durh.L.I. Killed O.R.2, wounded O.R.2.	

Confidential.

50th Division

Administrative Staff

War Diary

From

1st August 1917.

To

31st August 1917.

Volume XXVIII.

Original

Army Form C. 2118.

50TH DIVISION.   WAR DIARY or INTELLIGENCE SUMMARY   AUGUST 1917.

(Erase heading not required.)

Instructions regarding War Diaries and Intelligence Summaries are contained in F. S. Regs., Part II. and the Staff Manual respectively. Title Pages will be prepared in manuscript.

Place	Date	Hour	Summary of Events and Information	Remarks and references to Appendices
Near BOISLEUX AU MONT – S.17.a.8.4.	AUG: 1			
	2.		Casualties – 151st Bde – 8th D.L.I. wounded O.R.1.	
			Casualties – 446th Field Coy RE killed O.R.2, wounded O.R.1.	
			151st Bde – 6th D.L.I. wounded 2/Lt.W.F.Dunne on 1st, O.R.1. 9th D.L.I. wounded O.R.1.	
			7th D.L.I.– wounded O.R.1 (gas).	
	3.		Casualties – Divl T.Ms – Wounded O.R.1 (gas).	
			50th D.A.C – wounded O.R.1.	
			149th Bde – 5th N.F. wounded O.R.2 (gas). 149 M.G.Coy killed O.R.1, wounded O.R.3.	
			151st Bde – 6th D.L.I. wounded O.R.2. 8th D.L.I. wounded O.R.5 (inc. 1 gas; 1 acc. discharge of rifle).	
			7th D.L.I. –Wounded O.R.1.	
	4.		Casualties – 149th Bde – 5th N.F. wounded O.R.1 (gas). 6th N.F. wounded O.R.1. 7th N.F. killed O.R.1.	
			151st Bde – 6th D.L.I. wounded 2/Lt.P.E.Watson on 4th. 8th D.L.I. killed O.R.3, wounded O.R.1.	
			2/2 N.F.A.– Wounded O.R.1 (gas).	
	5.		Casualties – 150th Bde – 4th E.Yorks wounded O.R.1 (gas bomb). 5th D.L.I. wounded O.R.1.	
			151st Bde – 5th Borders killed O.R.1. No.151 M.G.Coy wounded O.R.1.	
	6.		Casualties – 250 Bde RFA – Wounded O.R.1.	
			446 Fld Coy RE – Killed O.R.1, wounded O.R.2.	
			151st Bde – 8th D.L.I. wounded O.R.1 self-inflicted. No.151 M.G.Coy wounded O.R.1.	
			7/DLI Pnrs – Wounded O.R.2.	
	7.		Transfers – 50th Division transferred from VII Corps to VI Corps at Noon on 7/8/17.	
			Casualties – Divl T.Ms – wounded O.R.2 (gas).	
			150th Bde – 4th East Yorks Regt – killed 2/Lt.H.S.Webster on 7th, wounded O.R.2 including 1 at duty.	
			151st Bde – 5th Borders wounded O.R.1 (acc. discharge of revolver). 7th D.L.I. Pnrs wounded O.R.1.	

Army Form C. 2118.

50th. Division.

Instructions regarding War Diaries and Intelligence Summaries are contained in F. S. Regs., Part II. and the Staff Manual respectively. Title Pages will be prepared in manuscript.

WAR DIARY
or
INTELLIGENCE SUMMARY
(Erase heading not required.)

August 1917.

Place	Date	Hour	Summary of Events and Information	Remarks and references to Appendices
	AUG: 8		Casualties - 150th Bde - 4th East Yorks O.R.1 reptd wounded at duty on 7th now rep. wounded. 4th Yorks wounded O.R.1.	
	9		Casualties - 150th Bde - 4th East Yorks wounded O.R.1. 4th Yorks wounded O.R.3 inc. 1 acc. 151st Bde - 5th Border Regt wounded O.R.2 inc. 1 at duty.	
	10		Casualties - 446 Fld Co RE - wounded O.R.1. 150th Bde - 4th Yorks killed O.R.1, wounded O.R.4. 5th D.L.I. wounded O.R.4 inc. 1 self-inflicted at duty, missing (believed prisoners) O.R.2. No.150 M.G.Coy wounded O.R.1. 151st Bde - 6th D.L.I. wounded O.R.1. 7/DLI Pnrs- Wounded O.R.1.	
	11		Casualties - 150th Bde - 5th Yorks killed O.R.1. 5th D.L.I. wounded O.R.1. 151st Bde - 8th D.L.I. killed O.R.1, wounded O.R.1. 9th D.L.I. wounded O.R.2.	
	12		Casualties - 150th Bde - 4th E.Yorks killed O.R.1, wounded O.R.3. 5th D.L.I. wounded O.R.1 self-inflicted. 151st Bde - 6th D.L.I. wounded O.R.1. 8th D.L.I. wounded O.R.3 inc. 2 at duty. 245 M.G.Co - wounded O.R.1.	
	13		Casualties - 149th Bde - 4th N.F. wounded O.R.1. 5th N.F. wounded O.R.1. 7th N.F. wounded O.R.2. 150th Bde - 5th D.L.I. 2/Lt(T/Lt)S.HUNT wounded at duty 13th. 2/2 (Nbn) Fd Ambce - wounded O.R.1.	
	14		Casualties - 149th Bde - 4th N.F. killed O.R.1, wounded O.R.2. 7th N.F. wounded O.R.1. 150th Bde - 4th E.Yorks wounded O.R.3 inc. 1 at duty.	

Army Form C. 2118.

WAR DIARY or INTELLIGENCE SUMMARY

(Erase heading not required.)

50th Division.

August 1917.

Instructions regarding War Diaries and Intelligence Summaries are contained in F.S. Regs., Part II. and the Staff Manual respectively. Title Pages will be prepared in manuscript.

Place	Date	Hour	Summary of Events and Information	Remarks and references to Appendices
	AUG: 15		Casualties - 251 Bde RFA - Killed O.R.2, wounded O.R.1 at duty.	
			149th Bde - 4th N.F. wounded O.R.8 inc. 6 Gas. 5th N.F. wounded O.R.1. 7th N.F. wounded O.R.2, missing O.R.2 did not return from patrol, both believed wounded, wounded 2/Lt.R.A.PRESCOTT on 15th.	
			150th Bde - 5th D.L.I. wounded O.R.1.	
			7/DLI Pnrs - killed 2/Lt.S.WALKER on 15th, O.R.1, wounded O.R.4.	
	16		Casualties - 250 Bde RFA - wounded O.R.1.	
			290 Bde RFA - wounded O.R.2.	
			50th D.A.C. - wounded O.R.4 at duty.	
			149th Bde - 4th N.F. wounded O.R.1. 7th N.F. killed O.R.2. 149 M.G.Co. killed (O.R.1	
			150th Bde - 4th E.Yorks Major T.J.MORRILL rep. missing 28th June 1917, now unofficially rep. wounded and prisoner. 150th T.M.B. wounded O.R.1.	
	17		Casualties - 149th Bde - 4th N.F. wounded O.R.1. 5th N.F. wounded O.R.1. 6th N.F. wounded O.R.1. No.149 M.Gun Coy killed O.R.2, wounded O.R.1.	
			150th Bde - 4th E.Yorks wounded O.R.6. 5th D.L.I. killed O.R.6, wounded O.R.2.	
	18		Casualties - 149th Bde - 4th N.F. wounded O.R.1. 6th N.F. killed O.R.3, wounded O.R.1, missing O.R.1 last seen as one of sentry group at 0.25.d.8.3. 7 p.m. 16th. 7th N.F. wounded O.R.1. 149th T.M.B. wounded O.R.2.	
			150th Bde - 5th D.L.I. killed O.R.1 acc. 150th T.M.B. wounded O.R.2 Gas.	
			151st Bde - 9th D.L.I. wounded O.R.3 acc.	
	19		Casualties - 149th Bde - 4th N.F. wounded O.R.1 at duty.	
			7/DLI Pnrs - wounded O.R.1.	
	20		Casualties - 250 Bde RFA - wounded O.R.2.	
			Divl Sigs - wounded O.R.1 at duty.	
			149th Bde - 5th N.F. wounded O.R.1.	
			150th Bde - 4th Yorks wounded O.R.1.	

2449 Wt. W14957/M90 750,000 1/16 J.B.C. & A. Forms/C.2118/12.

Army Form C. 2118.

50th Division.

WAR DIARY
or
INTELLIGENCE SUMMARY
(Erase heading not required.)

August 1917.

Instructions regarding War Diaries and Intelligence Summaries are contained in F. S. Regs., Part II. and the Staff Manual respectively. Title Pages will be prepared in manuscript.

Place	Date	Hour	Summary of Events and Information	Remarks and references to Appendices
	AUG: 21		Casualties – 149th Bde – 4th N.F. wounded O.R.1. 6th N.F. wounded O.R.1. 151st Bde – 5th Border Regt wounded O.R.3. 9th D.L.I. killed O.R.3, wounded O.R.5., inc. 1 acc.	
	22		Casualties – 7/Fld CoRE – wounded a/Capt J.B.GLUBB on 21st, O.R.1. 149th Bde – 4th N.F. wounded O.R.3. 151st Bde – 6th D.L.I. wounded O.R.1. 8th D.L.I. wounded O.R.2 inc. 1 acc. 9th D.L.I. wounded O.R.1. No.151 M.G.Coy wounded O.R.1. 7/DLI Pnrs – Killed O.R.1, wounded O.R.2.	
	23		Casualties – 7/Fld Co RE– wounded O.R.1. Divl Sig. Co– wounded O.R.1. 149th Bde – 4th N.F. wounded 2/Lt F.G.PEDDIE at duty on 22nd, O.R.2. 151st Bde – 9th D.L.I. wounded O.R.2 inc. 1 at duty.	
	24		Casualties – 251 Bde RFA– wounded O.R.1 at duty. 151st Bde – 6th D.L.I. wounded O.R.1.	
	25		Casualties – 149th Bde – 4th N.F. wounded O.R.1. 6th N.F. killed O.R.1 wounded O.R.1 151st Bde – 6th D.L.I. wounded 2/Lt.T.J.BURTON at duty on 25th, O.R.1.	
	26		Casualties – 250 Bde RFA– wounded O.R.5 inc. 1 at duty. 149th Bde – 6th N.F. wounded O.R.3. 7th N.F. wounded O.R.1. 151st Bde – 8th D.L.I. wounded O.R.2.	
	27		Casualties – Divl T.Ms – wounded O.R.1. 149th Bde – 5th N.F. wounded O.R.3. 6th N.F. wounded O.R.1 acc.	
	28		Casualties – 250 Bde RFA– wounded O.R.2 at duty. 151st Bde – 9th D.L.I. wounded O.R.1.	
	29		Casualties – 150th Bde – 4th E.Yorks wounded O.R.2. 245 M.G.Coy– wounded O.R.1.	

Army Form C. 2118.

WAR DIARY
or INTELLIGENCE SUMMARY

50th Division.

August 1917.

(Erase heading not required.)

Instructions regarding War Diaries and Intelligence Summaries are contained in F. S. Regs., Part II. and the Staff Manual respectively. Title Pages will be prepared in manuscript.

Place	Date	Hour	Summary of Events and Information	Remarks and references to Appendices
	AUG: 30		Casualties - 150th Infy Bde - 4th E.Yorks wounded O.R.1, 4th Yorks wounded 2/Lt.G.R.COLE on 19th.	
			151st Infy Bde - 5th Border Regt wounded O.R.1.	
	31		Casualties - Divl T.Ms - wounded O.R.1 at duty.	
			150th Infy Bde - 4th E.Yorks wounded O.R.1. 5th Durh.L.I. wounded O.R.2.	
			151st Infy Bde - 9th D.L.I. wounded O.R.1 at duty.	

CONFIDENTIAL

50th Division.

Administrative Staff

War Diary

From 1st September 1917

To 30th September 1917.

Volume XXIX.

ORIGINAL

50th DIVISION.
SEPTEMBER, 1917.

ADMINISTRATIVE WAR DIARY or INTELLIGENCE SUMMARY.

Army Form C. 2118.

Place	Date	Hour	Summary of Events and Information	Remarks and references to Appendices
	Septr			
Near BOISLEUX AU-MONT — S.17.a.34.	1		Bt.Maj.A.G.F.Isaao MC, G.S.O.2 this Divn proceeded on 30/8/17 to take up duties of G.S.O.2 10th Corps. Capt.L.W.Kentish, DSO., Royal Fuslrs, assumed duties of G.S.O.2 this Division on 31/8/17. Casualties :- 251st Bde RFA — wounded O.R.2, includes 1 at duty. 50th T.M.Bgde — wounded O.R.1. 151st Infy Bde— 5th Border Regt — wounded O.R.1; 8th D.L.I. wounded 2/Lt.W.WOODWARD on 1st.	
	2		Casualties — 50th Divnl Ammn Column — wounded O.R.1. 151st Infy Bde — 6th D.L.I. wounded O.R.2; 8th D.L.I. killed O.R.1.	
	3		Casualties — 50th T.M.Bde — wounded O.R.1. 150th Infy Bde — 5th Yorks Regt killed O.R.1. 151st Infy Bde — 8th D.L.I. wounded O.R.3. 7th D.L.I. Pnrs— wounded O.R.2.	
	4		Casualties — 251st Bde RFA — wounded O.R.1. 150th Infy Bde— 4th E.Yorks wounded O.R.1. 7th D.L.I.Pnrs— wounded O.R.1.	
	5		Casualties — 150th Infy Bde — 5th Yorks wounded 2/Lt.T.A.WILLIAMS on 5th, O.R.11 — all Gas. 5th D.L.I. wounded 2/Lt.J.A.BROMLEY on 4th, O.R.3 — gas. 150th T.M.Battery wounded O.R.2 includes 1 Gas. 7th D.L.I.Pnrs — wounded O.R. 10 — gas.	
	6		Casualties — 50th T.M.B. — wounded O.R.4 (inc. 2 gas and 2 acc.). 149th Infy Bde — 4th N.F. wounded O.R.2 (inc.1 gas). 150th Infy Bde — 4th E.Yorks wounded O.R.1. 4th Yorks wounded 2/Lt.R.EDWARDS, 2/Lt.P.L.LEIGH-BREESE (gas), O.R.16 (inc.14 gas). 5th Yorks wounded O.R.9 gas.	

50TH DIVISION.   **SEPTEMBER 1917.**

ADMINISTRATIVE
WAR DIARY
OF
INTELLIGENCE SUMMARY.
(Erase heading not required.)

Army Form C. 2118.

Instructions regarding War Diaries and Intelligence Summaries are contained in F. S. Regs., Part II, and the Staff Manual respectively. Title pages will be prepared in manuscript.

Place	Date	Hour	Summary of Events and Information	Remarks and references to Appendices
	Sept 6 (Con)		150th Infy Bde - 5th D.L.I. killed O.R.1, wounded O.R.2.	
			151st Infy Bde - 6th D.L.I. wounded O.R.1. 5th Border wounded O.R.1 (acc.)	
			7th D.L.I.Pnrs - wounded O.R.2 (gas).	
	7		Casualties -	
			7th Fld Co RE - wounded O.R.2 (gas).	
			149th Infy Bde - 4th N.F. wounded O.R.3 (gas).	
			150th Infy Bde - wounded O.R.1 4th E.Yorks. 4th Yorks wounded O.R.2 (gas).	
	8		Casualties -	
			149th Infy Bde - 4th N.F. O.R. killed 1, wounded O.R.3 (inc. 1 at duty). 5th N.F. wounded O.R.3.	
			150th Infy Bde - 4th E.Yorks wounded O.R.1. 5th D.L.I. wounded O.R.1.	
			7th D.L.I. - wounded O.R.1 (gas).	
	9		Casualties -	
			149th Infy Bde - 7th N.F. wounded O.R.1. 149th M.G.Coy killed O.R.1.	
			150th Infy Bde - 4th E.Yks wounded O.R.2. 5th Yks wounded O.R.1. 5th D.L.I. wounded O.R.2.	
	10		Casualties -	
			149th Infy Bde - 5th N.F. killed O.R.1, wounded 2/Lt. A.P.LETTS, O.R.2. 7th N.F. wounded O.R.1 acc.	
			150th Infy Bde - 4th Yks wounded acc. O.R.1. 5th Yks killed O.R.2.	
	11		Casualties -	
			7th Fld Co RE - wounded O.R.2 (gas).	
			149th Infy Bde - 7th N.F. wounded O.R.1.	
			150th Infy Bde - 4th Yks wounded O.R.2 (gas). 5th D.L.I. wounded O.R.1.	
	12		Casualties -	
			149th Infy Bde - 5th N.F. wounded O.R.3.	
			150th Infy Bde - 4th E.Yks killed O.R.2, wounded O.R.3. No.150 T.M.B. killed O.R.3, wounded O.R.1.	
	13		Casualties -	
			149th Infy Bde - 6th N.F. wounded O.R.1.	

Army Form C. 2118.

50th DIVISION.   SEPTR 1917.

ADMINISTRATIVE WAR DIARY or INTELLIGENCE SUMMARY.

(Erase heading not required.)

Instructions regarding War Diaries and Intelligence Summaries are contained in F. S. Regs., Part II. and the Staff Manual respectively. Title pages will be prepared in manuscript.

Place	Date	Hour	Summary of Events and Information	Remarks and references to Appendices
	Sept. 14		Casualties - 250th Bde RFA - wounded O.R.2. 50/Div Signals - wounded O.R.1. 149th Infy Bde - 4th N.F. killed O.R.2. wounded O.R.1. 5th N.F. wounded O.R.1. 150th Infy Bde - No.150 T.M.B. wounded O.R.2(acc). 151st Infy Bde - 8th D.L.I. wounded O.R.1.	
	15		A minor operation by three Companies 9th D.L.I. and 1 Coy 8th D.L.I. nr CHERISY. Casualties - 7th Fld Co RE - wounded O.R.1. 149th Infy Bde - No.149 M.G.Coy wounded O.R.1.	
	16		Casualties - operation near CHERISY 15th and 16th. 149th Infy Bde - 4th N.F. killed Lt.J.HOPE-WALLACE, wounded O.R.1. 7th N.F. wounded O.R.1. 150th T.M.B. killed O.R.1. wounded O.R.4. 150th Infy Bde - 150 T.M.B. wounded O.R.4. 151st Infy Bde - 6/DLI killed O.R.1. wounded O.R.4. 8th DLI wounded Capt.H.McNIFF, O.R.10. 9th DLI killed 2/Lt.H.HALL, MC, O.R.4. wounded 2/Lt.H.STRACHAN, 2/Lt(A/Capt)T.HARKER, Lt_A/Capt) E.C.PALMER, Lt.G.H.VOS-UTERLLNEGE. 8th Bn attd, Lt.G.A.MARSHALL, 8th Bn attd at duty, O.R. killed 4, wounded 18 (inc. 8 at duty) Missing blvd killed 3. 151st T.M.B. wounded 2/Lt.G.L. PARKINSON, 9th DLI attd, killed O.R.1. wounded O.R.4. 250th Bde RFA - wounded O.R.1. T.M.Bde - Y/50 Btty wounded Lt.E.S.HURST, killed O.R.4. wounded O.R.2. 7th Fld Co RE - wounded O.R.2. 50/Div.Signals - wounded O.R.1. Bvt.Lt-Col.H.KARSLAKE, CMG., DSO., R.A. - From G.S.O.1 this Divn to G.S.O.1 4th Division.	
	17		Casualties.- 151st Infy Bde - 8th D.L.I. killed O.R.1. wounded O.R.2. (acc. discharge of a revolver). 151 M.G.Coy wounded O.R.1. Bt.Lt-Col. E.C.ANSTEY, R.A. - from attd this Divn to be G.S.O.1.	
	18		Casualties.- 151st Infy Bde - 5th Border Regt wounded O.R.1 acc. 151 M.G.Co. wounded O.R.1 at duty.	

ADMINISTRATIVE WAR DIARY of INTELLIGENCE SUMMARY.

(Erase heading not required.)

Army Form C. 2118.

50th DIVISION. **SEPTR 1917.**

Instructions regarding War Diaries and Intelligence Summaries are contained in F. S. Regs., Part II. and the Staff Manual respectively. Title pages will be prepared in manuscript.

Place	Date	Hour	Summary of Events and Information	Remarks and references to Appendices
	Sept 19		Casualties -	
			149th Infy Bde - 5th N.F. Killed 2/Lt.W.E.S.POOLE, O.R.1, wounded O.R.1.	
			150th Infy Bde - 5/DLI wounded OR1 acc. 6th N.F. wounded OR1.	
			151st Infy Bde - 5th Border Regt wounded O.R.2. 9/DLI wounded O.R.2 inc. 1 at duty.	
	20		Casualties -	
			50/Div Signals - wounded O.R.1 acc.	
			149th Infy Bde - 6/N.F. Killed O.R.1, wounded O.R.1.	
			151st Infy Bde - 5th Border Regt wounded O.R.2. 151 M.G.Coy wounded O.R.1.	
			7th D.L.I. Pnrs - wounded O.R.1 at duty.	
	21		Casualties -	
			149th Infy Bde - 5th N.F. killed O.R.1, wounded 2/Lt.H.ARMSTRONG, O.R.4, inc. 2 acc. by kicking an old bomb in long grass.	
			151st Infy Bde - 5th Border Regt wounded O.R.1. 9th DLI wounded O.R.1.	
			7th DLI Pnrs - Killed O.R.1.	
			RAMC - 2/2 Fd Ambce - wounded O.R.1. 1/3rd Fd Ambce - wounded O.R.1.	
	22		Casualties -	
			50/Div Signals - wounded O.R.1 at duty.	
			149th Infy Bde - 4th N.F. attd 5th N.F. wounded 2/Lt.F.S.SHARLAND.	
			151st Infy Bde - 8th DLI wounded O.R.2. 8th DLI wounded 2/Lt.H.B.C.WATT	
	23		Casualties -	
			150th Infy Bde - 4th E.Yks wounded O.R.1. 5th Yks Killed O.R.1, wounded O.R.8 inc. 1 at duty.	
			151st Infy Bde - 6th DLI Killed O.R.1, wounded O.R.1.	
			Major A.G.B.BOURNE, R.H.A. attd proceeded to 11th Division as G.S.O.2.	
	24		Casualties -	
			7th Fld Co RE - wounded O.R.1.	
			151st Infy Bde - 6th DLI wounded O.R.2 inc. 1 at duty. 8th DLI wounded O.R.2 inc. 1 acc.	

ADMINISTRATIVE WAR DIARY or INTELLIGENCE SUMMARY.

Army Form C. 2118.

50th DIVISION.   SEPTR 1917.

Place	Date	Hour	Summary of Events and Information	Remarks and references to Appendices
	Sept 25		Casualties :-	
			150th Infy Bde - 4th E.Yks wounded O.R.4 (inc. 1 at duty). 4th Yks wounded O.R.1 at duty.	
			5th D.L.I. wounded O.R.1.	
			151st Infy Bde - 5th Borders wounded O.R.2 (acc) premature burst of bomb. 6th DLI killed O.R.1.	
			8th DLI wounded O.R.1.	
			7th DLI PHrs - killed O.R.1.	
	26		Casualties :-	
			251st Bde RFA - killed Major F.M.ARMSTRONG, wounded 2/Lt.S.DICKINSON, wounded at duty 2/Lt.	
			R.H.BAILEY, wounded O.R.2.	
			150th Infy Bde - 4th Yks wounded O.R.2 (gas).	
			151st Infy Bde - 9th DLI killed O.R.1, wounded O.R.4. No.151 M.G.Co wounded O.R.1.	
	27		Casualties :-	
			150th Infy Bde - 4th Yks wounded O.R.1 (gas). 5th DLI wounded O.R.3 inc. 1 at duty.	
			151st Infy Bde - 5th Border Regt wounded O.R.3. 6th DLI wounded O.R.3 inc. 1 at duty.	
			9th DLI wounded O.R.3.	
	28		Casualties :-	
			150th Infy Bde - 5th DLI killed O.R.1, wounded O.R.1, wounded acc. 2/Lt.J.YOUNG and Lt.O.J.	
			WILLIAMS, latter at duty. 1 O.R. bursting of a Very pistol when fired.	
			151st Infy Bde - 9th DLI wounded O.R.1. 5th Border Regt. wounded 2/LT.O.GILLESPIE.	
	29		Casualties :-	
			181st Co RE - O.R. wounded 1.	
			150th Infy Bde - 4th E.Yks wounded O.R.1 acc.	
	30		Casualties :-	
			149th Infy Bde - 7th N.F. wounded O.R.3.	
			150th Infy Bde - 4th E.Yorks killed O.R.1, wounded O.R.2.	

CONFIDENTIAL

ORIGINAL

Vol 31

50th Division
Administrative Staff
War Diary

From :- 1st October 1917

To :- 31st October 1917

Volume XXX.

50TH DIVISION.

ADMINISTRATIVE WAR DIARY or INTELLIGENCE SUMMARY.

OCTOBER 1917.

Army Form C. 2118.

Instructions regarding War Diaries and Intelligence Summaries are contained in F. S. Regs., Part II. and the Staff Manual respectively. Title pages will be prepared in manuscript.

(Erase heading not required.)

Place	Date	Hour	Summary of Events and Information	Remarks and references to Appendices
BOISLEUX-AU-MONT.	OCTR 1		Casualties - 50th Divl Trench Mortars killed O.R.1. 149th Infantry Bde – 4th N.F. wounded O.R.1 gas. 5th N.F. wounded O.R.1. 7th N.F. wounded O.R.3. 150th Infantry Bde– 4th East Yorks wounded O.R.2. 5th Yorks wounded O.R.1. No:245 M.Gun Coy – Killed O.R.2.	
	2		Casualties - 149th Infantry Bde – 7th N.F. wounded O.R.1. Killed 150th do = 4th E.Yorks 2/Lt.R.SNOWDON/O.R.1. 5th Yorks wounded O.R.1. 2/Lt.G.S.BAILEY, 7th Duke of Wellington's West Riding Regt attd. 7th Durh.L.I. Pnrs – Wounded at duty 2/Lt.J.H.R.MASSEY. Commdg 1/1st Cambridgeshire Regt, Major (T/Lt-Col.) E.P.A.RIDDELL, D.S.O./assumed command 149th Infantry Bde with rank of T/Brig-General vice Brig-Gen.H.C.REES, DSO. invalided.	
	3		Casualties - 149th Infantry Bde – 6th N.F. wounded O.R.1. 7th N.F. wounded O.R.2. 150th Infantry Bde – 5th Yorks wounded O.R.1.	
	4		Casualties - 50th Divl Trench Mortars – wounded O.R.1. 149th Infantry Bde – 7th N.F. wounded O.R.1. 150th Infantry Bde – 5th Yorks wounded O.R.1. 5th Durh.L.I. wounded O.R.1.	
	5			
ACHIET-LE-PETIT.	6		Division, less Artillery, moved from Camp near BOISLEUX-AU-MONT, near CHERISY, to ACHIET-LE-PETIT Rest Area. Divl H.Q. at ACHIET LE PETIT. 149th Bde at GOURCELLES LE COMTE. 150th Bde at ACHIET LE PETIT. 151st Bde at GOMIECOURT.	

Army Form C. 2118.

WAR DIARY
or
INTELLIGENCE SUMMARY.

(Erase heading not required.)

Place	Date	Hour	Summary of Events and Information	Remarks and references to Appendices
ACHIET-LE-PETIT.	6 (Contd)		Divl Artillery H.Q. – ACHIET LE PETIT – remainder with 51st Division in Line. No:245 M.Gun Coy – ACHIET LE PETIT. R.E. H.Q. – ACHIET LE PETIT. 7th D.L.I. Pnrs – COURCELLES LE COMTE. Divl Train – ACHIET LE PETIT. No:23 Divnl Supply Column – BEAUMETZ. 1/1st Nbn Fld Ambce – GOMIECOURT. 2/2nd Nbn Fld Ambce – COURCELLES LE COMTE. 1/3rd Nbn Fld Ambce – ½ mile West of ACHIET LE GRAND. A. V. C. – COURCELLES LE COMTE.	
	7		Casualties :- 50th Divl Trench Mortars wounded O.R.3 inc. 1 at duty.	
	8		Casualties :- 50th Divl Trench Mortars wounded O.R.2 inc. 1 at duty.	
	9			
	10			
	11			
	12			
	13			
	14			
	15			
	16			
	17			

Army Form C. 2118.

WAR DIARY
or
INTELLIGENCE SUMMARY.
(Erase heading not required.)

Instructions regarding War Diaries and Intelligence Summaries are contained in F. S. Regs., Part II. and the Staff Manual respectively. Title pages will be prepared in manuscript.

Place	Date	Hour	Summary of Events and Information	Remarks and references to Appendices
LEDERZEELE	18		Division, on transfer to Fifth Army, moved to ZEGGERS CAPPELLE AREA, and is temporarily under 2nd Corps, with Div.H.Q. including C.R.E., A.D.M.S., Divl Train, at LEDERZEELE,* 149th Infy Bde ARNEKE, 150th Infy Bde with 7th N.F. and 7th D.L.I. Pnrs at RUBROUCK, 151st Infy Bde ERINGHEM. (* less 7th N.F. and 7th D.L.I.)	
	19			
PROVEN	20		On transfer of Division from 2nd to 14th Corps, Fifth Army,; Divl H.Q. moved to PROVEN CENTRAL CAMP, 149th Infy Bde to P.5 AREA, PROVEN, 151st Infy Bde to ARNEKE AREA. Brig-Gen.N.J.G.CAMERON, C.M.G., Cameron Highrs, G.O.C. 151st Infantry Bde, proceeded to assume command of 49th Division, with temp. rank of Major General. Lt-Col.C.J.MARTIN, D.S.O., H.L.I. assumed command of 151st Infantry Bde. Colonel R.BURRITT, Canadian Local Forces, attd G.S., Divl H.Q. proceeded to take up duties of G.S.O.2, 12th Division.	
	21		150th Infy Bde from RUBROUCK to PROVEN.	
	22		151st Infantry Bde from ARNEKE to PROVEN. 50th Divisional Artillery from VI Corps Area to PROVEN AREA. Transfer of Division to 14th Corps, Fifth Army, completed.	
	23			
ELVERDINGHE	24		Division moved into line in relief of 17th Division, with Divl H.Q., C.R.A., C.R.E., A.D.M.S., and D.A.D.O.S. at ELVERDINGHE CHATEAU. 149th Infy Bde in Line. 150th Infy Bde WHITE MILL, ELVERDINGHE. 151st Infy Bde SERINGAPATAM CAMP X.28.d.5.3.; 7th Durh.L.I. Pnrs near WHITE MILL, ELVERDINGHE. Divl Train A.12.c.1.4. (Ref. Sheets D,27,28 1/40,000).	
	25		Bombs dropped in vicinity of ELVERDINGHE. Casualties - 250th Bde R.F.A. - killed 2/Lt.T.N.ASKWITH, wounded O.R.2. 151st Infy Bde - 6th Durh.L.I. wounded 2/Lt.R.W.RAGG, O.R.13.	

Army Form C. 2118.

(4).

WAR DIARY
or
INTELLIGENCE SUMMARY.
(Erase heading not required.)

Instructions regarding War Diaries and Intelligence Summaries are contained in F. S. Regs., Part II. and the Staff Manual respectively. Title pages will be prepared in manuscript.

Place	Date	Hour	Summary of Events and Information	Remarks and references to Appendices
ELVERDINGHE	26		ATTACK. O.R.8.	
			Casualties –	
			Divl Artillery = 250 Bde RFA killed O.R.2, wounded 2/Lt.A.F.DUNN / 251st Bde RFA killed O.R.2, wounded O.R.2.	
			149th Infy Bde = 7th N.F. 2/Lt. (A/Capt.) R.A.BROWN wounded.	
			150th Infy Bde = 4th E.Yorks killed Capt.K.A.WILSON-BARKWORTH. 5th Yorks wounded O.R.4.	
			151st Infy Bde = 6th Durh.L.I. wounded O.R.10 inc. 1 at duty. 8th D.L.I. wounded Capt.R.H. WHARRIER and 1 O.R.. 9th D.L.I. wounded O.R.2 accidental.	
			7th D.L.I. Pnrs– Killed O.R.3, wounded O.R.4.	
			447th Nbn Fld Co RE – wounded O.R.3.	
			1/1st Nbn Fld Ambce – wounded O.R.1.	
			2/2nd Nbn Fld Ambce – wounded O.R.4.	
	27		Casualties –	
			Divl Artillery = 250 Nbn Bde RFA O.R. killed 4, wounded 3 inc 2 gas. 251 Nbn Bde killed 2, wounded 6.	
			Royal Engineers = 50th Divl Signal Co RE O.R. wounded 1.	
			149th Infy Bgde = 4th N.F. wounded 2/Lts R.WOOD, A.W.LEARY, H.B.BELL 7th N.F. attd, A/Capt. G.E.CHARLEWOOD, wounded O.R. 123. 5th N.F. wounded 2/Lt.F.W.HILL, 2/Lt. T.M.SCOTT 6th N.F. attd, O.R. 143. 6th N.F. wounded O.R. 30. 7th N.F. wounded O.R.118. 149 M.G.Coy wounded 2/Lt.C.M.G.WARD MGC attd, O.R. 10.	
			150th Infy Bde = 4th Yorkshire Regt wounded 2/Lt.R.K.SMITH, O.R.2, Missing O.R.1.	
			151st Infy Bde = 6th D.L.I. O.R. killed 1, wounded 9. 9th D.L.I. 2/Lt.T.W.ROWLANDS wounded at duty, O.R. killed 5 wounded 2 (inc. 4 at duty).	
			7th D.L.I. Pnrs = wounded 4 O.R.	
	28		Casualties –	
			250th Bde RFA = wounded 1 O.R. at duty.	
			149th Infy Bde = 4th N.F. 2/Lts J.R.RUDDOCK and R.A.B.SIMPSON wounded, 17 O.R. killed. 5th N.F. 2/Lt(A/Capt) E.BISSET and 2/Lts A.R.PARK and W.CARR wounded, 2/Lt.P.SHAW 6th NF attd wounded and missing. 20 O.R. killed,	

(5).

Army Form C. 2118.

WAR DIARY
or
INTELLIGENCE SUMMARY.
(Erase heading not required.)

Instructions regarding War Diaries and Intelligence Summaries are contained in F. S. Regs., Part II. and the Staff Manual respectively. Title pages will be prepared in manuscript.

Place	Date	Hour	Summary of Events and Information	Remarks and references to Appendices
ELVERDINGHE	28 (Contd)		Casualties —	

149th Infy Bde (Contd) — 6th N.F. 2/Lt. R.S.GREENFIELD MC 7th N.F. attd wounded, 10 O.R. killed.
7th N.F. officers killed Hon Capt & Qr-Mr R.P.NEVILLE MC, Lieut. A.P. STRONG, 2/Lt.J.H.SHAW 6th N.F. attd, Lt.H.K.TEMPERLEY 6th N.F. attd, 2/Lt.R.THOMPSON MC 6th N.F. attd, Lt.R.L.GUY 6th N.F. attd, Lt.F.A. BROWN 6th N.F. attd, Lt.S.D.S.TUCKER 6th N.F. attd, 2/Lt.D.L.YOUNG 4th N.F. attd, 2/Lt.G.D.DOUGET 4th N.F. attd.
officers wounded and missing — 2/Lt.J.A.SCOTT, 4th N.F. attd. killed O.R.30.
No:149 M.Gun Coy — Lt.F.W.BRICKMAN wounded, O.R. 5 killed, 10 wounded, 1 missing.
149th T.Mortar Battery — O.R.1 wounded.

150th Infy Bde — 4th Yorkshire Regt 2/Lt.R.K.SMITH wounded, 13 O.R. wounded.
5th Yorkshire Regt Lt(A/Capt)G.F.G.REES and 2/Lt.J.D.BRYDON wounded, 3 O.R. W.
5th Durham L.Infy O.R. killed 12, wounded 10.

151st Infy Bde — 9th Durh.L.Infy O.R. killed 2.
7th D.L.I. Pnrs — O.R. killed 3, wounded 66 (inc. 50 gas shell).
1/1st Nbn Fld Ambce — O.R. wounded 2 inc. 1 gas shell.
1/3rd Nbn Fld Ambce — O.R. wounded 2 " 1 "

| | 29 | | Casualties — | |

Divnl Artillery — 250th Bde RFA — 2/Lt.P.W.BOBBYER wounded (gas), O.R. killed 1, wounded 4 (inc. 1 at duty and 2 gas shell).
Divnl R.Engineers — 447th Fld Co RE — O.R. wounded 1.
149th Infy Bde — 4th N.F. — 2/Lts D.A.SMITH and W.RUDDY killed, 2/Lts R.G.RAYNER and H.STOBBS missing. O.R. wounded 38, missing 108.
5th N.F. — 2/Lt.W.G.VERRILL 2nd NF attd killed. Lieut F.HASWELL, 2/Lt.R.GRAY and Lt.H.T.PAPE wounded (Lt.Pape at duty), 2/Lts W.C.MAY and W.W.WILKIN missing. O.R. killed 40, wounded 6, missing 230.
6th N.F. — O.Rs killed 9, wounded 7, missing 5.
7th N.F. — O.Rs killed 14, wounded 31, missing 41.
No:149 M.Gun Coy — Lt.E.W.BRICKMAN pre rep W now rep "K".

Army Form C. 2118.

(6).

WAR DIARY
or
INTELLIGENCE SUMMARY.
(Erase heading not required.)

Instructions regarding War Diaries and Intelligence Summaries are contained in F. S. Regs., Part II. and the Staff Manual respectively. Title pages will be prepared in manuscript.

Place	Date	Hour	Summary of Events and Information	Remarks and references to Appendices
ELVERDINGHE	29 Con'd		Casualties -	
			149th Infy Bde (Con'd) - Bde H.Q. - 4th Cl. Chap. The Rev P.LOOBY, CF "M" (R.C.).	
			150th Infy Bde - 4th Yorks Rgt - Lt(A/Capt)H.M.C.I.HOLLINGWORTH and 2/Lt.T.S.GEORGE wounded.	
			5th Yorks Rgt - O.Rs killed 6, wounded 26.	
			5th Durh.L.I. - O.Rs killed 12, wounded 39.	
			151st Infy Bde - 2/Lt.R.J.STOCKDALE wounded at duty.	
			6th Durh.L.I. - O.Rs wounded 7, missing 11.	
			8th Durh.L.I. - O.Rs wounded 1, missing 1.	
			9th Durh.L.I. - 2/Lt.J.DICK killed, 2/Lt.C.D.B.CLUFF, 8th attd 9th Bn. "W".	
			O.Rs killed 6, wounded 20, missing 2.	
			7th D.L.I. Pnrs - O.Rs 2 wounded (1 gas shell).	
			1/1st Nbn Fd Ambce - O.Rs wounded 1.	
	30		Casualties -	
			Divnl Arty - 250th Bde RFA - Lt.J.HOPWOOD wounded (gas) at duty. O.Rs killed 1, wounded 11 inc. 7 gas and 4 at duty.	
			Divnl R.E. - 446th Fld Coy - O.Rs wounded 2 inc. 1 at duty.	
			Divl Sig. Coy - O.Rs wounded 2 inc. 1 at duty.	
			150th Infy Bde - 4th East Yorks - Lt(A/Capt) M.HURTLEY wounded.	
			4th Yorks Rgt - O.Rs killed 1, wounded 21.	
			5th Yorks Rgt - 2/Lt.A.PHILIP wounded, O.R. wounded 16.	
			5th Durh.L.I. - O.Rs killed 2, wounded 24.	
			150 M.G. Coy - O.Rs killed 1, wounded 6.	
			150 T.M.Bty - O.Rs wounded 1.	
			151st Infy Bde - 6th Durh.L.I. - Lt.F.W.THE wounded, O.R. wounded 3.	
			9th Durh.L.I. - O.Rs missing 3.	
			7/D.L.I. Pnrs - O.Rs wounded 30 (inc. 21 gas), missing 3.	
			1/3 Nbn F.Amb. - O.R. wounded 4 inc. 3 gas.	
			1/1 do - O.R. wounded 1 gas.	
			2/2nd do - O.R. wounded 1 gas.	
			2 O.R. 4th N.F. prev. rep. "M" now rejoined.	

(7).

WAR DIARY
or
INTELLIGENCE SUMMARY.
(Erase heading not required.)

Army Form C. 2118.

Instructions regarding War Diaries and Intelligence Summaries are contained in F. S. Regs., Part II. and the Staff Manual respectively. Title pages will be prepared in manuscript.

Place	Date	Hour	Summary of Events and Information	Remarks and references to Appendices
ELVERDINGHE	31		Casualties —	
			250th Nbn Bde RFA — O.Rs killed 2, wounded 3 (inc. 2 gas).	
			251st Nbn Bde RFA — O.Rs wounded 1.	
			Divnl R.E.—	
			447 Nbn Fd Co RE — O.Rs wounded 1.	
			149th Infantry Bde.—	
			5th N.Fus — O.Rs wounded 2.	
			150th Infantry Bde.—	
			4th E.Yorks Regt — 2/Lt.H.B.DREWITT killed, 2/Lts E.LAWRENCE and E.W.ALLCHORN wounded, O.Rs killed 3, wounded 15.	
			4th Yorks Regt — Lt.H.C.HALE wounded, O.Rs killed 7, wounded 24.	
			5th Durham L.Infy — 2/Lt.G.H.BARKER wounded, O.Rs killed 1, wounded 27 (inc. 16 gas) Missing believed killed O.R.1.	
			No:150 M.Gun Coy — 2/Lt.G.R.ACTON wounded, O.Rs wounded 6.	
			151st Infantry Bde.— wounded O.R.2 inc. 1 S.I.W.	
			5th Border Regt — wounded Lt.W.L.Campbell and 2/Lt.P.Walker, O.Rs wounded 2. missing 1.	
			7th Durh.L.I. Pnrs — O.Rs killed 1, wounded 5.	
			Divnl Train — O.Rs wounded 1.	
			Divnl Ammn Column — O.Rs wounded 1.	
			1/3 Nbn Fd Ambce — wounded 2/Lt.R.JARRET and 6 O.Rs.	
			244th Divl E.Coy. —	
			4th N.F. — 18 O.R. prev rep "M" now rep "K".	
			do — 3 " " " "M" " " "W".	
			do — 24 " " " "M" " " "Unwounded".	
			5th N.F. — 5 " " " "M" " " since-rejoined.	

CONFIDENTIAL

ORIGINAL

50th Division

Administrative Staff

War Diary

From :- 1st November 1917

To :- 30th November 1917.

Volume XXXI

Army Form C. 2118.

50TH DIVISION.

ADMINISTRATIVE WAR DIARY or INTELLIGENCE SUMMARY.

(Erase heading not required.)

NOVEMBER 1917.

Instructions regarding War Diaries and Intelligence Summaries are contained in F. S. Regs, Part II. and the Staff Manual respectively. Title pages will be prepared in manuscript.

Place	Date	Hour	Summary of Events and Information	Remarks and references to Appendices
ELVERDINGHE.	1		Casualties -	
			50th Divnl Artillery.-	
			250th (Nbn) Bde RFA — O.Rs killed 2 wounded 4.	
			251st (Nbn) Bde RFA — O.Rs wounded 1.	
			50th Divnl R.E.-	
			7th Field Coy R.E. — O.Rs wounded 1.	
			446th (Nbn) Fd Co RE — O.Rs wounded 4.	
			447th (Nbn) Fd Co RE — Lt.T.Forster wounded 31/10/17.	
			Divnl Signal Coy R.E.— O.Rs wounded 3.	
			149th Infantry Brigade.-	
			4th North'd Fuslrs — Wounded Capt.R.W.Cranage (50th Divl Sig.Co.RE) "gas" 31/10/17, O.R.1.	
			6th do — Wounded O.Rs 1.	
			7th do — O.Rs 6 killed, 51 wounded 12 missing.	
			150th Infantry Brigade.-	
			4th East Yorkshire R.— 2/Lt.W.Stamper wounded (gas) 31/10/17.	
			5th Durham L.Infy — O.Rs 5 missing.	
			No:150 M.Gun Coy — Lt(A/Capt) G.Hudson and 2/Lt W.J.S.Ranken, M.G.C. wounded gas 31/10/17, O.Rs 1 killed, 1 missing.	
			151st Infantry Brigade.-	
			5th Border Regiment — 2/Lt(A/Capt) & Adjt J.Thomson killed 31/10/17, O.Rs 10 wounded.	
			6th Durham L.Infy — O.Rs 1 wounded.	
			8th do — O.Rs 1 wounded.	
			9th do — O.Rs 1 wounded.	
			7th Durh.L.I. Pnrs — 2/Lt(A/Capt) T.F.Forster killed 31/10/17. 2/Lt(A/Capt) H.Stewart and 2/Lt(A/Capt) W.A.Ridout wounded 31/10/17.	
			50th Divnl Train — O.Rs 1 wounded.	
			1/1st (Nbn) Fd Amboe — O.Rs 9 wounded.	
			M.M.Police — O.Rs 2 wounded.	
			No:149 M.G.Coy — 8 O.R. prev. rep. "W" now rep. "unwounded"	
			4th North'd F. — 1 O.R. prev. rep. "M" 28/10/17 now rep. "rejoined".	

50th DIVISION.

ADMINISTRATIVE
WAR DIARY
or
INTELLIGENCE SUMMARY.
(Erase heading not required.)

Army Form C. 2118.

NOVR. 1917.

Instructions regarding War Diaries and Intelligence Summaries are contained in F. S. Regs., Part II. and the Staff Manual respectively. Title pages will be prepared in manuscript.

Place	Date	Hour	Summary of Events and Information	Remarks and references to Appendices
ELVERDINGHE		2	CASUALTIES.	
			50th Divnl Artillery.	
			250th (Nbn) Bde RFA — O.Rs 6 killed, 5 wounded.	
			251st (Nbn) Bde RFA — O.Rs 1 wounded.	
			50th Divnl R.E.	
			446th (Nbn) Fld Co RE — O.Rs 1 wounded.	
			447th (Nbn) Fld Co RE — O.Rs 2 killed, 1 wounded.	
			149th Infantry Bgde.	
			4th North'd Fuslrs — Killed 2/Lts S.C.Smith and H.L.Weir 31/10/17.	
			6th do — Killed O.Rs 6.	
			7th do — Wounded 2/Lt.R.G.Soper 31/10/17.	
			150th Infantry Bgde.	
			4th East Yorks Rgt — O.Rs killed 3, wounded 13.	
			4th Yorkshire Regt — O.Rs killed 1, wounded 10.	
			5th do — Wounded Lt.H.Ganis 30/10/17 and 6 O.R.	
			5th Durham L.Infy — O.Rs wounded 6, missing 1.	
			No:150 M.Gun Coy — Wounded at duty Lt.A.L.Jenner and 2/Lt.P.H.Grimshaw, O.Rs killed 1, wounded 9.	
			151st Infantry Bgde.	
			6th Durham L.Infy — O.Rs wounded 2, missing 3.	
			8th do — O.Rs wounded 1.	
			7th Durh.L.I. Pnrs — O.Rs wounded 8.	
			1/1st (Nbn) Fld Amboe — O.Rs wounded 3.	
			1/3rd do — O.Rs wounded 1.	
			2/2nd do — Wounded Capt.J.Dunbar and 4 O.Rs.	
		3	50th Divnl Artillery.	
			250th (Nbn) Bde RFA — 2/Lt.G.H.Wilson and 33 O.Rs wounded 2/11/17.	
			251st do — 2 O.Rs wounded.	
			50th Divnl R.E. —	
			Divnl Signal Coy RE — 2/Lt(A/Lt) W.R.Stewart R.E. and 9 O.R. wounded 2/11/17.	
			149th Infantry Bgde.	
			6th North'd Fuslrs — 1 O.R. wounded.	

50th DIVISION.

NOVR 1917.

Instructions regarding War Diaries and Intelligence Summaries are contained in F.S. Regs., Part II. and the Staff Manual respectively. Title pages will be prepared in manuscript.

ADMINISTRATIVE
WAR DIARY
or
INTELLIGENCE SUMMARY.
(Erase heading not required.)

Army Form C. 2118.

Place	Date	Hour	Summary of Events and Information	Remarks and references to Appendices
ELVERDINGHE	3 Contd		CASUALTIES.	
			150th Infantry Brigade.—	
			4th East Yorks Regt — 2 O.R. wounded.	
			7th Durh.L.I. Pnrs — 13 O.R. wounded.	
			1/1st (Nbn) M.V.Sect.— 1 O.R. wounded.	
			151st Infantry Bgde.—	
			5th Border Regiment — 2/Lt(A/Capt) E.L.Henderson, Scott.R. attd wounded 3/11/17, O.Rs wounded 6.	
			8th Durham L.Infy — O.Rs 1 killed, 1 wounded, 3 missing.	
			No:151 M.Gun Coy — 1 O.R. wounded.	
			Lt.J.Hopwood, 250th Bde RFA prev. rep. "W" at duty now rep. "W".	
		4	50th Divnl Artillery.—	
			250th (Nbn) Bde RFA — O.Rs wounded 18.	
			251st do — O.Rs wounded 4.	
			50th Divnl R.E.—	
			Divl Sig. Coy R.E.— 8 O.R. wounded.	
			149th Infantry Bgde.— 2/Lt.V.G.Rowe wounded 4/11/17.	
			7th North'd Fuslrs — 1 O.R. wounded.	
			150th Infantry Bgde.—	
			4th East Yorks Regt — 1 O.R. wounded.	
			151st Infantry Bgde.—	
			5th Border Regiment — 2 O.R. wounded.	
			6th Durham L.Infy — 5 O.R. wounded.	
			8th do — 6 O.R. wounded.	
			9th do — 1 O.R. wounded.	
			No:151 M.Gun Coy — 1 O.R. wounded.	
			7th Durh.L.I. Pnrs — 3 O.R. wounded, 2 O.Rs missing.	
			1/1st (Nbn) Fld Ambce — 2 O.Rs wounded.	

50th DIVISION.

NOVR 1917.

Instructions regarding War Diaries and Intelligence Summaries are contained in F. S. Regs., Part II. and the Staff Manual respectively. Title pages will be prepared in manuscript.

Army Form C. 2118.

ADMINISTRATIVE WAR DIARY or INTELLIGENCE SUMMARY.

(Erase heading not required.)

Place	Date	Hour	Summary of Events and Information	Remarks and references to Appendices
ELVERDINGHE	5		CASUALTIES:-	
			50th Divnl Artillery.—	
			250th (Nbn) Bde RFA — 9 O.R. wounded.	
			251st do — 1 O.R. wounded.	
			50th Divnl R.E.—	
			446th (Nbn) Fld Co RE — 1 O.R. wounded.	
			Divnl Signal Coy RE — 3 O.R. wounded.	
			149th Infantry Bgde.—	
			6th North'd Fuslrs — 2 O.R. wounded.	
			150th Infantry Bgde.—	
			4th East Yorks Regt — O.Rs wounded 2, missing 1.	
			151st Infantry Bgde.—	
			5th Border Regiment — O.Rs wounded 2.	
			6th Durham L.Infy — O.Rs killed 1.	
			8th do — O.Rs killed 1, wounded 10.	
			9th do — Lt(T/Lt-Col) R.B.Bradford, VC MC wounded at duty 5/11/17, O.Rs 9. "W".	
			No:151 M.Gun Coy — O.Rs wounded 1.	
			1/1st (Nbn) Fld Ambce. — O.Rs wounded 1.	
			2/2nd (Nbn) Fld Ambce — Wounded Capt.G.D.Eccles RAMC at duty (gas) 5/11/17, O.Rs 17 Gas.	
			1/3rd (Nbn) Fld Ambce — Wounded O.Rs 13.	
	6		50th Divnl Artillery.—	
			250th (Nbn) Bde RFA — Wounded Lt.W.B.Williams (gas) and 34 O.Rs. 5/11/17.	
			251st do — wounded 1 O.R.	
			50th Divnl R.E.—	
			Divnl Signal Coy R.E. — Killed O.Rs 1.	
			150th Infantry Bgde.	
			4th East Yorks Regt — 4 O.Rs wounded.	
			5th Durham L.Infy — 1 O.R. wounded.	
			151st Infantry Bgde.—	
			5th Border Regiment — Killed 2/Lt(A/Capt) J.C.Laidlaw Scott,R. attd, 2/Lt.E.J.Pursglove, 2/Lt.M.A.Burke - all 6/11/17. Wounded 2/Lt.C.H.Corbett 5/11/17. O.R. "W". 7.	
			8th Durham L.Infy — O.Rs 1 killed, 8 wounded.	
			9th do — O.Rs 3 killed, 7 wounded.	

50th DIVISION.

NOVR 1917.

Army Form C. 2118.

ADMINISTRATIVE WAR DIARY or INTELLIGENCE SUMMARY.

(Erase heading not required.)

Place	Date	Hour	Summary of Events and Information	Remarks and references to Appendices
ELVERDINGHE		6 Cond		
		7	**CASUALTIES.**	
			151st Infantry Bgde.—	
			No.151 M.Gun Coy — O.Rs 1 killed, 2 wounded.	
			7th Durh.L.I. Pnrs — Wounded 2/Lt.L.F.Smith and 2/Lt.S.H.M.Larkham 6/11/17. O.Rs 4 killed and 14 wounded.	
			1/1st (Nbn) Fld Ambce — 1 O.R. wounded.	
			2/2nd do — 1 O.R. wounded.	
			50th Divnl Artillery.—	
			250th (Nbn) Bde RFA — 3 O.R. wounded.	
			251st do — 1 O.R. wounded.	
			50th Divnl R.E.—	
			446th (Nbn) Fld Co RE — 2 O.R. wounded.	
			149th Infantry Bgde.—	
			6th North'd Fuslrs — 2 O.R. wounded.	
			150th Infantry Bgde.—	
			4th East Yorkshire Regt — 1 O.R. wounded.	
			151st Infantry Brigade.—	
			5th Border Regt — 2 O.R. wounded.	
			9th Durham L.Infy — 4 O.R. wounded.	
			No:151 M.Gun Coy — 1 O.R. wounded.	
			2/2nd (Nbn) Fld Ambce — 1 O.R. wounded.	
			TOTAL CASUALTIES — 24/10/17 to 7/11/17.	
			K. W. M. Total.	
			Officers :— 25 64 5 94	
			O.Rs :— 282 1475 383 2140	
			TOTALS:— 307 1539 388 2234 (inc. 341 Off. & O.R. gas).	
		8	**50th Divnl Artillery.—** Wounded (gas) Lt (A/Capt) A.H.Leathart and 6 O.Rs.	
			250th (Nbn) Bde RFA — O.Rs 1 killed and 2 wounded.	
			50th Divnl R.E.—	
			446th (Nbn) Fld Co RE — O.Rs 1 killed and 2 wounded.	
			447th do — O.Rs 1 wounded.	

50th DIVISION.

NOVR 1917.

ADMINISTRATIVE WAR DIARY or INTELLIGENCE SUMMARY.

Army Form C. 2118.

(Erase heading not required.)

Instructions regarding War Diaries and Intelligence Summaries are contained in F.S. Regs., Part II. and the Staff Manual respectively. Title pages will be prepared in manuscript.

Place	Date	Hour	Summary of Events and Information	Remarks and references to Appendices
ELVERDINGHE	8 Contd		CASUALTIES:—	
			150th Infantry Brigade.—	
			4th East Yorks Regt — Wounded 2/Lt.G.W.Drewery wounded 7/11/17 and 1 O.R.	
			151st Infantry Brigade.—	
			8th Durham L.Infy — O.Rs killed 1, wounded 1.	
			151st T.Mortar Btty — 1 O.R. wounded.	
			1/1st (Nbn) Fld Ambce — 1 O.R. wounded.	
			2/2nd do — 1 O.R. wounded.	
			1/3rd do — 1 O.R. wounded.	
	9		50th Divnl Artillery.—	
			250th (Nbn) Bde RFA — Wounded (gas, at duty) — Major F.G.D.Johnson DSO, Capt (A/Maj) F.R.A. Shiel, Lts V.H.Jowett and R.M.Graham, 2/Lt.P.Grange. 2/Lt.R.L.Elder "gas".	
			H.Q., 50th D.A. — 1 O.R. killed.	
			149th Infantry Bgde.—	
			6th North'd Fuslrs — O.Rs killed 3, wounded 5.	
			No:149 M.Gun Coy — 1 O.R. wounded.	
EPERLECQUES	10		CASUALTIES.—	
			50th Divnl Artillery.—	
			250th (Nbn) Bde RFA — O.Rs killed 1, wounded 22 (inc. 1 at duty and 17 gas at duty).	
			251st do — O.Rs 1 wounded.	
			150th Infantry Bgde.—	
			5th Yorkshire Regt — 1 O.R. killed.	
			Divl H.Q. less R.Artillery moved to EPERLECQUES on relief by 17th Division. 151st Infy Bde Group (inc. D.H.Q.) moved by rail and road from ELVERDINGHE to EPERLECQUES area (detraining Station WATTEN) = locations as follows :—	
			Divl H.Q. — HOULLE. 8th D.L.I. — HOULLE. 151 T.M.Bty — MOULLE. 1/1st F.Ambce MOULLE.	
			151st Infy Bde H.Q. — HOULLE. 9th D.L.I. — do Div.Sig.Coy — EPERLECQUES. HQ Div Tr EPERLECQUES	
			5th Border Regt — MOULLE. No.151 M.G.Co.MOULLE. 244 D.E.Coy — do No.3 Coy HOULLE.	
			6th Durham L.Infy — LE HAUT.	

50th Division.

Army Form C. 2118.

7.

ADMINISTRATIVE WAR DIARY or INTELLIGENCE SUMMARY.

(Erase heading not required.)

NOVR. 1917.

Instructions regarding War Diaries and Intelligence Summaries are contained in F. S. Regs., Part II. and the Staff Manual respectively. Title pages will be prepared in manuscript.

Place	Date	Hour	Summary of Events and Information	Remarks and references to Appendices
EPERLECQUES	11		Casualties - 250th Bde RFA wounded 2 (inc. 1 gas). Signal Coy RE killed O.R.1. 150th Infy Bde Group moved by rail from ELVERDINGHE to EPERLECQUES Area (detraining station WATTEN) less 4th East Yorks Regt. Locations as follows :- Bde H.Q. TOURNEHEM. 150th T.M.Bty - MENTQUE. 4th Yorks do No.245 M.G.Coy - HELLEBROUCQ. 5th Yorks LA COMMUNE. 447th Fld Co RE - NORTBECOURT. 5th D.L.I NORTLEULINGHEM. 2/2 Nbn Fld Amb - BAYENHEM. No:150 M.G.Coy - MENTQUE. No.4 Coy Train - WESTROVE.	
	12		Casualties - 250th Bde RFA wounded O.R.4 (inc. 3 gas). 251st Bde RFA wounded O.R.2. 7th Durh.L.I. Pnrs wounded O.R.2. killed O.R.1.	
	13		Casualties - 50th Divl Signal Co RE wounded O.R.1. Lt. (T/Capt.) R.Boys Stones, M.C., 9th D.L.I., G.S.O.3, 50th Division, appointed Bde Major, 53rd Infantry Brigade. 149th Infantry Bde Group (personnel) moved by rail from ELVERDINGHE to EPERLECQUES area (detraining station WATTEN) Locations as follows:- Bde H.Q. - SERQUES. No:149 M.G.Coy - OUESTMONT. 4th N.F. - ZUDROVE. 149th T.M.Btty - WATTEN. 5th N.F. - SERQUES. Div.Burial Party - ZUDROVE. 6th N.F. - BAYENHEM. Div.Salvage Coy - ZUDROVE. 7th N.F. - SERQUES. No.2 Coy Train - GANSPETTE. Concentration of Division (less R.A., 7th D.L.I., 4th East Yorks, 7th Field Coy, 1/3rd Fld Amblce) in EPERLECQUES Area complete.	
	14		2/Lt.E.Greville Jones, M.C., 5th D.L.I. apptd G.S.O. 3rd Grade, 50th Division (vice Lt. R.Boys Stones, M.C., 9th D.L.I. apptd Bde Major, 53rd Infy Bde.). Casualties - 250th Bde RFA wounded O.R.2. 251st Bde RFA killed O.R.1, wounded O.R.3. 7th D.L.I. wounded O.R.2 (gas). "M" 8th D.L.I. wounded O.R.2 prev. rep.	
	15		Casualties - 250th Bde RFA wounded 1 O.R. at duty. 251st Bde RFA wounded O.R.3, killed O.R.4.	

50th Division.

Army Form C. 2118.

8.

ADMINISTRATIVE
WAR DIARY
or
INTELLIGENCE SUMMARY.

(Erase heading not required.)

NOVR., 1917.

Instructions regarding War Diaries and Intelligence Summaries are contained in F. S. Regs., Part II. and the Staff Manual respectively. Title pages will be prepared in manuscript.

Place	Date	Hour	Summary of Events and Information	Remarks and references to Appendices
EPERLECQUES	16		Casualties - 250th Bde RFA wounded Lt. (A/Capt.) U.W.Dickinson, 2/Lt.N.H.A.BECKINGHAM (both "gas" at duty). O.R. wounded 36 inc. 32 "gas". 251st Bde RFA O.Rs wounded 5 inc. 4 "gas". 4th East Yorks Regt - O.R. killed 1.	
	17		Casualties - 7th D.L.I. Pnrs wounded O.R.4.	
	18		Casualties - 250th Bde RFA - O.R. wounded 7 (inc. 6 "gas"). 251st Bde RFA - O.R. killed 1, wounded 4 (inc. 1 at duty).	
	19		Casualties - 250th Bde RFA - O.Rs wounded 3 (gas). 251st Bde RFA - O.R. wounded 2. 446th and 447th (Nbn) Fld Cos R.E. moved to ELVERDINGHE from WATTEN by rail, and were administered by 1st Division.	
	20		Casualties - 250th Bde RFA - wounded (gas, at duty) 5 O.Rs. ~~wounded O.R.1.~~ 251st Bde RFA wounded O.R.1.	
	21		Casualties - 250th Bde RFA - Missing O.R.1. 50th D.A.Col. - Wounded O.R.2. T.M.Battery - Wounded O.R.1. 7th D.L.I.Pnrs- Wounded O.R.1 at duty.	
	22		Casualties - 150th Infy Bde - 4th E.Yorks Regt 2/Lt.E.W.ALLCHORN reptd "w" 31/10/17 since died of Wounds. 4th Yorks Regt Lt.H.C.HALE reptd wounded 31st Octr since died of wounds. 7th Durh.L.I. - 2/Lt.F.GRAHAM wounded 28/10/17 not prev. reptd. 250th Bde RFA - O.Rs wounded 3.	

50th DIVISION.

ADMINISTRATIVE
WAR DIARY
or
INTELLIGENCE SUMMARY.
(Erase heading not required.)

NOVR., 1917.

Army Form C. 2118.

Instructions regarding War Diaries and Intelligence Summaries are contained in F. S. Regs., Part II. and the Staff Manual respectively. Title pages will be prepared in manuscript.

Place	Date	Hour	Summary of Events and Information	Remarks and references to Appendices
EPERLECQUES	23		Casualties - 251st Bde R.F.A. - O.R. wounded 1.	
	24		Casualties - 251st Bde R.F.A. - O.R. wounded 1. 7th D.L.I. Pnrs - O.R. wounded 2.	
	25		Casualties - 250th Bde R.F.A. - O.R. killed 3, wounded 1.	
	26			
	27		Casualties - 7th Durh.L.I. Pnrs - O.R. wounded 1 at duty.	
	28		Casualties - 50th Divl Sig. Coy RE - O.R. wounded 1 at duty.	
	29		Casualties - 251st Bde R.F.A. - O.R. wounded 2. 50th Divl T.M.Bde - O.R. wounded 3.	
	30		Casualties - 250th Bde R.F.A. - Wounded Lt. (A/Capt.) G.CHAPMAN, M.C.	

CONFIDENTIAL

ORIGINAL

50th Division

Administrative Staff

War Diary

From :- 1st December 1917

To :- 31st December 1917

Volume XXXII

50TH DIVISION.

ADMINISTRATIVE WAR DIARY or INTELLIGENCE SUMMARY.

DECEMBER 1917.

Army Form C. 2118.

Instructions regarding War Diaries and Intelligence Summaries are contained in F. S. Regs., Part II. and the Staff Manual respectively. Title pages will be prepared in manuscript.

(Erase heading not required.)

Place	Date	Hour	Summary of Events and Information	Remarks and references to Appendices
EPERLECQUES.	DEC. 1		CASUALTIES. 250th Bde RFA wounded O.R.1.	
	2		CASUALTIES. 251st Bde RFA wounded O.R.1. 149th and 150th Infy Bdes exchanged billets to facilitate training – locations now as follows:–	
			150th Infy Bde H.Q. – SERQUES.	
			4th East Yorks Regt – BAYENGHEM.	
			4th Yorkshire Regt – LE BAS.	
			5th do – ZUDROVE.	
			5th Durham L.Infy – SERQUES.	
			No.150 M.Gun Coy – OUESTMONT.	
			150th T.M.Battery – WATTEN DAM.	
			No.4 Coy Divl Train – BLEUEMAISON.	
			149th Infy Bde H.Q. – TOURNEHEM.	
			4th North'd Fuslrs – LA RONVILLE.	
			5th do – TOURNEHEM.	
			7th do – NORTBEULINGHEM.	
			No:149 M.Gun Coy – TOURNEHEM.	
			149th T.M.Battery – TOURNEHEM.	
			No.2 Coy Divl Train – WESTROVE.	
			7th Fld Coy R.E. and 7th D.L.I. Pnrs rejoined Division from ELVERDINGHE Area and are located as follows:– 7th Field Coy R.E. INGLINGHEM; 7th D.L.I. Pnrs GANSPETTE.	
	3		CASUALTIES. 251st Bde RFA wounded O.R.2.	
	4		CASUALTIES. 251st Bde RFA O.Rs killed 2, wounded 1.	
	5		CASUALTIES. 50th Divl Ammn Column O.Rs wounded 1.	
	6		CASUALTIES. 251st Bde RFA wounded O.R.1 (Gas).	
	7			
	8			

50th DIVISION.

Army Form C. 2118.

Instructions regarding War Diaries and Intelligence Summaries are contained in F. S. Regs., Part II. and the Staff Manual respectively. Title pages will be prepared in manuscript.

ADMINISTRATIVE WAR DIARY or INTELLIGENCE SUMMARY.

(Erase heading not required.)

DECEMBER 1917.

Place	Date	Hour	Summary of Events and Information	Remarks and references to Appendices
EPERLECQUES.	DEC 9		Part of Transport of 150th Infy Bde plus No.151 M.G.Coy, 7th Field Coy RE and 2/2nd (Nbn) Fld Ambce moved to BRANDHOEK area staging night at ZERMEZEELE.	
	10		150th Infy Bde plus No.151 M.G.Coy, 7th Field Coy RE and 2/2nd (Nbn) Fld Ambce moved from SERQUES Area to BRANDHOEK Area by rail. Part of Transport of 149th Infy Bde plus No.245 M.G.Coy, 446th (Nbn) Fld Coy RE and 1/1st (Nbn) Fld Ambce moved to BRANDHOEK Area staging night at ZERMEZEELE.	
	11		150th Infy Bde plus No.151 M.G.Coy moved forward from BRANDHOEK Area to Support Area, POTIJZE, in relief of 19th Infy Bde. 4th East Yorks, 5th D.L.I., No.150 M.G.Coy and No.151 M.G.Coy proceeded by train from BRANDHOEK Station, and Bde H.Q., 4th Yorks and 5th Yorks, and 150th T.M.Battery by march route via VLAMERTINGHE-YPRES Road. 149th Infy Bde plus No.245 M.G.Coy, 446th (Nbn) Fld Co RE and 1/1st (Nbn) Fld Ambce moved by rail from EPERLECQUES to BRANDHOEK Area (Bde H.Q. located at BRANDHOEK). Part of transport of 151st Infy Bde plus 7th D.L.I.Pnrs, 447th (Nbn) Fld Co RE and 1/3rd (Nbn) Fld Ambce moved from EPERLECQUES to BRANDHOEK Area, staging night at ZERMEZEELE.	
	12		151st Infy Bde plus 7th D.L.I.Pnrs, 447th (Nbn) Fld Coy and 1/3rd (Nbn) Fld Ambce moved by rail from EPERLECQUES Area to BRANDHOEK Area (Bde H.Q. located BRANDHOEK). 150th Infy Bde relieved 98th Infy Bde (33rd Divn) in line. Bde H.Q. ISRAEL HOUSE. 149th Infy Bde relieved 98th Infy Bde (33rd Divn) in Support Area. Bde H.Q. CONVENT, YPRES.	
BRANDHOEK.	13		Divl H.Q., less C.R.E. moved from EPERLECQUES to BRANDHOEK (Rear Div.H.Q.). CASUALTIES. 150 Infy Bde - 4th E.Yks Regt wounded O.R.3. 5th Yorks Regt killed O.R.1, wounded at duty Lt.T.H.GAUNT, O.R.3 inc. 1 at duty. 5th D.L.I. killed O.R.3, wounded O.R.1. No.150 M.G.Coy wounded O.R.3 gas, at duty. Divl Artillery - 251st Bde RFA wounded O.R.1 (Gas).	

50th DIVISION.

Army Form C. 2118.

ADMINISTRATIVE WAR DIARY or INTELLIGENCE SUMMARY.

(Erase heading not required.)

DECEMBER 1917.

Instructions regarding War Diaries and Intelligence Summaries are contained in F.S. Regs., Part II. and the Staff Manual respectively. Title pages will be prepared in manuscript.

Place	Date	Hour	Summary of Events and Information	Remarks and references to Appendices
BRANDHOEK.	DECR 14		CASUALTIES. 150th Infy Bde – 4th E.Yks Regt killed O.R.1, wounded O.R.5 inc. 1 at duty. 5th Yorks Regt O.Rs killed 1, wounded 4. 5th D.L.I. O.Rs wounded 5, missing 1. 151st Infy Bde – No.151 M.G.Coy O.Rs wounded 1. Divl Art'y – 250th Bde RFA O.Rs wounded 1.	
	15		CASUALTIES. 150th Infy Bde – 4th E.Yorks Regt O.Rs killed 3, wounded 10. 5th Yorks Regt O.Rs wounded 2. 5th D.L.I. O.Rs wounded 4. 7th D.L.I.Pnrs – wounded 2/Lt.J.R.BAILES.	
	16		150th Infy Bde moved to Reserve being located in BRANDHOEK Area – Bde H.Q. BRANDHOEK. 151st Infy Bde relieved 149th Infy Bde in Support Area – Bde H.Q. CONVENT, YPRES. 149th Infy Bde relieved 150th Infy Bde in Front Line – Bde H.Q. ISRAEL HOUSE. CASUALTIES. 149th Infy Bde – 5th N.F. O.Rs wounded 2. 7th N.F. O.Rs killed 3, wounded 8. 150th Infy Bde – 5th Yorks Regt O.Rs killed 2, wounded 9. 5th D.L.I. O.Rs killed 1, wounded 9 inc. 1 at duty. 151st Infy Bde – No.151 M.G.Coy O.Rs wounded 3. 7th Durh.L.I.Pnrs – O.Rs wounded 1. R.A.M.C. – 1/1st (Nbn) Fld Ambce – O.Rs wounded 3.	
YPRES (Advcd H.Q.) BRANDHOEK (Rear H.Q.)	17		Divnl H.Q. less D.A.A.G. and D.A.Q.M.G., A.D.M.S., D.A.D.V.S., D.A.D.O.S., and H.Q. Train moved from BRANDHOEK to Advd Div.H.Q. Ramparts YPRES at 10 a.m. CASUALTIES. 149th Infy Bde – 4th N.F. O.Rs wounded 1. 5th N.F. O.Rs killed 2, wounded 8. 6th N.F. O.Rs wounded 12. 7th N.F. O.Rs wounded 2. 150th Infy Bde – 5th Durh.L.I. O.Rs killed 1.	

50th DIVISION.

ADMINISTRATIVE WAR DIARY or INTELLIGENCE SUMMARY.

DECEMBER 1917.

Army Form C. 2118.

Place	Date	Hour	Summary of Events and Information	Remarks and references to Appendices
YPRES – Advd H.Qrs. BRANDHOEK – Rear H.Q.	DEC 18		CASUALTIES. 149th Infy Bde – 4th N.F. wounded O.R.8. 150th Infy Bde – 4th E.Yorks Regt – wounded Lt (A/Capt) R.MONGE on 18/12/17, wounded O.R.3. 5th D.L.I. missing O.R.1. 151st Infy Bde – 5th Border Regt wounded O.R.3. No.151 M.G.Coy wounded O.R.1. No:245 M.G.Coy – O.Rs killed 4, wounded 10. R.A.M.C. – 1/1st (Nbn) Fld Ambce killed O.R.1.	
	19		CASUALTIES. 149th Infy Bde – 4th N.F. wounded O.R.1. 6th N.F. wounded O.R.2. 149th T.M.Btty wounded O.R.1. 150th Infy Bde – 4th Yorks Regt wounded O.R.1. 151st Infy Bde – 5th Border Regt killed O.R.1, wounded O.R.2. 6th D.L.I. wounded Lt.G.P.RUDGE 7th D.L.I. attd, O.R.3. 7th D.L.I.Pnrs – Wounded at duty 2/Lt.R.LAWSON, wounded O.R.2. No.245 M.G.Coy – wounded O.R.1.	
	20		151st Infy Bde (in Support Area) relieved 149th Infy Bde in Front Line – Bde H.Q. ISRAEL HOUSE. 149th Infy Bde moved to Reserve Area, BRANDHOEK – Bde H.Q. BRANDHOEK. 150th Infy Bde (in Reserve) relieved 151st Infy Bde in Support – Bde H.Q. CONVENT, YPRES. CASUALTIES. 149th Infy Bde – 5th N.F. wounded O.R.5.	
	21		CASUALTIES. 149th Infy Bde – 4th N.F. O.Rs killed 5, wounded 8. 7th N.F. O.Rs wounded 1. 150th do – 4th E.Yorks Regt wounded at duty Lt.J.RUTHVEN, wounded O.R.1. 151st do – 5th Border Regt O.Rs killed 1, wounded 2. 6th D.L.I. wounded O.R.2. 8th D.L.I. wounded O.R.3, missing O.R.3.	
	22		CASUALTIES. 150th Infy Bde – 4th E.Yorks Regt wounded O.R.1. 151st do – 5th Border Regt wounded O.R.4. 9th D.L.I. wounded O.R.2 (inc. 1 at duty). 7th D.L.I.Pnrs – Killed O.R.2.	

50th DIVISION.

ADMINISTRATIVE WAR DIARY or INTELLIGENCE SUMMARY.

Army Form C. 2118.

DECEMBER 1917.

Instructions regarding War Diaries and Intelligence Summaries are contained in F. S. Regs., Part II. and the Staff Manual respectively. Title pages will be prepared in manuscript.

Place	Date	Hour	Summary of Events and Information	Remarks and references to Appendices
Advd H.Q. YPRES.	DECR 23		CASUALTIES. Divl Artillery - 251st Bde RFA wounded O.R.2. 150th Infy Bde - 5th Yorks Regt O.Rs killed 1, wounded 3. 151st Infy Bde - 8th D.L.I. wounded O.R.3. No.151 M.G.Coy wounded O.R.1.	
Near H.Q. BRANDHOEK.	24		CASUALTIES. 150th Infy Bde - 4th Yorks Regt Killed O.R.2, wounded Hon Lt & Q.Mr T.TAFT on 23/12/17 and O.R.9 (inc. 2 at duty). 151st Infy Bde - 5th Border Regt wounded O.R.3 (gas). 6th D.L.I. wounded O.R.9 (inc. 1 acc. and 2 gas). 8th D.L.I. wounded O.R.1 (gas). 9th D.L.I. wounded O.R.2 (gas). No.4 Section 50th Divl Signal Coy RE wounded O.R.2. 50th Divl Train - wounded O.R.1.	
	25		CASUALTIES. Divnl Arty. - 251st Bde RFA wounded O.R.1 (at duty). 150th Infy Bde - 4th E.Yorks Regt wounded O.R.3 (inc. 1 gas). 4th Yorks Regt wounded O.R.2. 5th Yorks wounded O.R.1 (gas). 5th D.L.I. wounded O.R.1 (gas). 150th Infy Bde relieved 151st Infantry Bde in Line - Bde H.Q. ISRAEL HOUSE. 149th Infy Bde relieved 150th Infantry Bde in Support - Bde H.Q. CONVENT, YPRES. 151st Infy Bde moved to Reserve - H.Q. BRANDHOEK.	
	26		CASUALTIES. 50th Divl Signal Coy RE - wounded O.R.2 (gas). 149th Infy Bde - 5th N.F. missing O.R.1 on 19/12/17. 150th Infy Bde - 4th E.Yorks Regt missing O.R.2 on 16/12/17, killed O.R.2, wounded O.R.6 on 26/12/17. 4th Yorks Regt wounded O.R.1 (gas). 5th Yorks Regt wounded O.R.1 (gas). 5th D.L.I. wounded O.R.1 (gas). 244th (Divl) Emp. Coy wounded O.R.4 (gas). Hon Lt & Q.Mr T.TAFT reptd wounded on 23/12/17 now reptd died of wounds 23/12/17. (4th Yorks Regt)	

50th DIVISION.

Army Form C. 2118.

ADMINISTRATIVE
WAR DIARY
or
INTELLIGENCE SUMMARY.
(Erase heading not required.)

Instructions regarding War Diaries and Intelligence Summaries are contained in F.S. Regs., Part II. and the Staff Manual respectively. Title pages will be prepared in manuscript.

DECEMBER 1917.

Place	Date	Hour	Summary of Events and Information	Remarks and references to Appendices
Advd H.Qrs YPRES. Rear H.Q. BRANDHOEK.	DEC. 27		CASUALTIES. Divnl Art'y - 250th Bde RFA killed O.R.1. 251st. Bde RFA wounded O.R.3 inc. 1 at duty. 149th Infy Bde - 4th N.F. killed O.R.1, wounded O.R.6. 150th Infy Bde - 4th E.Yorks Regt O.Rs killed 3, wounded 7. 4th Yorks Regt O.Rs killed 1, wounded 2. 5th Yorks Regt O.Rs killed 1, wounded 4.	
	28		CASUALTIES. 149th Infy Bde - 4th N.F. wounded at duty 2/Lt.J.G.NAPIER. No.149 M.G.Coy wounded O.R.3 (gas). 150th Infy Bde - 4th Yorks Regt O.Rs killed 1, wounded 7, inc. 4 gas and 1 at duty. 5th Yorks Regt killed Lt.F.G.DANBY and 2/Lt.W.H.COLES, wounded O.R.2.	
	29		149th Infy Bde relieved 150th Infy Bde in front line - Bde H.Q. ISRAEL HOUSE. 151st Infy Bde relieved 149th Infy Bde in Support - Bde H.Q. CONVENT, YPRES. 150th Infy Bde moved to Reserve. CASUALTIES. 7th Field Coy R.E. - wounded O.R.2. 149th Infy Bde - No.149 M.G.Coy wounded O.R.1 gas. 150th Infy Bde - 5th Yorks Regt killed O.R.2, wounded Lt.F.GREEN died of wounds 28/12/17. 5th D.L.I. wounded O.R.3.	
	30		CASUALTIES. Divnl Art'y - 251st Bde RFA O.Rs killed 1, wounded 1. 149th Infy Bde - 4th N.F. wounded O.R.2. 150th Infy Bde - 4th Yorks Regt O.Rs killed 2, wounded 1. No.245 M.Gun Coy - wounded O.R.12 (gas).	
	31		CASUALTIES. Divnl Art'y - 251st Bde RFA wounded Capt(A/Maj) W.P.NESS-WALKER, AC 30/12/17, died of wounds 31/12/17, wounded O.R.1. 50th Divnl Amm Col. wounded O.R.1. 149th Infy Bde - 4th N.F. wounded O.R.1. 7th N.F. killed O.R.3. 2/Lt.A.BURR wounded 31/12/17, wounded O.R.10. 149th T.M.Battery wounded O.R.5. 150th Infy Bde - 4th Yorks Regt wounded O.R.4 (Gas).	

APPENDIX I.

ESTABLISHMENT OF AMMUNITION AT
MAIN DIVISIONAL DUMP - CAMBRIDGE DUMP.

S. A. A.	...	...	...	1,000,000
Mills Hand Grenades	...	...)		(at least 75%
Mills Rifle Grenades	...	...)	30,000	(to be Mills (Rifle Grenades.
No.20 or 24 Rifle Grenades		...	10,000	
"P" Smoke Grenades	...	...	500	
Stokes Shell	...	...	...	2,000
Cartridges, Green	...	...	2,000	
Cartridges, Yellow	...	...	200	
Ring Charges	...	...	2,500	
Verey 1" White	...	...	10,000	
" 1½" "	...	...	2,500	

Flares   )
Rockets.   )
Pistol, Webley.) As may be ordered from time to time.
etc.   )

----------oOo----------

EB.

APPENDIX II.

WATER SUPPLY ARRANGEMENTS.

1. **WATER SUPPLY EAST OF POPERINGHE.**

The initial water points for the supply of drinking water are located as follows, (Sheet 28): water bottles, water carts and water tank lorries can refil at these points :-

Tank No. 4 at	G.7.d.9.5.	yielding daily	7,400 gallons.
5	G.3.c.7.2.	—	25,250 "
8	G.15.b.2.8.	—	11,700 "
9	H.14.a.9.8.	—	7,400 "
11	G.10.c.4.9.	—	15,500 "
14	H.8.b.9.9.	—	5,000 "
14a	H.2.d.8.3.	—	3,200 "
14b	H.3.c.2.5.	—	3,200 "
32	G.16.c.5.1.	—	4,000 "
48	G.12.a.9.9.	—	5,000 "

2. **FORWARD WATER POINTS.**

    (a) YPRES, I.8.b.1.9. Canvas tanks, capacity 38,000 gallons, yield 40,000 gallons a day.
        Water filtered and chlorinated before delivery to pump.
    (b) Canvas Tanks, WIELTJE, C.26.b.3.5., capacity 31,000 galls
        Filled by 4" pipe line from I.8.b.1.9.
    (c) Canvas Tank, OXFORD ROAD, C.29.c.5.15, capacity 8,000 gallons supplied by 4" main from I.8.b.1.9.
    (d) Canvas Tanks, MILL COT, I.5.a.4.7. capacity 13,000 galls supplied by 4" main from I.8.b.1.9.

The above points have water bottle and dixie fillers and stand pipes for filling water carts.

    (e) Canvas Tanks, BRIDGE HOUSE, C.21.a.2.7., capacity 8,000 galls supplied by 4" main from I.8.b.1.9.
    (f) Canvas Tanks, KANSAS CROSS, D.14.c.4.8. capacity 18,000 gallons. Supplied by 4" main from I.8.b.1.9.
    (g) Canvas Tanks HILL 37 D.20.a.7.8. capacity 32,000 galls. Supplied by 4" main from I.8.b.1.9.
    (h) Canvas Tanks ABRAHAM HEIGHTS, D.16.b.7.5. capacity 18,000 gallons.

Points (e), (f), (g), and (h) have water bottle and dixie fillers.
    Points (c) and (g) have hand pumps for filling carts.
    Point (h) has a stand pipe for filling carts.

(OVER)

(Water Supply Arrangements (sheet 2)

3.   The Horse Water Supply is from Water Points, existing streams and ponds and from wells and long shallow wells dug by the Units themselves.

Corps Horse Water Points are located as follows :-

(i) x No. 1 Trough   -   G.12.c.3.8.
     x   2   "   -   G.11.a.8.2.
     x   3   "   -   G.10.a.9.7.
     x   4   "   -   G.6.a.2.3.
     x   5   "   -   H.7.a.2.1.
     x   6   "   -   H.7.c.4.9.
        GOLDFISH Trough   -   H.11.b.1.1.
        DICKEBUSCH BECK I   -   H.18.c.4.9.
        DICKEBUSCH BECK II   -   H.18.b.6.3.
        CHATEAU EAST Trough   -   H.11.b.8.9.

            x - Piped Supply.

(ii) Shallow Wells.

    G.5.c.4.9.   G.10.b.1.4.   H.7.a.4.8.
    G.5.d.4.7.   G.11.a.8.3.   G.12.a.9.9.
    G.6.c.4.2.   G.10.d.7.3.   G.10.b.1.3.
    G.10.d.1.2.   G.11.d.6.1.   G.11.d.5.9.
    G.12.c.8.5.   G.12.b.8.8.   G.12.d.7.4.
    G.16.b.2.5.   G.17.a.7.7.   G.17.a.5.7.
    G.13.a.4.5.   G.18.b.5.3.   H.7.b.3.2.
    G.4.c.1.9.   G.3.d.2.8.   G.3.c.4.8.
    G.9.c.4.4.   G.9.a.8.4.   G.9.b.1.5.
    G.14.a.1.6.   G.9.d.3.4.   G.10.c.3.2.
    G.15.b.9.4.   G.14.b.5.6.   G.15.a.3.3.
    G.15.b.2.9.

The wells are provided with pumps and troughs and can water 40 horses at a time.

APPENDIX III.

SALVAGE SCHEME.

(1) HEADQUARTERS.   The Headquarters of the Divisional Salvage Coy will be at the Prison, YPRES.

(2) AREA.   The Divisional Area will be divided into three sub-areas :-

"A" Sub Area - East of OXFORD and CAMBRIDGE Roads.
"B" Sub Area - East of YPRES.
"C" Sub Area - West of YPRES.

The responsibility for the salvage of these areas will be as follows :-

"A" Sub Area - by the Brigade in the Line.
"B" and "C" Sub Areas - by the Divisional Salvage Coy.

It is to be clearly understood that this fixing of responsibility for the salvaging of these sub areas in no way relieves Units throughout the Division from assisting in the work of Salvage.

All Units in "B" and "C" Sub Areas will have a Salvage Dump in close proximity to their lines. The position of these Dumps will be reported to Div.H.Q. and O.C. Salvage Coy, forthwith.

The O.C. Salvage Coy. will be responsible for clearing these unit Dumps periodically into the Main Divisional Dump.

(3) WORK TO BE CARRIED OUT.

It is essential that the work to be carried out by the Divisional Salvage Coy. and by the personnel detailed by the Brigade in Reserve, is done with a thoroughness which will ensure that fresh ground is not started on till that which is being worked on is absolutely clear.
To carry this out, the work will be done on the following lines :-
The O.C. Salvage Co. will divide "B" Sub area into three sectors - and allot a section of the Salvage Coy. to each sector.
Each N.C.O. i/c of a Section will be given by O.C. Salvage Co. a map, showing the boundary of the Sector he is allotted.
Salvaging in each Sector will then be carried out by map squares - each map square will be thoroughly salved, and when clear of everything, the O.C. Salvage Co. will, if satisfied, shade in the map square that has been cleared on the N.C.Os map, and initial it.   Work on a fresh square will on no account be started till the square being worked on is absolutely clear.
Exactly the same principle will be adopted for the salving of "C" sub area.
The O.C. Salvage Coy will shade in on his map, which will show the boundary of the Divisional Area, the squares worked on, as they become clear.   These maps will be sent to Div.H.Q. for inspection, with the weekly Salvage return.

(4) DUMPS.

Main Divisional Dump - Prison, YPRES, & I.5.a.4.9.
Divisional Ordnance Store - H.7.c.central.

The Brigade in the line will arrange its own Dumps - but will clear them to the Main Divisional Dump at OXFORD ROAD, I.5.a.4.9.

"B" Sub-Area, will have three Salvage Dumps; one in each sector. The siting of these Dumps will be dependent on the map square being worked on, and will be selected by the O.C. Salvage Coy. The sites of these Dumps should be easily accessible to transport, and be cleared to Main Divisional Dump at Prison, YPRES, under orders of O.C. Salvage Coy.

"C" Sub-area Dumps are dependent on the map square being worked on, and will be selected by the O.C. Salvage Coy. accordingly, under the same principle as that for "B" Sub-area; salvaged material being cleared to Div'l Ordnance Store Dump at H.7.c. central under the orders of the O.C. Salvage Coy.

(5) SALVING OF R.E. MATERIAL.

The O.C. Salvage Co., and all units, are urged to do their utmost in the salvaging of R.E. material, particularly the following, of which there is a shortage :-
    (a) Corrugated iron sheets, straight or curved.
    (b) Steel shelters.
    (c) Joists.
    (d) Rails.
    (e) Screw posts.
    (f) Structural steelwork of all kinds.

A considerable amount of the above mentioned material can be salved from the old German lines.

All salved R.E. material in "A" Sub-area will NOT be taken to the Main Divisional Salvage Dump, but will be collected in the advanced R.E. Dumps.

(6) ORDNANCE.

The D.A.D.O.S. will ensure that he acquires from the Main Divisional Dump, any stores which are wanted for use by the Division.

(7) AMMUNITION.

All S.A.A., Grenades, and other Ammunition will be dumped separately on a site to be selected by O.C. Salvage Coy., near a road in the area being worked on.
The O.C. Coy. will report to Div.H.Q. periodically the amount and nature of ammunition salved and so dumped. The D.A.Q.M.G. will keep a record of this and so far as possible, make use of it, by transporting it to the Main Divisional Ammunition Dump - for use of troops in the line - care being taken that this Ammunition is issued from Main Divisional Dump for use first.
"Blinds of all descriptions (enemy or otherwise) are on no account to be touched, but map location reported to Div.H.Q.
Detonated grenades will, under arrangements to be made by the D.A.Q.M.G. be examined, and de-detonated if necessary before being dealt with.

(10) ARMBANDS.

Armbands will be worn at all times by the personnel of the Salvage Coy, any deficiencies should be replaced at once by demand on the D.A.D.O.S.

APPENDIX IV.

BURIAL SCHEME.

1. **DIVISIONAL BURIAL OFFICER.**
Lieut. J.C. TETLEY, 7th Bn. Durham Light Infy (Pnrs) is Divisional Burial Officer, and is in charge of the Divisional Burial Party. He is quartered at POTIJZE.

2. **MARKING OF GRAVES AND EFFECTS.**
Graves will be marked with a disc on a wire rod, which will be stuck in the ground at the head of the grave :-

A number of these rods and discs is in possession of the Divisional Burial Officer.

3. **RATION BAGS.**
The Divisional Burial Officer also possesses a supply of ration bags, for packing the personal effects of the dead.

4. **DUTIES OF THE DIVISIONAL BURIAL OFFICER.**
(a) In case of heavy fighting, to distribute the personnel engaged in collecting the dead so as to ensure the whole front being systematically searched.
(b) To bury the dead at sites selected by him.
(c) Proper marking of graves. (see para.2).
(d) To collect, and hand over to the Divisional Salvage Officer, the arms and equipment from the dead.
(e) To collect personal effects of the dead, place them together with the red identity disc in a ration bag, and forward them to the D.A.G., 3rd Division.
(f) On completion of a burial, to keep an accurate record in accordance with the following pro-forma :-

Map Reference. Location etc.	Tablet No.	Reg. No.	Rank	Unit.	Date of Burial.	and Name.

(g) To inform Units of particulars of burials carried out by his party.
(h) To carry out all orders relating to the burial of British soldiers.

5. **BURIAL BY UNITS.**
When a burial is made by a Unit, the following procedure should be adopted:-
(a) The grave should be marked as laid down in para. 2.
(b) All personal effects and the red identity disc to be placed in a ration bag or packet, and sent to the Divisional Burial Officer.
(c) A nominal roll, in the form laid down in para. 4 (f) will be completed by the Officer in charge of the burial, and forwarded to the Divisional Burial Officer.
(d) When more than one person is buried in the same grave, the bodies will be buried from left to right in the same order in which they are entered in the roll form, and the disc hung on the wire rod will be placed above the top left-hand corner of the grave. The extreme right limit of the grave should be marked by a wooden peg.

(OVER)

NOTE:- A supply of wire rods and discs (marked with Divisional Sign and serial number), also a supply of ration bags for effects (sub para. (b) above) will be kept at the Divisional Burial Officer's Office at I.3.d.7.6.

The Divisional Burial Officer now has a supply of prepared crosses (as used by the G.R.U.) and copper foil tablets for marking them. These may be obtained (ready printed) on the shortest notice, provided Units send particulars to the D.B.O.

6. CEMETERIES.
Reference Sheet 28 1/40,000.

BRANDHOEK	G.12.b.3.4.
VLAMERTINGHE	H.9.c.0.3.
ASYLUM YPRES	H.12.d.9.7.
DIVISIONAL YPRES	H.11.d.9.1.
Prison, YPRES	I.7.b.05.40.

Forward Cemeteries.

TYNE COTT	D.17.a.0.2.
MITCHELL'S FARM	D.20.c.20.15.
C.D.2.	D.11.d.50.50.
C.D.1.	D.11.d.0.2.
LEVI COTT.	D.21.a.50.50.
KINK CORNER.	D.26.a.9.4.

BATHS AND CLOTHING.
(Contd). 8.

Baths. YPRES. I.8.c.2.7.

1 N.C.O. found by Corps; 4 O.Rs by Division.
For use of Brigade in Support and Corps and Army Troops.
A large supply of socks is kept at BRANDHOEK, and YPRES for the use of Units, in exchange for wet socks. Baths
The whole of the establishment, including those staffed by personnel found by the Corps, are run under the supervision of the Divisional Baths Officer.

PACK ANIMAL ORGANISATION. 9.

(a) For <u>normal requirements</u> (i.e. transport of rations, water, and the normal ammunition requirement to the trenches.)
50 pack saddles are issued per brigade, in addition to the ordinary establishment of saddles.
These are distributed to the Units of the Brigade, each of which forms a pack train, consisting of its ordinary pack animals and light draught animals fitted with the additional pack saddles.

(b) For <u>Special Services</u> (i.e. abnormal ammunition requirements, transport of special reserve rations, water, etc.)
50 pack saddles are issued to S.A.A. Section D.A.C. A special pack section, the Officers and N.C.Os of which have previously reconnoitred the routes to the trenches, is thus formed.
This section, or portion of it, is allotted by Divisional Headquarters to Brigades, as found necessary for special work.

H.Q., 50th Div.
11th Decr. 1917.

[signed] Colonel,
A.A. & Q.M.G., 50th Division.

D.R.O. Distribution.

4th Northd. Fusiliers.
5th Northd. Fusiliers. F
6th Northd. Fusiliers.
7th Northd. Fusiliers.
Brigade Transport Officer.

Reference Para. 9 above.
The Brigade Transport Officer will arrange to take all surplus pack saddles on his charge.

[signed] Captain,
Staff Captain,
149th Infantry Brigade.

14/12/17.

50th Division
Administrative Staff
War Diary

From: 1st January 1918
To: 31st January 1918

Volume XXXIII.

50th Division.

Army Form C. 2118.

ADMINISTRATIVE WAR DIARY or INTELLIGENCE SUMMARY.

JANUARY, 1918.

(Erase heading not required.)

Instructions regarding War Diaries and Intelligence Summaries are contained in F. S. Regs., Part II. and the Staff Manual respectively. Title pages will be prepared in manuscript.

Place	Date	Hour	Summary of Events and Information	Remarks and references to Appendices
YPRES (Advd D.H.Q.) BRANDHOEK (Rear D.H.Q.)	JAN: 1	149th	150th Infy Bde relieved 151st Infy Bde in Support - Bde H.Q. Convent YPRES. 151st Infy Bde relieved 149th Infy Bde in Front Line - Bde H.Q. ISRAEL HOUSE. 149th Infy Bde moved to BRANDHOEK Area. - Bde H.Q. BRANDHOEK. CASUALTIES. R.E. - 446th Fld Coy RE O.R. wounded 6 (inc. 2 at duty). 149th Bde - 4th N.F. O.R. wounded 1. 6th N.F. O.R. killed 1, wounded 2. 7th N.F. O.R. killed 4, wounded 1. 4 O.R. rep. "W" 30/12/17 should read 3 O.R. killed on that date. No:245 M.Gun Coy - O.R. wounded 3 (gas).	
	2		CASUALTIES. 149th Bde - 4th N.F. O.Rs killed 1. 149th T.M.Btty O.R. wounded 3 (at duty). 150th Bde - 4th Yorks Rgt Killed O.R.1. 151st Bde - 9th D.L.I. wounded O.R.6 (inc. 1 at duty). No:245 M.G.Coy - O.R. wounded 1 (gas).	
	3		149th Infy Bde moved to WATOU Area - Bde H.Q. WATOU. CASUALTIES. R.E. - 50th Divl Signal Coy RE O.R. wounded 1 (gas). 446th Fld Co RE O.R. wounded 3. 150th Bde - 4th Yorks O.Rs killed 1, wounded 1. 5th Yorks O.R. wounded 1 (gas). 151st Bde - 8th D.L.I. O.R. wounded 1 (at duty). 9th D.L.I. O.Rs wounded 2. 7th D.L.I.Pnrs - O.Rs wounded 1 (1/1/18).	
	4		150th Infy Bde moved to WINNEZEELE Area - Bde H.Q. WINNEZEELE. CASUALTIES. R.F.A. - 250th Bde O.Rs killed 2, wounded 9. 50th D.A.C. O.Rs wounded 1 (at duty). 149th Bde - No.149 M.Gun Coy O.Rs wounded 1. 150th Bde - 4th Yorks O.Rs wounded 3. 151st Bde - /O.Rs wounded 3 (inc. 1 at duty). 9/D.L.I.	

Army Form C. 2118.

(2)

ADMINISTRATIVE
WAR DIARY
or
INTELLIGENCE SUMMARY.
(Erase heading not required.)

Instructions regarding War Diaries and Intelligence Summaries are contained in F. S. Regs., Part II. and the Staff Manual respectively. Title pages will be prepared in manuscript.

Place	Date	Hour	Summary of Events and Information	Remarks and references to Appendices
STEENVOORDE (Rue de Carnot.)	JAN. 5		CASUALTIES. R.F.A. - 251st Bde O.R. wounded 1.	
	6		Divnl Hd-Qrs moved by road from YPRES and BRANDHOEK to STEENVOORDE (Corps Reserve) on relief by 33rd Division. 151st Infantry Bde relieved in front line by 19th Infy Bde (33rd Division). Bde H.Q. - Convent, YPRES. Later moved to EECKE area - Bde H.Q. EECKE. CASUALTIES. 150th Bde - 4th Yorks O.R. wounded 1 (at duty, 5/1/18).	
	7		CASUALTIES. 150th Bde - R.A.M.C. attd 4th Yorks Capt.E.S.SIMPSON wounded 6/1/18 (gas). 5th Yorks Lieut. E.A.LISTER wounded (gas) 6/1/18. 151st Bde - 5th Borders O.R. wounded 1. 9th D.L.I. attd Lt.A.A.CAMPBELL wounded (at duty) 6/1/18.	
	8		Relief of 50th Divnl Artillery by 33rd Divnl Artillery completed. 50th D.A. in POPERINGHE Area.	
	9			
	10			
	11			
	12			
	13		Capt.H.J.GWYTHER, MC., took up duties of Bde Major, 151st Infy Bde.	
	14			
	15		Move of 50th Divnl Artillery to THIEMBRONNE Area from POPERINGHE Area completed. In G.H.Q. Reserve.	

Army Form C. 2118.

(3)

ADMINISTRATIVE WAR DIARY
or
INTELLIGENCE SUMMARY.

(Erase heading not required.)

Instructions regarding War Diaries and Intelligence Summaries are contained in F. S. Regs., Part II. and the Staff Manual respectively. Title pages will be prepared in manuscript.

Place	Date	Hour	Summary of Events and Information	Remarks and references to Appendices
	JAN: 16		150th Infy Bde moved from STEENVOORDE to TILQUES Area – Bde H.Q. HALLINES.	
	17		151st Infy Bde moved from EECKE Area to TILQUES Area – Bde H.Q. at BOESDINGHEM. CASUALTIES. 7th Durh.L.I.Pnrs Lt.H.J.LITTLE wounded (gas) 8/1/18 (not prev. rep.)	
	18		149th Infy Bde moved from WATOU to TATINGHEM Area – Bde H.Q. TATINGHEM.	
WIZERNES.	19		Divnl H.Q. moved from STEENVOORDE to WIZERNES.	
	20			
	21			
	22			
	23			
	24			
	25			
	26			
	27		50th Divl Art'y commenced move from THIEMBRONNE Area to POPERINGHE Area. 149th Infy Bde completed move by road and rail to YPRES Area – Bde H.Q. at YPRES.	

(A8:04) D. D. & L., London, E.C. Wt W1771/M2031 750,000 5/17 **Sch. 52** Forms/C2118/14

(4)

Army Form C. 2118.

ADMINISTRATIVE WAR DIARY
or
INTELLIGENCE SUMMARY.

(Erase heading not required.)

Instructions regarding War Diaries and Intelligence Summaries are contained in F. S. Regs., Part II. and the Staff Manual respectively. Title pages will be prepared in manuscript.

Place	Date	Hour	Summary of Events and Information	Remarks and references to Appendices
	JAN: 28		150th Infy Bde completed move by road and rail to BRANDHOEK - YPRES Area. Bde H.Q. BRANDHOEK.	
	29		Move of 50th D.Art'y to POPERINGHE Area completed. Relief in front line of 98th Infy Bde (33rd Divn) by 149th Infy Bde completed - 149th Infy Bde H.Q. at D.20.c.8.9.	
Ramparts, YPRES.	30		151st Infy Bde completed move by road and rail to BRANDHOEK Area - Bde H.Q. BRANDHOEK. Divnl H.Q. moved from WIZERNES to YPRES. CASUALTIES. 149th Infy Bde - 5th N.F. wounded 2/Lt.H.L.WRIGLEY, O.R.2. 6th N.F. killed O.R.1. 7th N.F. wounded O.R.1.	
	31		CASUALTIES. 149th Bde - 5th N.F. killed O.R.1.	

50TH (NORTHUMBRIAN) DIVISION.

ADMINISTRATIVE STAFF "A & Q"

WAR DIARY

FEBRUARY

1918

VOLUME NO. XXXIV.

50TH DIVISION.

ADMINISTRATIVE WAR DIARY or INTELLIGENCE SUMMARY.

Army Form C. 2118.

(Erase heading not required.)

FEBRUARY 1918.

Instructions regarding War Diaries and Intelligence Summaries are contained in F.S. Regs., Part II. and the Staff Manual respectively. Title pages will be prepared in manuscript.

Place	Date	Hour	Summary of Events and Information	Remarks and references to Appendices
Advd D.H.Q. RAMPARTS, YPRES. Rear D.H.Q. BRANDHOEK.	FEB:	1	CASUALTIES:- 149th Infy Bde - 5th N.F. wounded O.R.1. 6th N.F. wounded O.R. 1.	
		2	150th Infy Bde relieved 149th Infy Bde in front line - Bde H.Q. D.20.c.8.9. 149th Infy Bde moved to Reserve Area, BRANDHOEK - Bde H.Q. BRANDHOEK 151st Infy Bde moved to Support Area - Bde H.Q. Convent, YPRES.	
		3	CASUALTIES:- 150th Infy Bde - 4th East Yorks Regt wounded O.R. 1.	
		4	CASUALTIES:- 7th Field Coy RE wounded O.R. 1. 150th Infy Bde - 5th D.L.I. killed O.R. 1. 8th D.L.I. wounded O.R. 1 (acc.)	
		5	CASUALTIES:- 150th Infy Bde - 4th E.Yorks missing O.R. 2. 5th D.L.I. wounded O.R. 4.	
		6	CASUALTIES:- 150th Infy Bde - 5th D.L.I. wounded O.R. 1. 151st do - 8th D.L.I. wounded at duty 2/Lt.J.R.BARR 6/2/18. 7th Durh.L.I.Pnrs - wounded O.R. 1. 151st Infy Bde relieved 150th Infy Bde in front line - Bde H.Q. D.20.c.8.9. 149th Infy Bde relieved 151st Infy Bde in Support area - Bde H.Q. Convent, YPRES. 150th Infy Bde moved to Reserve area BRANDHOEK - Bde H.Q. BRANDHOEK.	
		7	CASUALTIES:- 151st Infy Bde - 8th D.L.I. 2/Lt.J.R.BARR reported wounded at duty now reptd wounded. 38th A.F.A. Bde - wounded O.R. 1.	
		8	CASUALTIES:- 151st Infy Bde - 8th D.L.I. wounded O.R. 1. 150th Infy Bde - 4th East Yorks 1 O.R. reptd missing night 4/5th Feb. now rejoined.	

50TH DIVISION.

FEBRUARY 1918.

ADMINISTRATIVE WAR DIARY or INTELLIGENCE SUMMARY.

(Erase heading not required.)

Army Form C. 2118.

Instructions regarding War Diaries and Intelligence Summaries are contained in F.S. Regs., Part II. and the Staff Manual respectively. Title pages will be prepared in manuscript.

Place	Date	Hour	Summary of Events and Information	Remarks and references to Appendices
	FEB:	9	CASUALTIES. 151st Infy Bde - No.151 M.Gun Coy wounded O.R. 1.	
		10	CASUALTIES. 251st Bde RFA - wounded O.R.1. 149th Infy Bde - 4th N.F. wounded O.R.2. 5th N.F. wounded O.R. 2. 151st Infy Bde - 5th Bord.R. wounded O.R.3 (inc. 1 at duty). 6th D.L.I. killed O.R. 2, missing O.R.1. 8th D.L.I. wounded O.R. 5 inc. 1 at duty. Divnl Front extended. 149th Infy Bde relieved 199th Infy Bde in front line - Bde H.Q. D.26.a.6.4. 151st Infy Bde moved to POTIJZE Support Area - Bde H.Q. Convent, YPRES.	
		11	151st Infy Bde moved to POTIJZE Support Area - Bde H.Q. Convent, YPRES. 150th Infy Bde relieved 151st Infy Bde in Left Sector - Bde H.Q. D.20.c.8.9.	
		12	7th N.F. transferred to 42nd Division and converted into Pioneer Battalion.⎫ on re-organisa- 9th D.L.I. transferred to 62nd Division " " " " ⎬ tion of 5th D.L.I. transferred from 150th Infy Bde to 151st Infy Bde ⎭ Divisions.	
		13	CASUALTIES. 7th Durh.L.I.Pnrs wounded O.R. 1. 5th Bord.R. transferred to 66th Division and converted into Pioneer Battalion on re-organisation of Divisions.	
		14	CASUALTIES. 149th Infy Bde - 6th N.F. wounded O.R. 1. 151st Infy Bde relieved 150th Infy Bde in Left Sector - Bde H.Q. D.20.c.8.9. 150th Infy Bde moved to Support Area, POTIJZE - Bde H.Q. Convent, YPRES.	
		15	CASUALTIES. 149th Infy Bde - 6th N.F. wounded O.R. 1. 151st Infy Bde - 8th D.L.I. wounded O.R. 1.	
		16	CASUALTIES. 151st Infy Bde - 8th D.L.I. wounded O.R. 2.	

50TH DIVISION.

FEBRUARY 1918.

Army Form C. 2118.

ADMINISTRATIVE WAR DIARY
or
INTELLIGENCE SUMMARY.

(Erase heading not required.)

Instructions regarding War Diaries and Intelligence Summaries are contained in F. S. Regs., Part II. and the Staff Manual respectively. Title pages will be prepared in manuscript.

Place	Date	Hour	Summary of Events and Information	Remarks and references to Appendices
	FEB: 17		CASUALTIES. 149th Infy Bde - 5th N.F. O.Rs killed 1, wounded 4. 150th Infy Bde - 4th Yorks wounded O.R. 1. 151st Infy Bde - 8th D.L.I. O.Rs killed 1, wounded 3, inc. 1 S.I.W.	
	18		CASUALTIES. 151st Infy Bde - 8th D.L.I. wounded O.R. 1.	
	19		CASUALTIES. Divnl R.E. - 7th Field Coy RE wounded O.R.1 at duty. 149th Infy Bde - 4th N.F. wounded O.R.1. 150th Infy Bde - 4th Yorks Regt wounded O.R. 1. 151st Infy Bde - 6th D.L.I. O.Rs killed 1, wounded 9, inc. 2 at duty. 150th Infy Bde relieved 151st Infy Bde in Left Sector - Bde H.Q. D.20.c.8.9. 151st Infy Bde moved to POTIJZE Support Area - Bde H.Q. Convent, YPRES.	
	20		CASUALTIES. 150th Infy Bde - 4th East Yorks wounded O.R.4. 5th Yorks Regt wounded O.R. 1. 19th Infy Bde (33rd Div.) relieved 151st Infy Bde in Support Area - Bde H.Q. Convent, YPRES. 151st Infy Bde Group moved by road and rail to TATINGHEM Area - Bde H.Q. TATINGHEM.	
	21		CASUALTIES. Divnl R.A. - 251st Bde RFA missing O.R.1. 149th Infy Bde - 6th N.F. wounded O.R. 1. 150th Infy Bde - 4th E.Yorks wounded O.R. 1. 4th Yorks wounded O.R. 1. 5th Yorks O.Rs killed 1, wounded 2 in front line - Bde H.Q. D.20.c.8.9.	
	22		19th Infy Bde relieved 150th Infy Bde in Support Area, POTIJZE - Bde H.Q. Convent, YPRES. 150th Infy Bde moved by road and rail to TILQUES Area - Bde H.Q. HALLINES.	
	23		CASUALTIES. 149th Infy Bde - 4th N.F. wounded O.R. 1. 149th Infy Bde moved by road and rail to TILQUES Area - Bde H.Q. BOISDINGHEM. Divisional H.Q. moved to WIZERNES.	
WIZERNES.				

50TH DIVISION.

FEBRUARY 1918.

Army Form C. 2118.

Instructions regarding War Diaries and Intelligence Summaries are contained in F. S. Regs., Part II. and the Staff Manual respectively. Title pages will be prepared in manuscript.

ADMINISTRATIVE WAR DIARY
or
INTELLIGENCE SUMMARY.
(Erase heading not required.)

Place	Date	Hour	Summary of Events and Information	Remarks and references to Appendices
	FEBY:	24	50th Divnl Artillery relieved/33rd Divnl Artillery – 50th D.A. H.Q. at THIEMBRONNE.	
		25	Colonel C.M.Cartwright, CB. CMG. appointed A.A. & Q.M.G., MARSEILLES Base.	
		26	Capt.A.C.H.Duke (Reserve of Officers), D.A.Q.M.G., 57th Division, appointed A.A. & Q.M.G., and took up duties.	
		27		
		28		
		29		
		30		

50th Divisional Administration

A. & Q.

50th (Northumbrian) DIVISION

MARCH 1918

CONFIDENTIAL
Original

WD 36

50th Division

Administrative Staff

War Diary

From: 1st March 1918.

To: 31st March 1918.

Volume XXXV.

Army Form C. 2118.

MARCH 1918.

50TH (NORTHUMBRIAN) DIVISION.
WAR DIARY
INTELLIGENCE SUMMARY.
(Erase heading not required.)

Instructions regarding War Diaries and Intelligence Summaries are contained in F. S. Regs., Part II. and the Staff Manual respectively. Title pages will be prepared in manuscript.

Place	Date	Hour	Summary of Events and Information	Remarks and references to Appendices
WIZERNES.	1			
	2			
	3			
	4			
	5			
	6			
	7			
	8			
	9		Division moved to Fifth Army Area. Divisional Headquarters to MOREUIL.	
MOREUIL.	10		DIVISIONAL HEADQUARTERS MOVED TO HARBONNIERES.	
HARBONNIERES	11		Captain S.J.Paget assumed duties as Brigade Major 149th Infantry Brigade, vice Lieut. T. Captain W.Anderson, DSO. MC. 8th North'l Fusiliers, to G.S.O. 2 37th Division., with temporary rank of Major. Division moved to Fifth Army Reserve area.	
	12			
	13			
	14			
	15			

Army Form C. 2118.

50TH (NORTHUMBRIAN) DIVISION.
WAR DIARY
of
INTELLIGENCE SUMMARY.

(Erase heading not required.)

Instructions regarding War Diaries and Intelligence Summaries are contained in F. S. Regs., Part II. and the Staff Manual respectively. Title pages will be prepared in manuscript.

Place	Date	Hour	Summary of Events and Information	Remarks and references to Appendices
HARBONNIERES.	15	—	Captain J.A. Bell, 7th Durham Light Infantry (Pioneers) assumed duties Staff Captain 149th Infantry Brigade, vice Captain G.S.Haggie, 5th North'd Fusiliers to England tour of duty.	
	16			
	17		Brigadier General C.Coffin, VC.DSO, G.O.C. 25th Infantry Brigade relinquished temporary command of 50th Division. Brigadier General A.U.Stockley, C.M.G. assumed temporary command of the 50th Division.	
	18			
	19		Captain F.H.Witts, MC. Irish Guards assumed duties of acting Brigade Major 150th Infantry Brigade, vice Captain J.N.Lumley, 13 Hussars to acting G.S.O. 2 3rd Division.	
	20			
BEAUMETZ.	21		Division moved to Fifth Army forward area. Divisional Headquarters to BEAUMETZ.	
Le MESNIL.	22		Divisional Headquarters withdrawn to Le Mesnil.	
VILLERS CARBONNEL	23		Divisional Headquarters moved to VILLERS CARBONNEL arriving about 11 a.m. and moved to FOUCAUCOURT.	
FOUCAUCOURT.				
VALLEY ST MARTIN.	24		Brigadier General A.U.Stockley, C.M.G. C.R.A. 50th Division relinquished temporary command of 50th Division on arrival of Brigadier General H.C.Jackson, DSO. to command. Brigadier General Jackson, DSO. 179th Infantry Brigade assumed command of Division with temporary rank of Major General, vice Major General Sir P.S.Wilkinson, KCMG. CB to England. Divisional Headquarters withdrawn to VALLEY ST. MARTIN about 1 mile behind FOUCAUCOURT.	

Army Form C. 2118.

50TH (NORTHUMBRIAN) DIVISION.
WAR DIARY
INTELLIGENCE SUMMARY.
(Erase heading not required.)

Instructions regarding War Diaries and Intelligence
Summaries are contained in F. S. Regs., Part II.
and the Staff Manual respectively. Title pages
will be prepared in manuscript.

Place	Date	Hour	Summary of Events and Information	Remarks and references to Appendices
VALLEY ST MARTIN	26		Divisional Headquarters withdrawn to HARBONIERES.	
HARBON- IERES.				
MARCELCAVE.	26		Divisional Headquarters withdrawn to MARCELCAVE.	
VILLERS BRETONNEUX.	27		Divisional Headquarters withdrawn to VILLERS BRETONNEUX.	
HANGARD. SOURDON.	28		Divisional Headquarters withdrawn to HANGARD about noon. Divisional Headquarters withdrawn in afternoon to SOURDON.	
SOURDON	29		Divisional Headquarters moved from SOURDON to BOVES.	
BOVES.				
BOVES.	30		Divisional Headquarters moved from BOVES to SAINS-EN-AMIENOIS.	
DOURIEZ	31		Division less Royal Artillery and one composite force (of 149th and 170th Infantry Brigades operating with 20th Division) withdrawn from the line. Divisional Headquarters moved to DOURIEZ.	
			LIST OF CASUALTIES INCURRED BY THE DIVISION DURING THE PERIOD 22nd to 31st March, 1918 is attached.	

50th (NORTHUMBRIAN) DIVISION.

LIST No 1 dated 24/3/18.

22nd March to 31st March, 1918.

UNIT.	DATE.	KILLED. O.R.	WOUNDED. O.R.	MISSING. O.R.	NAMES OF OFFICERS.	REMARKS.
ROYAL ENGINEERS.						
7th Field Company R.E.	22/3/18.	-	1	1a	2/Lt. H.A.BESON, R.E. 7th Field Coy. RE.	W. a wounded.
446th (Nbn) Field Coy. R.E.	"	-	-	-	Capt. (A/Lt.Col.) W. ROB.MC. KOYLI. attd 4th N.F.	W.
149th INFANTRY BRIGADE.						
4th North'd Fusiliers	"	1	2	-	LIEUT. J.V.COCKBURN 4th N.F.	K.
150TH INFANTRY BRIGADE.						
4th E. Yorkshire Regt.	"	1	2	5	CAPT. T.W.GREGORY, 4th E. Yorkshire Regt.	K.
	"	8	1	1	2/Lt. G.W.DREWERY, 4th E. Yorkshire Regt.	K.
					2/LT. H. KETTLE, 4th E. Yorkshire Regt.	W & M b1d P of W
					Lieut. T.G.HOLLIS, 4th E. Yorkshire Regt.	W & M b1d P of W
151st INFANTRY BRIGADE.					LIEUT. F.E.FURLEY.	K.
5th Durham Light Infantry.	23/3/18.	13	1	6	2/LIEUT. C.R.INGHAM,	M.
6th Durham Light Infantry.	"	1	1	3¾	2/LIEUT. R.E.HATFIELD	M b incl. 1 at M
8th Durham Light Infantry.	"	-	1	16b	2/LIEUT. H. NEEDHAM	L. duty,
50TH M.G.BATTALION.	22/23/3/18.	5	4	20 2b 7b	LIEUT G.D.TIBBITTS. MORO attd do	W at duty.
7th DURHAM LIGHT INFY Pers.	23/3/18.	2	2	3 -	Captain(A/Lt.Col.)B.H.CHARLTON MC. 4th Yorkshire Regt.	
					LIEUT(A/Capt) J.S.SAINSBRIDGE. 4th Yorks R.K.	K.
					Bt. MAJOR H.BROWN. DSO.MC. 5th attd do	K.
					CAPTAIN J.K.H.HESSLER. 5th Durham L.I.	K.
					2/LIEUT. H.J.W.SCOTT, do	W.
					CAPTAIN F. BERRIFORD.DLI. attd 8th DLI.	W.
					LIEUT. W.S.H.BEDDAL. 50th Bn. M.G.C.	W.
					(Shewn W.S. in Arty List column 1565 K.)	
					2/LIEUT. R.B. MASON. 50th Bn. M.G.C.	W.
					2/Lieut T.A. BAXTER. do	K.
					2/LIEUT. ATTWATER. do	K.
					2/LIEUT. L.E. PHILLIPS do	W.
					LIEUT P.H.HIGHT, do	M.
					2/LIEUT T. WAINWRIGHT. do	M.
					CAPTAIN J.R.HOUFTON. do	W & M.
					LIEUT (A/Major) G.D.R.DOBSON 7th DL.I.	W.
					Lieut J.HETHERINGTON. do	W.
	7	22	13	103 7.64		

UNIT. (LIST NO 2). 25/3/18	DATE.	KILLED.		WOUNDED.		MISSING.		NAMES OF OFFICERS.	REMARKS.
		O.	O.R.	O.	O.R.	O.	O.R.		
149TH INFANTRY BRIGADE.	22/3/18.							LIEUT (A/CAPT) H.G.KING. MC. NF attd 4th N.F.	M.
149th T.M.Battery.	"			1	2			do A.FINLAYSON 6th HLI	W.
4th North'd Fusiliers.	"		12	1	73	4	103	LIEUT T.C.LUND. 4th N.F.	M.
5th North'd Fusiliers.	"		9		33		73	2/LIEUT T.TIBBS. N.F. attd 4th N.F.	K.
6th North'd Fusiliers.	"		20	3	50	3a	190	2/LIEUT L.R.CHEVREAU do	K.
attd 149th Bde H.Q.								2/LIEUT T. NETTLESHIP. do	W.
1st Camb. Regt.	"				1			2/LIEUT C.J.MACKINTOSH 20th N.F. attd 5th N.F.	K.
2nd Suffolk Regt.	"				1b			2/LIEUT W.H.J.MARKHAM. N.F. attd 5th N.F.	M.
150TH INFANTRY BRIGADE.	23/3/18.							2/LIEUT T.A.CROFTS N.F. attd 5th N.F.	M.
5th Yorkshire Regt.					9		8c	LIEUT C..BAIDEN, 4th attd 6th N.F.	W & M
								2/LIEUT J.H.MILTON. do	W & M
								LIEUT G.A.OSWALD, 6th North'd Fusiliers.	W & M
a includes 1 wounded.								LIEUT S.J.B.STANTON. do	W
b includes 1 at duty,								LIEUT 1. do	W
c wounded.		2	41	4	169	9	338.	CAPTAIN K.M.DRUMMOND do	W

(LIST NO 3.) dated 29th March, 1918.									
149th INFANTRY BRIGADE.	27/3/18.							Bt. LT. COL. WILKINSON ,DSO KOSB & E.Yorks R	W.
4th North'd Fusiliers.	"			1				(Bt. Lt. Col /3/18 London Gazette /3/18)	
5th North'd Fusiliers.	"			1				2/LIEUT W. ADAMSON 4th North'd Fus.	W.
6th North'd Fusiliers.	"			1				2/LIEUT H. WHITE. 4th attd 5th N.F.	W.
150TH INFANTRY BRIGADE.								LIEUT T.V.THOMPSON (since D. of W. 28/3/18)	
4th E. Yorkshire Regt.	"			1				N.F. attd 5th N.F.	W.
5th Yorkshire Regt.	"			1				CAPTAIN H.D.K.DAVIES, 8th North'd Fus.	W.
5th attd 4th Yorks Regt	"			1				LIEUT J.V.TOWNSEND, 5th Yorkshire Regt.	W.
attd 150th T.M.B.	"			1				2/LIEUT R. CAMPBELL, 5th attd 4th Yorks Regt	W.
151ST INFANTRY BRIGADE.	"			4				attd 150th T.M.Battery.	
5th Durham Light Infantry.	"							2/LIEUT H.A.L.CHABEN, 5th Durham L.I.	W.
8th Durham Light Infantry.	"			2				2/LIEUT E. LINES, do	W.
50TH BN. M.G. CORPS.	"							MAJOR A.L.RIMES. do	W.
151st M.G. Company.	"							LIEUT P.J.STOCKDLE, do	W.
ROYAL ENGINEERS.	"							Capt(T/Lt.Col) J.A. MARTIN.MC. KOYLI. 8 h DLI.	W.
7th Field Coy. RE.	"					1a		T/LIEUT. A.E.JONES. 151st M.G.Company. W at duty	
H.Q. 50th Division.	"					2a		2/LIEUT. H.T.J.KEENS, do	W.
R.A.M.C.									
1/1st (Nthn) Field Ambulance.	29/3/18.					1b		a accidental,	
		1		14	4	1b		b at duty.	

LIST NO. 4. dated 30th March, 1918.

UNIT.	DATE.	KILLED. OF.	KILLED. O.R.	WOUNDED. O.	WOUNDED. O.R.	MISSING. O.	MISSING. O.R.	NAMES OF OFFICERS.
ROYAL ENGINEERS.								
7th Field Company. R.E.	27/3/18.	—	—	1	1	—	—	T/CAPTAIN S.J.PAGET, Bde Major 149th Infantry Brigade. M.bld K.
do	28/3/18.	—	1	—	10	—	—	CAPTAIN J.A.BELL, 7th D.L.I. (Pnrs) do W.
447th Field Coy. R.E.	28/3/18.	—	—	1	—	—	1	Staff Captain 149th Inf. Bde. W. Lieut (A/Major) H.A.BAKER. RE. 7th Field Coy. W.
149TH INFANTRY BRIGADE H.Q.	"	—	—	1	—	—	—	MAJOR A.J.D.CHIVERS. RE. 447th Field Coy. W.
150TH INFANTRY BRIGADE.	"	—	—	—	—	—	—	LIEUT J.C.C.BRUCE. do W.
4th Yorkshire Regt.	28/3/18.	—	—	1	—	—	—	LIEUT. R. EDWARDS. 4th Yorkshire Regt. W.
151ST INFANTRY BRIGADE.		—	—	—	—	—	—	LIEUT H. GREEN. MC. 5th Durham Light Infy. W.
5th Durham Light Infy.	27/3/18.	—	—	2	—	—	2	2/LIEUT. J.C.SMITH, DLI. attd do W.
								CAPTAIN L.W.TAYLOR. 5th Durham L.I. W & M.
								LIEUT. J.M.SLACK, DLI. attd do M.

LIST NO. 5. dated 31st March, 1918.

UNIT.	DATE.	KILLED. OF.	KILLED. O.R.	WOUNDED. O.	WOUNDED. O.R.	MISSING. O.	MISSING. O.R.	NAMES OF OFFICERS.
H.Q. 50th Division.	29/3/18.	—	—	1	1	—	—	Captain A.W.Smith, 8th Cheshire Regt Intelligence Officer 50th Divn. W.
ROYAL ARTILLERY								T/LIEUT (A/Capt) J.A.HUDSON RE. attd 50 D.A. W.
H.Q.	"	—	—	—	—	—	—	CAPT (A/MAJOR) E.G.ANGUS. MC. 250th Bde RFA. W.
R.E. attd H.Q.	21/3/18.	—	—	1	3	—	1	2/LIEUT J.FERGUSON. RA. 250th Bde RFA. W.
250th Bde, R.F.A.	"	—	2	2	20	—	4	Major (T/Lt. Col.)F.W.ROBSON. DSO. 5th Yorkshire Reg t Comdg 6th DLI. K.
251st Bde R.F.A.	28/3/19.	—	2	—	4	—	—	LIEUT (A/CAPT) H.WALTON.MC. 6th DLI. K.
do	31/3/18.	—	1	—	3	—	—	2/LIEUT. H.R.PINKNEY, DLI. 6th DLI. W.
50th Divl. Amn. Col.	"	—	—	—	11	—	—	2/LIEUT H. ORTON, 5th attd 6th D.L.I. W.
151ST INFANTRY BRIGADE.	"	—	—	—	1	—	—	2/LIEUT. A.A.HORROD, 6th Durham L.I. W.
6th Bn. Durham LI.	25/3/18.	3	—	5	—	3a	—	2/LIEUT. J.C.HESLOP. 6th Durham L.I. W.
8th Bn. Durham L.I.	24/3/18.	1	1	2	1	1b	—	CAPTAIN R. PEBERDY, 6th Durham L.I. W.
7TH DURHAM L.I. (PIONEERS):	23/3/18.	—	—	—	4	—	—	LIEUT D.F.CHARLTON, LI. attd 6th D.L.I. M.
do	24/3/18.	1	4	—	14	—	—	Lieut A.DOBSON, 6th Durham L.I. M.
do	25/3/18.	1	5	—	32	—	1	Lieut T.J.BURTON, 6th Durham L.I. W.
do	26/3/18.	—	2	—	9	—	50	2/LIEUT E.A.TIMPERTON 4th attd 6th D.L.I. W.
do	27/3/18.	1	4	—	—	—	—	Captain H.J.Moylam, 8th Durham L.I. K.
do	28/3/18.	1	8	2	56	—	—	LIEUT H.S.MACKINLAY, 8th Durham L.I. K.
do	29/3/18.	—	2	—	8	—	—	2/LIEUT H.L.FISHER, DLI. attd 8th DLI. W.
do	30/3/18.	—	—	—	1	—	—	CAPTAIN T.E.SLATER. RB. R.A.C. attd 8th DLI.M bld P.W.

LIST NO 5 continued.

	DATE.	KILLED		WOUNDED		MISSING		NAMES OF OFFICERS.
		O.	O.R.	O.	O.R.	O.	O.R.	
H.N.L.T.								LIEUT (A/CAPT) H. THOMPSON. 7th D.L.I. (Pnrs) K.
ROYAL ENGINEERS.								LIEUT J.D.KNIGHT, 7th D.L.I. (Pnrs). K.
447th (Nbn) Field Coy.	27/3/18.	-	-	-	4	-	-	2/LIEUT. E. WILSON, DLI. attd 7th D.L.I. K.
do	23/3/18.	-	1	-	10	-	-	LIEUT. H.J. LITTLE K 7th D.L.I.(Pnrs) K.
50th Bn. M.G.Corps,	25/3/18.	-	-	-	1	-	-	LIEUT E.H.HOPPER. 7th D.L.I.(Pnrs) W.
do	26/3/18.	-	-	-	8d	-	-	2/LIEUT. R.C.ROBINSON. DLI. attd 7th DLI. Pnrs. W.
do	27/3/18.	1	1	-	9	-	2	2/LIEUT. G. NIXON 7th D.L.I. Pnrs. W.
do	28/3/18.	-	2	-	6	-	-	2/LIEUT. K. TINDLE. do (shown as TINDALL in AL)M.
do	29/3/18.	-	-	-	2	-	-	
do	30/3/18.	-	-	-	3	-	-	a. includes 1 Bld D. of W.
do	31/3/18.	-	2	-	2	-	-	b. Bld Wounded.
R.A.M.C.								c. Wounded.
2/2nd (Nbn) Field Ambulance.	30/3/18.	-	-	-	1	-	-	d. includes 1 at duty.
do	31/3/18.	-	-	-	-	-	-	
		8.	35	14/	213	5	9	

LIST NO 6. dated 7th April, 1918.

149TH INFANTRY BRIGADE.								LIEUT (A/CAPT) W.B.HICKS, 4th N.F. W.& M 28/3/18
4th North'd Fus.	26/3/18.	-	-	-	-	-	-	LIEUT (A/Capt) T.A.L. THOMPSON. MC. 4th N.F. W. 27/3/18
do	27/3/18.	-	-	-	3	-	-	2/LIEUT. F. SIDDELEY. N.F. attd 4th N.F. W. "
do	30/3/18.	-	-	-	-	-	-	2/LIEUT. J.G. CLARKE. 4th N.F. W. "
5th North'd Fusiliers.	26/3/18.	-	-	6	1	1a	-	LIEUT (A/Capt) E.L. DOBSON. 4th N.F. W. "
do	27/3/18.	-	-	4b	-	1	-	LIEUT. G DAVIES 4th N.F. W. 26/3/18
do	30/3/18.	-	-	2c	20	-	-	CAPTAIN L.R.PROCTOR. N.F. attd 5th N.F. W. 27/3/18
6th North'd Fusiliers.	27/3/18.	1	-	3	10	1a	-	LIEUT J.B. WILSON. MC. 5th North'd Fus. W. at duty "
do	1/1/18	-	-	2	2	-	-	2/LIEUT. O. YOUNG. 5th North'd Fusiliers. W. "
do	28/3/18.	-	-	-	-	-	-	LIEUT C.V.PARKS. 5th North'd Fusiliers. W. "
149th T.M. Battery.	27/3/18.	-	-	1	1	-	-	CAPTAIN (A/Lt.Col.) N.I. WRIGHT. DSO. XXX
150TH INFANTRY BRIGADE.								7th attd 5th North'd Fusiliers. W. "
4th E. Yorkshire Regt.	25/3/18.	-	-	-	-	-	-	2/LIEUT. A COULSON. N.F. attd 5th N.F. M. 30/3/18
do	26/3/18.	-	-	-	-	-	1	LIEUT. L.W. HOWARD. 5th North'd Fusiliers. W. "
do	28/3/18.	-	-	-	-	-	-	CAPTAIN J.C.LEASK. do W. "
do	29/3/18.	-	-	-	-	-	-	2/LIEUT. T.A.HERDMAN. 4th attd 5th North'd Fus.W. 27/3/13
do	31/3/18.	-	-	-	-	-	-	2/LIEUT. S.E.H. ALLEN. 5th Devons attd 5 thN.F. K. 27/3/3
		1c	-	.20	-	3	-	LIEUT (A/CAPT) H. ARIST OKG.MC. 5th attd 6th N.F. W.
								2/LIEUT A.V.DAVIES. 7th attd 4th N.F. W.
								2/LIEUT J.H.BROWNRIGG. N.F. ATTD 6th N.F. W.

LIST NO. 6. continued.

UNIT.	DATE.	KILLED. O. O.R.	WOUNDED. O. O.R.	MISSING. O. O.R.	NAMES OF OFFICERS.
150TH INFANTRY BRIGADE.					
4th Yorkshire Regt.	22/3/18.	3 -	- -	- -	2/LIEUT. T. HALL. 4th N.F. attd 5th N.F. W & M 27/3/18.
do	23/3/18.	- -	2 -	- -	LIEUT. E.S. FOTHERBY, 6th North'd Fus. W. 23/3/18
do	25/3/18.	- -	- -	1 -	LIEUT. J.L.HOWELLS. 21st N.F. attd 6th N.F. W. "
do	27/3/18.	- -	- -	1 -	LIEUT. S. BROWN. 6th North'd Fusiliers. W. 1/4/18.
do	26/3/18.	- -	3 -	1 -	LIEUT. (A/Capt) JL.G.THOMAS.4th N.F.att 149 TMB. W. 27/3/18
do	28/3/18.	- -	- -	1 -	2/LIEUT. S.B.WILSON. 4th E.Yorkshire Regt. M. 25/3/18.
do				1e	Bt.LT.COL. W.T.WILKINSON. DSO. KOSB 4 E.Yorks R.W. 23/3/18.
do	31/3/18.	- -	3 -	- -	(List No. 5 note W. 27/3/18)
5th Yorkshire Regt.	25/3/18.	1 -	1 -	- -	2/LIEUT. P. GREEN. 4th E. Yorkshire Regt. M. 28/3/18.
do	26/3/18.	2 -	3 -	3d	2/LIEUT A FOSTER. E.Yorks attd 4th E.Yorks R.W. 29/3/18.
do	27/3/18.	- -	7 -	1 -	LIEUT. E. JARMAN. 4th E.Yorks Regt. W. 31/3/18
do	28/3/18.	- -	1 -	- -	2/LIEUT. A PRATT. 4th E.Yorkshire Regt. W. "
do	29/3/18.	- -	1 -	- -	CAPTAIN C.T.A.POLLOCK. Inns of Court OTC.
do	30/3/18.	4 -	1e	- -	attd 4th E.Yorks Regt.
			1 -		2/LIEUT S. WATERHOUSE. 4th E.Yorkshire Regt. M. "
					2/LIEUT. C. BROOKE. E.Yorks attd 4th E.Yorks R. M. "
					2/LIEUT. E.R.CHARLTON. 4th E.Yorkshire Regt. K. "
					2/LIEUT. G. THOMPSON. 4th E.Yorkshire Regt. W. "
150th T.M.Battery.	29/3/18.	- -	1e	- -	2/LIEUT W.S.CARRATT. "
	31/3/18.	- -	3b	- -	LIEUT. (A/Capt) D. SPURWAY, 4th Yorks Regt. K. 23/3/18.
151ST INFANTRY BRIGADE.					2/LIEUT. T.A. HYSLOP. MC. Yorks Regt
5th Durham L.I.	1/4/18.	- -	2 -	- -	attd 4th Yorks Regt. K. "
do					LIEUT. (A/Capt) C.N.C.STIFF.4th Yorkshire Regt.K. "
6th Durham L.I.	26/3/18.	2 -	- -	- -	2/LIEUT. W.L.SNOWBALL. do W. "
					2/LIEUT. J.G.HARDWICK. Yorks Regt attd 4th Yorks W. "
					2/LIEUT. H.SCORER. 4th Yorkshire Regt. W. "
					2/LIEUT. T.L.BEYNON. Yorks Regt attd 4th Yorks R.W.23/3/18.
					2/LIEUT ARC STEIN. 4th Yorkshire Regt. W. "
					LIEUT (A/Capt) A.R.POWYS. M. "
					2/LIEUT. W. TROTTON. M. "
					LIEUT. M. MACHAY. W. "
					2/LIEUT. D.J.E.LAMB.MC. 5th attd 4th Yorks R.W. 25/3/18.
					2/LIEUT. G.A.GREEN. Yorks Regt attd 4th Yorks R.M. 26/3/18.
					2/LIEUT. W.E.COOK. 4th Yorkshire Regt. W & M.28/3/18.
					LIEUT H.L.HARRISON. 4th Yorkshire Regt. W. 30/3/18.
					LIEUT S.R.DOBINSON. Yorks Regt attd 4th Yorks R K. 31/3/18.
					2/LIEUT W. FLETCHER. 4th Yorkshire Regt. W. "
					LIEUT H.P.GREGORY. 5th Yorkshire Regt. W & M. 25/3/18.
					LIEUT A HEPTON. "

a. wounded, b. includes 1 at duty.
c. date unknown; d. includes 2 wounded, e. at duty.

LIST NO. 6 continued.

NAMES OF OFFICERS.

2/LIEUT W.N.PEARSON. Yorks Regt. attd 5th Yorks Regt.	W & M	25/3/18.
2/LIEUT. J. BATTYE. 5th Yorkshire Regt.	K.	"
CAPTAIN W.E.E.GARROD. "	W.	"
2/LIEUT. L.S.WALLGATE. "	W.	"
LIEUT. E.R.WINSER. "	W.	"
LIEUT. (A/Capt) C.R.HURWORTH. "	K.	26/3/18.
LIEUT. H.E. EVANS.	K.	"
2/LIEUT. C.W.STODDART, 3rd attd 5th Yorks Regt.	W.	26/3/18
2/LIEUT. A.H.STRONG, 7th attd 5th Yorks Regt.	M.	"
2/LIEUT. W.G.MORRIS. Yorks Regt. attd 5th Yorkshire Regt.	W.	27/3/18
CAPTAIN G. THOMPSON. MC. 5th Yorkshire Regt.	W.	28/3/18.
CAPTAIN (A/Lt.Col).J.A.R.THOMSON. "	W at duty	29/3
2/LIEUT. C. CROPPER. Yorks Regt attd 5th Yorks Regt.	W.	30/3/18.
2/LIEUT. G.F.OAKDEN.4th E. Yorks attd 150th T.M.Bty.	W.	28/3/18.
MAJOR J. ELMER. 5th Durham Light Infantry	W. at duty	29/3/18
2/LIEUT. F. WILLIAMS. DLI attd 5th D.L.I.	W.	31/3/18.
LIEUT E.C.HOLMES. 5th Durham L.I.	W.	"
2/LIEUT G. WILKINSON. "	W at duty	"
2/LIEUT. A HANLEY. D.L.I. attd 5th D.L.I.	W.	1/4/18.
2/LIEUT. W. THOMPSON. 5th Durham L.I.	W.	"
2/LIEUT. T. SHARKEY. 6th Durham L.I.	K.	26/3/18.
2/LIEUT A.R.BURN. D.L.I. attd 6th D.L.I.	K.	"

DATE.	UNIT.	KILLED. O.R.	WOUNDED. O.R.	MISSING. O.R.
	149TH INFANTRY BRIGADE.			
23/3/18	4th North'd Fusiliers.	16	90	48a in. 12 M.bd W.
to				in. 3 M.bd K.
29/3/18	5th North'd Fusiliers.	12	113	83b in.47 M.bd P.W.
	6th North'd Fusiliers.	-	44	21c in. 9 wounded.
	149th T.M.Battery.	-	3	4d in. 2 wounded.
	1st Cam. Regt. attd 149th Inf.Bde.	-	1	-
	7th N.F. 149th Bde H.Q.	-	1	1
	50th Div. Sig. Coy.RE attd 149th Bde H.Q.	1	2	-
	150TH INFANTRY BRIGADE.			
21/3/18	4th E.Yorkshire Regt.	26	140	251e in.23 wounded.
to	4th Yorkshire Regt.	10	35	27f in. 2 wounded.
29/3/18.	do	14	89	173g in. 9 wounded.
	5th Yorkshire Regt.	42	190	44h in. 12 wounded
	150th T.M.Battery.	-	1	3
	R.A.M.C. 1/1st (Nbn) Field Ambulance.	-	-	6
22/3/18	**151ST INFANTRY BRIGADE.**			
to	5th Durham Light Infantry.	28	160	90
31/3/18	6th Durham Light Infantry.	34	172b	55a a in. 3 wounded b in. 4 at duty
	8th Durham Light Infantry.	18	130	71c c incl. 6 w.
	151st T.M.Battery.	-	3	-
		201	1198	879

CASUALTY WIRE NO. A. 80 dated 5/4/18.

UNIT.	DATE.	KILLED. O.	KILLED. O.R.	WOUNDED. O.	WOUNDED. O.R.	MISSING. O.	MISSING. O.R.	NAMES OF OFFICERS.
8th North'd Fusiliers.	27/3/18.	-	-	1	7	-	-	Capt(A/Lt.Col.)F.Robinson, DSO. R.Innis Fus. W. Commanding, 8th N.F.
50th Bn. M.G.Corps,	-	-	3	-	11	-	-	
Casualty wire A.24 dated 5/4/18.								a. at duty.
ROYAL ARTILLERY. 250th Bde, R.F.A.	31/3/18.	-	-	1a	1	-	-	2/Lt. K.M.Goodenough, RA. (S.R.) 250th Bde RFA.Wat duty
Casualty wire No. A 49 dated 5/4/19. 250th Bde R.F.A.	-	-	-	1	18	-	-	Lt. Col. R. Chapman, CMG. DSO. 250th Bde RFA. W.
4th E.Yorkshire Regt.	23/3/18.	-	-	-	-	1	-	2/Lt. G.F.Stephenson, 4th E.Yorkshire Regt. M.
250th Bde R.F.A.	-	-	-	-	2	-	-	
251st Bde R.F.A.	28/3/18. 29/3/18.	-	-	-	1 1	-	-	
150th INFANTRY BRIGADE. 4th E.Yorkshire Regt.	26/3/18.	-	-	1	X	-	-	Lieut C. Earle, 4th E.Yorkshire Regt. W.
1/3rd (Nbn) Field Amb.	-	-	-	-	3	-	-	

50th Div. QX/4763/50.   S E C R E T.

50TH DIVISION ADMINISTRATIVE INSTRUCTIONS NO: 35.
Ref. 50th Division Warning Order No:180 now being put into operation.

1. **ENTRAINING INSTRUCTION.-**

    Brigades will detail Officers not under rank of Captain to superintend entrainment of their Brigades. Names of Officers selected to be reported to this Office by wire.

    All the trains consist of 1 Officers Carriage, 17 flat trucks, and 30 covered trucks. Each flat truck will take on average of 4 axles.

    Each covered truck will take 40 men or 8 H.D.Horses or 8 L.D.Horses or Mules.

    No personnel or stores will be allowed in the brake vans at either end of the train. No covered truck should be used for baggage as it restricts the space available for personnel.

    All Units except Infantry will arrive complete at Entraining Stations 3 hours before the time of the departure of their train. Infantry Battalions Transport will arrive at Entraining Stations 3 hours before times of departure of their trains.

    Infantry personnel will arrive at entraining stations 1½ hours before the time of departure of their trains.

    All Infantry Battalions and Pioneer Battalions will detail their own loading parties, strength 1 Officer and 30 other ranks who will also unload trains at detraining stations. All other Units will be responsible for their own loading and unloading of their trains under Officers detailed for the purpose. Complete marching out states, shewing number of men, horses, G.S.wagons, Limbered G.S.Wagons, and 2-wheeled vehicles and bicycles will be sent down to R.T.O. 3½ hours before time of departure of trains. Each portion of limbered G.S.Wagons will be counted as a 2-wheeled vehicle on the state.

    Supply and baggage wagons will accompany their Units in every case.

    The entraining of all Units must be completed half an hour before the time of departure of the trains.

    Breast ropes for horse trucks must be provided by the Units themselves; ropes for lashing vehicles on the flat trucks will be provided by the railway. Senior Officer on each train will be in command of the train, and will detail picquets for each end of the train at all stops to prevent troops leaving. All doors of covered trucks and carriages on the right hand side of the train when on the main line must be kept closed. Arrangements will be made by the A.P.M. to control traffic on the road approaches to the entraining station. No troops or transport will be allowed to enter the yard without orders. Waterbottles must be carried full.

    Arrangements will be made by formations and units for the watering of horses before entraining and also at HOUR'S Halt at TAINQUES, if M.L.O. there reports to O.C., Train that there is time.

2. **ADVANCED PARTIES.-** consist of 1 Officer per Brigade and 1 Officer and 2 other ranks per Unit with bicycles who will entrain 2 trains earlier than their Unit from respective entraining stations. These advance parties will report to Administrative Commandant VILLERS BRETONNEUX for instructions. They will meet their units on detraining (approximately 6 hours later than themselves and act as guides).

3. Surplus kit will be dumped as instructed in D.R.O.No:5790 dated 6th March, 1916, and a list sent to this office as soon as possible stating the weight in terms of cwts- approximately.

4. **LEAVE.-** All parties due to proceed on leave 2 days after their Units entrain will be left behind with instructions to report to D.D.O. at ST.OMER Station or Detail Barracks, ST.OMER with 1 clear days rations.

(2).

Instructions about leave in New Area will be issued later. Leave lorries will not run to-day and afterwards.

D.D.O. travels with 21.50 train from ST.OMER on 9th inst.

5. AREA STORES.-
All Area Stores will be collected at Unit Headquarters if there is not time to return them to Area Commandant.

A list of these will be sent to Area Commandant and a copy to Divisional H.Qrs.

6. ORDNANCE STORES.-
These will be closed to-day and will move with Divisional Canteen, Divisional Gas School and Clothing Store from WIZERNES at 15.41 hours on 8th instant under orders of D.A.D.O.S.

7. LORRIES FOR BLANKETS.-
Guides for these will report to Divisional H.Qrs. "Q" Office at 9 a.m. to-day for the following :-

Infantry Brigades ... 4 each.
Machine Gun Batt'n. ... 4

Lorries of Infantry Brigades and Machine Gun Battalion will be kept by Brigades and Machine Gun Battalion until all their Units have entrained and will then be ordered to return to the Square, WIZERNES for further orders.

All other Units requiring lorries will report by wire the hour and place at which they will require them when they will be supplied.

8. SUPPLIES.-
All troops, except Divisional Artillery, will entrain with rations and forage up to and including for consumption 10th instant, and Divisional Artillery for consumption on 11th instant.

9. REAR PARTIES.-
These will not be left but C.O's. of all Units will arrange that all billets are left in a thoroughly clean and sanitary condition, obtaining certificates from Area Commandants to that effect as far as possible.

9.

8th March, 1918.

(sd) A.DUKE, Lt-Col.,
AA & QMG., 60th Division.

N.B.- Schedule of train time-table from entraining station is attached.

SECRET.

STARTING HOURS OF TRAINS.

Reference provisional programme for move issued with 50th
Division Warning order No.189 dated 25.3.18.

Train.	Date.	From WIZERNES.
No. 1	8th.	18.14.
No. 2.	8th.	21.14.
No. 3.	9th.	0.14.
No. 4.	9th.	3.14.
No. 5.	9th.	6.14.
No. 6.	9th.	9.14.
No. 7.	9th.	12.14.
No. 8	9th.	15.14.
No. 9.	9th.	18.14.
No.10.	9th.	21.14.
No.11.	10th.	0.14.
No.12.	10th.	–

Detrain ... BOVES.

A. & Q.

50th (NORTHUMBRIAN) DIVISION

APRIL 1918.

Casualty lists attached

APRIL 1918.

50TH (NORTHUMBRIAN) DIVISION.
WAR DIARY

(Erase heading not required.)

Army Form C. 2118.

Instructions regarding War Diaries and Intelligence Summaries are contained in F. S. Regs., Part II. and the Staff Manual respectively. Title pages will be prepared in manuscript.

Place	Date	Hour	Summary of Events and Information	Remarks and references to Appendices
DOURIEZ	1			
	2			
	3			
ROBECQ	4		Division (less Artillery) moved by bus to Robecq Area. Divisional Headquarters at ROBECQ	
	5			
	6			
	7			
MERVILLE	8		Division moved to MERVILLE Area. Divisional Headquarters at White Chateau.	
	9			
	10			
	11			
LA MOTTE THIENNES	12		Divisional Headquarters (less General Staff) withdraw to LA MOTTE Chateau and later the same day to THIENNES.	
	13			
Advd.D.H.Q. THIENNES Rear D.H.Q. WITTES	14		Divisional Headquarters, less General Staff and C.R.E., moved to WITTES.	

Army Form C. 2118.

50TH (NORTHUMBRIAN) DIVISION.
WAR DIARY
~~INTELLIGENCE SUMMARY~~

(Erase heading not required.)

Instructions regarding War Diaries and Intelligence Summaries are contained in F. S. Regs., Part II. and the Staff Manual respectively. Title pages will be prepared in manuscript.

Place	Date	Hour	Summary of Events and Information	Remarks and references to Appendices
ROQUETOIRE	15			
	16		Division withdrawn from front line Divisional Headquarters moved to ROQUETOIRE.	
	17			
	18			
	19			
AIRE, Rue de St Omer.	20		Division moved to AIRE Area. Divisional Headquarters to AIRE.	
	21			
	22		Lieut. A.F.SOAMES, Dorset Yeomanry, assumed duties as A.D.C. and Camp Commandant, Headquarters, 50th Division.	
	23			
	24			
	25			
	26		Division ordered to move to Southern portion of Front.	
	27			
ARCIS LE PONSART under IX Corps	28		Divisional Headquarters established at ARCIS-LE-PONSART.	
	29		Lieut. H.C.COOPER, 2nd Northumberland Fusiliers (attached 1/5th Loyal North Lancs) assumed duties as A.D.C. to G.O.C., 50th Division.	
	30		Complete list of casualties during the month is attached.	

50TH (NORTHUMBRIAN) DIVISION.

CASUALTY RETURN, NOON 8th April 1918 to NOON, 9th April 1918.

UNIT.	DATE.	KILLED. O.	KILLED. O.R.	WOUNDED O.	WOUNDED O.R.	MISSING. O.	MISSING. O.R.	REMARKS.
151ST INFANTRY BRIGADE.								
5th Durham Light Infantry	9/4/18	*	-	-	2	-	-	
6th Durham Light Infantry	"	-	-	7	10	-	-	
50TH BN. M.G. CORPS.	"	-	-	1	2	-	-	
TOTALS.		-	-	8	14	-	-	

NAMES OF OFFICERS.

```
 * 2/Lt. J.L.GOTT, D.L.I. attached 6th Durham Light Infy.      Wounded  9/4/18.
   Lieut. R.GREEN, MC, 6th Durham Light Infantry                  "       "
   Lieut. C.L.J.REES, 8th attched 6th Durham Light Infantry       "       "
   2/Lieut. G.H.KING, D.L.I. attd 6th Durham Light Infantry.      "       "
   P.H.B.LYON, MC, 6th Durham Light Infantry                      "       "
   2/Lieut L.C.WATSON, 6th Durham Light Infantry                  "       "
   Captain J.A.MACKENZIE, M.B. RAMC, attd. 6th Durham Light Infy. "       "
** 2/Lieut E.W.DERBYSHIRE, 50th Bn. M.G.Corps.                    "       "
```

* Column 1431 e Army List. ** Shewn as E. Column 1570 e Army List.

H.Q. 50th Div.,
9th April 1918.

(sd) W. McCRACKEN, Major,
for D.A.A.G. for Major General,
Commanding 50th (North"bn) Division.

50TH (NORTHUMBRIAN) DIVISION.

CASUALTY RETURN. NOON 9/4/18 to NOON 10/4/18

UNIT.	KILLED. O.	KILLED. O.R.	WOUNDED. O.	WOUNDED. O.R.	MISSING. O.	MISSING. O.R.	DATE.	REMARKS.
ROYAL ARTILLERY.								
446th Field Coy. R.E.	-	-	-	1a	-	-	9/4/18	a at duty
do.	-	1	-	-	-	-	10/4/18	
149th INFY BRIGADE.								
4th Northd Fusiliers	-	-	-	4	-	-	9/4/18.	
6th Northd Fusiliers	-	-	-	2	-	-	"	
R.E. Signals attd.								
149th Inf. Bde. H.Q.	-	-	-	1	-	-	"	
150TH INFY BRIGADE.								
4th E.Yorkshire Regt.	-	-	-	5	-	-	"	
5th Yorkshire Regt.	-	-	-	5	-	-	"	
152st INFY BRIGADE.								
5th Durh. Light Infy.	-	-	2	25	-	-	"	
6th Durh. Light Infy.	-	-	2	21	-	-	"	
8th Durh. Light Infy.	-	-	2	17	-	-	"	
151st T.M.Battery.	-	-	2	3	-	-	"	
50th Bn. M.F.Corps	-	-	2	3	-	-		
R.A.M.C.								
2/2nd North'bn Field Ambulance R.A.M.C.	-	-	-	1	-	-	"	
7th Durh. Light Infy. (Pioneers)	-	2	1	29	-	-	"	
TOTALS.	-	3	9	118	-	-		

TOTAL BY CATEGORIES.

Shell Fire	1
Rifle & M.G. fire	129
Total.	130

(sd) W. McCRACKEN, Major, for Lt.Col.
A.A.& Q.M.G. for Maj-Gen.,
Commanding 50th Division.

(P.T.O.

NAMES OF OFFICERS.

		WOUNDED.		
5th Durh. Light Infy.	Capt. P.WOOD, DSO	WOUNDED	9/4/18.	
do.	2/Lt. G.MAXWELL, DLI	"	"	
6th Durh. Light Infy.	2/Lt. B.R.LEATHERBARROW,	"	"	
do.	Hon.Capt & Q.M. W.M.Hope	"	"	Promoted Hon. Capt. London Gazette 28/2/18.
8th Durham.L.Infy.	Capt. R.H.GUEST-WILLIAMS	"	"	
do.	2/Lt. A.E.THOMSON DLI.	"	"	
50th Bn. M.G.Corps	2/Lt. L.R.BUTLIN, MC.	"	"	
do.	2/Lt. H.T.MADDOCKS	"	"	
7th Durh. Light Infy.	Lieut. F.C.TILBROOK.	"	"	

LIST NO. 3.

50TH (NORTHUMBRIAN) DIVISION.

CASUALTIES NOON 10/4/18 to NOON 11/4/18.

UNIT.	Date.	KILLED O.	KILLED O.R.	WOUNDED O.	WOUNDED O.R.	MISSING O.	MISSING O.R.	REMARKS.
ROYAL ARTILLERY.								
251st Brigade R.F.A.	31/3/18.	-	-	-	1a	-	-	a at duty.
do	7/4/18.	-	-	-	1	-	-	
ROYAL ENGINEERS.								
447th Field Coy. R.E.	10/4/18.	-	-	-	1	-	-	
149TH INFY. BDE.								
4th North'd Fusiliers.	11/4/18.	-	-	1	46	-	-	
5th do	"	-	-	-	53	-	-	
6th do	"	-	-	1	97	-	-	
150TH INFY BDE.								
4th E.Yorks Regt.	"	-	-	-	33	-	-	
4th Yorks Regt.	"	-	-	2	13	-	-	
5th Yorks Regt.	"	-	-	-	1	-	-	
151ST INFY BDE.								
5th Durham L.I.	10/4/18.	-	-	1	-	-	-	
"	9/4/18.	1	-	-	16	1	-	
6th "	"	1	-	1	5	4	-	
8th "	"	-	-	-	3	-	-	
151st T.M.Battery.	"	1	-	1	-	-	-	
7th DURHAM L.I. (Pnrs).	11/4/18.	-	-	2	17	-	-	
50th Bn. M.G.Corps.	10/4/18.	-	-	2	20	-	-	
	11/4/18.	-	-	1	-	-	-	
TOTALS.		3	-	12	307	5	-	

NAMES OF OFFICERS.

4th North'd Fusiliers.	2/LIEUT. C.H.DAVISON.	Wounded 11/4/18
6th North'd Fusiliers.	Lieut H. ROBINSON. 4th N.F.	do
4th Yorkshire Regiment.	MAJOR A. GRAHAM,	do
do	2/LIEUT. H.W.IBBETSON, Yorks Regt.	do
5th Durham Light Infy.	2/LIEUT. G. WILKINSON.	Killed 9/4/18.
do	LIEUT. G.H.CARRINGTON.	Missing, "
6th Durham Light Infy.	LIEUT. CL. TYERMAN.	Killed. "
do	2/LIEUT. R.A.WILSON, 4th D.L.I.	Wounded "
do	LIEUT (A/Capt) J.F.G.AUBIN. MC.	Missing, "
do	LIEUT (A/Capt) G. KIRKHOUSE.	" "
do	LIEUT. D.B.SCOTT.	" "
do	2/LIEUT F. SHIRTLIFFE, DLI.	" "
151st T.M. Battery.	LIEUT (A/Capt) R. CURRY, 8th D.L.I.	Killed "
do	2/LIEUT. W.R.LENG. 5th D.L.I.	Wounded "
7th D.L.I. (Pnrs).	LIEUT. F.J.ILES.	" 11/4/18.
do	LIEUT. S. PROBERT.	" "
50th Bn. M.G. Corps.	LIEUT. A.M.JONES. MC.	" 10/4/18.
do	2/LIEUT. G. BURGOINE.	" "
do	LIEUT. A.L.JENNER. MC.	" 11/4/18.
5th Durham Light Infy.	2/LIEUT. H. FAWCETT.	" 10/4/18.

Major.
D.A.A.G. for Major General.
Commanding, 50th (North'bn) Division.

12/4/18.

LIST NO. 4.

50TH (NORTHUMBRIAN) DIVISION.

CASUALTIES NOON 11/4/18 to NOON 12/4/18.

UNIT.	Date.	KILLED. O.	KILLED. O.R.	WOUNDED. O.	WOUNDED. O.R.	MISSING. O.	MISSING. O.R.	REMARKS.
149TH INFANTRY BDE.								
4th North'd Fus'lrs.	12/4/18.	–	–	2	59	–	–	
5th North'd Fus'lrs.	"	–	–	1	26	–	–	
6th North'd Fus'lrs.	"	–	–	–	51	–	–	
149th T.M.Battery.	"	–	–	1	2	–	–	
150TH INFANTRY BDE.								
4th E. Yorkshire Regt.	"	–	–	1	5	–	–	
4th Yorkshire Regt.	"	–	–	–	23	–	–	
5th Yorkshire Regt.	"	–	–	–	7	–	–	
151ST INFANTRY BDE.								
5th Durham Light Infy.	"	–	–	1	50	–	–	
6th Durham Light Infy.	"	–	–	–	15	–	–	
8th Durham Light Infy.	"	–	–	2	30	–	–	
7TH DURHAM LIGHT INFY. (PIONEERS)	"	–	–	–	58	–	–	
50th BN. M.G. CORPS.	"	–	–	2	13	–	–	
R.A.M.C.								
1/1st (North'n) Field Ambulance.	"	–	–	–	1	–	–	
2/2nd do	"	–	–	–	1	–	–	
50th Divl. Signal Coy. RE	"	–	–	–	1	–	–	
TOTALS.		–	–	10	346	–	–	

Attached Units.

34th Divl. Arty.								
152nd Bde. R.F.A.	11/4/18.	–	1	1	16	–	–	
GRAND TOTAL.		–	1	11	362	–	–	

NAMES OF OFFICERS, overleaf.

LIST NO. 5

50TH (NORTHUMBRIAN) DIVISION.

CASUALTIES FROM NOON 12/4/18 - NOON 13/4/18.

UNIT.	Date.	KILLED. O.	KILLED. O.R.	WOUNDED. O.	WOUNDED. O.R.	MISSING. O.	MISSING. O.R.	REMARKS.
ROYAL ENGINEERS.								
446th (Nbn) Field Coy.	12/4/18	1	-	-	1	-	-	
447th do.	"	-	1	1	2	-	-	
50th Divl. Signal Coy.	11/4/18	-	-	-	1	-	-	
do.	12/4/18	-	2	-	4	-	-	
149TH INFANTRY BRIGADE.								
4th Northd Fusiliers	12/4/18	-	-	-	14	-	-	
5th do.	"	-	-	1	13	-	-	
6th do.	"	-	1	1	7	-	-	
149th T.M. Battery	"	-	-	-	1	-	-	
150TH INFANTRY BRIGADE.								
4th E. Yorkshire Regt.	"	-	-	-	7	-	-	
4th Yorkshire Regt.	"	-	1	-	13	-	-	
5th do.	"	-	-	-	3	-	-	
150th T.M. Battery	"	-	-	-	1	-	-	
151ST INFANTRY BRIGADE.								
5th Durham L.I.	"	-	-	-	11	-	-	
6th do.	"	-	-	-	13	-	-	
8th do.	"	-	-	-	7	-	-	
50TH BN. M.G.CORPS.	"	-	-	-	9	-	-	
7TH DURHAM L.I.(PIONEERS)	"	-	-	1	18	-	-	
R.A.M.C.								
1/1st (NBN) Field Ambulance	"	-	-	-	1	-	-	
1/3rd do.	"	-	-	-	1	-	-	
		1	5	4	127	-	-	

NAMES OF OFFICERS.

446th (Nbn) Field Coy. R.E.	LIEUT. J.R.W.WILLIAMS, MC,RE,TF.	KILLED	12/4/18.
447th do.	LIEUT. C.R.PORTER, RE, TF	WOUNDED	"
5th Northd Fusiliers	2/LIEUT. J.E.RIGBY, NF.	"	"
6th do.	LIEUT. R.D.VERNON. NF.	"	"
7th Durham L.I.(Pioneers)	2/LIEUT. J.F.MADDISON, DLI	"	"

(sd) C.DUKE.Lt.Col.
A.A. & Q.M.G. for Major General,
Commanding 50th (North:bn) Division.

H.Q. 50th Div.,
13th April 1918.

LIST NO. 6.

50TH (NORTHUMBRIAN) DIVISION.

CASUALTIES NOON 13/4/18 - NOON 14/4/18.

UNIT.	Date.	KILLED. O.	KILLED. O.R.	WOUNDED. O.	WOUNDED. O.R.	MISSING. O.	MISSING. O.R.	REMARKS.
ROYAL ENGINEERS.								
446th (Nbn) Field Coy.	12/4/18.	-	-	-	5	-	-	
50th Div. Sig. Coy.	9/4/18.	-	-	-	1	-	-	
149TH INFANTRY BRIGADE.								
5th North'd Fuslrs.	13/4/18.	-	-	-	1	-	-	
151ST INFANTRY BRIGADE.								
Headquarters.	"	-	-	-	1	-	-	
6th Durham L.I.	"	-	-	1	1	-	-	
8th Durham L.I.	"	-	-	-	4	-	-	
7th DURHAM L.I.(Pnrs)	11/4/18	1	-	2	19	2	-	
A.P.M. (5th N.F. attd)	13/4/18.	-	-	-	1	-	-	
50TH BN. M.G.CORPS.	"	-	-	-	1	-	-	
R.A.M.C.								
1/1st (Nbn) Field Ambulance.	"	-	1	-	-	-	-	
TOTALS.		1	1	3	34	2	-	

NAMES OF OFFICERS.

6th Durham Light Infy.		
R.A.M.C. attached.	CAPTAIN J.G.HILL, MB.	WOUNDED.13/4/18
7th Durham L.I. (Pnrs).	CAPTAIN W.M.MORANT,	KILLED 11/4/18.
do	LIEUT. F.W.R.NESBITT,	WOUNDED. " "
do	2/LIEUT. J. COLMAN (shewn as COLEMAN in ARMY LIST)	" "
do	LIEUT (A/Capt) A.T.R.HUDSON,	MISSING. " "
do	LIEUT. A.E.HOPSON.	" "

CORRECTION.

LIST NO. 2.

LIEUT F.C.TILBROOK, 7th DURHAM LIGHT INFANTRY (PIONEERS) reported wounded 9/4/18 now reported Died of Wounds.

First Army "A".
XIth Corps "A".
"Q".
    14/4/18

Lt. Col.
A.A. & Q.M.G. for Major General.
Commanding, 50th (North'bn) Division.

LIST NO 7.

50TH (NORTHUMBRIAN) DIVISION.

CASUALTIES FROM NOON 1/4/18 - NOON 15/4/18.

UNIT.	DATE.	KILLED O.	O.R.	WOUNDED O.	O.R.	MISSING O.	O.R.	REMARKS
149TH INFANTRY BRIGADE.								
4th North'd Fusiliers.	14/4/18.	-	-	-	14	-	-	
5th North'd Fusiliers.	"	-	-	-	5	-	-	
6th North'd Fusiliers.	"	-	-	-	1	-	-	
149th T.M. Battery.	"	-	-	-	2	-	-	
150TH INFANTRY BRIGADE.								
4th E. Yorkshire Regt.	"	-	-	-	9	-	-	
4th Yorkshire Regt.	"	-	-	-	12	-	-	
5th Yorkshire Regt.	11/4/18	-	-	2	-	-	-	
do	14/4/18	-	-	-	19	-	-	
151ST INFANTRY BRIGADE.								
5th Durham Light Infy.	"	-	-	-	5	-	-	
7TH DURHAM LIGHT INFY. (Pioneers).	8-14/4/18.	-	24	-	6	-	5	5 a. w. unded.
50TH BN. M.G.CORPS.	11/4/18.	-	-	2	1	4	-	
R.A.M.C.								
1/3rd (Nbn) Field Ambulance.	14/4/18.	-	-	-	2	-	-	
		-	24	4	76	4	5	

NAMES OF OFFICERS.

5th Yorkshire Regt.	2/LIEUT. R. SPEIGHT, Yorks Regt.	WOUNDED 11/4/18
do	CAPTAIN F.B.PARKER, Yorks Regt.	" "
50th BN. M.G. CORPS.	LIEUT. J.W.YOUNGS, MGC. 11/4/18 (Died of wounds 12/4/18)
do	2/LIEUT. H.M.PARSONS, MGC.	WOUNDED 11/4/18
do	LIEUT (A/Capt) W.R.THOMSON, MGC.	MISSING "
do	2/LIEUT. R.HAZELEY, MGC.	" "
do	2/LIEUT. H.M.BALMI, MGC.	" "
do	2/LIEUT. T. LEE, MGC.	" "

CORRECTION.

LIST NO 6.

LIEUT. A.L.M.HUDSON. AND LIEUT A.E.HOPSON. 7th Durham Light Infantry Pioneers reported missing now reported wounded and missing 11/4/18.

H.Q. 50th Divn.
15th April, 1918.

Lt.Col.
A.A. & Q.M.G. for Major General.
Commanding, 50th (North'bn) Division.

LIST NO. 8.

50TH (NORTHUMBRIAN) DIVISION.

CASUALTIES FROM 8/4/18 to 15/4/18.

UNIT.	DATE.	KILLED. O.	KILLED. O.R.	WOUNDED. O.	WOUNDED. O.R.	MISSING. O.	MISSING. O.R.	REMARKS.
149TH INFANTRY BRIGADE.								
Headquarters.	8-15/4/18.	-	2	-	2	-	1	
4th North'd Fusiliers.	"	-	4	-	-	-	226	
"	10/4/18.	-	-	1	-	-	-	
"	12/4/18.	-	-	1	-	-	-	
5th North'd Fusiliers.	8-15/4/18.	-	8	-	-	-	474	
"	10/4/18.	-	-	-	-	1a	-	a. wounded.
"	11/4/18.	1	-	-	-	4	-	
"	12/4/18.	-	-	2	-	1	-	
6th North'd Fusiliers.	8-15/4/18.	-	31	-	52	-	257.	
"	10/4/18.	1	-	5	-	1	-	
"	11/4/18.	-	-	1	-	1	-	
"	12/4/18.	-	-	-	-	1b	-	b. bld Killed
149th T.M. Battery.	8-15/4/18.	-	1	-	3	-	-	
151ST INFANTRY BRIGADE.								
Headquarters.	8-15/4/18.	-	-	-	2	-	-	
"	12/4/18.	-	-	1c	-	-	-	c. at duty.
5th Durham L.I.	8-15/4/18.	-	20	-	-	-	342.	
"	11/4/18.	-	-	2	-	2	-	
8th Durham L.I.	9/4/18.	1	-	-	-	1	-	
8th Durham L.I.	8-15/4/18.	-	18	-	52	-	221.f.	incl. 65 W
"	10/4/18.	1	-	-	-	3d	-	d Incl. 1 Pris 1 bld. K. 1 Bld. P.
"	11/4/18.	1	-	2	-	1e	-	e. bld P.
"	12/4/18.	1	-	-	-	-	-	
151st T.M. Battery.	8-15/4/18.	-	4	-	11	-	-	
TOTAL.		6	88.	16.	122.	16.	1521.	

CORRECTIONS.

LIST NO. 1.
CAPTAIN J.M. MACKENZIE. MB. RAMC. reported W. 9/4/18 now reported (D. of W. 9/4/18).

LIST NO. 3.

2/LIEUT. C.H. DAVISON, 4th North'd Fusiliers reported Wounded 11/4/18 now reported DIED OF WOUNDS. 11/4/18.

LIEUT (A/Capt) J.F.G. AUBIN. MC. LIEUT (A/Capt) G. KIRKHOUSE. LIEUT D.B. SCOTT. and 2/LIEUT F. SHIRTLIFFE. D.L.I. all 6th D.L.I. reported MISSING 9/4/18 now reported KILLED 9/4/18.

LIST NO 4.

LIEUT E.W. STILES, 7TH North'd Fusiliers, attached 149th T.M. Battery reported WOUNDED 12/4/18 now reported DIED OF WOUNDS 13/4/18.

LIST NO. 6-

CAPTAIN J.G. HILL. MB. R.A.M.C. should read "attached 6th North'd Fusiliers.

NAMES OF OFFICERS, overleaf.

H.Q. 50th Divn.
16/4/18.

Lt. Col.
A.A. & Q.M.G. for Major General.
Commanding, 50th (North'bn) Division

NAMES OF OFFICERS.

4th North'd Fusiliers.	CAPTAIN J.S.J.ROBSON.MC.	WOUNDED.	10/4/18.
"	2/LIEUT. J.B.BROWN. NF.	"	12/4/18.
5th North'd Fusiliers.	LIEUT. J.W.LOUGH.	W. & M.	10/4/18.
"	LIEUT. A.J.FIELD.	KILLED.	11/4/18.
"	CAPTAIN F.W.GRIMLING.	MISSING	"
"	CAPTAIN G. BRANFOOT.	"	"
"	LIEUT. R.G.SMITH.	"	"
"	2/LIEUT. P. GRAHAM.4 NF.	"	"
"	LIEUT (A/Capt) A. MORRIS.	WOUNDED.	12/4/18.
"	LIEUT. C.V.ALDER.	"	"
"	LIEUT. F.G.HUTCHINSON.	MISSING	"
	(Shewn as HUTCHISON in Army List).		
6th North'd Fusiliers.	LIEUT G.E.JESSOP.8th W.Yorks.	KILLED	10/4/18.
"	LIEUT. A. TOON	WOUNDED.	"
"	LIEUT. H. WAUGH.	"	"
"	LIEUT. A.W.LEECH.	"	"
"	LIEUT. G.B.ARMSTRONG.	"	"
"	2/LIEUT. E. PICKERSGILL, 4th N.F.	"	"
"	LIEUT. S. MORPETH.	MISSING.	"
"	CAPTAIN F. DAWSON. MC.	WOUNDED.	11/4/18.
"	2/LIEUT. G.M.WAGGOTT. NF.	MISSING.	"
"	XX/LIEUT. A. THOMPSON.	MISSING (B'ld K.)	12/4/18.
151st Infantry Brigade Headquarters.	CAPTAIN H.J.GWITHER. MC. MANCHESTER REGT. BDE MAJOR.	WOUNDED at duty.	"
5th Durham Light Infy.	2/LIEUT. A.R.BYGRAVE.	WOUNDED	11/4/18.
"	2/LIEUT. R.J.GRANT. MC.	"	"
6th Durham Light Infy.	LIEUT G.F.ROWE.	MISSING.	"
"	LIEUT. C.L.HADDON (HADDON) DLI.	"	"
6th Durham Light Infy.	CAPTAIN G.E.CARDEW, 4th Devons.	KILLED.	9/4/18.
"	2/LIEUT. R. RAILTON. DLI.	MISSING.	"
8th Durham Light Infy.	CAPTAIN H.B.HOLDSWORTH.	KILLED.	10/4/18.
"	LIEUT. A. RANSON.	MISSING. (Prisoner of War).	"
"	2/LIEUT. H. I'ANSON.	MISSING (B'ld KILLED)	"
"	2/LIEUT. R. BURDON. D.L.I.	MISSING. (B'ld PRISONER)	"
"	CAPTAIN F.M.WEEKS (Capt N.F.)	KILLED	11/4/18.
"	2/LIEUT. M.A.SMITH (Recently commissioned)	WOUNDED.	"
"	2/LIEUT. A.G.N.GREEN.	MISSING (B'ld PRISONER)	"
"	LIEUT. A.V.MCLARE. MC.	KILLED	12/4/18.
"	LIEUT J. BLAIR.	WOUNDED.	11/4/18

LIST NO. 10.

50TH (NORTHUMBRIAN) DIVISION.

CASUALTIES.

UNIT.	DATE.	KILLED. O. O.R.	WOUNDED. O. O.R.	MISSING. O. O.R.	REMARKS.
149TH INFANTRY BRIGADE.					
4th North'd Fusiliers.	10/4/18.	— —	— —	1a —	a Wounded.
do	12/4/18.	— —	1 —	— —	
5th North'd Fusiliers.	16/4/18.	— —	1 —	— —	
150TH INFANTRY BRIGADE.					
4th E.Yorkshire Regt.	8-17/4/18.	— —	3 —	5 b —	b incl. 1 W.
do	16/4/18.	— —	— 2	— —	
4th Yorkshire Regt.	8-17/4/18.	— —	2 —	— —	
5th Yorkshire Regt.	do	— —	— —	4c —	c incl. 3 W.
150th T.M.Battery.	do	— —	1 —	— —	
151ST INFANTRY BRIGADE.					
6th Durham L.I.	16/4/18.	— —	1 —	— —	
50th Bn. M.G.Corps.	9/4/18.	— —	— 2d	— —	d at duty.
do	10/4/18.	— 2	— 11	— 2a	
do	12/4/18.	— 7	— —	— 1a	
do	13/4/18.	— —	— —	— 1e	e Bld K.
do	8-17/4/18.	— —	— —	— 30	
50th Divl. Signal Coy.	9/4/18.	— —	— 2	— —	
M.M.P.	13/4/18.	— —	— X	— 1	
TOTALS.		— 9	8 18	10 35.	

NAMES OF OFFICERS.

4th North'd Fusiliers.	2/LIEUT. A.N.LAWSON.	W & M 10/4/18
do	2/LIEUT. W.A.KIPLING.	WOUNDED. 12/4/
5th North'd Fusiliers.	LIEUT. COL. A. IRWIN.	" 16/4/1
	(LIEUT. COL. London Gazette 12/3/18.)	
4th E.Yorkshire Regt.	LIEUT. (A/Capt) C.M.SLACK. MC.	MISSING. 8-17/4/
do	CAPTAIN J. RUTHVEN.	" "
do	2/LIEUT. R. THOMPSON.	" "
do	2/LIEUT. A.T.WOODCOCK,	" "
do	CAPTAIN (A/Major) H.B.JACKSON. MC.	W & M. "
do	2/LIEUT. G. THOMPSON.	WOUNDED. "
do	2/LIEUT. S.J.ELVIN.	" "
do	LIEUT. T.W.ANDREWS, 5th E.Yorks.	" "
4th Yorkshire Regt.	LIEUT (A/Capt) F.D.FARQUHARSON, 5th Bn. R. Scots.	" "
do	2/LIEUT. H.E.WEBB-Yorks Regt.	" "
5th Yorkshire Regt.	2/LIEUT. W.H.ALLIS. Yorks Regt.	" & M.
do	CAPTAIN E.M.ROBSON. MC.	" & M "
do	2/LIEUT. J.W.BROWN, Yorks Regt.	" & M "
do	2/LIEUT. G.W.LAWSON. Yorks Regt.	MISSING. "
150th T.M.Battery.	2/LIEUT. J. MARGERRISON. Yorks Regt.	WOUNDED. "

CORRECTION.

LIST NO. 8. 5th North'd Fusiliers. Unit report correct name of LIEUT F.G.HUTCHISON is as now stated.

H.Q. 50th Divn.
17th April, 1918.

Lt.O.
A.A. & Q.M.G. for Major General
Commanding, 50th (North'bn) Division

LIST NO 11.

50TH (NORTHUMBRIAN) DIVISION.

CASUALTIES.

UNIT.	DATE.	KILLED. O.	O.R.	WOUNDED. O.	O.R.	MISSING. O.	O.R.	REMARKS.
150TH INFANTRY BRIGADE.								
4th E. Yorkshire Regt.	8-17/4/18.-		18	-	65	-	246a	a incl. 11 Wound
4th Yorkshire Regt.	"		16	-	107	-	191	
5th Yorkshire Regt.	"		10	-	55	-	209	
151ST INFANTRY BRIGADE.								
8th Durham Light Infy.	"		19	-	19	-	339b	b incl. 2 ounde
			65	-	246	-	985	

(signed) Lt. Col.
A.A. & Q.M.G. for Major General
Commanding, 50th (North'bn) Division.

H.Q. 50th Divn.
18th April, 1918.
First Army A. Alth Corps. A. "G".

On His Majesty's Service.

Duplicate

50th Division
Administrative Staff
War Diary

From :- 1st May 1918
To :- 31st May 1918

Volume XXXVIII.

50 D
A.Q
18

Army Form C. 2118.

MAY 1918.

50TH (NORTHUMBRIAN) DIVISION.

WAR DIARY
or
INTELLIGENCE SUMMARY.

(Erase heading not required.)

Instructions regarding War Diaries and Intelligence Summaries are contained in F. S. Regs., Part II. and the Staff Manual respectively. Title pages will be prepared in manuscript.

Place	Date	Hour	Summary of Events and Information	Remarks and references to Appendices
AROIS-le-PONSART.	1.			
	2.			
	3.			
	4.			
	5.		Divisional Headquarters remained at AROIS-le-PONSART until 12 noon. Advanced Divisional Headquarters (less Rear "Q") moved to Chateau, BEAURIEUX at 12 noon.	
Rear DHQ. AROIS-le-PONSART Adv. DHQ. BEAURIEUX				
BEAURIEUX	6.		Rear Divisional Headquarters arrived at BEAURIEUX. D.H.Q. now established at White Chateau, BEAURIEUX.	
	7.			
	8.			
	9.			
	10.			
	11.			
	12.			
	13.			
	14.			
	15.			

Army Form C. 2118.

WAR DIARY
or
INTELLIGENCE SUMMARY.
(Erase heading not required.)

Instructions regarding War Diaries and Intelligence Summaries are contained in F. S. Regs., Part II. and the Staff Manual respectively. Title pages will be prepared in manuscript.

Place	Date	Hour	Summary of Events and Information	Remarks and references to Appendices
BEAURIEUX	16.			
	17.			
	18.			
	19.			
	20.			
	21.			
	22.			
	23.		The General Officer Commanding Division presented Medal Ribbons to Officers, Warrant Officers, Non-Commissioned Officers and Men on the battalion parade ground at North End of MAIZY Bridge, at 6 p.m. Names of recipients and precis of acts for which recommended is attached.	APPENDIX I.
	24.			
	25.			
	26.			
Adv. DHQ. BEAURIEUX Rear DHQ Chateau REVILLON.	27.		Rear Divisional Headquarters withdraw to the Chateau at REVILLON, at 3 a.m. and later withdraw to BASLIEUX. Later the same day Rear D.H.Q. withdraw to DRAVEGNY. The following casualties to Staff Officers occurred during the day:- General Staff. 2/Lt. R.K.Milne, Intelligence Officer, wounded.	

Original

50th Division.

Administrative Staff

War Diary

From: 1st May 1918
To: 31st May 1918

Volume XXXVIII

Army Form C. 2118.

50TH (NORTHUMBRIAN) DIVISION.
WAR DIARY
INTELLIGENCE SUMMARY.
(Erase heading not required.)

MAY 1918.

Instructions regarding War Diaries and Intelligence Summaries are contained in F. S. Regs., Part II. and the Staff Manual respectively. Title pages will be prepared in manuscript.

Place	Date	Hour	Summary of Events and Information	Remarks and references to Appendices
AROIS-le-PONSART.	1.			
	2.			
	3.			
	4.			
Rear DHQ. AROIS-le-PONSART Adv. DHQ. BEAURIEUX	5.		Divisional Headquarters remained at AROIS-le-PONSART until 12 noon. Advanced Divisional Headquarters (less Rear "Q") moved to Chateau, BEAURIEUX at 12 noon.	
BEAURIEUX	6.		Rear Divisional Headquarters arrived at BEAURIEUX. D.H.Q. now established at White Chateau, BEAURIEUX.	
	7.			
	8.			
	9.			
	10.			
	11.			
	12.			
	13.			
	14.			
	15.			

Army Form C. 2118.

WAR DIARY
*
INTELLIGENCE SUMMARY.
(Erase heading not required.)

Instructions regarding War Diaries and Intelligence Summaries are contained in F. S. Regs., Part II. and the Staff Manual respectively. Title pages will be prepared in manuscript.

Place	Date	Hour	Summary of Events and Information	Remarks and references to Appendices
BEAURIEUX	16.			
	17.			
	18.			
	19.			
	20.			
	21.			
	22.			
	23.		The General Officer Commanding Division presented Medal Ribbons to Officers, Warrant Officers, Non-Commissioned Officers and Men on the battalion parade ground at North End of MAIZY Bridge, at 6 p.m. Names of recipients and precis of acts for which recommended is attached.	APPENDIX I.
	24.			
	25.			
	26.			
Adv. DHQ. BEAURIEUX Rear DHQ Chateau REVILLON.	27.		Rear Divisional Headquarters withdraw to the Chateau at REVILLON, at 3 a.m. and later withdraw to BASLIEUX. Later the same day Rear D.H.Q. withdraw to DRAVEGNY. The following casualties to Staff Officers occurred during the day:— General Staff. 2/Lt. R.K.Milne, Intelligence Officer, wounded.	

Army Form C. 2118.

WAR DIARY
of
INTELLIGENCE SUMMARY.
(Erase heading not required.)

Instructions regarding War Diaries and Intelligence Summaries are contained in F. S. Regs., Part II. and the Staff Manual respectively. Title pages will be prepared in manuscript.

Place	Date	Hour	Summary of Events and Information	Remarks and references to Appendices
	27.(cont)		Administrative Service and Departments. Major W.McCracken, Argyll & Suth. Hldrs. DAQMG 50th Div.) Missing. Col. A.Milne Thompson, CMG, RAMC,(TF). ADMS 50th Div.) Major R.M.Handfield Jones, RAMC. DADMS 50th Div.)	
			149th Infantry Brigade. Commander Brig-General E.P.A.Riddell, DSO. Wounded.	

			150th Infantry Brigade.
			  Commander Brig-General H.C.Rees, DSO. Wounded and Missing.
			  Brigade Major Captain F.H.Witts, MC. Wounded.
			  Staff Captain Captain J.G.Redfern. Wounded.	

			151st Infantry Brigade.
			  Commander Brig-General O.T.Martin, DSO. Killed.
			  Brigade Major Captain H.J.Gwyther, MC. Wounded.	

DRAVEGNY	28.		Rear Divisional Headquarters moved from DRAVEGNY to LHERY via ARCIS-le-PONSART, CRUGNY, SAVIGNY and FAVEROLLES.	
LHERY.			Orders received to move Rear D.H.Q. to CUILES.	
LHERY CUILES IGNY-le- JARD.	29.		D.H.Q. moved to the Chateau, CUILES at 2 a.m. and later withdrew over the MARNE via PONT-a-BINSON to IGNY-le-JARD.	
IGNY-le- JARD. BREUIL.	30.		D.H.Q. moved from IGNY-le-JARD to BREUIL.	
VERT-la GRAVELLE.	31.		D.H.Q. moved via OBRAIS, CONGY, JOCHES, COIZARD to VERT-la-GRAVELLE and was established at the Mairie.	
			A list of casualties incurred by Division during operations on the AISNE is attached.	APPENDIX II.

APPENDIX

II

LIST NO. 1.

50TH (NORTHUMBRIAN) DIVISION.

C A S U A L T I E S.

UNIT.	DATE.	KILLED. O. O.R.	WOUNDED. O. O.R.	MISSING. O. O.R.	REMARKS.
50th Divl. H.Q.	27/5/18	- -	- -	4 a -	(a Bld P. of W. (incl. 1 Wounded.
ROYAL ENGINEERS.					
Headquarters.) RAMC attached)	"	- -	- -	1 -	
7th Field Coy. RE.	"	1 -	1 -	2 b -	b incl. 1 Wounded.
446th Field Coy. RE.	"	- -	4 -	5 -	
447th Field Coy. RE.	"	- -	4 -	5 -	
149TH INFANTRY BRIGADE.					
Headquarters.	"	- -	3 -	- -	
4th North'd Fus.	"	1 -	1 -	- -	
5th North'd Fus.	"	- -	- -	1c -	c Wounded.
6th North'd Fus.	"	- -	- -	1d -	d Bld P. of W.
150TH INFANTRY BRIGADE.					
Headquarters.	"	- -	2 -	1d -	
4th Yorkshire Regt.	"	- -	- -	1d -	
5th Yorkshire Regt.	"	- -	- -	1d -	
151ST INFANTRY BRIGADE.					
Headquarters.	"	- -	1 -	1e -	e Bld Killed.
50TH BN. M.G.CORPS.	"	1 -	5 -	5 -	
Army Chaplains Dept.) Attd 50th Divn.)	"	1 -	1 -	1f -	f Wounded. Bld P. of W.
TOTAL.		4 -	18 -	30 -	

NAMES OF OFFICERS.

50th Divl. H.Q.   COLONEL A MILNE-THOMSON, A.D.M.S. 50th Divn.   MISSING. Bld P. of W.

"   L/Capt (T/Major) R.A.L.HENFIELD-JONES,RAMC. D.A.D.M.S. 50th Divn.   "

"   MAJOR E. McCRACKEN. Argyll & Suth'd Highrs. D.A.Q.M.G. 50th Divn.   "

"   2/Lt. R.F.MILNE. Intelligence Officer, 50th Divn.   (Wounded).

RAMC. attd 50th)   T/Capt. D. GILLESPIE, RAMC, TO.   MISSING.
Divl. Engineers)

7th Field Coy. RE Lieut (A/Major) A.F.Baldwin, RE.   KILLED.
"   Lieut. R.G.POTTER, RL. RE.   WOUNDED.
"   Lieut (A/Capt) F.J.SLATTERY, RE. TC.   WOUNDED & MISSING.
"   2/Lt. N.F.SHARP, RE. RL.   MISSING.
446th Field Coy.RE. Lieut. R.A.DUPRE, RE. TF.   WOUNDED.
"   Lieut. E.F.G.AMOS. RE. TF.   "
"   Lieut. R.J.JONES, RE. TF.   "
"   2/Lt. G.L.REDINGTON. RE. TF.   "
447th Field Coy.RE. MAJOR A.G.RAINSFORD-HANNAY,DSO. RE.   MISSING.
"   Lieut R.J.HOGG. RE.TF.   "
"   LIEUT R.E.HEAY. RE.TF.   "
"   LIEUT E.C.YOUNG. RE.TF.   "
"   LIEUT T.A.BUSHELL. RE.TF.   "

2.

NAMES OF OFFICERS. continued.

149th Inf.Bde.H.Q.	Brigadier Genl. E.P.A.RIDDELL. DSO. Commanding, 149th Inf. Bde.	WOUNDED.
	Lieut D.A.BROWN, Queens Regt. attd 149th Inf. Bde. Signal Officer.	"
	Capt. G.F.PEGG. General List. attd 149th Inf. Bde. H.Q.	"
4th North'd Fus.	Major T/Lt.Col. B.D.GIBSON. DSO.	KILLED.
"	Lieut. W.H.NICHOLSON.	WOUNDED.
5th North'd Fus.	Capt. N.M.NORTH.	WOUNDED AND MISSING.
6th North'd Fus.*	Major (A/Lt.Col.) E.TEMPERLEY.	MISSING. Bld. P. of W.
150th Inf. Bde. H.Q.	Capt. F.H.WITTS, MC. Irish Guards. Bde. Major 150th Inf.Bde.	WOUNDED.
"	Capt. J.G.REDFERN, 4th E.Yorks Regt. Staff Capt. 150th Inf. Bde.	"
"	Brig. Genl. H.C.REES. DSO. Commanding, 150th Inf. Bde.	MISSING. Bld P. of W.
4th Yorkshire Regt.*	T/Major (A/Lt.Col) R.E.D.KENT.	" " "
5th Yorkshire Regt.	Capt (A/Lt.Col.) J.A.R.THOMSON.	" " "
151st Inf. Bde. H.Q.	Capt H.J.GWYTHER. MC. Manchester Regt. Bde Major 151st Inf. Bde.	WOUNDED.
"	Brig. Genl. C.T.MARTIN. DSO. Commanding, 151st Inf. Bde.	~~MISSING Bld~~ KILLED.
50th M. G. Bn.	LIEUT. G.B.COOTE.	KILLED.
"	* Lt. A/Major J.S.DAWBARN. MGC.	WOUNDED.
"	* Lt. A/Capt. L.C.TOMLINSON. MGC.	"
"	* Lt. A/Major R.C.Moon. 4th Yorks RegtMGC	"
"	* Lt. A/Capt. H.W.Fletcher. MGC.	"
"	Lt. A.M.MORRISON. MGC.	"
"	* Capt A/Major M.B.DOUGLAS. MGC.	MISSING.
"	* Capt. A/Major G.R.McPHAIL. MGC.	"
"	* Lt. A/Capt. T.H.NEEDHAM. MGC.	"
"	* Lt. A/Capt. A.O.COOPER. MGC.	"
"	Lt. T.W.WALDING. MGC.	"
"	Lt. B.BURDETT. MGC.	"
"	Lt. J.R.GRAHAM. MGC.	"
"	Lt. I.A.LAUDER. MGC.	"
"	Lt. F.MUNRO. MGC.	"
"	Lt. H.T.P.TEAGUE. MGC.	"
"	Lt. G.C.ODOM. MGC.	"
"	Lt. A. SPENCER. MGC.	"
"	Lt. C.J.BURTON. MGC.	"
"	2/Lt. J.E.INGRAM. MGC.	"
"	2/Lt. F.BETHELL. MGC.	"
"	2/Lt. R.S.ROBERTSON. MGC.	"
"	2/Lt. J.S.McVEY. MGC.	"
"	2/Lt. W.J.S.RANKEN. MGC.	"
"	2/Lt. R. ROPNER. MGC.	"
"	Lieut. W.T.HUNTER. RE. ATTD	
ARMY CHAPLAINS DEPT.		
attached 6th N.F.	Rev. G.A.H.BISHOP. CF.	KILLED.
" 4th E.Yorks.	Rev. J.L.A.EDWARDS. CF.	WOUNDED. Bld P. of W.
" 50th D.A.C.	Rev. C.D.JOB. CF.	WOUNDED.

*Recommended for promotion to acting rank but not gazetted.

H.Q. 50th Divn.
30th May, 1918.

Lieut. Col.
A.A. & Q.M.G. 50th (North'bn) Division; for G.O.C.

GXth Corps "A".
"G".

APPENDIX I

50TH (NORTHUMBRIAN) DIVISION.

OFFICERS, W.Os, N.C.Os AND MEN TO BE PRESENTED WITH MEDAL RIBBONS BY GENERAL OFFICER COMMANDING 50TH (NORTHUMBRIAN) DIVISION ON 23RD MAY, 1918.

Lt. (A/Capt) Thomas Richard GINGER, 4th Yorkshire Regiment.

For most conspicuous gallantry and skill in leading his men during the period March 22nd to April 1st 1918 in the neighbourhood of DONART.

For rallying two Companies of his Battalion after the capture of NORBESCOURT FARM and on many subsequent occasions shewing initiative and skill in the handling of his men.

Awarded M.C.

T/Capt. David GILLESPIE, RAMC attd H.Q. 50th Divl R.E.

Throughout the operations on the 27th and 28th March 1918, in the vicinity of HARBONNIERES and CAIX, this Officer attended to the wounded and arranged for their removal under fire. Owing to his coolness and fine example the work of removing wounded men under difficult conditions was successfully carried out.

Awarded M.C.

No.463038 A/Cpl Henry Armstrong SADLER, 50th Divl Signal Coy RE.

For conspicuous gallantry and devotion to duty between 1st and 13th February 1917.

This N.C.O. shewed a fine example of coolness and personal bravery in the face of danger.

Awarded D.C.M.

On a previous occasion this N.C.O. shewed great bravery and devotion to duty in laying and repairing lines under hostile shell fire.

Awarded M.M.

No.463076 Spr Edward MOLE, 50th Divl Signal Coy RE.

On the night of Octr 30/31st 1917, this man when all the linesmen at his post were wounded or gassed repaired breaks under intense shell fire and displayed great coolness and gallantry under continuous heavy shelling.

Awarded D.C.M.

No.24/250267 Corpl BOLD, A.S.C. 50th Divl Train.

During the 2nd Battle of YPRES when the wheel of his vehicle was shattered by shell fire. Obtaining a spare wheel from a disabled vehicle in the vicinity he repaired his wagon under heavy shell fire and completed the delivery of rations to Brigade Hd-Qrs.

Awarded D.C.M.

-2-

No: 463185 Sgt George REDHEAD, 50th Divl Signal Coy RE.

Near LANGEMARCK on the night of the 25/26th Octr 1917, this N.C.O. brought up the Signal Section under intense shell fire and on 26th maintained visual signalling from Advanced Station under heavy shell fire.

Awarded M.M.

During the period March 22nd to 1st April 1918 this N.C.O. displayed the utmost endurance and devotion to duty.
By unfailing cheerfullness and determination he rendered most valuable service.

Awarded BAR to MM.

No: 463025 Spr James William BARRAS, 50th Div.Sig.Co RE.

During operations on the SOMME on 5th/6th Novr 1916 this N.C.O. man was employed on repair of signal lines for 20 consecutive hours under heavy shell fire.
Spr Barras though wounded by shrapnel by his gallantry and perseverance communication was maintained with Advanced Bde H.Q.

Awarded M.M.

Later, at LANGEMARCK between 24th and 26th Octr 1917 Spr Barras laid and repaired cable under heavy and continuous shell fire, continuously, day and night, for three days.

Awarded BAR to MM.

No: 24287 Spr Thomas Mornington WATSON, 50th Bn. M.Gun Corps.

On the 5th Novr 1916 during operations on the SOMME when a gun which had gone forward had been knocked out of action, Sgt Watson passing through a heavy barrage reached the captured position and brought his gun into action. Later, when more ammunition was required, he returned to the dump carrying ammunition up to his gun.

Awarded M.M.

Later, on 23rd April 1917, for conspicuous during ARRAS operations.

Awarded BAR to MM.

No: 463027 A/2/Cpl James HAMILTON, 50th Divnl Signal Co RE.

For gallantry and devotion to duty on 4th April 1918, when acting as Linesman between Divl H.Q. and Arty Bde H.Q. in vicinity of JENTELLES.

Awarded M.M.

No: 236938 Spr Robert McHUGH, 50th Divl Sig. Co RE.

Near LANGEMARCK on night of Octr 27/28th 1917, when all other means of communication had failed, Spr McHugh maintained visual communication forward to Bde H.Q. under continuous heavy shelling.

Awarded M.M.

No:25626 Spr (A/L/Cpl) Bernard John ROWE, 50th Divl Sig Co RE.

Near LANGEMARCK, on 21st Novr 1917 though suffering from gas posioning, this Spr continued to repair lines under heavy shell fire. Owing to his superd courage and ~~effort~~ courageous efforts communications for which he was responsible were maintained.

Awarded M.M.

No:463097 Spr Ralph Hamilton LAWS, 50th Div.Sig.Co.RE

Between the 29th and 31st Octr 1917 in the vicinity of LANGEMARCK Spr Laws repaired lines continuously for 70 hours under heavy and continuous shell fire and by his magnificient work when most of the linesmen at the advanced post were wounded and gassed communication was maintained.

Awarded M.M.

No:500559 Spr Thomas James GUNTER, 50th Div.Sig.Co.RE

Between Octr 29th and 31st 1917 in the vicinity of LANGEMARCK he maintained and repaired forward telephone lines under intense shell fire and gas bombardment. Continuing his gallant work, although badly gassed, until relieved two days later.

Awarded M.M.

No:428850 Pnr John FOLEY, 50th Divl Sig.Co.RE

For gallantry and devotion to duty on the 4th April 1918. By his untiring work under most dangerous circumstances and in a critical situation he laid and repaired communications during a period of 48 hours.

Awarded M.M.

No:457907 L/Cpl Joseph William MAY, R.E., H.Q. 50th Divl RE.

This N.C.O. regardless of his personal safety dressed wounded in the open at ELVERDINGHE on 31st Oct 1917 during an intense bombing raid. His prompt and pluck action undoubtedly saved life.

Awarded M.M.

No:200231 C.Q.M.S. YOUNG, 4th Yorkshire R.

For gallant and consistent good work during the SOMME battle. On night of 15/16th Septr 1916 this N.C.O. went into No Man's Land and brought in under heavy machine gun fire his Coy Officer who was badly wounded.

Awarded M.M.

No:200536 Cpl Ernest PEACOCK, 4th Yorkshire R.

After his L.Gun team had become casualties this N.C.O. by skilfully handling his gun covered the withdrawal of the troops remaining at his post until all his ammunition was expended. He then brought his gun out of action, being the last man to withdraw.

Awarded M.M.

- 4 -

No: 33011 Cpl MORGAN, 4th Yorkshire Regt.

At POLYGON WOOD on the 23rd Octr 1917 this N.C.O. was in charge of the L.Gun posts. He displayed courage and initiative in going out to No Man's Land and single handed bringing in three German prisoners.

Awarded M.M.

No: 200107 L/Cpl PENNOCK, 4th York.R.

During the SOMME operations in Septr 1916 this N.C.O. maintained communication between Bde and Coy H.Q. in spite of intense bombardment.

Awarded M.M.

No: 201586 Pte William LUMLEY, 4th York.R.

On 24th Septr 1917 during a heavy enemy attack, in spite of intense barrage, Pte Lumley brought his gun into action in a forward position and by opening a heavy enfilading fire materially contributed to the failure of the enemy attack.

Awarded M.M.

No: 36124 Pte TURNER, 4th York.R.

For extreme gallantry displayed while taking part in the successful daylight raid on Decr 13th 1917.

Awarded M.M.

No: 28267 Pte RICHARDSON, 4th Yorkshire Regt.

On July 18th 1917 in spite of enemy shell fire he assisted his L.Gun team to keep up a steady enfilading fire on advancing enemy. Although wounded he remained at his gun until the enemy was beaten off.

Awarded M.M.

No: 23521 Sgt ACKLAM, 50th Bn. M.G.C.

For gallantry and devotion to duty on Septr 15th 1916, during operations on the SOMME.

Awarded M.M.

No: 24302 Sgt John William GLENNEL, 50th Bn. M.G.C.

For gallantry and coolness in action during the operations on the SOMME in Septr 1916.
This N.C.O. was in charge of two guns which were sent up to replace damaged guns in captured positions. By skilfully placing his guns he materially assisted in stopping the German counter attack.

Awarded M.M.

No: 71346 Sgt Thomas DRIFFILL, 50th Bn M.G.C.

At PASSCHENDAELE on Feby 9th 1918 this N.C.O. displayed absolute disregard of danger and shewed consummate coolness in clearing six guns from a SEINE Dump under most difficult circumstances.

Awarded M.M.

No:63625 L/Cpl Iziah CHANDLER,
50th Bn.M.G.C.

During the operations on the SOMME from Mch 22nd to Apl 1st 1918 he displayed great coolness and steadiness ~~unfire-fire~~ under fire setting a splendid example to his comrades. By initiative and energy the advance of the enemy was materially delayed.

Awarded M.M.

No:72379 Pte William BAXTER,
50th Bn. M.G.C.

During an attack on the SOMME on the morning of 14th Novr 1916 it was mainly due to this man's energy and courageous tenacity that his L.Gun post was maintained though heavily pressed by the enemy.

Awarded M.M.

No:72392 Pte Michael HALL.
50th Bn. M.G.C.

This man was continually employed as Forward section runner during special operations south of HOUTHULST FOREST between Octr 25/28th 1917. In spite of intense enemy fire and under worst possible weather conditions, this man worked consistently and rendered invaluable service to his Company, as runner and guide to M.Gun teams coming into the line.

Awarded M.M.

No:15411 Pte Archibald SPENCER,
50th Bn.M.G.C.

During the operations near HOUTHULST FOREST on 25th Octr 1917 this man carried messages through a heavy barrage and displayed great bravery while acting in the capacity of runner for which employment he volunteered.

Awarded M.M.

No:4369 Pte Stephen MUMFORD.
50th Bn.M.G.C.

In the PASSCHENDAELE Sector during the night Feb. 9th 1918 this man shewed the greatest skill and coolness when clearing guns from SEINE Dump by Horse Transport under most trying circumstances.

Awarded M.M.

No:70415 Pte Henry BAPTIST,
50th Bn. M.G.C.

During the SOMME operations March 23rd to Apl 1st 1918 he shewed absolute disregard for shell and M.Gun fire while carrying out his duties as runner.

Awarded M.M.

No:T4/250398 C.S.M. WALKER,
A.S.C. 50th Divl Train.

For zeal and ability displayed in the performance of his work, and for untiring devotion to duty since arrival in France in Apl 1915.

Awarded M.M.

- 6 -

No:T4/250253 C.Q.M.S. EGGLESTON, A.S.C. 50th Divl Train.	For unswerving loyalty and devotion to duty since arrival in France in April 1915. Awarded M.M.
No:T4/250230 Dvr WILSON, A.S.C. 50th Divl Train.	For consistent good service and devotion to duty since arrival in France in April 1915. Awarded M.M.
No:S/4539 S/Sgt (A/S.Condt) Bertie FIELD, A.O.C., H.Q. 50th Div.	At ALBERT on 8th Feb. 1917 while Ordnance stores were being heavily shelled this N.C.O. by his courage and good example was mainly instrumental in removing to a place of safety a large quantity of valuable Government stores. Awarded M.M.
No:483060 Sgt James Arthur HINSON, R.E., H.Q. 50th Divl R.E.	For consistent good work and reliability and unfailing cheerfulness at all times. Awarded M.S.M.
No:250167 A/Q.M.S. Bertie STODDART, 6th D.L.I. attd H.Q., 50th Division.	For consistent and unfailing good service and devotion to duty during the period April 1915 to Decr. 1917 whilst performing the duties of Qr-Mr-Sgt on 50th Divisional H.Q. Awarded M.S.M.
No:T4/250303 S.S.M. Thomas Frederick SIDDLE, A.S.C. 50th Divl Train.	This W.O. has carried out his duties with zeal and energy since arrival in France in April 1915 and has at all times performed excellent service. Awarded M.S.M.
No:T4/252100 S.Sgt Hugh Percy NICHOLSON, A.S.C., 50th Divl Train att H.Q. 50th Division.	For consistent good work and devotion to duty since April 1915. Awarded M.S.M.

APPENDIX I

50TH (NORTHUMBRIAN) DIVISION.

OFFICERS, W.Os, N.C.Os AND MEN TO BE PRESENTED WITH MEDAL RIBBONS BY GENERAL OFFICER COMMANDING 50TH (NORTHUMBRIAN) DIVISION ON 23RD MAY, 1918.

Lt. (A/Capt) Thomas Richard GINGER, 4th Yorkshire Regiment.

For most conspicuous gallantry and skill in leading his men during the period March 22nd to April 1st 1918 in the neighbourhood of DOMART.

For rallying two Companies of his Battalion after the capture of NORBESCOURT FARM and on many subsequent occasions shewing initiative and skill in the handling of his men.

Awarded M.C.

T/Capt. David GILLESPIE, RAMC attd H.Q. 50th Divl R.E.

Throughout the operations on the 27th and 28th March 1918, in the vicinity of HARBONNIERES and CAIX, this Officer attended to the wounded and arranged for their removal under fire. Owing to his coolness and fine example the work of removing wounded men under difficult conditions was successfully carried out.

Awarded M.C.

No.463038 A/Cpl Henry Armstrong SADLER, 50th Divl Signal Coy RE.

For conspicuous gallantry and devotion to duty between 1st and 13th February 1917.

This N.C.O. shewed a fine example of coolness and personal bravery in the face of danger.

Awarded D.C.M.

On a previous occasion this N.C.O. shewed great bravery and devotion to duty in laying and repairing lines under hostile shell fire.

Awarded M.M.

No.463076 Spr Edward MOLE, 50th Divl Signal Coy RE.

On the night of Octr 30/31st 1917, this man when all the linesmen at his post were wounded or gassed repaired breaks under intense shell fire and displayed great coolness and gallantry under continuous heavy shelling.

Awarded D.C.M.

No.T4/250267 Corpl BOLD, A.S.C. 50th Divl Train.

During the 2nd Battle of YPRES when the wheel of his vehicle was shattered by shell fire. Obtaining a spare wheel from a disabled vehicle in the vicinity he repaired his wagon under heavy shell fire and completed the delivery of rations to Brigade Hd-Qrs.

Awarded D.C.M.

— 2 —

No: 463185 Sgt George REDHEAD, 50th Divl Signal Coy RE.

Near LANGEMARCK on the night of the 25/26th Octr 1917, this N.C.O. brought up the Signal Section under intense shell fire and on 26th maintained visual signalling from Advanced Station under heavy shell fire.

Awarded M.M.

During the period March 22nd to 1st April 1918 this N.C.O. displayed the utmost endurance and devotion to duty.
By unfailing cheerfullness and determination he rendered most valuable service.

Awarded BAR to MM.

No: 463025 Spr James William BARRAS, 50th Div.Sig.Co RE.

During operations on the SOMME on 5th/6th Novr 1916 this N.C.O. man was employed on repair of signal lines for 20 consecutive hours under heavy shell fire.
Spr Barras though wounded by shrapnel by his gallantry and perseverance communication was maintained with Advanced Bde H.Q.

Awarded M.M.

Later, at LANGEMARCK between 24th and 26th Oct 1917 Spr Barras laid and repaired cable under heavy and continuous shell fire, continuously, day and night, for three days.

Awarded BAR to MM.

No: 24287 Spr Thomas Mornington WATSON, 50th Bn. M.Gun Corps.

On the 5th Novr 1916 during operations on the SOMME when a gun which had gone forward had been knocked out of action, Sgt Watson passing through a heavy barrage reached the captured position and brought his gun into action. Later, when more ammunition was required, he returned to the dump carrying ammunition up to his gun.

Awarded M.M.

Later, on 23rd April 1917, for conspicuous during ARRAS operations.

Awarded BAR to MM.

No: 463027 A/2/Cpl James HAMILTON, 50th Divl Signal Co RE.

For gallantry and devotion to duty on 4th April 1918, when acting as Linesman between Divl H.Q. and Arty Bde H.Q. in vicinity of JENTELLES.

Awarded M.M.

No: 236938 Spr Robert McHUGH, 50th Divl Sig. Co RE.

Near LANGEMARCK on night of Octr 27/28th 1917, when all other means of communication had failed, Spr McHugh maintained visual communication forward to Bde H.Q. under continuous heavy shelling.

Awarded M.M.

No:25626 Spr (A/L/Cpl) Bernard John ROWE, 50th Divl Sig Co RE.

Near LANGEMARCK, on 21st Novr 1917 though suffering from gas posioning, this Spr continued to repair lines under heavy shell fire. Owing to his superd courage and ~~effort~~ courageous efforts communications for which he was responsible were maintained.

Awarded M.M.

No:463097 Spr Ralph Hamilton LAWS, 50th Div.Sig.Co.RE

Between the 29th and 31st Octr 1917 in the vicinity of LANGEMARCK Spr Laws repaired lines continuously for 70 hours under heavy and continuous shell fire and by his magnificient work when most of the linesmen at the advanced post were wounded and gassed communication was maintained.

Awarded M.M.

No:500559 Spr Thomas James GUNTER, 50th Div.Sig.Co.RE

Between Octr 29th and 31st 1917 in the vicinity of LANGEMARCK he maintained and repaired forward telephone lines under intense shell fire and gas bombardment. Continuing his gallant work, although badly gassed, until relieved two days later.

Awarded M.M.

No:428850 Pnr John FOLEY, 50th Divl Sig.Co.RE

For gallantry and devotion to duty on the 4th April 1918. By his untiring work under most dangerous circumstances and in a critical situation he laid and repaired communications during a period of 48 hours.

Awarded M.M.

No:457907 L/Cpl Joseph William MAY, R.E., H.Q. 50th Divl RE.

This N.C.O. regardless of his personal safety dressed wounded in the open at ELVERDINGHE on 31st Oct 1917 during an intense bombing raid. His prompt and pluck action undoubtedly saved life.

Awarded M.M.

No:200231 C.Q.M.S. YOUNG, 4th Yorkshire R.

For gallant and consistent good work during the SOMME battle. On night of 15/16th Septr 1916 this N.C.O. went into No Man's Land and brought in under heavy machine gun fire his Coy Officer who was badly wounded.

Awarded M.M.

No:200536 Cpl Ernest PEACOCK, 4th Yorkshire R.

After his L.Gun team had become casualties this N.C.O. by skilfully handling his gun covered the withdrawal of the troops remaining at his post until all his ammunition was expended. He then brought his gun out of action, being the last man to withdraw.

Awarded M.M.

- 4 -

No:33011 Cpl MORGAN, 4th Yorkshire Regt.	At POLYGON WOOD on the 23rd Octr 1917 this N.C.O. was in charge of the L.Gun posts. He displayed courage and initiative in going out to No Man's Land and single handed bringing in three German prisoners. Awarded M.M.
No:200107 L/Cpl PENNOCK, 4th York.R.	During the SOMME operations in Septr 1916 this N.C.O. maintained communication between Bde and Coy H.Q. in spite of intense bombardment. Awarded M.M.
No:201586 Pte William LUMLEY, 4th York.R.	On 24th Septr 1917 during a heavy enemy attack, in spite of intense barrage, Pte Lumley brought his gun into action in a forward position and by opening a heavy enfilading fire materially contributed to the failure of the enemy attack. Awarded M.M.
No:36124 Pte TURNER, 4th York.R.	For extreme gallantry displayed while taking part in the successful daylight raid on Decr 13th 1917. Awarded M.M.
No:26267 Pte RICHARDSON, 4th Yorkshire Regt.	On July 18th 1917 in spite of enemy shell fire he assisted his L.Gun team to keep up a steady enfilading fire on advancing enemy. Although wounded he remained at his gun until the enemy was beaten off. Awarded M.M.
No:23521 Sgt ACKLAM, 50th Bn. M.G.C.	For gallantry and devotion to duty on Septr 15th 1916, during operations on the SOMME. Awarded M.M.
No:24302 Sgt John William GLENNEL, 50th Bn. M.G.C.	For gallantry and coolness in action during the operations on the SOMME in Septr 1916. This N.C.O. was in charge of two guns which were sent up to replace damaged guns in captured positions. By skilfully placing his guns he materially assisted in stopping the German counter attack. Awarded M.M.
No:71346 Sgt Thomas DRIFFILL, 50th Bn M.G.C.	At PASSCHENDAELE on Feby 9th 1918 this N.C.O. displayed absolute disregard of danger and shewed consummate coolness in clearing six guns from SEINE Dump under most difficult circumstances. Awarded M.M.

No:63625 L/Cpl Iziah CHANDLER,
  50th Bn.M.G.C.

During the operations on the SOMME from Mch 22nd to Apl 1st 1918 he displayed great coolness and steadiness ~~under fire~~ under fire setting a splendid example to his comrades. By initiative and energy the advance of the enemy was materially delayed.

Awarded M.M.

No:72379 Pte William BAXTER,
  50th Bn. M.G.C.

During an attack on the SOMME on the morning of 14th Novr 1916 it was mainly due to this man's energy and courageous tenacity that his L.Gun post was maintained though heavily pressed by the enemy.

Awarded M.M.

No:72392 Pte Michael HALL.
  50th Bn. M.G.C.

This man was continually employed as Forward section runner during special operations south of HOUTHULST FOREST between Octr 25/28th 1917. In spite of intense enemy fire and under worst possible weather conditions, this man worked consistently and rendered invaluable service to his Company, as runner and guide to M.Gun teams coming into the line.

Awarded M.M.

No:15411 Pte Archibald SPENCER,
  50th Bn.M.G.C.

During the operations near HOUTHULST FOREST on 25th Octr 1917 this man carried messages through a heavy barrage and displayed great bravery while acting in the capacity of runner for which employment he volunteered.

Awarded M.M.

No:4369 Pte Stephen MUMFORD.
  50th Bn.M.G.C.

In the PASSCHENDAELE Sector during the night Feb. 9th 1918 this man shewed the greatest skill and coolness when clearing guns from SEINE Dump by Horse Transport under most trying circumstances.

Awarded M.M.

No:70415 Pte Henry BAPTIST,
  50th Bn. M.G.C.

During the SOMME operations March 23rd to Apl 1st 1918 he shewed absolute disregard for shell and M.Gun fire while carrying out his duties as runner.

Awarded M.M.

No:T4/250398 C.S.M. WALKER,
  A.S.C. 50th Divl Train.

For zeal and ability displayed in the performance of his work, and for untiring devotion to duty since arrival in France in Apl 1915.

Awarded M.M.

APPENDIX II

LIST NO. 1.

50TH (NORTHUMBRIAN) DIVISION.

CASUALTIES.

UNIT.	DATE.	KILLED.		WOUNDED.		MISSING.		REMARKS.
		O.	O.R.	O.	O.R.	O.	O.R.	
50th Divl. H.Q.	27/5/18	-	-	-	-	4 a	-	(a Bld P. of W. (incl. 1 Wounded.
ROYAL ENGINEERS.								
Headquarters.) RAMC attached)	"	-	-	-	-	1	-	
7th Field Coy. RE.	"	1	-	1	-	2 b	-	b incl. 1 Wounded
446th Field Coy. RE.	"	-	-	4	-	3	-	
447th Field Coy. RE.	"	-	-	-	-	5	-	
149TH INFANTRY BRIGADE.								
Headquarters.	"	-	-	3	-	-	-	
4th North'd Fus.	"	1	-	1	-	-	-	
5th North'd Fus.	"	-	-	-	-	1c	-	c Wounded.
6th North'd Fus.	"	-	-	-	-	1d	-	d Bld P. of W.
150TH INFANTRY BRIGADE.								
Headquarters.	"	-	-	2	-	1d	-	
4th Yorkshire Regt.	"	-	-	-	-	1d	-	
5th Yorkshire Regt.	"	-	-	-	-	1d	-	
151ST INFANTRY BRIGADE.								
Headquarters.	"	-	-	1	-	1e	-	e Bld killed.
50TH BN. M.G.CORPS.	"	1	-	5	-	3	-	
Army Chaplains Dept.) attd 50th Divn.)	"	1	-	1	-	1f	-	f Wounded. Bld P. of W.
TOTAL.		4	-	18	-	39	-	

NAMES OF OFFICERS.

50th Divl. H.Q.	COLONEL A MILNE-THOMSON, A.D.M.S. 50th Divn.	MISSING. ~~Bld P. of W.~~
"	T/Capt (T/Major) R.R.HANDFIELD-JONES,RAMC. D.A.D.M.S. 50th Divn.	"
"	MAJOR A. McCRACKEN. Argyll & Suth'd Highrs. D.A.Q.M.G. 50th Divn.	"
"	2/Lt. R.K.MILNE. Intelligence Officer, 50th Divn.	" (Wounded).
RAMC. attd 50th) Divl. Engineers)	T/Capt. D. GILLESPIE, RAMC. TC.	MISSING.
7th Field Coy. RE.	Lieut (A/Major) W.F.Baldwin, RE.	KILLED.
"	Lieut. H.G.POTTLE, MC. RE.	WOUNDED.
"	Lieut (A/Capt) F.J.SLATTERY,RE.TC.	WOUNDED & MISSING.
"	2/Lt. H.F.SHARP. RE. TC.	MISSING.
446th Field Coy.RE.	Lieut. H.A.DUPRE. RE. TF.	WOUNDED.
"	Lieut. E.F.G.AMOS. RE.TF.	"
"	Lieut. R.J.JONES. RE.TF.	"
"	2/Lt. G.E.REMINGTON. RE.TF.	"
447th Field Coy.RE.	MAJOR A.G.RAINSFORD-HANNAY,DSO. RE.	MISSING. P/W.
"	Lieut H.J.HOGG. RE.TF.	"
"	LIEUT R.H.REAY. RE.TF.	"
"	LIEUT E.W.YOUNG. RE.TF.	"
"	LIEUT T.H.RUSSELL. RE.TF.	"

NAMES OF OFFICERS. continued.

149th Inf.Bde.H.Q.	Brigadier Genl. E.P.A.RIDDELL. DSO. Commanding, 149th Inf. Bde.	WOUNDED.
	Lieut D.A.BROWN, Queens Regt. attd 149th Inf. Bde. Signal Officer.	"
	Capt. G.F.PEGG. General List. attd 149th Inf. Bde. H.Q.	"
4th North'd Fus.	Major T/Lt.Col. B.D.GIBSON. DSO.	KILLED.
"	Lieut. W.R.NICHOLSON.	WOUNDED.
5th North'd Fus.	Capt. H.R.NORTH.	WOUNDED AND MISSING.
6th North'd Fus.*	Major (A/Lt.Col.) E.TEMPERLEY.	MISSING. Bld. P. of W.
150th Inf. Bde. H.Q.	Capt. F.H.WITTS,MC. Irish Guards. Bde. Major 150th Inf.Bde.	WOUNDED.
"	Capt. J.G.REDFERN, 4th Yorks Regt. Staff Capt. 150th Inf. Bde.	"
"	Brig. Genl. H.C.REES. DSO. Commanding, 150th Inf. Bde.	MISSING. Bld P. of W.
4th Yorkshire Regt.*	T/Major (A/Lt.Col) R.E.D.KENT.	" " "
5th Yorkshire Regt.	Capt (A/Lt.Col.) J.A.R.THOMSON.	" " "
151st Inf. Bde. H.Q.	Capt H.J.GWYTHER. MC. Manchester Regt. Bde Major 151st Inf. Bde.	WOUNDED.
"	Brig. Genl. C.T.MARTIN. DSO. Commanding, 151st Inf. Bde.	KILLED.
50th M. G. Bn.	Lieut. G.B.COOPE.	KILLED.
"	* Lt. A/Major J.S.DAWBARN. MGC	WOUNDED.
"	* Lt. A/Capt. L.C.TOMLINSON. MGC.	"
"	* Lt. A/Major R.C.Moon. 4th Yorks Regt.MGC	"
"	* Lt. A/Capt. H.W.Fletcher. MGC.	"
"	Lt. A.H.MORRISON. MGC.	"
"	* Capt A/Major H.B.DOUGLAS. MGC.	MISSING.
"	* Capt. A/Major G.R.McPHAIL. MGC.	"
"	* Lt. A/Capt. T.R.NEEDHAM. MGC.	"
"	* Lt. A/Capt. A.O.COOPER. MGC.	"
"	Lt. T.W.WALDING. MGC.	"
"	Lt. E.DURDETT. MGC.	"
"	Lt. J.R.GRAHAM. MGC.	"
"	Lt. I.A.LAUDER. MGC.	"
"	Lt. F.MUNRO. MGC.	"
"	Lt. H.T.P.TEAGUE. MGC.	"
"	Lt. G.C.ODOM. MGC.	"
"	Lt. A. SPENCER. MGC.	"
"	Lt. C.J.BURTON. MGC.	"
"	2/Lt. J.S.INGRAM. MGC.	"
"	2/Lt. F.BETHEL. MGC.	"
"	2/Lt. R.S.ROBERTSON. MGC.	"
"	2/Lt. J.S.McVEY. MGC.	"
"	2/Lt. W.J.S.RANKEN. MGC.	"
"	2/Lt. R. HOPNER. MGC.	"
"	Lieut. W.T.HUNTER. RE. ATTD	"

ARMY CHAPLAINS DEPT.

attached 6th N.F.	Rev. G.A.H.BISHOP. CF.	KILLED.
" 4th E.Yorks.	Rev. J.L.A.EDWARDS.CF.	WOUNDED. Bld P. of W.
" 50th D.A.C.	Rev. O.O.JOB. CF.	WOUNDED.

*Recommended for promotion to acting rank but not gazetted.

H.Q. 50th Divn.   Lieut. Col.
30th May, 1918.   A.A. & Q.M.G. 50th (North'bn) Division, for G.O.C.

IXth Corps "A".

50TH (NORTHUMBRIAN) DIVISION.   LIST No. 2.

CASUALTIES FROM 27TH May, 1918 to date.

OFFICERS.

UNIT.	K.	W.	M.	Remarks.
ARTILLERY.				
250th Bde R.F.A.	1	2	19 a.	a. Includes 1 wounded.
251st Bde R.F.A.	-	1	19 a.	
50th Divl. Amn. Col.	-	-	3 b.	b. Includes 1 Bld Killed.
50th T.M. Batteries.	-	2	3 c.	c. Includes 1 wounded 1 Bld K.
149TH INFANTRY BRIGADE.				
Headquarters.	-	-	1	
4th North'd Fus.	1	5d	16e	d. Includes 1 D. of W.
				e. Includes 2 wounded.
5th North'd Fus.	4	4d	6a	
6th North'd Fus.	-	3g	18h	g. Includes 1 Gas.
				h. Includes 4 wounded.
149th T.M. Battery.	-	-	4	
150TH INFANTRY BRIGADE.				
4th E. Yorkshire Regt.	1	3	24a	
4th Yorkshire Regt.	-	2	16e	
5th Yorkshire Regt.	-	2	22	
151ST INFANTRY BRIGADE.				
Headquarters.	-	1	-	(Gas).
5th Durham L.I.	1	3j	29	j. Includes 1 Gas.
6th Durham L.I.	2	5	7	
8th Durham L.I.	2	2	19k	k. Includes 6 wounded.
151st T.M. Battery.	-	1	-	
7TH DURHAM L.I. Pnrs.	1	2	-	
TOTAL.	15	35	191	

NAMES OF OFFICERS.

250th Bde R.F.A.	LIEUT T.F.A. RICHARDSON. RFA. TF.	KILLED	27/5/18.
"	LIEUT J. HOPWOOD. MC. RFA. TF.	WOUNDED.	"
"	2/LT. P. GRANGE. MC. RA.	"	"
"	LIEUT H.R. HORNSBY. MC. RFA. TF.	WOUNDED & MISSING.	"
"	2/LT. H.W. ABEY. RA. SR.	MISSING.	"
"	LIEUT. R.J. BARDSLEY. RA. SR.	"	"
"	LT. (A/Major) G. CHAPMAN. MC. TF.	"	"
"	LIEUT. J.P. HUTCHINSON. MC. RFA. TF.	"	"
"	2/LT. K.M. GOODENOUGH. MC. RA. SR.	"	"
"	2/LT. D.H. COSTAR. RA. SR.	"	"
"	LIEUT. E. DARLING. MC. RFA. TF.	"	"
"	LIEUT. E.C. EARLE. RFA. TF.	"	"
" attached.	LIEUT REES. U.S.M.O.R.C.	"	"
251st Bde R.F.A.	LIEUT. COL. F.B. MOSS-BLUNDELL. DSO. RFA. TF.	"	"
"	LT. (A/Capt) B.K. BARTON. MC. RFA. TF.	"	"
"	LIEUT. A.S. WITHERINGTON. RFA. TF.	"	"
"	2/LT. E.D. TUDHOPE. RA. SR. (Signal Offr).	"	"
"	Capt (A/Major) W.H.H. HUTCHINSON. MC. RFA. TF.	"	"
"	LIEUT. T.M. GATHERAL. RFA. TF.	"	"
"	LIEUT. L.R. WILLIAMS. RFA. TF.	"	"

NAMES OF OFFICERS.

251st (Nbn) Bde R.F.A.

Major G.D.NANTES, R.A.	Missing	27/5/18.
Lt.C.O.FRANK, R.F.A. TF.	"	"
2/Lt.H.BULLING, R.F.A. TF.	"	"
2/Lt.T.POWELL, R.A. SR.	"	"
Capt(A/Maj) W.GOLDING, MC R.F.A. TF	"	"
Lt.J.L.GIBSON, R.F.A. TF.	"	"
2/LT.W.T.MERCER, R.F.A. TF.	"	"
Lt.F.W.SOPWITH, MC. R.F.A. TF.	"	"
Lt.G.E.PATTON, R.F.A. TF.	"	"
2/Lt.W.E.CLARK, R.F.A. TF.	"	"
2/Lt.G.W.PARKES (shewn in Army L. as "PARKER"	"	"
Lt.W.J.SULLIVAN, U.S. R.A.M.C. attd	Wounded	"
Lt.W.S.GALL, R.F.A. TF.	" & Missing	"

50th Divnl Ammn Col.

Lt.W.A.DENHAM, R.F.A. TF.	Missing	"
2/Lt.I.H.WHITE, R.A. SR.	"	"
Lt.W.W.WHYTE, R.F.A. TF.	" bvd Killed	"

50th T.Mortar Batteries.

Capt.W.C.HAND, DSO. MC. R.G.A.	Wounded	"
Lt.T.SAMPLE, R.F.A. TF.	"	"
2/Lt.G.H.B.CLARKE, R.F.A. TF.	" & Missing	"
Lt(A/Capt) S.R.C.PLIMSOLL, MC. R.F.A. TF.	Missing bvd "K"	"
2/Lt.F.J.HODDER, R.F.A. TF.	"	"

149th INFANTRY BRIGADE.
Headquarters.

Lt.P.W.LOVELL, 6th North'd F.	Missing	"

4th North'd Fusrs.

~~Lt.L.S.CHEESERIGHT~~ CHEESERIGHT, 8th N.F.	Killed	"
2/Lt.J.A.GREANEY, R.D.F.	Wounded	"
2/Lt.D.FIRTH, N.F.	"	30/5/18.
2/Lt.J.E.FARWELL, N.F.	"	"
Lt.R.H.SMALLWOOD, N.F.	"(D of W)	27/5/18.
~~2/Lt.J.C.NAPIER, 4th N.F.~~	~~"~~	
2/Lt.H.R.REES	Missing	"
2/Lt.H.R.TULLEY, 8th N.F.	"	"
Lt(A/Capt) J.V.GREGORY, MC. 6th N.F.	Wounded & Missg	"
2/Lt.W.L.McLEAN, N.F.	" " "	"
Lt(A/Capt) A.WILLIS, 8th N.F.	Missing	"
2/Lt.J.W.MARSDEN, N.F.	"	"
Lt.J.J.HOLME, 6th N.F.	"	"
2/Lt.F.G.PEDDIE, MC.,	"	"
2/Lt.W.JONES, N.F.	"	"
2/Lt.H.E.FINILAY, N.F.	"	"
Capt.R.ALLEN.	"	"
2/Lt.A.E.MORRIS, N.F.	"	"
2/Lt.A.H.ROYLE, N.F.	"	"
2/Lt.W.~~MAXFIELD~~ MAXFIELD, N.F.	"	"
Lt.H.H.HARRISON, N.F.	"	"
Lt.F.J.IVES,	"	"

5th North'd Fusrs.

2/Lt J.E.PORRITT, N.F.	Killed	27/5/18.
2/Lt.J.H.McMURDO	"	"
2/Lt.J.McMEEKEN, N.F.	"	"
2/Lt.J.B.SLACK, N.F.	"	"
2/Lt.E.PHILLIPS, N.F.	Wounded (D of W)	"
2/Lt.J.H.YOUNG, N.F.	"	"
2/Lt.R.S.BOWIE, N.F.	"	"
2/Lt.E.V.SARGENT		
2/Lt.R.T.DENNIS, R.I.R.	Missing	28/5/18.
Capt.H.G.DODDS	"	27/5/18.
2/Lt.S.WEATERTON, N.F.	"	"
2/Lt.L.J.ROSS, R.I.R.	"	"
2/Lt.R.H.QUINE, N.F.	"	"
2/Lt.W.E.PRIESTNALL, N.F.	Wounded & Missing	"

6th North'd Fusrs.

Major A.D.S.ROGERS	Wounded	"
Capt.J.N.MacKENZIE, MC. MB. RAMC attd	Missing	"
Capt.H.GRAHAM, N.F.	"	"
Capt.R.E.M.HEANLEY, 84th Training Res.	"	"
Lt.J.WATSON, N.F.	"	"
Lt.H.V.RUSSELL	Wounded & Missing	"
2/Lt.A.P.ANDERSON, D.L.I.	Missing	"
Lt.W.R.DODDS, N.F.	Wounded & Missing	"
Lt.W.M.McLARE, N.F.	Missing	"
Lt.J.W.CRAIG CRAKE.	"	"
Lt.C.O.MARSHALL, N.F.	"	"
2/Lt.J.GRAY, N.F.	"	"
2/Lt.A.E.GLANVILLE, R.D.F.	Wounded & Missing	"
Lt(A/Capt) J.G.GARRARD, MC. 5th N.F.	" " "	"
2/Lt.E.D.SURTEES, N.F.	Wounded (GAS)	"
Capt(A/Maj.) J.G.LEATHART, MC.	"	2/6/18.
2/Lt.C.B.McCOMB, R.I.R.	Missing	27/5/18.
2/Lt.W.J.DAVID, N.F.	"	"
2/Lt.A.S.TAYLOR, N.F.	"	"
2/Lt.I.R.LEES (not shewn in Army L.)	"	"
2/Lt.J.S.STOKOE, N.F.	"	"

149th Trench Mortar Battery.

Lt(A/Capt) J.M.BENSON, 4th N.F.	"	"
2/Lt.J.SOWERBY, N.F. attd 6th Bn.	"	"
2/Lt.C.TOLKIEN, 8th attd 4th N.F. (shewn in Army L. "TOLKEIN").	"	"
2/Lt.A.E.BROWN, 5th N.F.	"	"

150TH INFANTRY BRIGADE.-
4th East Yorkshire Regt.

Major H.R.HASLETT, R.I.R.	"	"
Capt.N.W.INGLEBY,	"	"
Lt.E.JOHNSTON	"	"
Capt.E.LAVERACK.	"	"
Lt.C.S.JOHNSON	"	"
Lt.W.E.HEWAT	"	"
2/Lt.S.FEARNLEY, 13th E.Yorks	"	"
Lt.P.S.MURRAY, MC. R.I.R.	"	"
Lt.H.F.STEPHENSON, R.I.R.	"	"
2/Lt.J.A.A.FLYNN, R.I.R.	Wounded & Missing	"
2/Lt.R.GIVEN, R.I.R.	Missing	"
2/Lt.B.C.BINER, R.I.R.	"	"
2/Lt.A.THRUSTLE, E.Yorks	W "	"
2/Lt.C.N.ROGAN	"	"
2/Lt.J.WALKER, E.Yorks (newly commd)	"	"
2/Lt.T.K.DIGBY, R.I.R.	"	"
2/Lt.S.F.BASTOW	"	"
2/Lt.A.C.SMITH, R.I.R. (newly commd)	"	"
2/Lt.W.C.WADDINGTON	"	"
2/Lt.H.R.HOLLIS	"	"
2/Lt.D.G.DANN, E.Yorks	"	"
2/Lt.C.W.CAMPBELL	"	"
2/Lt.E.WILLISON, D.L.I. att 7th Bn	"	"

150TH INFY BDE (Contd).
4th East Yorkshire Regt (Contd).

2/Lt.W.WATSON, E.Yorks	Missing	27/5/18.
Lt(A/Capt) O.PHILLIP	Wounded	"
2/Lt.H.PEARSON	"	"
2/Lt.P.BOLTON, 8th E.Yorks	"	"
Capt.G.W.YOUNG, 8th E.Yorks	Killed	"

4th Yorkshire Regt.-

Lt.J.F.JOHNS, York.R.	Wounded	"
Lt.H.R.B.BAILEY, York.R.		"
Capt(A/Maj.) L.NEWCOMB E,	Missing	"
2/Lt(A/Capt) W.L.GORING, MC. 6th Yorks	"	"
Capt.H.N.CONSTANTINE, MC.	"	"
Lt.D.W.W.S.PURCELL, York.R.	"	"
Lt.C.K.KELK, 5th Yorkshire R.	"	"
Lt.R.W.M.CLOSE	"	"
Lt.T.WIGGINS	"	"
Lt.J.C.STORY, York.R.	"	"
Lt.G.W.MACKAY, 5th York.R.	" bvd wounded	"
Lt.T.A.ROBSON, 5th York.R.	"	"
2/Lt.H.E.WEBB, York.R.	Wounded & Missing	"
2/Lt.W.H.JONES, York.R.	Missing	"
2/Lt.A.W.APPLEBY,	"	"
2/Lt.J.H.DERRETT	"	"
2/Lt.W.R.HOLMES	"	"
2/Lt.A.G.V.MARSH, R.I.R.	"	"
2/Lt.C.W.STIRK (newly commd)	"	"
2/Lt.H.A.CLIDERO	"	"

5th Yorkshire Regt.

Lt(A/Capt) P.D.J.WATERS MC.	Wounded	"
2/Lt.W.JACKSON, York.R.	"	"
Capt.G.THOMPSON, MC.	Missing	"
Lt.(A/Capt) & Adjt A.S.WOOD, 4th York.R.	"	"
Capt.G.MOSELEY	"	"
Capt.E.H.WEIGHELL	"	"
Lt(A/Capt) H.G.AMIS	"	"
Lt.G.H.SMITH	"	"
Lt.J.E.E.WINSTON	"	"
Lt.G.W.COOPER, 81st Training Reserve	"	"
Lt.C.B.R.REES	"	"
Lt.H.W.KNIGHT, York.R.	"	"
Lt.E.A.LISTER	"	"
2/Lt.J.M.ATKINSON	"	"
2/Lt.F.BARROWCLIFF, 8th Yorks	"	"
2/Lt.C.L.KING, 7th Yorks	"	"
2/Lt.H.T.ROBSON, York.R.	"	"
2/Lt.W.PATTERSON, York.R.	"	"
2/Lt.L.RYMER	"	"
2/Lt.T.J.CAVANAGH, R.I.R.	"	"
2/Lt.S.F.JOWETT (newly commd)	"	"
2/Lt.P.LAWSON, 13th Yorks	"	"
2/Lt.R.J.CHARTERS, R.I.R.	"	"
2/Lt.R.CARNAGHAN, R.I.R.	"	"

151ST INFANTRY BRIGADE.-
Headquarters.-

Lt.S.G.WOOD, MC. 7th N.Fant 50th Div.Sig.Co.	Wounded gas	"

5th Durham Light Infy.-

Capt.J.A.N.HESSLER	Killed	"
Capt.E.A.MEEK, MC.	Wounded	"
Lt.W.A.CAMPBELL	"	"
2/Lt.H.R.C.McMONAGEE, R.I.R.	" (gas)	"
2/Lt.K.McN.PHILLIPS, N.F.	Missing	"
Capt.A.B.HILL	"	"
Capt.W.N.J.MOSCROP, MC	"	"
Capt.J.McMINN, R.I.R.	"	"

151ST INFANTRY BRIGADE.-

5th Durham Light Infy.-

Lt.O.J.~~GRAHAM, M.C.~~ WILLIAMS, MC.	Missing	27/5/18.
Lt.R.W.G.ROBINSON	"	"
Lt.A.L.B.CHILDE, 7/8th W.Yorks	"	"
Lt.C.WEST	"	"
2/Lt.E.I.LOWES	"	"
2/Lt.P.GODDING, R.I.R.	"	"
2/Lt.T.SCOTT, D.L.I.	"	"
2/Lt.J.LEIGH, N.F.	"	"
2/Lt.W.S.WRAY, N.F.	"	"
2/Lt.C.A.F.THORNTON, W.Yorks	"	"
2/Lt.J.C.M.PEACOCK, D.L.I.	"	"
2/Lt.P.BALMER	"	"
2/Lt.R.J.HADDON, D.L.I.	"	"
2/Lt.G.F.PATTINSON, D.L.I.	"	"
2/Lt.W.S.KIRKUP, D.L.I.	"	"

6th Durham Light Infy.-

Lt.A.M.CLARE, M.D. R.A.M.C. attd	Killed	"
2/Lt.J.C.GARRITT, 8th W.Yorks	"	"
2/Lt.R.H.HALLAS, 8th W.Yorks	Wounded	"
Capt(A/Maj.) T.B.HESLOP	"	"
2/Lt.J.G.PORTEOUS, 7/8th W.Yorks	"	"
2/Lt.J.W.WELDON, 7/8th W.Yorks	"	"
2/Lt.S.S.PEMBERTON do	"	"
2/Lt.J.L.GOTT, D.L.I.	Missing	"
2/Lt.A.B.GILES, 5th D.L.I.	"	"
Lt.R.GREEN, MC.	"	"
Lt.E.A.ARMBRISTER, 8th D.L.I.	"	"
Capt.W.B.HANSELL	"	"
Lt(A/Capt) P.H.B.LYON, MC.	"	"
Lt.A.M.BROWN,	"	"

8th Durham Light Infy.-

Lt.W.BIGG	Killed	"
2/Lt.F.W.HARRISON	WOUNDED+MISSING	"
Lt.N.CLARK	Wounded	"
2/Lt.J.BRAMWELL	"	"
Lt(A/Capt) R.H.WHARRIER, MC.	" & Missing	"
Capt.J.W.E.TURNBULL	" " "	"
2/Lt.R.H.HILL.	" (gas)& Missing	"
Lt.A.L.WILSON.	" " "	"
Lt.C.C.DUGDALE, D.L.I.	" " "	"
Lt.W.C.HATHERAL, R.I.R.	" & Missing	"
Capt.F.W.B.JOHNSON	Missing	"
Lt(A/Capt) & Adjt J.H.BURRELL	"	"
Capt.H.WILKINSON, D.L.I.	"	"
Lt(A/Capt) J.HUTCHINSON	"	"
2/Lt.F.C.ARKLESS, D.L.I.	"	"
Lt.R.H.MONTGOMERY, R.I.R.		
A.E.		
Lt.F.C.S.HARRISON.	"	"
Lt.E.A.PIKE	"	"
Lt.D.SLOANE, R.I.R.	"	"
Lt.M.HOPPER	"	"
2/Lt.C.A.MACE, D.L.I.	"	"
Lt.T.E.McQUISTON, R.I.R.	"	"
Capt A. SIEWING, U.S. R.A.M.C. attd	"	"

151st Trench Mortar Battery.-

2/Lt.W.R.WORRALL, 8th W.Yorks	"	"

7th DURH.L.I.PIONEERS.

2/Lt(A/Maj.) R.DICKSON	Killed	"
2/Lt.F.WOODS	Wounded	"
2/Lt.J.P.JUDSON	"	"

LIST No. 2.

50TH (NORTHUMBRIAN) DIVISION.

CASUALTIES FROM 27TH May, 1918 to date.

OFFICERS.

UNIT.	K.	W.	M.	Remarks.
ARTILLERY.				
250th Bde R.F.A.	1	2	10 a.	a. Includes 1 wounded.
251st Bde R.F.A.	-	1	19	
50th Divl. Amn. Col.	-	-	3 b.	b. Includes 1 Bld Killed.
50th T.M.Batteries.	-	2	3 c.	c. Includes 1 wounded 1 Bld K.
149TH INFANTRY BRIGADE.				
Headquarters.	-	-	1	
4th North'd Fus.	2	4	16 d	d. Includes 1 D. of W.
				e. Includes 2 wounded.
5th North'd Fus.	-	4	9	
6th North'd Fus.	-	3g	18h	g. Includes 1 Gas.
				h. Includes 4 wounded.
149th T.M. Battery.	-	-	4	
150TH INFANTRY BRIGADE.				
4th E.Yorkshire Regt.	1	3	24	
4th Yorkshire Regt.	-	1	19	
5th Yorkshire Regt.	-	2	22	
151ST INFANTRY BRIGADE.				
Headquarters.	-	1	-	(Gas).
5th Durham L.I.	1	2j	20	j. Includes 1 Gas.
6th Durham L.I.	2	5	7	
8th Durham L.I.	1	2	19k	k. Includes 6 wounded.
151st T.M.Battery.	-	1	-	
7TH DURHAM L.I. Pnrs.	1	2	-	
TOTAL.	11	35	191	

NAMES OF OFFICERS.

250th Bde R.F.A.	LIEUT T.F.A.RICHARDSON, RFA.TF.	KILLED	27/5/18.
"	LIEUT J.HOPWOOD, MC. RFA.TF.	WOUNDED.	"
"	2/LT. P. GRANGE, MC. RA.	"	"
"	LIEUT H.R.HORNSBY, MC. RFA.TF.	WOUNDED & MISSING.	"
"	2/LT. H.W.ABEY. RA. SR.	MISSING.	"
"	LIEUT. R.J.BARDSLEY, RA. SR.	"	"
"	LT. (A/Major) G.CHAPMAN, MC. TF.	"	"
"	LIEUT. J.P.HUTCHINSON, MC. RFA.TF.	"	"
"	2/LT. K.M.GOODENOUGH, MC. RA. SR.	"	"
"	2/LT. D.H.CPSTAR, RA. SR.	"	"
"	LIEUT. E. DARING, MC. RFA. TF.	"	"
"	LIEUT. E.C.EARLE. RFA. TF.	"	"
" attached.	LIEUT W.REES. U.S.M.O.R.C.	"	"
251st Bde R.F.A.	LIEUT. COL. F.B.MOSS-BLUNDELL. DSO. RFA. TF.	"	"
"	LT. (A/Capt) B.K.BARTON. MC. RFA. TF.	"	"
"	LIEUT. A.S.WITHERINGTON. RFA. TF.	"	"
"	2/LT. E.D.TUDHOPE. RA. SR. (Signal Offr).	"	"
"	Capt (A/Major) W.R.H.HUTCHINSON. MC. RFA. TF.	"	"
"	LIEUT. T.H.GATHERAL. RFA. TF.	"	"
"	LIEUT. L.R.WILLIAMS. RFA. TF.	"	"

NAMES OF OFFICERS.

251st (Nbn) Bde R.F.A.

Major G.D.NANTES, R.A.	Missing	27/5/18.
Lt.C.C.FRANK, R.F.A. TF.	"	"
2/Lt.H.BULLING, R.F.A. TF.	"	"
2/Lt.T.POWELL, R.A. SR.	"	"
Capt(A/Maj) W.GOLDING, MC R.F.A. TF	"	"
Lt.J.L.GIBSON, R.F.A. TF.	"	"
2/Lt.W.T.MERCER, R.F.A. TF.	"	"
Lt.F.W.SOPWITH, MC. R.F.A. TF.	"	"
Lt.C.E.PATTON, R.F.A. TF.	"	"
2/Lt.W.E.CLARKE R.F.A. TF.	"	"
2/Lt.G.W.PARKES (shewn in Army L. as "PARKER"	"	"
Lt.W.J.SULLIVAN, U.S. R.A.M.C. attd	Wounded	"
Lt.W.S.GALL, R.F.A. TF.	" & Missing	"

50th Divnl Ammn Col.

Lt.W.A.DENHAM, R.F.A. TF.	Missing	"
2/Lt.I.H.WHITE, R.A. SR.	"	"
Lt.W.W.WHYTE, R.F.A. TF.	" bvd Killed	"

50th T.Mortar Batteries.

Capt.W.C.HAND, DSO. MC. R.G.A.	Wounded	"
Lt.T.SAMPLE, R.F.A. TF.	"	"
2/Lt.G.H.B.CLARKE, R.F.A. TF.	" & Missing	"
Lt(A/Capt) S.R.C.PLIMSOLL, MC. R.F.A. TF.	Missing bvd "K"	"
2/Lt.F.J.HODDER, R.F.A. TF.	"	"

149th INFANTRY BRIGADE.
Headquarters.
Lt.P.W.LOVEL, 6th North'd F.	Missing	"

4th North'd Fusrs.
~~Lt.T.G.............. CHEESERIGHT, 6th N.F.~~	~~Killed~~	~~"~~
2/Lt.J.A.GREANEY, R.D.F.	Wounded	"
2/Lt.D.FIRTH, N.F.	"	30/5/18.
2/Lt.J.E.FARWELL, N.F.	"	"
Lt. SMALLWOOD, N.F.	Wounded (D of W)	27/5/18.
~~2/Lt.J.C.NAPIER, 4th N.F.~~		
2/Lt.K.R.REES	Missing	"
2/Lt.H.E.TULLEY, 8th N.F.	"	"
Lt(A/Capt) J.V.GREGORY, MC. 6th N.F.	Wounded & Missg	"
2/Lt.W.L.MCLEAN, N.F.	" "	"
Lt(A/Capt) A.WILLIS, 8th N.F.	Missing	"
2/Lt.J.W.MARSDEN, N.F.	"	"
Lt.J.J.HOLME, 6th N.F.	"	"
2/Lt.F.G.PEDDIE, MC.,	"	"
2/Lt.W.JONES, N.F.	"	"
2/Lt.H.E.FINDLAY, N.F.	"	"
Capt.R.ALLEN.	"	"
2/Lt.A.E.MORRIS, N.F.	"	"
2/Lt.A.H.BOYLE, N.F.	"	"
2/Lt.W.MAXFIELD, N.F.	"	"
Lt.H.H.HARRISON, N.F.	"	"
Lt.F.J.IVES,	"	"

2.

5th North'd Fusrs.

Lt.J.E.PORRITT, N.F.	Killed	27/5/18.
2/Lt.J.H.McMURDO	"	"
2/Lt.J.McMEEKEN, N.F.	"	"
2/Lt.J.B.SLACK, N.F.	"	"
2/Lt.E.PHILLIPS, N.F.	Wounded (D of W)	"
2/Lt.J.H.YOUNG, N.F.	"	"
2/Lt.R.S.BOWIE, N.F.	"	"
2/Lt.E.V.SARGENT	"	"
2/Lt.R.T.DENNIS, R.I.R.	Missing	28/5/18.
Capt.H.G.DODDS	"	27/5/18.
2/Lt.S.WEATERTON, N.F.	"	"
2/Lt.L.J.ROSS, R.I.R.	"	"
2/Lt.R.H.QUINE, N.F.	"	"
2/Lt.W.E.PRIESTNALL, N.F.	Wounded & Missing	"

6th North'd Fusrs.

Major A.D.S.ROGERS	Wounded	"
Capt.J.N.MacKENZIE, MC. MB. RAMC attd	Missing	"
Capt.H.GRAHAM, N.F.	"	"
Capt.R.E.M.HEANLEY, 84th Training Res.	"	"
Lt.J.WATSON, N.F.	"	"
Lt.H.V.RUSSEL	Wounded & Missing	"
2/Lt.A.P.ANDERSON, D.L.I.	Missing	"
Lt.W.R.DODDS, N.F.	Wounded & Missing	"
Lt.W.M.McLARE, N.F.	Missing	"
Lt.J.W.CRAIG CRAKE.	"	"
Lt.C.O.MARSHALL, N.F.	"	"
2/Lt.J.GRAY, N.F.	"	"
2/Lt.A.E.GLANVILLE, R.D.F.	Wounded & Missing	"
Lt(A/Capt) J.G.GARRARD, MC. 5th N.F.	" " "	"
2/Lt.E.D.SURTEES, N.F.	Wounded (GPS)	"
Capt(A/Maj.) J.G.LEATHART, MC.	"	2/6/18.
2/Lt.C.B.McCOMB, R.I.R.	Missing	27/5/18.
2/Lt.W.J.DAVID, N.F.	"	"
2/Lt.A.S.TAYLOR, N.F.	"	"
2/Lt.I.R.LEES (not shewn in Army L.)	"	"
2/Lt.J.S.STOKOE, N.F.	"	"

149th Trench Mortar Battery.

Lt(A/Capt) J.M.BENSON, 4th N.F.	"	"
2/Lt.J.SOWERBY, N.F. attd 6th Bn.	"	"
2/Lt.C.TOLKIEN, 8th attd 4th N.F. (shewn in Army L. "TOLKEIN").	"	"
2/Lt.A.E.BROWN, 5th N.F.	"	"

150TH INFANTRY BRIGADE.-
4th East Yorkshire Regt.

Major H.R.HASLETT, R.I.R.	"	"
Capt.N.W.INGLEBY,	"	"
Lt.E.JOHNSTON	"	"
Capt.E.LAVERACK.	"	"
Lt.C.S.JOHNSON	"	"
Lt.W.E.HEWAT	"	"
2/Lt.S.FEARNLEY, 13th E.Yorks	"	"
Lt.P.S.MURRAY, MC. R.I.R.	"	"
Lt.H.F.STEPHENSON, R.I.R.	"	"
2/Lt.J.A.A.FLYNN, R.I.R.	Wounded & Missing	"
2/Lt.R.GIVEN, R.I.R.	Missing	"
2/Lt.B.C.BINER, R.I.R.	"	"
2/Lt.A.THRUSTLE, E.Yorks	"	"
2/Lt.C.N.ROGAN	"	"
2/Lt.J.WALKER, E.Yorks (newly commd)	"	"
2/Lt.T.K.DIGBY, R.I.R.	"	"
2/Lt.S.F.BASTOW	"	"
2/Lt.A.C.SMITH, R.I.R. (newly commd)	"	"
2/Lt.W.C.WADDINGTON	"	"
2/Lt.H.R.HOLLIS	"	"
2/Lt.D.G.DANN, E.Yorks	"	"
2/Lt.T.W.CAMPBELL	"	"
2/Lt.E.WILLISON, 7th D.L.I. att 7th Bn	"	"

3.

150TH INFY BDE (contd).
4th East Yorkshire Regt (Contd).

2/Lt.V.WATSON, E.Yorks	Missing	27/5/18.
Lt.(A/Capt) C.PHILLIP	Wounded	"
2/Lt.H.PEARSON	"	"
2/Lt.F.BOLTON, 8th E.Yorks	"	"
Capt.G.V.YOUNG, 8th E.Yorks	Killed	"

4th Yorkshire Regt.-

Lt.J.V.JOHNS, York.R.	Wounded MISSING	"
Lt.H.T.B.BAILEY, York.R.	WOUNDED + "	"
Capt(A/Maj.) L.BEECOMB E.	Missing	"
2/Lt(A/Capt) W.L.GORING, MC. 8th Yorks	"	"
Capt.H.B.CONSTANTINE, MC.	"	"
Lt.W.V.S.PURCELL, York.R.	"	"
Lt.C.F.KELK, 5th Yorkshire R.	"	"
Lt.R.W.M.CLOSE	"	"
Lt.T.WIGGINS	"	"
Lt.J.C.STORY, York.R.	" bvd wounded	"
Lt.G.G.V.MACKAY, 5th York.R.	"	"
Lt.T.A.ROBSON, 5th York.R.	Wounded & Missing	"
2/Lt.H.F.WEBB, York.R.	Missing	"
2/Lt.W.H.JONES, York.R.	"	"
2/Lt.A.W.APPLEBY,	"	"
2/Lt.J.H.DERRETT	"	"
2/Lt.W.B.HOLMES	"	"
2/Lt.A.G.V.MARSH, R.I.R.	"	"
2/Lt.C.W.STIRK (newly commd)	"	"
2/Lt.H.A.CLIDERO		

5th Yorkshire Regt.

Lt(A/Capt) P.D.J.WATERS	Wounded	"
2/Lt.W.JACKSON, York.R.	"	"
Capt.G.THOMPSON, MC.	Missing	"
Lt.(A/Capt) & Adjt A.C.WOOD, 4th York.R.	"	"
Capt.C.MOSELEY	"	"
Capt.R.H.MITCHELL WRIGHILL	"	"
Lt(A/Capt) H.C.AMIS	"	"
Lt.C.H.SMITH	"	"
Lt.J.H.E.WINSTON	"	"
Lt.C.E.COOPER, 21st Training Reserve	"	"
Lt.C.B.R.REES	"	"
Lt.H.W.KNIGHT, York.R.	"	"
Lt.E.A.LISTER	"	"
2/Lt.J.H.ATKINSON	"	"
2/Lt.F.BARROWCLIFF, 8th Yorks	"	"
2/Lt.C.L.KING, 7th Yorks	"	"
2/Lt.H.T.ROBSON, York.R.	"	"
2/Lt.V.PATTERSON, York.R.	"	"
2/Lt.L.HYMER	"	"
2/Lt.T.J.CAVANAGH, R.I.R.	"	"
2/Lt.S.F.JOWETT (newly commd)	"	"
2/Lt.P.LAWSON, 13th Yorks	"	"
2/Lt.R.J.CHARTERS, R.I.R.	"	"
2/Lt.R.CARNACHAN, R.I.R.	"	"

151ST INFANTRY BRIGADE.-
Headquarters.-

Lt.E.G.WOOD, MC. 7th N.Fatt 50th Div.Sig.Co.	Wounded gas	"

5th Durham Light Infy.-

Capt.J.A.N.WHEELER	Killed	"
Capt.F.A.HUNK, MC.	Wounded	"
Lt.W.A.CAMPBELL	" (gas)/MISSING	"
2/Lt.H.R.C.McMONAGLE, R.I.R.	"	"
2/Lt.F.McM.PHILLIPS, N.F.	Missing	"
Capt.A.B.HILL	"	"
Capt.W.H.J.MOSCROP, MC	"	"
Capt.J.McMINN, R.I.R.		

4.

151ST INFANTRY BRIGADE.-

5th Durham Light Infy.-
Lt.O.J.GRAHAM, M.C. WILLIAMS	Missing	27/5/18.
Lt.R.W.G.ROBINSON	"	"
Lt.A.L.B.CHILDE, 7/8th W.Yorks	"	"
Lt.C.WEST	"	"
2/Lt.E.I.LOWES	"	"
2/Lt.P.GODDING, R.I.R.	"	"
2/Lt.T.SCOTT, D.L.I.	"	"
2/Lt.J.LEIGH, N.F.	"	"
2/Lt.W.S.WRAY, N.F.	"	"
2/Lt.O.A.P.THORNTON, W.Yorks	"	"
2/Lt.J.C.M.PEACOCK, D.L.I.	"	"
2/Lt.P.BALMER	"	"
2/Lt.R.J.HADDON, D.L.I.	"	"
2/Lt.G.F.PATTINSON, D.L.I.	"	"
2/Lt.W.S.KIRKUP, W.I.	"	"

6th Durham Light Infy.-
Lt.A.W.CLARE, M.D. R.A.M.C. attd	Killed	"
2/Lt.J.C.GARBUTT, 8th W.Yorks	"	"
2/Lt.R.H.HALLAS, 8th W.Yorks	Wounded	"
Capt(A/Maj.) T.B.HESLOP	"	"
2/Lt.J.D.PORTEOUS, 7/8th W.Yorks	"	"
2/Lt.J.W.WELDON, 7/8th W.Yorks	"	"
2/Lt.S.S.PEMBERTON do	"	"
2/Lt.J.L.GOTT, D.L.I.	Missing	"
2/Lt.A.R.GILES, 5th D.L.I.	"	"
Lt.R.GREEN, MC.	"	"
Lt.E.A.ARMBRISTER, 8th D.L.I.	"	"
Capt.W.B.HATSELL	"	"
Lt(A/Capt) P.H.B.LYON, MC.	"	"
Lt.A.N.BROWN,	"	"

8th Durham Light Infy.-
Lt.W.BIGG	Killed	"
2/Lt.F.W.HARRISON	WOUNDED + MISSING.	"
Lt.N.CLARK	Wounded	"
2/Lt.J.BRAMWELL	"	"
Lt(A/Capt) R.H.WHARRIER, MC.	" & Missing	"
Capt.J.W.E.TURNBULL	" " "	"
2/Lt.R.H.HILL.	" (gas)& Missing	"
Lt.A.L.WILSON.	" " "	"
Lt.C.C.DUGDALE, D.L.I.	" " "	"
Lt.W.C.HATHERAL, R.I.R.	" & Missing	"
Capt.F.W.B.JOHNSON	Missing	"
Lt(A/Capt) & Adjt J.H.BURRELL	"	"
Capt.H.WILKINSON, D.L.I.	"	"
Lt(A/Capt) J.HUTCHINSON	"	"
2/Lt.F.C.ANKLESS, D.L.I.	"	"
Lt.S.H.MONTGOMERY, R.I.R.	"	"
A.F.		
Lt.F.C.S.HARRISON.	"	"
Lt.E.A.PIKE	"	"
Lt.D.SLOANE, R.I.R.	"	"
Lt.N.HOPPER	"	"
2/Lt.C.A.HAGE, D.L.I.	"	"
Lt.T.E.McQUISTON, R.I.R.	"	"
Capt.--SIEWING, U.S. R.A.M.C. attd	"	"

151st Trench Mortar Battery.-
2/Lt.W.R.WORRALL, 8th W.Yorks	"	"

7th DURH.L.I.PIONEERS.
2/Lt(A/Maj.) R.DICKSON	Killed	"
2/Lt.F.WOODS	Wounded	"
2/Lt.J.P.JUDSON	"	"

List No: 3.

50th (Northumbrian) Division.

CASUALTIES FROM 27th MAY 1918 TO DATE.

OFFICERS.

UNIT.	K.	W.	M.	REMARKS.
149th INFY BDE.-				
4th North'd Fus.	-	-	2	
5th do	-	-	1	
6th do	-	1	-	
150th INFY BDE.-				
Headquarters	-	1	1	
4th East Yorks R.	-	1	1	
4th Yorkshire R.	-	1	-	
5th do	-	-	1	
151st INFY BDE.-				
8th Durh.L.I.	-	2	12	
7th DURH.L.I.PNRS	-	1	16	
	-	7	34	

NAMES OF OFFICERS.

149th INFY BDE.
4th North'd Fus.
  Capt. F.C.H.BENNETT, M.B. R.A.M.C. attd   Missing   27/5/18.
  2/Lt.J.A.McINTYRE, N.F.   "   "
5th North'd Fus.
  2/Lt.J.BRYCE, R.I.R.   "   "
6th North'd Fus.
  2/Lt.J.E.SIMMONDS, N.F.   Wounded   "

150th INFY BDE.-
4th E.Yorkshire Regt.
  2/Lt.J.C.W.BEALE, E.Yorks   "   "
  Lt.GD TIBBETTS, M.O.R.C. attd   Missing   "
4th Yorkshire Regt.
  Lt.P.I.LEIGH-BREESE   Wounded s.s.   "
5th Yorkshire Regt.
  Lt.J.A.WHITE, M.O.R.C. attd   Missing   "
Bde Headquarters.
  2/Lt.C.A.KENNEDY, R.E.   "   "
  Capt.T.H.HUTCHINSON, 4th Yorks   Wounded   "

151st INFY BDE.-
8th Durh.L.I.
  Lt.C.H.SYMES, 4th Gloucesters   Missing   "
  2/Lt.A.S.BOSTOCK, E.Yorks 8th D.L.I.   "   "
  2/Lt.R.S.ELLIOTT, 8th D.L.I.   WOUNDED MISSING   "
  Lt.C.D.ROBERTS   "   "
  2/Lt.B.THOMPSON   "   "
  Lt.L.W.WILSON, R.I.R.   "   "
  2/Lt.E.B.F.ARTHY, 7th D.L.I.   WOUNDED MISSING   "
  2/Lt.W.F.G.PRIEST, 9th D.L.I.   "   "
  2/Lt.H.PALMER, W.Yorks   "   "
  2/Lt.H.C.HOWELL, W.Yorks   "   "
  2/Lt.T.F.GRAVES, R.I.R.   "   "
  2/Lt.C.BROWN, D.L.I.   "   "
  Lt.G.P.NUDGE, 7th D.L.I.   "   "
  2/Lt.A.G.BREWER, 14th D.L.I.   W "   "

(2)

7th Durh.L.I. Pnrs.

Lt(A/Capt) J.E.SCOTT	Wounded gas	27/5/18.
Lt(A/Capt) & Adjt W.F.LAING, MC.	Missing	"
Capt. H.JOSEPH	"	"
Lt. R.LAWSON	"	"
Lt. S. PROBERT	"	"
Lt(A/Capt) R.F.W.PARKER, A.C.C.	"	"
Lt. R.V.ILES	"	"
2/Lt. J.P.B.GREY	"	"
Lt. G.W.BOSUSTOW	"	"
2/Lt. F.C.MAJOR, D.L.I.	"	"
Lt. F.GRAHAM	"	"
Lt. L.J.FOSTER	"	"
2/Lt. P.GIBSON, D.L.I.	"	"
Lt. P.WALKER	"	"
Lt. S.N.CARTER	"	"
Lt(A/Capt) L.BENNETT	"	"

MAJOR,
D.A.A.G. for Maj.-General,
Commanding 50th (Northumbrian) Division.

4/6/18.

CORRECTIONS.

LIST No.2.

4th North'd Fus.	2/Lt.J.C.NAPIER rep. "Wounded 27/5/18" now rep. sick to hospital.
8th North'd Fus.	2/Lt.W.M.DODDS should read "2/Lt.W.R.DODD"
4th E.Yorks R.	2/Lt.J.WALKER, E.Yorks (newly commd) should read "2/Lt.J.W.WALKER, E.Yorks (newly commd)
6th Durh.L.I.	2/Lt.J.G.PORTEOUS should read "2/Lt.J.D. PORTEOUS".
4th North'd Fus.	Lt. L.S.CHEESERIGHT, 8th N.F. reported killed now reported with Unit

LIST NO. 5.

50TH (NORTHUMBRIAN) DIVISION.

CASUALTIES FROM 27TH MAY, 1918 TO DATE.

UNIT.	DATE.	KILLED. O. O.R.	WOUNDED. O. O.R.	MISSING. O. O.R.	REMARKS
ARTILLERY.					
250th Bde R.F.A.	27/5/18	— 2	— 35	— —	152a a Incl.
251st Bde R.F.A.	"	— 2	— 6	— —	206b17 W. 5 Bld K.
" R.E. Sub.Section.	"	— —	— —	— 4	18 b Incl.
" R.A.M.C.	"	— —	— —	— —	2 3 W.
" R.A.F.	"	— —	— —	— —	2
50th D.A.C.	"	— 6	— 13	— —	18 c Incl.
50th T.M.Bn.	"	— —	— 7	— —	67c 3 W.
149TH INF. BDE.					
Headquarters.					
Sig. Coy. RE	"	— —	— 3	— —	1
4th N.F.	"	— 2	— 1	— —	1
5th N.F.	"	— —	— 2	— —	1
6th N.F.	"	— 1	— 1	— —	—
4th North'd Fus.	"	— 2	— 37	— —	485.
5th North'd Fus.	"	— 10	— 97	— —	539
6th North'd Fus.	"	— 9	— 46	— —	530
T.M. Battery.	"	— 2	— 7	— —	31
TOTAL.		— 33	— 253	— —	1837.

CORRECTIONS.

LIST NO. 3.
5th Durham L.I. 2/Lt. R.S. ELLIOTT reported Missing now reported Wounded.

Actual O.R. casualties for 150th Infantry Brigade will be forwarded without delay.

H.Q. 50th Divn.
9th June, 1918.

R.C.Olive / Major.
D.A.A.G. for Major General,
Commanding, 50th (North'bn) Division.

List No: 3.

50th (Northumbrian) Division.

CASUALTIES FROM 27th MAY 1918 TO DATE.

OFFICERS.

UNIT.	K.	W.	M.	REMARKS.
149th INFY BDE.-				
4th North'd Fus.	-	-	2	
5th do	-	-	1	
6th do	-	1	-	
150th INFY BDE.-				
Headquarters	-	1	1	
4th East Yorks R.	-	1	1	
4th Yorkshire R.	-	1	-	
5th do	-	-	1	
151st INFY BDE.-				
6th Durh.L.I.	-	2	12	
7th DURH.L.I. PNRS	-	1	16	
	-	7	34	

NAMES OF OFFICERS.

149th INFY BDE.
4th North'd Fus.
Capt. F.C.H.BENNETT, M.B. R.A.M.C. attd — Missing — 27/5/18.
2/Lt. J.A.McINTYRE, N.F. — " — "
5th North'd Fus.
2/Lt. J.BRYCE, P.I.R. — " — "
6th North'd Fus.
2/Lt. J.E.SIMMONDS, N.F. — Wounded — "
150th INFY BDE.-
4th E.Yorkshire Regt.
2/Lt. J.C.W.BEALE, E.Yorks — " — "
Lt. GD TIBBETTS, M.O.R.C. attd — Missing — "
4th Yorkshire Regt.
Lt. P.L.LEIGH-BREESE — Wounded s.s. — "
5th Yorkshire Regt.
Lt. J.A.WHITE, M.O.R.C. attd — Missing — "
Bde Headquarters.
2/Lt. C.A.KENNEDY, R.E. — " — "
Capt. T.H.HUTCHINSON, 4th Yorks — Wounded — "
151st INFY BDE.-
6th Durh.L.I.
Lt. G.H.SYKES, 4th Gloucesters — Missing — "
2/Lt. A.S.BOSTOCK, W.Yorks 8th D.L.I. — " — "
2/Lt. R.S.ELLIOTT, 8th D.L.I. — WOUNDED MISSING — "
Lt. G.D.ROBERTS — " — "
2/Lt. R.THOMPSON 5DLI — " — "
Lt. L.E.WILSON, R.I.R. — " — "
2/Lt. E.F.ANTHY, 7th D.L.I. — WOUNDED MISSING — "
2/Lt. W.E.C.PRIEST, 8th D.L.I. — " — "
2/Lt. H.PALMER, W.Yorks — " — "
2/Lt. H.C.HOWELL, W.Yorks — " — "
2/Lt. T.F.GRAVES, R.I.R. — " — "
2/Lt. C.BROWN, D.L.I. — " — "
Lt. C.P.BUDGE, 7th D.L.I. — " — "
2/Lt. A.C.BREWER, 14th D.L.I. — W+ " — "

List. No.4.

50th (Northumbrian) Division.

CASUALTIES FROM 27TH MAY 1918 TO DATE.

OTHER RANKS.

UNIT.	K.	W.	M.	REMARKS.
244th (Divl) Employment Coy.	-	4a	31	a includes 3 at duty.
M.M.P.	-	-	1	
Traffic Control Personnel attached A.P.M.				
4th Northd Fusiliers.)	-	-	1b	b wounded.
6th Northd Fusiliers.)	-	-	1b	
5th Yorkshire Regt.)	-	-	1	
5th Durham Light Infy.)	-	-	2c	c includes 1 wounded
6th Durham Light Infy.)	-	-	1	
Divisional Headquarters.				
A.S.C.	1	-	1	
R.A.M.C.)	-	-	7	
244th D. Empt. Coy.)	-	-	2	
Dragoon Guards)	-	-	1	
Suffolk Regt.)	-	1	-	
4th Northd Fus.)	-	-	1	
5th Northd Fus.)	-	1	3	
4th Yorkshire R.)	-	-	1	
5th Yorkshire R.)	-	1	-	
5th Durham Light Infy.)	-	-	1	
6th Durham Light Infy.)	-	-	2	
8th D.L.I. (Pnrs))	-	-	6	
D.A.D.O.S.				
A.O.C.)	-	-	1	
6th Durham LgI. att.)	-	-	2	
244th D. Empt. Coy.)	-	-	1	believed wounded
50th Divisional Train.	1	5	4	
R.A.M.C.				
1/1st Nbn. Field Amb.	1	10	70	
2/2nd Nbn. Field Amb.	-	3	14	
1/3rd Nbn. Field Amb.	4	6	15	
50th Div. Salvage Coy.				
244th D. Empt. Coy.)	-	1	13	
7th Durham L.I.)	-	1	-	
Royal Engineers.				d includes 1 believed W.
7th Field Coy. R.E.	1	-	86d	and 1 believed Gassed.
446th do.	1	27e	18f	e includes 3 gas. 5 at duty.
447th do.	2	3	137	f includes 4 wounded.
Signal Company R.E.	-	2	27g	g Wounded.
5th Northd Fus. att.)	-	-	1	
5th Durham L.I.)	-	-	1	
6th Durham L.I.)	-	-	1	
7th Durham L.I.)	-	-	1	
9th Durham L.I.)	-	-	1	
9th Royal Scots.)	-	-	1	
7th Durham L.I. (Pioneers).	2	35	488	
	13	100	945.	

List No.4.

50th (Northumbrian) Division.

CASUALTIES FROM 27th MAY 1918 TO DATE.

OTHER RANKS.

UNIT.	K.	W.	M.	REMARKS.
244th (Divl) Employment Coy.	-	4a	51	a includes 3 at duty
M.M.P.	-	-	1	
Traffic Control Personnel attached A.P.M.				
4th Northd Fusiliers)	-	-	1b	b wounded
6th Northd Fusiliers)	-	-	1b	
5th Yorkshire Regt.)	-	-	1	
5th Durham Light Infy.)	-	-	2c	c includes 1 wounded
6th Durham Light Infy.)	-	-	1	
Divisional Headquarters				
A.S.C.)	1	-	1	
R.A.M.C.)	-	-	7	
244th (Divl) Empt. Coy.)	-	-	2	
Dragoon Guard)	-	-	1	
Suffolk Regt.)	-	1	-	
4th Northd Fusiliers)	-	-	1	
5th Northd Fusiliers)	-	1	3	
4th Yorkshire Regt.)	-	-	1	
5th Yorkshire Regt.)	-	1	-	
5th Durham Light Infy.)	-	-	1	
6th Durham Light Infy.)	-	-	2	
7th Durham Light Infy.)	-	-	8	
D.A.D.O.S.				
A.O.C.)	-	-	1	
6th D.L.I. attd.)	-	-	2	
244th D. Empt. Coy.)	-	-	1	Believed wounded
50th Divisional Train.	1	5	4	
R.A.M.C.				
1/1st Nbn. Field Amb.	1	10	70	
2/2nd Nbn. Field Amb.	-	8	14	
1/3rd Nbn. Field Amb.	4	6	15	
50th Div. Salvage Coy.				
244th D. Empt. Coy.)	-	1	13	
7th Durham Light Infy.)	-	1	-	
Royal Engineers.				d includes 2 believed W.
7th Field Coy. R.E.)	1	-	86d	and 1 believed Gassed.
446th do.)	1	27e	18f	e includes 5 Gas.5 at duty
447th do.)	2	3	137	f includes 4 wounded.
Signal Company R.E.)	-	2	27	1 Wounded.
5th Northd Fusiliers att)	-	-	7	
5th Durham Light Infy.)	-	-	1	
6th Durham Light Infy.)	-	-	1	
7th Durham Light Infy.)	-	-	1	
9th Durham Light Infy.)	-	-	1	
9th Royal Scots)	-	-	2	
7th Durham Light Infy.(Pnrs)	2	35	469	
	13	100	948	

List No.5.

50TH (NORTHUMBRIAN) DIVISION.

CASUALTIES FROM 27/5/18 TO DATE.

UNIT.	DATE.	KILLED.		WOUNDED.		MISSING.		REMARKS.
		Off.	O.R.	Off.	O.R.	Off.	O.R.	
151st Inf. Bde.								
Bde. H.Q.	27/5/18.	-	-	-	8	-	6	(a) Inc. 7 Gas.
5th D.L.I.	"	-	2	1	19	2	568	
6th D.L.I.	"	-	2	-	20	2	478	(b) Inc. 18 "W"
8th D.L.I.	"	1	7	1	47a	-	441b	
T.M.Bty.	"	-	-	-	8	-	-	(c) injured acc.
50th Bn. M.G.C.	"	-	10	-	53	-	366	
R.A.M.C.								
2/2nd Nbn. F.Amb.	6/6/18.	-	-	10	-	-	-	
		1	21	3	147	4	1859.	

OFFICERS' NAMES.

5th Durham L.I.	2/Lt. G.Tunnel,	Wounded	27/5/18.
"	R.Blayney	"	"
"	W.Harris	"	"
6th Durham L.I.	" B.Howarth, E. Yorks.	Missing	"
"	" G.A.Gray	"	"
8th Durham L.I.	Lt. R.J.Fraser, D.L.I.	Killed.	"
	2/Lt. W.A.Mason, R.D.F.	Wounded	"
2/2nd Nbn.F.Amb.	T/Capt. T.R.Robertson, MB	injured acc.	6/6/18.

CORRECTIONS.

List No.2.
5th D.L.I. - 2/Lt. H.R.C.McMonagle, R.I.R. reported "W" gas, now
  reported Missing.
8th D.L.I. - 2/Lt. F.W.Harrison, reported "K" now reported Wounded
  and Missing.

List No.3.
6th D.L.I. - F.B.P.Arthy, 7th D.L.I. - rep. Missing now rep. Wounded.
  A.G.Brewer, rep. Missing, now rep. Wounded and Missing.

(sd) C.DUKE, Lieut-Colonel,
A.A. & Q.M.G., for Major General,
Commanding 50th (Northumbrian) Division.

H.Q. 50th Div.,
7th June 1918.

List No.5.

50TH (NORTHUMBRIAN) DIVISION.

CASUALTIES FROM 27/5/18 TO DATE.

UNIT.	DATE.	KILLED Off.	KILLED O.R.	WOUNDED Off.	WOUNDED O.R.	MISSING Off.	MISSING O.R.	REMARKS.
151st Inf. Bde.								
Bde. H.Q.	27/5/18.	-	-	-	8	-	6	(a) Inc. 7 Gas.
5th D.L.I.	"	-	2	1	19	2	568	
6th D.L.I.	"	-	2	-	20	2	478	(b) Inc. 18 "W"
8th D.L.I.	"	1	7	1	47a	-	441b	
T.M.Bty.	"	-	-	-	8	-	-	(c) injured acc.
50th Bn. M.G.C.	"	-	10	-	53	-	366	
RR.A.M.C.								
2/2nd Nbn. F.Amb.	6/6/18.	-	-	-	10	-	-	
		1	21	3	147	4	1859.	

OFFICERS' NAMES.

5th Durham L.I.	2/Lt. G.Tunnel,	Wounded	27/5/18.
"	R.Blayney	"	"
"	W.Harris	"	"
6th Durham L.I.	" B.Howarth, E. Yorks.	Missing	"
"	" G.A.Gray	"	"
8th Durham L.I.	Lt. R.J.Fraser, D.L.I.	Killed.	"
	2/Lt. W.A.Mason, R.D.F.	Wounded	"
2/2nd Nbn.F.Amb.	Capt. T.R.Robertson, MB	injured acc.	6/6/18.

CORRECTIONS.

List No.2.
5th D.L.I. - 2/Lt. H.R.C.McMonagle, R.I.R. reported "W" gas, now reported Missing.
8th D.L.I. - 2/Lt. F.W.Harrison, reported "K" now reported Wounded and Missing.

List No.3.
6th D.L.I. - F.B.P.Arthy, 7th D.L.I. - rep. Missing now rep. Wounded.
A.G.Brewer, rep. Missing, now rep. Wounded and Missing.

H.Q. 50th Div
7th June 1918.

(sd) C.DUKE, Lieut-Colonel,
A.A. & Q.M.G., for Major General,
Commanding 50th (Northumbrian) Division.

(2)

7th Durh.L.I. Pnrs.

Lt(A/Capt) J.E.SCOTT	Wounded gas	27/5/18.
Lt(A/Capt) & Adjt W.F.LAING, MC.	Missing	"
Capt. H.JOSEPH	"	"
Lt. R.LAWSON	"	"
Lt. S.PROBERT	"	"
Lt(A/Capt) R.W.W.PARKER, A.C.C.	"	"
Lt. R.V.ILES	"	"
2/Lt. J.P.R.GREY	"	"
Lt. C.W.BOSUSTOW	"	"
2/Lt. P.C.MAJOR, D.L.I.	"	"
Lt. P.GRAHAM	"	"
Lt. L.J.FOSTER	"	"
2/Lt. P.GIBSON, D.L.I.	"	"
Lt. P.WALKER	"	"
Lt. S.N.CARTER	"	"
Lt(A/Capt) L.BENNETT	"	"

MAJOR,
D.A.A.G. for Maj.-General,
Commanding 50th (Northumbrian) Division.

4/8/18.

CORRECTIONS.

LIST No. 2.
- 4th North'd Fus.   2/Lt. J.C.NAPIER rep. "Wounded 27/5/18" now rep. sick to hospital.
- 8th North'd Fus.   2/Lt. W.M.DODDS should read "2/Lt. W.R.DODD"
- 4th E.Yorks R.   2/Lt. J.WALKER, E.Yorks (newly commd) should read "2/Lt. J.W.WALKER, E.Yorks (newly commd)
- 8th Durh.L.I.   2/Lt. J.G.PORTEOUS should read "2/Lt. J.D. PORTEOUS".
- 4th North'd Fus.   Lt. L.S.CHEESERIGHT, 8th N.F. reported killed now reported with Unit

LIST NO. 6.

50TH (NORTHUMBRIAN) DIVISION.

CASUALTIES FROM 27TH MAY, 1918 TO DATE.

UNIT.	DATE.	KILLED. O. O.R.	WOUNDED. O. O.R.	MISSING. O. O.R.	REMARKS
ARTILLERY.					
250th Bde R.F.A.	27/5/18	– 2	– 35	–	132a 3 Incl.
251st Bde R.F.A.	"	– 2	– 9	–	206b17 W.
" "	)				3 Bld K.
" R.E.Sub.Section.	)"	– –	– –	– +	15 b Incl.
" R.A.M.C.	)"	– –	– –	– –	2 3 W.
" R.A.F.	)"	– –	– –	– –	2
50th D.A.C.	"	– 5	– 15	–	16 c Incl.
50th T.M.Bs.	"	– –	– 7	–	67c 3 W.
149TH INF. BDE.					
Headquarters.)					
Sig. Coy. RE)	"	– –	– 3	–	1
4th N.F.)	"	– 1	– 1	–	1
5th N.F.)	"	– –	– 2	–	1
6th N.F.	"	– 1	– 1	–	–
4th North'd Fus.	"	– 2	– 37	–	485.
5th North'd Fus.	"	– 10	– 97	–	536
6th North'd Fus.	"	– 9	– 46	–	530
T. M. Battery.	"	– 2	– 7	–	31
TOTAL.		– 35	– 258	–	1827.

CORRECTIONS.

LIST NO. 5.
6th Durham L.I. 2/Lt. R.S.ELLIOTT reported Missing now reported Wounded.

Actual O.R. casualties for 150th Infantry Brigade will be forwarded without delay.

Major.
D.A.A.G. for Major General.
H.Q. 50th Divn.
8th June, 1918.
Commanding, 50th (North'bn) Division.

List No.8.

50TH (NORTHUMBRIAN) DIVISION.
CASUALTIES FROM 27/5/18 TO DATE.

UNIT.	DATE.	KILLED Offrs.	KILLED O.R.	WOUNDED Off.	WOUNDED O.R.	MISSING Off.	MISSING O.R.	REMARKS.
150th Inf. Bde.								
4th E. Yorks	27/5/18.	-	8	-	20	-	644	
4th Yorks.	"	-	2	-	26	6	605a	a includes 1 W.
5th Yorks.	"	-	11	-	25	1	688	and Q Bld Killed.
151st Inf. Bde.								
HQ, 8th D.L.I. att.	"	-	-	-	-	-	1	
		-	21	-	71	7	1938.	

NAMES OF OFFICERS.

4th Yorks.
   Lt.(A/Capt) R.M.Howes.   Missing.   27/5/18.
   Lt. R.Gates, 5th Yorks.   "   "
   Lt. J.A.Hamlyn, Yorks Regt.   "   "
   2/Lt. W.A. Shooter, R.I.R.   "   "
   2/Lt. L.Brewin, Yorks Regt.   "   "
   2/Lt. A.E.Bedford, 9th Yorks.   "   "

5th Yorks.
   2/Lt. W.Lowther, Yorks Regt.   "   "

CORRECTIONS.

List No.2.

4th E. Yorks Regt.
   2/Lt. A.Thrustle, E.Yorks, Missing 27/5/18 should read
"2/Lt. A.V.Thrustle, E. Yorks, Wounded and Missing 27/5/18.

4th Yorks.
   Lt. J.F.Johns, Yorks Regt reported Wounded now reported Missing.
   Lt. E.R.B.Bailey, Yorks Regt. reported Wounded now reported Wounded and Missing.

H.Q. 50th Div.,
9th June 1918.

(sd) C.DUKE, Lieut-Colonel,
A.A. & Q.M.G.for Major General,
Commanding 50th (Northumbrian) Division.

List No.3.

50TH (NORTHUMBRIAN) DIVISION.

CASUALTIES FROM 27/5/18 TO DATE.

UNIT.	DATE.	KILLED. Offrs.	KILLED. O.R.	WOUNDED. Off.	WOUNDED. O.R.	MISSING. Off.	MISSING. O.R.	REMARKS.
150th Inf. Bde.								
4th E. Yorks	27/5/18.	-	8	-	20	-	644	
4th Yorks.	"	-	2	-	23	6	605a	a includes 1 W.
5th Yorks.	"	-	11	-	25	1	689	and O Bld killed.
151st Inf. Bde.								
HQ, 8th D.L.I. att."		-	-	-	-	-	1	
		-	21	-	71	7	1938.	

NAMES OF OFFICERS.

4th Yorks.
  Lt. (A/Capt) R.M.Howes.   Missing.   27/5/18.
  Lt. R.Gates, 5th Yorks.   "   "
  Lt. J.A.Hamlyn, Yorks Regt.   "   "
  2/Lt. W.A. Shooter, R.I.R.   "   "
  2/Lt. L.Brewin, Yorks Regt.   "   "
  2/Lt. A.E.Bedford, 9th Yorks.   "   "

5th Yorks.
  2/Lt. W.Lowther, Yorks Regt.   "   "

CORRECTIONS.

List No.2.

4th E. Yorks Regt.
  2/Lt. A.Thrustle, E.Yorks, Missing 27/5/18 should read
"2/Lt. A.V.Thrustle, E. Yorks, Wounded and Missing 27/5/18.

4th Yorks.
  Lt. J.F.Johns, Yorks Regt reported Wounded now reported Missing.
  Lt. E.R.B.Bailey, Yorks Regt. reported Wounded now reported Wounded
   and Missing.

                                        (sd) C.DUKE, Lieut-Colonel,
H.Q. 50th Div.,   A.A. & Q.M.G.for Major General,
9th June 1918.   Commanding 50th (Northumbrian) Division.

50TH (NORTHUMBRIAN) DIVISION.

CASUALTIES FROM 27/5/18 TO DATE.

UNIT.	Date.	KILLED. Off.	KILLED. O.R.	WOUNDED. Off.	WOUNDED. O.R.	MISSING. Off.	MISSING. O.R.	Names of Officers.
7th Durham L.I. (Pioneers).	27/5/18.	-	-	-	-	1	-	Capt. E.J. PRESPER, RAMC.
6th Northd Fus.	30/5/18	1	-	-	-	-	-	Lt. A.R. HALL.
1/1st Nbn. F.Amb.	27/5/18.	-	-	1	-	-	-	Hon. Capt. & Q.Mr. T. BARRADELL.
50th Div.Sig.Coy.	"	-	-	-	-	1	-	Lt. D.V.L. CRADDOCK, 9th Durham L.I.
4th Northd Fus.	"	-	-	-	-	1	-	Capt. D.T. TURNER.
		1	-	1	-	3	-	

50TH (NORTHUMBRIAN) DIVISION.

CASUALTIES FROM 27/5/18 TO DATE.

UNIT.	Date.	KILLED. Off.	KILLED. O.R.	WOUNDED. Off.	WOUNDED. O.R.	MISSING. Off.	MISSING. O.R.	Names of Officers.
7th Durham L.I. (Pioneers).	27/5/18.	—	—	—	—	1	—	Capt. E.J. PRESPER, RAMC
6th Northd Fus.	30/5/18	1	—	—	—	—	—	Lt. A.R. HALL.
1/1st Nbn. F.Amb.	27/5/18.	—	—	1	—	—	—	Hon. Capt. & Q.Mr. T. BARRADELL.
50th Div. Sig. Coy.	"	—	—	—	—	1	—	Lt. D.V.L. CRADDOCK, 9th Durham L.I.
4th Northd Fus.	"	—	—	—	—	1	—	Capt. D.T. TURNER.
		1	—	1	—	3	—	

Original.

50th Division.

Administrative Staff

War Diary

From 1st June 1918

To 30th June 1918

Volume XXXIX.

Army Form C. 2118.

50TH (NORTHUMBRIAN) DIVISION.

WAR DIARY
&
INTELLIGENCE SUMMARY.

(Erase heading not required.)

JUNE 1918.

Instructions regarding War Diaries and Intelligence Summaries are contained in F. S. Regs., Part II. and the Staff Manual respectively. Title pages will be prepared in manuscript.

Place	Date	Hour	Summary of Events and Information	Remarks and references to Appendices
VERT LA GRAVELLE	1.		Division (Less Composite Battalion) withdrawn from the line and concentrated around VERT LA GRAVELLE, with Divisional Headquarters at VERT LA GRAVELLE. Bt.Lieut-Colonel (T/Brig-General) F.J.Marshall, CMG, DSO, Seaforth Highlanders assumed duty as General Officer Commanding 150th Infantry Brigade. Capt. J.A.D.Perrins, Welsh Guards, assumed duty as Brigade Major, 150th Infantry Brigade.	
	2.		50th Composite Brigade in process of formation.	
	3.			
	4.			
	5.		CASUALTIES. R.A.M.C. 1/1st (Nbn) Field Ambulance, Wounded, Hon.Capt. & Q.M. T.Barradell, 27/5/18. 50th Div.Signal Company. Lt. D.V.L.Craddock, Missing, 27/5/18. Captain J.C.Latter, MC, 5th Lanc Fusiliers assumed duty as Staff Captain, 150th Infantry Brigade. Captain W.Tong, MC, assumed duty as Brigade Major, 151st Infantry Brigade. Captain A.J.Trousdell, MC, 3rd R.I.F. assumed duty as Brigade Major 149th Infantry Brigade.	
	6.		CASUALTIES. 149th Inf. Bde. 4th Northd Fusiliers Capt. D.T.Turner, Missing, 27/5/18. 50th Composite Brigade proceeded by bus to forward area. Lt.Col. J.Clay, R.A.M.C., T.F. assumed duties as A.D.M.S. with temporary rank of Colonel. Capt. E.H.Veitch, 8th Durham L.I., Staff Captain 151st Infantry Brigade proceeded to England for 6 months tour of duty. Capt. J.A.Bell, 7th Durham, L.I. assumed duty as Staff Captain 151st Inf. Bde, 6/8/18.	
	7.		CASUALTIES. 149th Inf. Bde. 4th N.F. Wounded O.R.2 : 5th N.F. Killed O.R.2 Wounded O.R. 9 : 6th N.F. Wounded 2/Lt. B.J.Browne, Royal Dublin Fusiliers, 7/6/18. 150th Inf. Bde. 4th E.Yorks Wounded O.R. 2 : 4th Yorks, KILLED O.R. 1, Wounded O.R. 3 :	

Army Form C. 2118.

WAR DIARY
INTELLIGENCE SUMMARY
(Erase heading not required.)

Instructions regarding War Diaries and Intelligence Summaries are contained in F. S. Regs., Part II. and the Staff Manual respectively. Title pages will be prepared in manuscript.

Place	Date	Hour	Summary of Events and Information	Remarks and references to Appendices
VERT LA GRAVELLE.	7.		CASUALTIES (Continued). 150th Inf. Bde. 5th Yorks R. Wounded Lt. & Q.M. P.J.Foord, O.R. 1 : T.M.Battery, Wounded O.R. 1. 151st Inf. Bde. 8th D.L.I. Wounded O.R. 1 : 6th D.L.I. Wounded O.R. 1. 50th Bn. M.G.C. Killed, O.R. 1, Wounded O.R. 6. R.A.M.C. 1/1st Mbn. Field Amb., Wounded 1(Died of wounds)Capt. W. Atkin, RAMC, TF, O.R. Wounded 1, Missing O.R. 3. Lt.Col. R.E.Sugden, DSO, 4th West Ridings assumed command of 151st Infantry Brigade with temporary rank of Brigadier General. Lt.Col. P.M.Robinson, CMG, Royal West Kent Regt assumed command of 149th Infantry Brigade with temporary rank of Brigadier General. Captain R.O.Hobson, MC, 12th N.F. assumed duty as G.S.O.3	
	8.		CASUALTIES. Royal Artillery. 251st Bde. R.F.A. Injured O.R. 1, 151st Inf Bde. 5th D.L.I. Wounded O.R. 1. 150th Inf. Bde. 5th Yorks, Wounded O.R. 1, Capt. F.H.Garraway, MO, London Regiment assumed duty as D.A.Q.M.G., with temporary rank of Major.	
CHATEAU MONTGIVREUX, MONDEMONT	9.		Division (Less Composite Brigade) moved to Mondemont Area, Divisional Headquarters moved to Chateau Montgivreux, near Mondemont.	
	10.		CASUALTIES. Royal Engineers. H.Q. Wounded at duty, 27/5/18, Lt.(A/Capt) C.W.M.Potts.	
	11.		CASUALTIES. 149th Inf. Bde. 4th N.F. Wounded O.R. 1 Gassed. 150th Inf. Bde. 4th Yorkshire Regt wounded O.R. 1. 50th Bn.M.G.C. wounded O.R. 3. Capt.H.J.MILLIGAN, RAMC, assumed duties as DADMS with temp. rank of Major.	

Army Form C. 2118.

WAR DIARY
INTELLIGENCE SUMMARY
(Erase heading not required.)

Instructions regarding War Diaries and Intelligence Summaries are contained in F. S. Regs., Part II. and the Staff Manual respectively. Title pages will be prepared in manuscript.

Place	Date	Hour	Summary of Events and Information	Remarks and references to Appendices
CHATEAU MONTGIVREUX, MONDEMENT.	12.		CASUALTIES. 149th Infy Bde - 4th N.F. wounded O.R.4 (inc. 1 gas). 5th N.F. wounded O.R.1 (gas). 6th N.F. wounded O.R.3. 151st Infy Bde - 5th D.L.I. wounded Lt(A/Capt) E.G.JONES, M.C. 11/6/18. Killed O.R.1, wounded O.R.1.	
	13.		CASUALTIES. 149th Infy Bde - 4th N.F. wounded O.R.1. 5th N.F. wounded O.R.1. 150th Infy Bde - 4th East Yorkshire Regt killed O.R.1. 151st Infy Bde - 5th D.L.I. killed O.R.2. 6th D.L.I. wounded O.R.1. 8th D.L.I. wounded O.R.1.	
	14.		CASUALTIES. 149th Infy Bde - 4th N.F. killed O.R.2, wounded O.R.3. 5th N.F. killed O.R.5, wounded O.R.9. 150th Infy Bde - 4th E.Yorks Rgt wounded O.R.1. 4th Yorks Rgt killed O.R.1, wounded O.R.3. 5th Yorkshire Regt killed O.R.4, wounded O.R.2. 151st Infy Bde - 8th D.L.I. wounded (at duty) Lt (A/Capt) B.M.WILLIAMS, wounded O.R.4.	
	15.		CASUALTIES. 149th Infy Bde - 5th N.F. wounded O.R.2.	
	16.		CASUALTIES. 149th Infy Bde - 4th N.F. missing O.R.1. 6th N.F. Lt.A.R.HALL killed 30/5/18.	
	17.		Division (less Comp. Bde) moved to LA NOUE AREA, with D.H.Q. at LA NOUE CHATEAU.	
CHATEAU LA NOUE.	18.		CASUALTIES. 50th Bn.M.Gun Corps - killed O.R.1, wounded O.R.1.	
	19.		CASUALTIES. 50th Bn.M.Gun Corps - killed O.R.1, wounded O.R.1. 50th Composite Brigade rejoined the Division from forward area.	
	20.			

Army Form C. 2118.

WAR DIARY

INTELLIGENCE SUMMARY

(Erase heading not required.)

Instructions regarding War Diaries and Intelligence Summaries are contained in F. S. Regs., Part II. and the Staff Manual respectively. Title pages will be prepared in manuscript.

Place	Date	Hour	Summary of Events and Information	Remarks and references to Appendices
CHATEAU LA NOUE.	21.			
	22.			
	23.			
	24.			
	25.			
	26.			
	27.			
	28.			
	29.			
	30.			

Vol 40

ORIGINAL

50th Division
Administrative Staff
War Diary

From: 1st July 1918
To: 31st July 1918

Volume XL.

50TH DIVISION.

Army Form C. 2118.

ADMINISTRATIVE
WAR DIARY
INTELLIGENCE SUMMARY.
(Erase heading not required.)

JULY, 1918.

Instructions regarding War Diaries and Intelligence Summaries are contained in F. S. Regs., Part II. and the Staff Manual respectively. Title pages will be prepared in manuscript.

Place	Date	Hour	Summary of Events and Information	Remarks and references to Appendices
LA NOUE CHATEAU.	JULY 1.			
	2.			
	3.		Division commenced to entrain for British Zone.	
HUPPY.	4.		Divnl H.Q. arrived in British Zone and established at HUPPY.	
	5.			
	6.			
	7.			
	8.			
	9.			
	10.			
	11.			
MARTIN EGLISE and HUPPY.	12.		'G' Staff and A.A. & Q.M.G. left HUPPY and established at MARTIN EGLISE.	
	13.		Maj.(Bt.Lt.Col.) C.P.HEYWOOD, CMG DSO., Coldstream Gds assumed duty as G.O.C. 150th Infy Bgde, with temporary rank of Brigadier-General.	
	14.		Bt.Lt.Col. (T/Brig.-Gen.) F.J.MARSHALL, CMG DSO., G.O.C. 150th Infy Bde appointed Asst Inspector on the Staff of the Inspector General of Training.	

50th DIVISION.

ADMINISTRATIVE WAR DIARY

JULY, 1918.

Army Form C. 2118.

Instructions regarding War Diaries and Intelligence Summaries are contained in F. S. Regs., Part II. and the Staff Manual respectively. Title pages will be prepared in manuscript.

(Erase heading not required.)

Place	Date	Hour	Summary of Events and Information	Remarks and references to Appendices
MARTIN EGLISE & HUPPY.	JULY 15.		Reduction of Division to Training Cadre. Surplus personnel in the Division despatched to Base Depots.	
GREGES.	16.		Divisional Hd-Qrs moved to GREGES. Division commenced to administer new Units; composition of Division:- **149th INFY BGDE.** **150th INFY BGDE.** **151st INFY BGDE.** 2nd Royal Dub.Fus. 7th Wiltshire Rgt. 1st K.O.Y.L.I. 3rd Royal Fuslrs. 2nd Bn. North'd Fus. 6th Royal Innis.F. 13th Black Watch 2nd Bn. Royal Mun.F. 4th K.R.R.C. (Scottish Horse). **PIONEERS.** 5th Royal Irish Regiment. (Pnrs).	
	17.			
	18.		50th Divnl Cadre Battalions moved to ROUXMESNIL Area.	
	19.			
	20.			
	21.			
	22.			
	23.			
	24.			
	25.			
	26.			
	27.			

50th DIVISION.
JULY, 1918.

ADMINISTRATIVE WAR DIARY

Army Form C. 2118.

Instructions regarding War Diaries and Intelligence Summaries are contained in F. S. Regs., Part II. and the Staff Manual respectively. Title pages will be prepared in manuscript.

(Erase heading not required.)

Place	Date	Hour	Summary of Events and Information	Remarks and references to Appendices
GREGES.	JULY 28.			
	29.			
	30.		Major R. de H. HALL, M.C., R.E. TF assumed duties as C.R.E. with actg rank of Lt-Colonel, vice Major (A/Lt.-Col) J.A. McQUEEN, DSO. MC. (sick in England).	
	31.			

50TH DIVISION — ADMINISTRATIVE STAFF.

- W A R   D I A R Y -
****

From 1st August 1918.
To 31st August 1918.

Vol. XLI.

50TH DIVISION.

AUGUST, 1918.

Army Form C. 2118.

ADMINISTRATIVE WAR DIARY or INTELLIGENCE SUMMARY.

(Erase heading not required.)

Instructions regarding War Diaries and Intelligence Summaries are contained in F. S. Regs., Part II. and the Staff Manual respectively. Title pages will be prepared in manuscript.

Place	Date	Hour	Summary of Events and Information	Remarks and references to Appendices
GREGES.	AUG: 1.			
	2.			
	3.			
	4.		Casualties - 250th Nbn Bde RFA wounded O.R.1.	
	5.		-do- - 250th Nbn Bde RFA wounded 2/Lt.T.E.FORSYTH, O.R. 1.	
	6.		-do- - 50th Divl T.Mortar Batteries Missing O.R. 2.	
	7.		-do- - 50th Divl Ammn Col. wounded O.R. 2. 50th Bn. M.G.Corps wounded O.R. 2.	
	8.		-do- - 250th Nbn Bde RFA killed O.R.1. 251st Nbn Bde RFA O.Rs killed 3, wounded 2. 50th Divnl T.Mortar Batteries wounded O.R. 1.	
	9.			
	10.		-do- - 50th Divl T.Mortar Batteries wounded O.R. 1.	
	11.		-do- - 250th Nbn Bde RFA wounded (gas) 2/Lt.D.H.BROWNLEE, O.R. 2.	
	12.		-do- - 250th Nbn Bde RFA wounded O.R. 1. 251st Nbn Bde RFA wounded O.R. 2.	
	13.		-do- - 250th Nbn Bde RFA wounded O.R. 3. 251st Nbn Bde RFA wounded O.R. 1.	
	14.		-do- - 250th Nbn Bde RFA O.Rs killed 1, wounded 6. 251st Nbn Bde RFA O.Rs kd 1 wd 3.	

50th DIVISION.

Army Form C. 2118.

AUGUST, 1918.

Instructions regarding War Diaries and Intelligence Summaries are contained in F. S. Regs., Part II. and the Staff Manual respectively. Title pages will be prepared in manuscript.

ADMINISTRATIVE WAR DIARY

INTELLIGENCE SUMMARY

(Erase heading not required.)

Place	Date	Hour	Summary of Events and Information	Remarks and references to Appendices
GREGES.	AUG: 15		Casualties - 250th Nbn Bde RFA wounded O.R. 2.	
	16		-do- 250th Nbn Bde RFA wounded 2/Lt.C.H.HODGSON MC, wounded O.R.2 (gas). 251st Nbn Bde RFA wounded O.R. 1.	
	17		-do- 250th Nbn Bde RFA O.Rs killed 1, wounded 17. 251st Nbn Bde RFA wounded (gas) 2/Lt.A.K.IRVINE, wounded O.R. 30.	
	18		-do- 250th Nbn Bde RFA wounded O.R. 3. DIVISIONAL HORSE SHOW held at DIEPPE.	
	19		-do- 250th Nbn Bde RFA wounded O.R. 2. 50th D.A.Col. wounded O.R. 2.	
	20		-do- 250th Nbn Bde RFA wounded O.R. 1.	
	21		-do- 250th Nbn Bde RFA wounded Lt(A/Capt) J.G.BROWELL MC, O.R. 3. 251st Nbn Bde RFA O.R. killed 1, wounded 1. 50th D.A.Col. wounded O.R. 2.	
	22		-do- 250th Nbn Bde RFA O.Rs killed 3, wounded 3. 251st Nbn Bde RFA wounded 2/Lt. MOODY-STUART, 2/Lt. T.J.GOODSELL, 2/Lt.G.P.HIBBERT and 2/Lt.A.W.WILSON. O.Rs killed 4, wounded 19.	
	23		-do- 250th Nbn Bde RFA O.Rs killed 1, wounded 9. 251st Nbn Bde RFA O.Rs *** wounded 1.	
	24		-do- 250th Nbn Bde RFA wounded O.Rs 8. 251st Nbn Bde RFA wounded (gas) 2/Lt.D.MORRIS, 2/Lt.F.C.STEWART, O.Rs 5.	
	25			
	26			
	27		-do- 250th Nbn Bde RFA O.Rs killed 1, wounded 6. 251st Nbn Bde RFA O.Rs killed 1.	

50th DIVISION.

Army Form C. 2118.

ADMINISTRATIVE
WAR DIARY
of
INTELLIGENCE SUMMARY.

(Erase heading not required.)

AUGUST, 1918.

Instructions regarding War Diaries and Intelligence Summaries are contained in F. S. Regs., Part II. and the Staff Manual respectively. Title pages will be prepared in manuscript.

Place	Date	Hour	Summary of Events and Information	Remarks and references to Appendices
GREGES.	AUG: 28		Major A.D'E.KNOX, R.W.Kent Regt joined as D.A.A.G., 50th Division. Major A.E.G.PALMER, D.S.O., M.C. left to take up appointment as D.A.A.G., XIII Corps.	
	29		Casualties - 251st Nbn Bde RFA wounded LT.H.C.MACNAMARA, wounded (at duty) 2/Lt.E.R.HEBBLE-THWAITE and 2/Lt.E.W.THOMAS.	
	30			
	31		Casualties - 250th Nbn Bde RFA killed 2/Lt.W.S.LAIDLAW, wounded O.R. 2. 251st Nbn Bde RFA wounded Capt. (A/Major) R.E.GORDON MC and 2/Lt.W.R.T.CHETWYND.	

50TH DIVISION - ADMINISTRATIVE STAFF.

W A R   D I A R Y.

From:- 1st SEPTEMBER 1918.
To:-   30th   "   "

VOLUME XLII.

Army Form C. 2118.

ADMINISTRATIVE WAR DIARY
INTELLIGENCE SUMMARY
(Erase heading not required.)

SEPTEMBER 1918.

Instructions regarding War Diaries and Intelligence Summaries are contained in F.S. Regs., Part II. and the Staff Manual respectively. Title pages will be prepared in manuscript.

Place	Date	Hour	Summary of Events and Information	Remarks and references to Appendices
GREGES	1/8			
	9			
	10		DIVL. SPORTS HELD ON RACE COURSE, DIEPPE.	
	11			
	12			
	13			
	14			
	15		MOVE OF DIVISION TO THIRD ARMY AREA COMMENCED	
	16		MOVE OF DIVISION COMPLETE. DIVL. HD. QRS. AT LUCHEUX Chateau	

Army Form C. 2118.

ADMINISTRATIVE WAR DIARY

INTELLIGENCE SUMMARY

(Erase heading not required.)

SEPTEMBER 1918.

Instructions regarding War Diaries and Intelligence Summaries are contained in F. S. Regs., Part II. and the Staff Manual respectively. Title pages will be prepared in manuscript.

Place	Date	Hour	Summary of Events and Information	Remarks and references to Appendices
LUCHEUX	17			
	18			
	19			
	20			
	21			
	22			
	23			
	24			

Army Form C. 2118.

ADMINISTRATIVE WAR DIARY of INTELLIGENCE SUMMARY.

(Erase heading not required.)

SEPTEMBER 1918.

Instructions regarding War Diaries and Intelligence Summaries are contained in F.S. Regs., Part II. and the Staff Manual respectively. Title pages will be prepared in manuscript.

Place	Date	Hour	Summary of Events and Information	Remarks and references to Appendices
LUCHEUX	25			
MONTIGNY	26		DIVISION MOVED TO FOURTH ARMY AREA - DIVL. HD. QRS. AT MONTIGNY Chateau	
	27		CASUALTIES - 250TH BDE. R.F.A. 1 O.R.	
	28		CASUALTIES - 250TH BDE. R.F.A. Wounded Lieut. E.S. HURST - O.R. 5 Killed O.R. 1	
			DIVISION MOVED TO THIRD CORPS AREA - DIVL. HD. QRS at COMBLES	
COMBLES.	29			
	30			

CONFIDENTIAL.

50th DIVISION - ADMINISTRATIVE STAFF.

W A R   D I A R Y.

From :- 1st OCTOBER, 1918.
To   :- 31st   "   "

VOLUME XLIII.

Army Form C. 2118.

ADMINISTRA[TIVE]
WAR DIARY
and
OCTOBER 1918 INTELLIGENCE SUMMARY.

(Erase heading not required.)

Instructions regarding War Diaries and Intelligence Summaries are contained in F. S. Regs., Part II. and the Staff Manual respectively. Title pages will be prepared in manuscript.

Place	Date	Hour	Summary of Events and Information	Remarks and references to Appendices
LIERA-MONT.	OCT.	1st	Divnl H.Q. (Rear) moved to LIERAMONT.	
		2		
		3		
		4		
EPEHY.		5	Divnl H.Q. (Rear) moved to EPEHY.	
		6	Capt.R.C.HOBSON MC, GSO 3 evacuated to C.C.S. (acc. injury).	
		7		
		8		
		9		
GUISANCOURT FARM.		10	Divnl H.Q. (Rear) moved to GUISANCOURT FARM.	
		11		
LE TROU AUX SOLDATS		12	Divnl H.Q. (Rear) moved to LE TROU AUX SOLDATS.	
		13	Lt-Col.E.C.ANSTEY, GSO 1, evacuated to C.C.S. (sick).	
		14	Total casualties - 1st Phase (from 1st to 14th Oct) - see Appendix "A" attached. Lt-Col.A.F.Miller MC, Notts & Derby Regt took up appointment as G.S.O.1.	
		15		
		16		

Army Form C. 2118.

ADMINISTRATIVE WAR DIARY

~~INTELLIGENCE SUMMARY.~~

OCTOBER 1918.

(Erase heading not required.)

Instructions regarding War Diaries and Intelligence Summaries are contained in F. S. Regs., Part II. and the Staff Manual respectively. Title pages will be prepared in manuscript.

Place	Date	Hour	Summary of Events and Information	Remarks and references to Appendices
LE TROU AUX SOLDATS	OCT. 17		Major Viscount G.R.ERLEIGH, M.C. Inns of Court took up appointment as D.A.A.G.	
	18			
	17		Major A.D'E.KNOX, D.A.A.G., proceeded to ENGLAND for three months course at Senior Officers' School, CAMBRIDGE.	
	19		Captain W.LAING-HAY, General List, took up appointment as G.S.O.3.	
	20		Lt-Col.A.K.GRANT, DSO., Royal West Kents, took up appointment as G.S.O.1.	
	21		Lt-Col.A.T.MILLER, M.C., Notts & Derby Regt, left to take up appointment as Instructor at Junior Staff School, CAMBRIDGE.	
	22			
	23			
	24			
	25			
	26			
	27			
	28			
	29			
LE CATEAU.	30		Casualties - Officers - See Appendix "A" attached. O.Ranks - " "B" " Divnl H.Q. moved to LE CATEAU.	
	31		Total casualties, 2nd phase 15/31st Octr - see Appendix "B" attd.	

50th DIVISION.

CASUALTIES.
(Officers)

	O.	OR
1st Phase:- 1st/14th OCT. 1918.	108 -	1918
2nd Phase:- Comm'g 15th OCT. 1918.	68 -	1143
Total:	176 -	3061

50th DIVNL HD.QRS.

Phase
1/14 Oct.   Injured.

Captain R.C. HOBSON, M.C. (5/10/18)

149th INFY BDE.

Phase
1/14 Oct.   3rd Roy.F.

KILLED.
Maj.(A/Lt-Col) E.H.Nicholson, DSO (4/10/18).
Lt. (A/Capt) R.T.O.Consterdine-Chadwick (4/10/18).
Lt.(T/Capt) & Adjt W.T.Humphreys (4/10/18).
Lt.E.C.Nepean (4/10/18).
T/Lt.R.A.L.Dadies (4/10/18).
Lieut.C.H.P.Cross (4/10/18).
T/Lt.P.J.T'Connor (4/10/18).
2/Lt.H.Marsh (4/10/18).
T/Capt.J.M.McLaggan MC RAMC (4/10/18).

Phase
comm'g   Nil.
15/Oct

WOUNDED.
Phase
1/14 Oct.
Lt(A/Capt) R.D.T.Woolfe (4/10/18).
2/Lt.J.M.Smith (4/10/18).

Phase
commg
15 Oct
T/Lt.W.E.Forster (17/10/18).
T/2/Lt.J.J.Laws (17/10/18).
T/2/Lt.H.B.Leavers (17/10/18).
2/Lt.W.P.Gaston (17/10/18).

Phase   MISSING.
1/14 Oct   Nil
Phase
commg   2/Lt.B.R.G.Rogers (17/10/18.
15/Oct.

- 2 -

13th (S.H.) BLACK WATCH.

Phase
1/14 Oct.   KILLED.
  Lt(A/Capt) & Adjt.A.Rawson (6/10/18).
  2/Lt.D.Bell (6/10/18).
  2/Lt.J.C.Forsyth (11/10/18).
Phase
comng
15/Oct
               Nil.

Phase   WOUNDED.
1/14 Oct
  Lt.R.Inglis (4/10/18)
  Lt.L.H.Jones (4/10/18)
  Capt.Hon.J.Dewar (5/10/18)
  Capt(A/Lt-Col) Hon. R.E.S.Barrington DSO (6/10/18)
  Capt.A.J.L.MacGregor MC (6/10/18)
  Lt.E.M.Firney (6/10/18)
  Lt.G.W.A.Rutherford (6/10/18)
  Lt.W.Forster (7/10/18)
  Lt.C.Kinlock (7/10/18)
  Lt.A.G.Hoard, MORC USA (at duty).
Phase
comng
15/Oct
  Lt.A.H.Skelton (17/10/18)
  Lt.R.Watson (17/10/18)
  2/Lt.S.J.Morgan (17/10/18)
  2/Lt.J.Mitchell (17/10/18)
  2/Lt.J.A.Keith (17/10/18)
  Lt.G.Robertson (18/10/18)

               MISSING.
Phase
1/14 Oct   Nil.
Phase
comng
15/Oct   Nil.

2nd ROYAL DUBLIN FUSILIERS.

KILLED.

Phase 1/14 Oct
- 2/Lt.W.Sutherland (8/10/18)
- Lt(A/Capt) M.Pedlow MC (12/10/18)

Phase coming 15/Oct
- T.2/Lt.F.A.Walkey (17/10/18)
- Lieut.C.W.Kidson (17/10/18)

WOUNDED.

Phase 1/14 Oct
- Lieut.D.C.A.Shepard (4/10/18)
- 2/Lt.J.W.Elvery (8/10/18)
- T/2/Lieut.E.A.Poulter (12/10/18)
- T/2/Lieut.J.T.M.Boulter (12/10/18)

Phase coming 15/Oct
- Capt.A.B.Bagley, M.C. (17/10/18)
- 2/Lieut.C.J.Byrne, D.C.M. (17/10/18)
- 2/Lieut.W.Humphrey (17/10/18)
- T/Capt.G.M.Crawford (18/10/18)
- Lieut.B.P.Glancy (18/10/18)
- 2/Lieut.J.V.Staples (18/10/18)

MISSING.

Phase 1/14 Oct — Nil.

Phase coming 15/Oct — Nil.

149th TRENCH MORTAR BATTERY.

NIL.

150TH INFANTRY BRIGADE.

2nd NORTH'D FUS.

Phase
1/14 Oct

KILLED.

Lt(A/Capt) H.S.King, M.C. (5/10/18)
Lieut.C.F.C.Carr-Ellison (4/10/18)
T/Lieut.W.H.Collings (3/10/18)
T.2/Lieut.J.C.Lumsden (11/10/18)

Phase
commg
15/Oct

T/Lieut.J.B.Wilson (18/10/18)

Phase
1/14 Oct

WOUNDED.

Lieut.H.A.Scarless (3/10/18)
Capt.(A/Major) C.R.Freeman, M.C. (4/10/18)
2/Lieut.C.Girdlestone (4/10/18)
2/Lieut.E.I.Williams (4/10/18)
2/Lieut.R.Bentley (4/10/18)
T.2/Lt.J.Lees Barton (6/10/18).
Lieut.A.K.Phillips (4/10/18)
Lieut.T.S.Crichton (4/10/18)
T/Lieut.H.E.Gardner (11/10/18)

Phase
commg
15/Oct

T.2/Lieut.J.C.Atkinson (17/10/18)

MISSING.
Nil.

Phase
1/14 Oct

INJURED.

Lieut.T.C.Dodd (6/10/18)

7th WILTSHIRE REGIMENT.

KILLED.

Phase
1/14 Oct

2/Lieut.C.Rogers (4/10/18)
Lieut.C.Penruddocke (4/10/18)
Lt(A/Capt) W.H.Socrer (7/10/18) D. of W.

Phase
commg
15/Oct

Nil.

WOUNDED.

Phase
1/14 Oct

Captain J.C.James (6/10/18)
2/Lieut.F.G.Sheppard (gas) (8/10/18)

Phase
~~1/15 Oct~~
commg
15/Oct

2/Lt.F.H.Robins (18/10/18)
T/Captain C.H.Sawtell (18/10/18)
2/Lt (A/Capt) R.A.F. Law, M.C. (18/10/18)
T/Lieut.H.P.Maskell (18/10/18)
2nd Lieut.F.Byrne (18/10/18)
2nd Lieut.E.J.Stanford (18/10/18)

MISSING

Nil.

2nd ROYAL MUNSTER FUSILIERS.

KILLED.

Phase
1/14 Oct

Lieut.C.M.J.Ryan, M.C. (4/10/18)
2nd Lieut.D.Daly (4/10/18)
2nd Lieut.J.King (4/10/18)
Captain J.O'Brien, M.C. (6/10/18)

2nd ROYAL MUNSTER FUS. (Contd)

Phase commg 15/Oct

KILLED.

Lieut.J.R.Howe (18/10/18)

Phase 1/14 Oct

WOUNDED.

T/Capt.E.R.H.Orford, M.C. (4/10/18)
2nd Lt. O.S.Ahern (4/10/18)
2nd Lt. J.J.Carson (3/10/18)
Lieut. F.T.McKeown (4/10/18)
Lieut. A.L.B.Stevens (4/10/18) at duty.
Lieut. R.L.Philpot (4/10/18)
2nd Lt.R.V.Flanagan (4/10/18)
Lieut.C.E.Baldwin (4/10/18)
Lieut.E.R.H.Hudson (4/10/18)
T/Capt.A.Keevil, M.C. (4/10/18)
Captain V.P.O'Malley, M.C. (7/10/18).
Lieut.E.E.Russell (8/10/18)
T/Lieut.E.D.Conran (14/10/18)

Phase commg 15/Oct

T/Lieut.M.Prendergast (16/10/18)
Captain S.W.Whateley (18/10/18)
Lieut.H.W.Clarke (18/10/18)
T.2/Lt.H.G.Carolin (16/10/18)
2nd Lieut.D.Minahan (18/10/18)

MISSING.

Nil.

151ST INFANTRY BRIGADE.

6th ROY. IRISH. FUS.

KILLED.

Phase 1/14 Oct

Lieut.G.R.L.Baillie (5/10/18)
2/Lieut.R.H.D.Cusile (5/10/18)
2/Lieut.J.A.Hicks (5/10/18)
Lt.(A/Capt.) H.T.Lutton (5/10/18)

Phase comng 15/Oct

T/Captain C.G.Barton, V.C. (17/10/18)
2/Lieut.J.H.Corscaden (17/10/18)
T/Lieut.J.J.C.Kermody (17/10/18)
2/Lieut.V.J.F.Wilson (17/10/18)
T.2/Lt.E.R.McKenny (18/10/18)

WOUNDED.

Phase 1/14 Oct

2/Lieut.J.Furney (5/10/18)
2/Lieut.D.Reid (5/10/18)
2/Lieut.H.C.Lewis (5/10/18)
T/Captain O.F.H.Smyth (5/10/18)
2/Lieut.H.A.Whiteside (5/10/18)
2/Lieut.H.Martin (5/10/18)
Lieut.A.E.Kelly (5/10/18)
2/Lieut.F.J.Little (5/10/18)

Phase comng 15/Oct

T/Lieut.H.St.G.Stewart (17/10/18)
T.2/Lieut.J.Crawford (17/10/18)
T.2/Lieut.A.A.V.Buchanan (17/10/18).
T.2/Lieut.E.R.McKenny (17/10/18) (at duty)

MISSING.

NIL.

1st K.O.Y.L.I.

KILLED.

Phase
1/14 Oct

Lieut.J.G.B.Ewinge (3/10/18)
2nd Lieut.P.J.Hill (3/10/18)
Tem/Lieut.P.C.Scott (8/10/18)

Phase)   T/Lieut.E.Tuke (17/10/18)
comng)   Lieut.C.A.H.Bromham (17/10/18)
18/Oct) Lieut.W.S.Scott (17/10/18)

WOUNDED.

Phase
1/14 Oct

T/Captain R.Meadows (3/10/18)
Capt.(A/Maj.) C. de Hoghton, M.C. (3/10/18)
2nd Lieut.D.Shires (3/10/18)
2nd Lieut.W.Brown (3/10/18)
2nd Lieut.L.Botterill (3/10/18)
2nd Lieut.J.G.Rudson (3/10/18)
2nd Lieut.F.J.Highman (3/10/18)
Lieut. K.Paterson (8/10/18)

Phase
comng
18/Oct

T/2/Lieut.L.H.Gaze (17/10/18)
Lieut.F.Roebuck (17/10/18)
T/Lieut.W.Harrold (17/10/18) (gas)
Captain T.F.H. Upton (17/10/18) (at duty)
Temp/Lieut.L.Franklin (18/10/18)

MISSING.

Nil.

4th K. R. R. C.

Phase 1/14 Oct

KILLED.

2nd Lieut.T.F.Mackay (3/10/18)
2nd Lieut.W.A.Fryer (3/10/18)
2nd Lieut.M.A.White (3/10/18)
Lieut.H.T.Preece (3/10/18)

Phase commg 15/Oct

T.2/Lt.J.L.Williams (10/10/18)

WOUNDED.

Phase 1/14 Oct

Capt.G.F.H.Hayhurst-Frence, M.C. (3/10/18)
Lieut.W.J.J.Macaulay, M.C. (3/10/18)
Lieut.H.C.M.Hardy (3/10/18)
2nd Lieut.S.F.S.Sutton (3/10/18)
2nd Lieut.J.C.Carl (3/10/18)
2nd Lieut.F.McBiven (3/10/18)
Tcap/Lieut.C.E.F.Munnion (8/10/18)
   -do-   P.G.C.Debnam (8/10/18)
T/2/Lieut.H.E.Gorsby (8/10/18)
   -do-   A.J.Austin (8/10/18) (at duty)

Phase commg 15/Oct

Capt.H.E.Antrobus (17/10/18)
Capt.G.B.Eden (17/10/18)
T/Capt. & Adjt A.F.Nutting, M.C. (17/10/18)
T.2/Lieut.R.M.A.Stewart (17/10/18)
Lieut.H.C.F.Holgate (17/10/18)
2nd Lieut.L.Pows-Jones (17/10/18)

151ST TRENCH MORTAR BATTERY.
WOUNDED.

Phase commg 15/Oct

T/Lieut.S.T.S.Walker (17/10/18)
T/Lieut.C.Wallace (18/10/18) (at duty)

5th BN. ROYAL IRISH REGT (PIONEERS).

KILLED.
Nil.

WOUNDED.
Nil.

MISSING.
Nil.

INJURED.

Phase
1/14 Oct   2nd Lieut.F.J.McNALLY (4/10/18)

50TH BN. M.G.C.

Phase
1/14 Oct   **KILLED.**
Nil.

Phase
coming
15/Oct   T/2/Lieut.A.HANCOCK (17/10/18)
         -do-   A.D.CRUICKSHANK (23/10/18)

WOUNDED.

Phase
1/14 Oct

A/Captain C.H.M.Toy (3/10/18)
2nd Lieut.A.D.Cruickshank (3/10/18)
    -do-   J.H.Harvie (7/10/18)

Phase
coming
15/Oct   2/Lt.E.A.W.Weller (17/10/18)
T/2/Lieut.A.R.Rodgers (17/10/18)
Temp./Lieut.J.S.Machin (17/10/18)
Capt.(A/Major) C.J.Brooks (17/10/18) at duty
T.2/Lieut.N.McL.Steel (23/10/18)

ROYAL ENGINEERS.

446th (NEL) FIELD COY R.E.

Phase
1/14 Oct

KILLED.

Nil.

Wounded.

Nil.

MISSING.

Nil.

Phase
commg
15/Oct

KILLED.
2/Lieut.T.W.Bennallack (17/10/18)

WOUNDED.
2/Lieut.C.W.Glazebrook (17/10/18)

MISSING.

Nil.

60th DIVISION.

CASUALTIES.
(Officers)

1st Phase:- 1st/14th OCT. 1918.   *108/1918*

2nd Phase:- Comng 16th OCT. 1918. *68/1143*

176 - 3061.

50th DIVN. R.G.A.

Phase
1/14 Oct.   Introd.

    Captain R.C. HOLKER, R.E. (5/10/18)

140th HVY BDE.

Phase
1/14 Oct.   3rd Pox.B.

THIRD.

Maj.(A/Lt-Col) E.T.Nicholson, DSO (4/10/18).
Lt. (A/Capt) R.T.C.Constantine-Turbick (4/10/18).
Lt. (T/Capt) & Adjt H.T.Humphreys (4/10/18).
Lt. E.C.Hopson (4/10/18).
T/Lt. F.A.L.Dadios (4/10/18).
Lieut.J. P.Cross (4/10/18).
T/Lt. D.J. Connor (4/10/18).
2/Lt.H.Marsh (4/10/18).
T/Capt.J.M.McFaggen MC RAMC (4/10/18).

Phase
coming   Nil.
15/Oct

LOSTWRD.

Phase
1/14 Oct.
Lt.(A/Capt) R.L.T.Woolfe (4/10/18).
2/Lt.J.M.Smith (4/10/18).

Phase
coming
15 Oct
T/Lt. W.E.Forster (17/10/18).
T/2/Lt.J.J.Lamb (17/10/18).
T/2/Lt.H.R.Leavers (17/10/18).
2/Lt.R.E.Gaston (17/10/18).

Phase   HUNDRED.
1/14 Oct   III
Phase
coming   2/Lt.R.R.C.Rogers (17/10/18.

- 2 -

13th (S.R.) BLACK WATCH.

Phase
1/14 Oct.   KILLED.
Lt(T/Capt) & Adjt.A.Lawson (8/10/18).
2/Lt.D.Bell (6/10/18).
2/Lt.J.S.Forsyth (11/10/18).

Phase
comng
15/Oct   Nil.

Phase   WOUNDED.
1/14 Oct
Lt.R.Inglis (4/10/18)
Lt.L.H.Jones (4/10/18)
Capt.Hon.J.Dewar (5/10/18)
Capt(A/Lt.Col) Hon. R.E.B.Barrington DSO (6/10/18)
Capt.A.J.L.MacGregor MC (6/10/18)
Lt.M.H.Firney (6/10/18)
Lt.O.W.A.Rutherford (6/10/18)
Lt.W.Forster (7/10/18)
Lt.C.Kinloch (7/10/18)
Lt.A.G.Heard, MORC USA (at duty).

Phase
comng
15/Oct
Lt.A.D.Sholton (17/10/18)
Lt.R.Watson (17/10/18)
2/Lt.C.J.Morgan (17/10/18)
2/Lt.J.Mitchell (17/10/18)
2/Lt.J.A.Keith (17/10/18)
Lt.A.Robertson (18/10/18)

             MISSING.
Phase
1/14 Oct   Nil.
Phase
comng
15/Oct   Nil.

- 3 -

2nd ROYAL IRISH RIFLES.

Phase
1/14 Oct   KILLED.
2/Lt. J.Sutherland (5/10/18)
Lt(A/Capt) F.Pellow MC (12/10/18)

Phase
COMING
15/Oct
T.Lieut. F.A.McKoy (17/10/18)
Lieut. C.J.Ridson (17/10/18)

Phase   WOUNDED.
1/14 Oct
Lieut. E.C.A.Shepard (4/10/18)
2/Lt. J.B.Elvery (5/10/18)
T/2/Lieut. D.A.Boulter (12/10/18)
T/2/Lieut. J.E.P.Boulter (12/10/18)

Phase
COMING
15/Oct
Capt. A.P.Bagley, M.C. (17/10/18)
2/Lieut. J.Byrne, D.C.M. (17/10/18)
2/Lieut. T.Humphrey (17/10/18)
T/Capt. C.M.Crawford (18/10/18)
Lieut. B.P.Glazy (18/10/18)
2/Lieut. J.T.Staples (18/10/18)

                    MISSING.
Phase
1/14 Oct   Nil.
Phase
COMING
15/Oct   Nil.

149th TRENCH MORTAR BATTERY.

                    Nil.

- 4 -

180TH INFANTRY BRIGADE.

2nd NORTH'D FUS.

Phase
1/14 Oct

KILLED.
Lt(A/Capt) T.T.King, M.C. (3/10/18)
Lieut. O.P.C.Carr-Ellison (4/10/18)
2/Lieut. T.R.Collings (6/10/18)
T.2/Lieut. S.G.Lumsden (11/10/18)

Phase
coming
15/Oct
T/Lieut. J.R.Wilson (18/10/18)

Phase
1/14 Oct

WOUNDED.
Lieut. B.A.Hawelock (5/10/18)
Capt.(A/Major) G.R.Procter, M.C. (4/10/18)
2/Lieut. G.Livingstone (4/10/18)
2/Lieut. E.L.Williams (4/10/18)
2/Lieut. R.Bentley (6/10/18)
T.2/Lt. J.Lees Barton (8/10/18)
Lieut. A.N.Phillips (4/10/18)
Lieut. T.L.Crighton (4/10/18)
T/Lieut. H.T.Gardner (11/10/18)

Phase
coming
15/Oct
T.2/Lieut. J.C.Atkinson (17/10/18)

MISSING.
NIL.

Phase
1/14 Oct

INJURED.
Lieut. T.C.Dodd (8/10/18)

- 2 -

7th DIVISIONAL ARTILLERY.

Phase
1/14 Oct   KILLED.

T/Lieut. B. Rogers (4/10/18)
Lieut. T. Fanshawcke (4/10/18)
Lt(A/Capt) W.H. Scorer (7/10/18) D. of W.

Phase
conng
15/Oct   Nil.

WOUNDED.

Phase
1/14 Oct
Captain J.C. James (6/10/18)
2/Lieut. F.J. Sheppard (gas) (6/10/18)

Phase
1/21 Oct
conng
15/Oct
2/Lt. W.H. Robins (18/10/18)
T/Captain C.H. Cartell (19/10/18)
T/Lt (A/Capt) R.A.F. Low, M.C. (19/10/18)
T/Lieut. L.P. Haskell (18/10/18)
2nd Lieut. E. Byrne (18/10/18)
2nd Lieut. C.J. Stanford (19/10/18)

MISSING

Nil.

2nd ROYAL MUNSTER FUSILIERS.

Phase   KILLED.
1/14 Oct
Lieut. C.H.J. Ryan, M.C. (4/10/18)
2nd Lieut. B. Daly (4/10/18)
2nd Lieut. J. King (4/10/18)
Captain J. O'Brien, M.C. (6/10/18)

2nd ROYAL MUNSTER FUS. (Contd)

Phase
CORPS
15/Oct

KILLED.

Lieut. J.H.Howe (13/10/18)

Phase
1/14 Oct

WOUNDED.

T/Capt. E.E.H.Orford, M.C. (4/10/18)
2nd Lt. O.S.Ahern (4/10/18)
2nd Lt. J.J.Carson (3/10/18)
Lieut. W.R.Boteoam (4/10/18)
Lieut. A.L.B.Stevens (4/10/18) at duty.
Lieut. P.L.Philpot (4/10/18)
2nd Lt. R.J.Flanagan (4/10/18)
Lieut. H.F.Baldwin (4/10/18)
Lieut. E.M.H.Stubbs (4/10/18)
T/Capt. A.Neovil, M.C. (4/10/18)
Captain V.H.O'Malley, M.C. (7/10/18).
Lieut. F.R.Russell (8/10/18)
T/Lieut. E.D.Conron (14/10/18)

Phase
CORPS
15/Oct

T/Lieut. T.Prendergast (16/10/18)
Captain S.H.Whateley (18/10/18)
Lieut. H.H.Clar e (18/10/18)
T.2/Lt. H.S.Carolin (18/10/18)
2nd Lieut. D.Hinehan (18/10/18)

MISSING.

Nil.

151st INFANTRY BRIGADE.

6th BN. DURHAM L.I.
KILLED.

Phase
1/14 Oct

Lieut. O.F.L.Baillie (5/10/18)
2/Lieut. E.L.H.Curtis (5/10/18)
2/Lieut. J.A.Hicks (5/10/18)
Lt.(A/Capt.) D.T.Sutton (5/10/18)

Phase
comg
15/Oct

T/Captain C.G.Barton, M.C. (17/10/18)
2/Lieut. J.H.Corcoran (17/10/18)
T/Lieut. J.J.C.Kennedy (17/10/18)
2/Lieut. V.J.F.Wilson (17/10/18)
T.2/Lt. G.E.McCarry (19/10/18)

WOUNDED.

Phase
1/14 Oct

2/Lieut. J.Turney (5/10/18)
2/Lieut. B.Todd (5/10/18)
2/Lieut. H.R.Lewis (5/10/18)
T/Captain C.F.H.Smyth (5/10/18)
2/Lieut. H.A.Whitworth (5/10/18)
2/Lieut. N.Martin (5/10/18)
Lieut. A.T.Kelly (5/10/18)
2/Lieut. P.J.Little (5/10/18)

Phase
comg
15/Oct

T/Lieut. R.St.G.Stewart (17/10/18)
T.2/Lieut. J.Crawford (17/10/18)
T.2/Lieut. A.S.V.Jackson (17/10/18).
T.2/Lieut. E.R.McCarry (17/10/18) (at duty)

MISSING.

NIL.

- 6 -

1st K.O.Y.L.I.

KILLED.

Phase
1/14 Oct
    Lieut. J.G.D.Swinge (8/10/18)
    2nd Lieut. P.J.Hill (8/10/18)
    2nd/Lieut. P.C.Scott (8/10/18)

Phase) T/Lieut. R.Rake (17/10/18)
comg) Lieut. G.A.P.Brenhan (17/10/18)
15/Oct) Lieut. P.C.Scott (17/10/18)

WOUNDED.

Phase
1/14 Oct
    T/Captain R.Meadows (8/10/18)
    Capt.(A/Maj.) G. de Hoghton, M.C. (8/10/18)
    2nd Lieut. A.Shirra (8/10/18)
    2nd Lieut. W.Brown (8/10/18)
    2nd Lieut. L.Botterill (8/10/18)
    2nd Lieut. J.G.Ridson (8/10/18)
    2nd Lieut. P.J.Highman (8/10/18)
    Lieut. L.Paterson (8/10/18)

Phase
comg
15/Oct
    T/2/Lieut. L.H.Case (17/10/18)
    Lieut. F.Roebuck (17/10/18)
    T/Lieut. W.Harrold (17/10/18) (gas)
    Captain T.F.W.Upton (17/10/18) (at duty)
    Temp/Lieut. L.Franklin (18/10/18)

MISSING.

NIL.

- 9 -

4th K.R.R.C.

Phase 1/14 Oct

KILLED.

2nd Lieut. T.F. Mackay (8/10/18)
2nd Lieut. E.A. Fryer (8/10/18)
2nd Lieut. H.A. White (8/10/18)
Lieut. H.E. Froome (8/10/18)

Phase ending 18/Oct

T.2/Lt. J.I. Williams (15/10/18)

WOUNDED.

Phase 1/14 Oct

Capt. A.F.H. Bayhurst-Franco, M.C. (8/10/18)
Lieut. R.J.G. Lousley, M.C. (8/10/18)
Lieut. E.G.H. Hardy (8/10/18)
2nd Lieut. J.P.C. Sutton (8/10/18)
2nd Lieut. J.C. Gard (8/10/18)
2nd Lieut. W. Nothven (8/10/18)
Temp/Lieut. T.E.F. Mannion (8/10/18)
 -do-   P.G.C. Dobson (8/10/18)
T/2/Lieut. H.S. Soreby (8/10/18)
 -do-   A.J. Austin (8/10/18) (at duty)

Phase ending 18/Oct

Capt. H.T. Antrobus (17/10/18)
Capt. G.R. Eden (17/10/18)
T/Capt. & Adjt A.F. Fritting, M.C. (17/10/18)
T.2/Lieut. R.E.A. Stewart (17/10/18)
Lieut. E.G.F. Holgate (17/10/18)
2nd Lieut. L. Pews-Jones (17/10/18)

181ST TRENCH MORTAR BATTERY.

WOUNDED.

Phase ending 18/Oct

T/Lieut. S.R.S. Walker (17/10/18)
T/Lieut. C. Wallace (18/10/18) (at duty)

- 10 -

5th Bn. ROYAL IRISH REGT. (PIONEERS).

KILLED.
Nil.

WOUNDED.
Nil.

MISSING.
Nil.

INJURED.
Phase
1/14 Oct 2nd Lieut. V.J. McMAHON (4/10/18)

50TH BN. M.G.C.

KILLED.
Phase
1/14 Oct   Nil.

Phase
comg
15/Oct   T/2/Lieut. A. HANCOCK (17/10/18)
          -do-   A.O. CHIPCHASE (25/10/18)

WOUNDED.
Phase
1/14 Oct
          A/Captain C.H.H. Toy (8/10/18)
          2nd Lieut. A.T. Cruickshank (8/10/18)
          -do-   J.H. Harvie (7/10/18)

Phase
comg
15/Oct   2/Lt. H.A.H. Feller (17/10/18)
          T/2/Lieut. A.H. Rodgers (17/10/18)
          Temp./Lieut. J.S. Inchin (17/10/18)
          Capt.(A/Major) C.J. Brooks (17/10/18) at duty
          T.P./Lieut. H. McL. Stool (25/10/18)

- 11 -

ROYAL ENGINEERS.

446th (Wx) FIELD COY. R.E.

KILLED.

Phase
1/14 Oct   Nil.

Spunded.

Nil.

MISSING.

Nil.

Phase
OCTRE
15/Oct   KILLED.
                  2/Lieut. W. J. Bernallock (17/10/18)

                  WOUNDED.
                  2/Lieut. F. T. Hazebrook (17/10/18)

                  MISSING.

                  Nil.

APPENDIX "A".

50th DIVISION.

ACTUAL CASUALTIES REPORTED FOR PHASE 1st to 14th OCTR., 1918.

UNIT.	KILLED.		WOUNDED		MISSING		DIED OF INJURIES		INJURED	
	O.	O.R.	O.	O.R.	O.	O.R.	O.	O.R.	O.	O.R.
DIVISIONAL HD.QRS.									1	
149th INFANTRY BDE.										
3rd Royal Fusrs	9	34	2	103	–	4	–	–	–	1
13th (SH) B.Watch	3	22	11	122	–	–	–	–	1	6
2nd Roy.Dub.Fus	2	28	4	160	–	3	–	–	–	1
Total Bde :-	14	84	17	385	–	7	–	–	1	8
150th INFANTRY BDE.										
2nd North'd Fus.	4	28	9	154	–	6	–	–	1	1
7th Wiltshire Rgt	3	34	2	168	–	11	–	–	–	2
2nd Roy.Mun.Fus.	4	47	13	202	–	21	–	–	–	–
Total Bde:-	11	109	24	524	–	38	–	–	1	3
151st INFANTRY BDE.-										
6th Roy.Innis.Fus	4	34	8	a189	–	16	–	–	–	1
1st K.O.Y.L.I.	3	34	8	181	–	11	–	–	–	–
4th K.R.R.C.	4	49	10	b151	–	9	–	–	–	1
Total Bde:-	11	117	26	521	–	36	–	–	–	2
5th BN. ROY.IR.RGT. (Pioneers)	–	2	–	3	–	–	–	1	1	1
50th BN. M.G.C.	–	8	1	47	–	1	–	–	–	1
ROYAL ENGINEERS.-										
447th Nbn Fd Co RE	–	–	–	3	–	–	–	–	–	–
7th Field Co RE	–	–	–	c2	–	–	–	–	–	–
FIELD AMBULANCES.										
1/1st Nbn Fd Ambce	–	–	–	3	–	–	–	–	–	–
2/2nd -do-	–	–	–	d6	–	–	–	–	–	–
1/3rd -do-	–	–	–	2	–	–	–	–	–	–
TOTAL DIVISION:-	36	320	68	1496	–	82	–	1	4	15

(a) Includes 4 Gas.
(b) Includes 4 Gas.
(c) Gas.
(d) Includes 1 Gas.

APPENDIX "B".

50th DIVISION.

UNIT.	KILLED.		WOUNDED		MISSING		DIED OF INJURIES		INJURED.	
	O.	O.R.	O.	O.R.	O.	O.R.	O.	O.R.	O.	O.R.
149th INFANTRY BDE.										
3rd Royal Fus.	-	9	4	67	1	10	-	-	-	-
13th B.Watch	-	31	5	123	1	1	-	-	-	2
2nd Roy.Dub.Fus.	2	33	7	a158	-	7	-	-	-	-
149th T.M.Battery	-	-	-	2	-	-	-	-	-	-
Total Bde:-	2	73	16	350	2	18	-	-	-	2
150TH INFANTRY BDE.-										
2nd North'd Fusrs	1	4	1	31	-	1	-	-	-	1
7th Wiltshire Regt	-	23	6	71	-	3	-	-	-	-
2nd Roy.Mun.Fusrs	1	25	5	71	-	13	-	-	-	-
Total Bde :-	2	52	12	173	-	17	-	-	-	1
151st INFANTRY BDE.-										
6th Royal Innis.Fus.	5	12	4	76	-	11	-	-	-	-
1st K.O.Y.L.I.	3	8	5	79	-	56	-	-	-	-
4th K.R.R.C.	1	17	6	94	-	4	-	-	-	-
151st T.M.Battery	-	-	2	6	-	1	-	-	-	-
Total Bde :-	9	37	17	255	-	72	-	-	-	-
5th ROY.IR.R.(PRS).	-	3	-	b38	-	-	-	-	-	-
50th BN. M.G.C.	3	16	4	54	-	3	-	-	-	1
DIVISIONAL ART'Y.-										
250th Bde R.F.A.	-	5	2	26	-	1	-	-	-	-
251st Bde R.F.A.	-	3	1	18	-	-	-	-	-	-
50th D.A.C.	-	-	-	3	-	1	-	-	-	-
ROYAL ENGINEERS.-										
7th Field Coy RE	1	2	1	4	-	-	-	-	-	-
446th Nbn Fd Co RE	-	-	-	-	-	-	-	-	-	-
447th -do-	-	-	-	c5	-	-	-	-	-	-
FIELD AMBULANCES.-										
1/3rd Nbn Fd Ambce	-	-	-	6	-	-	-	-	-	-
TOTAL DIV. :-	17	191	53	932	2	112	-	-	-	4

(a) Includes 24 Gas.
(b) Includes 1 Gas.
(c) Gas.

50th. DIVISION.

APPENDIX I.

ACTUAL CASUALTIES REPORTED FOR PHASE 1st. to 14th. OCTOBER 1918.

UNIT.	KILLED.		WOUNDED.		MISSING.		DIED OF INJURIES.		INJURED.	
	O.	O.R.	O.	O.R.	O.	O.R.	O.	O.R.	O.	O.R.
DIVNL. HD. QRS.	--	--	--	--	--	--	--	--	1.	--
149. INFY. BDE.--										
3rd. Royal Fus.	9.	34.	2.	105.	--	4.	--	--	--	1.
13th. B. Watch.	3.	23.	11.	123.	--	--	--	--	1.	6.
2nd. Roy.Dub.Fus.	2.	29.	4.	160.	--	3.	--	--	--	1.
TOTAL BDE.	14.	86.	17.	388.	--	7.	--	--	1.	8.
150. INFY. BDE.--										
2nd.North'd.Fus.	4.	27.	9.	146.	--	20.	--	--	1.	1.
7th.Wilts. R.	3.	33.	2.	165.	--	15.	--	--	--	2.
2nd.Roy.Mun.Fus.	4.	47.	13.	186.	--	35.	--	--	--	--
TOTAL BDE.	11.	107.	24.	497.	--	70.	--	--	1.	3.
151. INFY. BDE.--										
6th.Roy.Innis.F.	4.	34.	6.	a189.	--	16.	--	--	--	1.
1st. K.O.Y.L.I.	3.	34.	8.	181.	--	11.	--	--	--	--
4th. K.R.R.C.	4.	49.	10.	b151.	--	9.	--	--	--	1.
TOTAL BDE.	11.	117.	24.	521.	--	36.	--	--	--	2.
7th.Bn.MGX.TH.RGT. (Pioneers).	--	2.	--	5.	--	--	--	1.	1.	1.
50th. Bn. M.G.CORPS.--	--	6.	1.	47.	--	1.	--	--	--	1.
ROYAL ENGINEERS.										
447th.(Hbn)Fd.Coy.	--	--	--	3.	--	--	--	--	--	--
7th. Field Coy.	--	--	--	62.	--	--	--	--	--	--
FIELD AMBULANCES.										
1/1st.(Hbn)F.A.	--	--	--	3.	--	--	--	--	--	--
2/2nd. --do--	--	--	--	d6.	--	--	--	--	--	--
1/3rd. --do--	--	--	--	2.	--	--	--	--	--	--
GRAND TOTAL.--	36.	318.	66.	1470.	--	114.	--	1.	4.	15.

(a) Includes 4 Gas.   (c) Gas.

(b) Includes 4 Gas.   (d) Includes 1 Gas.

APPENDIX II.

PRISONERS OF WAR CAPTURED.

1st. Phase - 31st/4th October 1918.

UNWOUNDED		30 Officers	1350 O.Rs.
Wounded.	"	2 "	113 "

TOTAL - 32 " 1463 "

Unwounded Prisoners taken between October 8th - October 11th.

belonged to the following Units :-

	Officers.	O.Rs.
21st. Res. Div.	3.	380.
25d. Div.	12.	827.
6th. Div.	4.	99.
Artillery, etc. (i.e. Units,)	2.	113.
& o from men of other Divns.)		
	22.	1329.

50th. Division. 'G'.   A.D.M.S. No............

          With reference to your G.X. 1249 dated 5th. inst. Below are
particulars of R.A.M.C. officers of the Division who require a copy
of the pamphlet.

Colonel   CLAY.   J.   48 Eldon Place.   Newcastle-on-Tyne.
Major.   MILLIGAN.H.J.M.C.Leven Grove Terrace.   Dumbarton.   Scot.
Lt.Col.   CRAVEN.   J.W.M.C.'Ashfield'.   Stocksfield-on-Tyne.
Major.   SHIELD.   H.M.C.Bamburgh.   Northumberland.
Captn.   ERRINGTON. R.M.C.11 Claremont Terrace.   Sunderland.
Captn.   CRAIG.   W.J.C.M.C.East Newport.   Fife.   N.B.
Captn.   COOPER.   W.M.C.95 Potternewton Lane,   Chappellerton, Leeds.
Captn.   BARRADELL.   M.C.71 St. Chad's Road.   Derby.
Lt.Col.   THOMPSON.W.A.   'Ely House' Princes Avenue. Hull.
Major.   RODGER.   J.M.C.The Nook.   Barry.   Carnaustie.   Scotland.
Captn.   GRIERSON.E.M.   4 Balmoral Terrce. Sth.Gosforth. Newcastle/Tyne.

                                                        Major R.A.M.C. for
10th. March 1919.   A.D.M.S. 50th. Division.

CONFIDENTIAL.

Vol 44

50th DIVISION - ADMINISTRATIVE STAFF.

WAR DIARY.

From :- 1st NOVEMBER, 1918.
To :- 30th "   "

VOLUME XLIV.

Army Form C. 2118.

50TH DIVISION.

ADMINISTRATIVE WAR DIARY

or

INTELLIGENCE SUMMARY.

(Erase heading not required.)

NOVR., 1918.

Instructions regarding War Diaries and Intelligence Summaries are contained in F. S. Regs., Part II. and the Staff Manual respectively. Title pages will be prepared in manuscript.

Place	Date	Hour	Summary of Events and Information	Remarks and references to Appendices
LE CATEAU	NOVR 1/3			
LA FAYT Fme	4		50th D.H.Q. (Rear) moved to LA FAYT Fme.	
LANNOY	5		50th D.H.Q. (Rear) moved to LANNOY.	
FONTAINE	6		50th D.H.Q. (Rear) moved to FONTAINE.	
NOYELLES	7		50th D.H.Q. (Rear) moved to NOYELLES.	
MONCEAU	8		50th D.H.Q. (Rear) moved to MONCEAU.	
"	9/10			
DOURLERS	11		50th D.H.Q. (Rear) moved to DOURLERS. Total casualties - 3rd Phase - 1/11th Novr., 1918 - Officers see Appendix 'A' attd. O.Ranks " 'B' " " " 'C' " Div. in action - see "Narrative of operations............................"	
	1/11 12		Commemoration Service, followed by presentation of medals, at DOURLERS, for 149th and 150th Infantry Brigades and Divisional Units.	
	13		Commemoration Service, followed by presentation of medals, at MONCEAU, for 151st Infantry Bde.	
	14		Commemoration Service followed by presentation of Medals, at ST REMY CHAUSSEE, for R.A. Units.	
	15/29			
	30		Practice assembly for visit of His Majesty the King.	

ACTUAL CASUALTIES FOR PHASE 1st to 11th NOVR 1918.

UNIT.	KILLED.		WOUNDED.		MISSING		INJURED	
	O.	O.R.	O.	O.R.	O.	O.R.	O.	O.R.
DIVISIONAL HD. QRS.								1
149th INFANTRY BDE.								
3rd Royal Fuslrs	1	14	5	88	-	6		1
13th (S.H.) B.Watch	1	28	2	98		2		1
2nd Roy.Dub.Fusrs	1	8	9	112	-	2		
149th T.M.Battery	-	-	-	2	-	-		
	3	50	16	300	-	8	-	2
150th INFANTRY BDE.								
2nd North'd Fusrs	-	11	4	113	-	12	-	-
7th Wiltshire Rgt	2	7	3	57	-	1	-	-
2nd Royal Mun.Fus.	1	7	3	61	-	2	-	-
	3	25	10	231	-	15	-	-
151st INFANTRY BDE.								
6th Roy.Innis.Fus.	-	29	7	150	1	3	-	-
1st K.O.Y.L.I.	3	27	4	115	-	17	-	-
4th K.R.R.C.	2	26	7	136	-	7	-	1
151st T.M.Battery	-	-	-	2	-	-	-	-
	5	82	18	403	1	32	-	1
5th ROY.IR.R.(PNRS).	-	7	1	10	-	-	-	-
50th BN. M.G.C.	1	3	1	19	-	1	-	-
DIVNL ARTILLERY.								
250th Nbn Bde RFA	-	1	-	5	-	-	-	-
251st -do-	-	-	1	1	-	-	-	-
50th T.M.Batteries	-	-	-	1	-	-	-	-
FIELD AMBULANCES.								
1/1st Nbn Fd Ambce	-	4	-	7	-	-	-	-
2/2nd -do-	-	-	-	3	-	-	-	-
1/3rd -do-	-	-	1	1	-	-	-	-
	12	172	48	981	1	56	1	3

GRAND TOTAL :- 62 Officers.
1212 O.Ranks.

APPENDIX I.

ACTUAL CASUALTIES FOR PHASE 1ST to 11TH NOVEMBER 1918.

UNIT.	KILLED.		WOUNDED.		MISSING.		INJURED.	
	O.	O.R.	O.	O.R.	O.	O.R.	O.	O.R.
DIVISIONAL HDQRS.							1	
149th INFANTRY BDE								
3rd Roy.Fus.	1	14	5	68	-	6	-	-
13th(S.H)B.Watch	1	28	2	98	-	-	-	1
2nd Roy.Dub.Fus.	1	8	9	112	-	2	-	1
149th T.M.B.	-	-	-	2	-	-	-	-
	3	50	16	300	-	8	-	2
150th INFANTRY BDE.								
2nd Northd Fus.	-	11	4	113	-	12	-	-
7th Wilts Regt.	2	7	3	57	-	1	-	-
2nd Roy.Mun.Fus.	1	7	3	61	-	2	-	-
	3	25	10	231	-	15	-	-
151st INFANTRY BDE.								
6th Roy.Innis.F.	-	29	7	150	1	8	-	-
1st K.O.Y.L.I.	3	27	4	115	-	17	-	-
4th K.R.R.C.	2	26	7	136	-	7	-	1
151st T.M.B.	-	-	-	2	-	-	-	-
	5	82	18	403	1	32	-	1
5th ROY.IR.REGT (Pioneers)	-	7	1	10	-	-	-	-
50TH BN. M.G.C.	1	5	1	19	-	1	-	-

/Div. Artillery

UNIT.	KILLED.		WOUNDED.		MISSING.		INJURED.	
	O.	O.R.	O.	O.R.	O.	O.R.	O.	O.R.
DIVL. ARTILLERY.								
250th Nbn Bde.	-	1	-	5	-	-	-	-
251st -do-	-	-	1	1	-	-	-	-
50th T.M.Bg.	-	-	-	1	-	-	-	-
FIELD AMBULANCES.								
1/1st Nbn Fd Amboo.	-	4	-	7	-	-	-	-
2/2nd -do-	-	-	-	3	-	-	-	-
1/3rd -do-	-	-	1	1	-	-	-	-
	12	172	48	981	1	56	1	3

GRAND TOTAL :- 62 Officers.
1212 Other Ranks.

G 773   (R)

26/09   50th Division

18 prs v. 15 prs

R.A. 711/3.

2nd Corps.

      In continuation of R.A. 711/3, dated 3rd inst -
G. H. Q. in their reply to the Army Commander's representation state that the rearmament of Territorial Force Divisions with 18 pdrs depends on the return of 15 pdr Mark IV guns from this country.   The replacement of the 50th Division Mark I guns by Mark IV cannot therefore be carried out.

                                John Headlam

                                Major General, R. A.,

2nd Army Hd. Qrs.,
    26th Septbr, 1915.

2nd Corps.
G. 905

50th Division.

The attached copy of correspondence which has taken place with reference to your G.X. 388 of 29/8/15, is forwarded for your information.

(sd) Alick Russell
Lt.Col
for B. G. G. S.

2nd Corps.
4/9/15.

2ND CORPS HEADQUARTERS.

No. .... Date 10/8/15.

Time .... p.m.

C.C.

B.G.G.S. ✓

G.2.

G.3.

I.g.

A.

Q.

R.A. to see

R.E.

File.

50 Div.
forwarded for your information.

R.A. 711/3/1.

II Corps,

        I am directed to inform you that, in reply to a representation regarding the rearmament of the 50th Divisional Artillery, the following has been received from G. H. Q. :-

    "In reply to your R.A. 705/3/1 of the 3rd August,
    "there is no prospect at present of any 15 pdr B.L.C.
    "mark IV guns becoming available to re-equip Territorial
    "Divisions armed with the mark I gun."

                                         John Headlam

                                             Major General, R. A.,

2nd Army Hd. Qrs.,
   10th August, 1915.

R.A. 711/3/1.

II Corps

I am directed to inform you that, in reply to a representation regarding the re-armament of the 50th Divisional Artillery, the following has been received from G.H.Q.,

> "In reply to your R.A. 705/3/1 of the 3rd August, there is no prospect at present of any 15 pdr B.L.C. mark IV guns becoming available to re-equip Territorial Divisions armed with the mark I gun".

2nd Army Hd.Qrs.
10th August, 1915.

(Sd) John Headlam.
Major-General. R.A.

2.

50th Division.

2nd Corps.
G. 258

Forwarded for your information.

2nd Corps.
10/8/15.

for B. G. G. S.

R.A. 711/3/5

2nd Corps.

With reference to 2nd Corps letter G 773, dated 30th August - I have to inform you that the Army Commander has this day made a further representation to G. H. Q. on the subject of the unsatisfactory state of the armament of the artillery of the 50th Division, and has urged the importance of replacing the 15 pr Mark I, B.L.C. equipment by Mark IV as soon as the latter becomes available.

John Headlam

Major General, R. A.,

2nd Army Hd. Qrs.,
    3rd Septbr, 1915.

R.A. 711/3.

2nd Corps.
———

In continuation of R.A. 711/3, dated 3rd instant G.H.Q. in their reply to the Army Commander's representation state that the rearmament of Territorial Force Divisions with 18 pdrs depends on the return of 15 pdr Mark IV guns from this country. The replacement of the 50th Division Mark I guns by Mark IV cannot therefore be carried out.

(Sd) John Headlam.
Major General, R.A.

2nd Army Hd.Qrs.
26th Septr.1915.

———

2nd Corps.
G. 577

50th Division.
———

The above is a copy of a minute received from the 2nd Army, forwarded for your information with reference to your G.X. 388 of 29/8/15, and in continuation of my G. 905 of 4/9/15.

(sd) W.H. Scaill
Major, G.S.
for B. G. G. S.

2nd Corps.
27/9/15.

Headquarters,

    50th Division.

At the end of last year we were told in a War Office letter that all 15-pdr Batteries proceeding abroad would have Mark 1V guns issued to them.   This was cancelled a week or 10 days before embarkation, and we were then told to bring out the guns in possession of Batteries.   These were all Mark 1, 15-pdrs.   I wish to bring to notice the following points connected with this equipment :-

1.   The guns are old, two have already been condemned for excessive scoring in the bore, four others are under suspicion and sentenced for re-examination after 50 or 100 rounds.   When scoring has once become marked, deterioration is often rapid, and it cannot be expected that these four guns can remain serviceable much longer, even if they are not condemned at the next inspection.   Also, worn guns do not shoot the same as those in a more serviceable condition.

All breech mechanisms are very worn, but are reported by the I. O. M. to be still serviceable.

There is a good deal of wear in the elevating and sighting gears, and this must affect the accuracy of shooting; most of the wear can be taken up in parts of the elevating gear and sights when the guns have been overhauled, but the wear of an elevating screw cannot be taken up.

The extensions to the shields not being flanged and being only supported by vertical brackets running from the old shield up the entire height of the extension, are markedly unstable;   the dial sight, to be accurate, must be so supported as to admit of the minimum of play when in use on the shield;   the present extension can never give this essential rigidity.

-2-

2. The difficulties of replacement of equipment, e.g.,

(a) A gun knocked out in action on the 24th May was not replaced until the 30th July; the old gun was then returned.

(b) Two limbers knocked out on 24th May have never been replaced.

(c) The provision and replacement of spare parts; it was months before any were provided, and everything has not been provided up to date.

3. The provision and supply of ammunition. There are at present about 3,200 rounds short in the Divisional Ammunition Column, and this deficiency is being increased from week to week, as the Divisional Ammunition Column is unable to fill up from any formation in rear. There are also supposed to be 50 rounds per gun (1,800 per Division) in the Ammunition Sub-park; they are not there, and I presume there are also none on the Lines of Communication.

4. Owing to some shell now being supplied having No. 80 fuzes and others No. 65A, different fuze scales are necessary.

5. There are no high explosive shell in 15-pdr equipment; for trench warfare they are desirable.

6. Owing to the height of the shield on the 15-pdr we find we often have to re-make emplacements previously occupied by an 18-pdr Battery.

I would therefore urge that the issue of 18-pdr equipment to the 15-pdr Field Artillery Brigades of this Division should be at once considered, and I would suggest that it is not necessary to wait until the whole of the 15-pdr batteries can be re-armed at one and the same time, but that a Brigade, or even a Battery, should be re-armed when the equipment is available. There are, I know, the objections regarding the supply of ammunition, and the inter-changeability of stores, but in view of the difficulty of getting 15-pdr guns, etc., replaced, and the present deficiency of 15-pdr ammunition, I consider that these objections lose much of their weight.

[signature]

Brig. Genl.,
C.R.A., 50th Division.

Hq. 50th D.A.
29. 8. 15.

50th. Divn.
G. X. 388

2nd. Corps.
----

1. I have received the attached report from my C. R. A. on the condition of the Guns and equipment of the Artillery of this Division, and desire to bring to the notice of the Corps Commander the situation of this Division as regards its Artillery.

2. As regards the supply of ammunition referred to in paragraph 3 of Brigadier-General Henshaw's report, the receipt of 2nd. Army No. Q/784/9 of the 28th. August reduces the establishment of ammunition to be carried in the Brigade and Divisional Ammunition Columns by nearly a half. This will doubtless do away with the present deficiency. It does not, however, alter the fact that there are now less rounds available in Divisional organizations than was previously considered necessary.

3. It may be fairly stated that apart from the howitzers, the artillery of this Division consists of 34 obsolescent Field Guns of which a proportion are quite unreliable. These are provided with an obsolete form of ammunition which renders the rate of fire slow when compared with that of modern guns; spare parts are obtained with difficulty or are unobtainable; any guns or limbers that may become damaged cannot be replaced. If this state of affairs is compared with that of any regular Division who have either forty-eight or fifty-four 18 pounders, it must be realized that the gun power of this Division is less than a half that now considered necessary.

4. I consider that the replacement of the present equipment by 18 pounder equipment is a matter of the utmost importance

P.T.O.

- 2 -

and I trust that Brigades or even batteries will be
re-armed as rapidly as possible.

                                                               P.S. Wilkinson Major-General,

29th. August 1915.   Commanding 50th. Division.

2nd Corps.
G. 773

2nd Army.

1. I cannot too strongly urge the importance of this subject.

2. The 50th Division are in a very inefficient state as regards their artillery equipment. The Division is holding a very important part of the line and should be re-equipped with 18 pounders at the earliest possible date.

3. There is no need to postpone the re-equipment of a single brigade or even of a single battery for the mere reason that 18 pounder guns are not yet available for the whole division. We will all willingly put up with any difficulties in the handling of two different natures of ammunition.

4. The worst guns should be scrapped at once and replaced by 18 pounders. This will have the further advantage of ensuring an adequate supply of ammunition for any 15 pounder guns which are still kept in action.

Charles Ferguson

Lieutenant-General.
Commanding 2nd Corps.

30/8/15.

2ND CORPS HEADQUARTERS.

No. 541   Date 27/9/15.

　　Time 10/55 a.m.

C.C.   ⎫
　　　 ⎬ Can I to 50 Div?   Yes
B.G.G.S.⎭   W.T.T

G.2. WTT

G.3.

I.g.

A. | To see H&l

Q. |

R.A.

R.E.

　　　　　　　　　　File.

2ND CORPS HEADQUARTERS.

No. 534 Date 3/9/15.

Time 5/53 pm.

O.C. ✓

B.G.G.S.

Previous correspondence attached.

I will forward a copy of the last letter to 50th D.V if you approve.

G.2

G.3

I.g.

A.

Q.

G 905 L
50 DW

R.A. as

R.E.

File.

50th Divn.
G.X.382

2nd Corps.

1. I have received the attached report from my C.R.A. on the condition of the Guns and equipment of the Artillery of this Division, and desire to bring to the notice of the Corps Commander the situation of this Division as regards its Artillery.

2. As regards the supply of ammunition referred to in paragraph 3 of Brigadier-General Henshaw's report, the receipt of 2nd Army No.Q/784/9 of the 28th August reduces the establishment of ammunition to be carried in the Brigade and Divisional Ammunition Columns by nearly a half. This will doubtless do away with the present deficiency. It does not, however, alter the fact that there are now less rounds available in Divisional organizations than was previously considered necessary.

3. It may be fairly stated that apart from the howitzers, the artillery of this Division consists of 54 obsolescent Field Guns of which a proportion are quite unreliable. These are provided with an obsolete form of ammunition which renders the rate of fire slow when compared with that of modern guns; spare parts are obtained with difficulty or are unobtainable; any guns or limbers that may become damaged cannot be replaced. If this state of affairs is compared with that of any regular Division who have either forty-eight or fifty-four 18 pounders, it must be realised that the gun power of this Division is less than a half that now considered necessary.

4. I consider that the replacement of the present equipment by 18 pounder equipment is a matter of the utmost importance and I trust that Brigades or even batteries will be re-armed as rapidly as possible.

29th August, 1915.

(sd) P.S. Wilkinson, Major-General,
Commanding 50th Division.

50th Divn.Artillery
S.C.768

G.X.309

Headquarters,
    50th Division.

At the end of last year we were told in a War Office letter that all 15-pdr Batteries proceeding abroad would have Mark IV guns issued to them. This was cancelled a week or ten days before embarkation, and we were then told to bring out the guns in possession of Batteries. These were all Mark 1, 15-pdrs. I wish to bring to notice the following points connected with this equipment:-

1. The guns are old, two have already been condemned for excessive scoring in the bore, four others are under suspicion and sentenced for re-examination after 50 or 100 rounds. When scoring has once become marked, deterioration is often rapid, and it cannot be expected that these four guns can remain serviceable much longer, even if they are not condemned at the next inspection. Also, worn guns do not shoot the same as those in a more serviceable condition.

All breech mechanisms are very worn, but are reported by the I.O.M. to be still serviceable.

There is a good deal of wear in the elevating and sighting gears, and this must affect the accuracy of shooting; most of the wear can be taken up in parts of the elevating gear and sights when the guns have been overhauled, but the wear of an elevating screw cannot be taken up.

The extensions to the shields not being flanged and being only supported by vertical brackets running from the old shield up the entire height of the extension, are markedly unstable; the dial sight, to be accurate, must be so supported as to admit of the minimum of play when in use on the shield; the present extension can never give this essential rigidity.

2. The difficulties of replacement of equipment, e.g.,
(a) A gun knocked out in action on the 24th May was not replaced until the 30th July; the old gun was then returned.
(b) Two limbers knocked out on 24th May have never been replaced.
(c) The provision and replacement of spare parts; it was months before any were provided, and everything has not been provided up to date.

3. The provision and supply of ammunition. There are at present about 3,200 rounds short in the Divisional Ammunition Column, and this deficiency is being increased from week to week, as the Divisional Ammunition Column is unable to fill up from any formation in rear. There are also supposed to be 50 rounds per gun (1,800 per Division) in the Ammunition Sub-park; they are not there, and I presume there are also none on the Lines of Communication.

4. Owing to some shell now being supplied having No.80 fuzes and others No.65A, different fuze scales are necessary.

5. There are no high explosive shell in 15-pdr equipment; for trench warfare they are desirable.

6. Owing to the height of the shield on the 15-pdr we find we often have to re-make emplacements previously occupied by an 18-pdr Battery.

I would therefore urge that the issue of 18-pdr equipment to the 15-pdr Field Artillery Brigades of this Division should be at once considered, and I would suggest that it is not necessary to wait until the whole of the 15-pdr batteries can be re-armed at one and the same time, but that a Brigade, or even a Battery, should be re-armed when the equipment is available. There are, I know, the objections regarding the supply of ammunition, and the interchangeability of stores, but in view of the difficulty of getting 15-pdr guns, etc, replaced, and the present deficiency of 15-pdr

ammunition

ammunition, I consider that these objections lose much of
their weight.

Hq.50th D.A.
29/8/15.

(Sd) C.E.Henshaw, Brig.Genl.,
C.R.A.,50th Division.

Copy for G

Q.C.1683.

Q/4134.

Second Army.

                                             D.D.O.S.
                                             2nd Army.
                                             63/208.

      Sufficient 18-pdr. equipments are now available for issue to the 50th Division in replacement of the 15-pdr B.L.C. equipments, which will be withdrawn and returned to the base with as little delay as possible, as the 15-pdr equipments are urgently required in England.

      D.O.S. has been requested to arrange with you direct the details of the replacement and withdrawal.

      All 15-pdr ammunition should be withdrawn from the ammunition wagons and limbers and returned to ammn. railhead before the guns, &c, are sent to the base.

      The sights dial No.1 and also section 15 stores in possession of the batteries will be retained for use with the 18-pdr guns.

      Kindly inform me by telegram as soon as the exchange has been completed.

G.H.Q.,   (sd) H. de Martelli. Major.,
12/11/15.   for Q.M.G.

                           2.

Headquarters.
   2nd Corps.

      Forwarded for information. Further instructions will be forwarded on receipt. No action should be taken till receipt of these.

H.Q., 2nd Army.   (sd) J.W.Hale. Colonel.
14/11/15.   D.D.O.S.
                           3.

50th Division.

      Forwarded for information.

Headquarters.   (sd) G.E.R.Kenrick. Lieut. Col.
2nd Corps.
15/11/15.   A.Q.M.G. 2nd Corps.

"C" Form (Duplicate).
MESSAGES AND SIGNALS.
Army Form C. 2123.

No. of Message

Handed in at Bar Office 12.20 p.m. Received

TO 2nd Corps

Sender's Number: Ra 928 Thirkell

AAA

Please forward for information of army commander report showing result of last inspection by IOM of guns 50th Division aaa any further information that may show present state of guns should be included

FROM PLACE & TIME: Second Army

ND CORPS HEADQUARTERS.

No. 170 Date 30/8/15.
Time 6/45 a.m.

C.C.

B.G.G.S.

G.2. as
G.3.
I.g.
A.}
Q.} to see
R.A. seen as
R.E.

G.   File _____.

G.773
to 2 Ary

2ND CORPS HEADQUARTERS.

No. 5741   Date 27/9/15.
         Time 10/50 a.m.

C.C. ⎫
      ⎬ Can to 50 Div?   Yes
B.G.G.S. ⎭   W.T.

G.2. WTF

G.3.

I.g.

A. ⎫ To cc HQ
Q. ⎭

R.A.

R.E.

File.

2ND CORPS HEADQUARTERS.

No. 534 Date 3/9/15.

Time 5/53 p.m.

O.C. ✓

B.G.G.S.

G.2

G.3

I.G.

A.

Q.

R.A. as

R.E.

Previous correspondence attached.

I will forward a copy of this last letter to 50th D.V if you approve.

as

G 905 L
50 DW

File.

13/54/2

Head Qrs. R.A. 50th Division

Vol I.   1.4 — 31.5.15.

apl '15
Dec '16

26/04

Accident by Shell

Trench 73, 50th Division. Aug/15.

p.p with p diary
HLC

NOT TO BE WRITTEN ON.

Records

To O/C 1st North'n Bde.

Sir,

I regret to report that, during firing (to register) this afternoon at about 4.15 p.m., one shell fell short & the base, with the fuze, grazed the parados of the shelter trench (behind the firing trench) &, entering a dug-out, wounded an infantry man, who, I regret to learn, has since died.

The rounds fired were as under
Rd 1. 3000 – Cor 160.
              Observed. 40 yds left. Graze plus
Rd 2. Cor 156 – 2950
              Observed. 40 yds left. Air. 10' high
                                                Range.
Rd. 3. Repeat.
              This was the round which caused the

2/

accident.

The map range had been worked
out by me some days ago as 2950.
Before firing I again verified this
on the 1/10000 map since supplied me.
As our trenches are shewn 250 yds
short - I considered I was safe in
firing at 3000 seeing that the
50% zone for the 15 pdr B.L.C
gun is 80 yds & the 100% consequently
320. yds. — seeing also that in
all previous shooting, (during which
no such accident has occurred) the
gun had been found to shoot pretty
closely to map range.

Mr Walker has now returned &
brought with him the head of the shell

3) with fuze attached.

From the marks on the fuze
it is evident that the fuze & head
were not supported by the central
tube as they should have been with
the consequent result that the
head has set back into the body
of the shell. This has expanded
the mouth of the body to such an
extent that at one place the
body has been expanded so as to
nearly clear one of the rotating (or traversing)
pins. When the shell burst this
pin has consequently left in the
head intact & unsheared.

I think from the marks that
the shell body (where expanded

able to recover any other
parts, this evening, which
could be of value in
trying to account for
the accident.

I examined the dug out
of which I attach a cross-
section. Nothing appeared
to have entered the dug out
except the nose & fuze.
The dotted line shows the
line of flight as judged
from the marks.

I have, Sir, the honour to be
Your obedient Servant

W E Walker
Lt.

Friday 30.7.15
8.30.pm.

To O.C. 1st Northumbrian Bde
R.F.A. (T.)

Sir,

In accordance with your orders just received by telephone I have to report as follows on the accident which took place in 73 trench this afternoon.

I was acting as F.O.O. in 73 trench during registering. Firing began about 3.45 pm. to register the enemy's trench near the point (I 11 a 4 - 2½) at which it crosses the ARMENTIÈRES – PÉRENCHIES Railway.

I observed from No 4 traverse (I 10 b 9½ - 6). The distance

(2)

between the trenches at this point is given by the Infantry as 260 yards. (Taken with Machine Gun Range Finder, Barr & Stroud type). I judged that my shell would fall on the Northern curve of the small salient in the enemy's trench not near the point I 11 a 4 - 2½. My observations for line refer to the fall of the shell right or left of this point.

I observed Round No 1 as

 "40 yds Left. Cxxxge. Over."

& Round No 2 as

 "40 yds Left Aim 10' high Range".

Round No 3 I did not

(3)

observe. I did hear it burst, apparently behind me & to my left.

One of my telephone operators immediately informed me that it had burst behind 73 trench.

I went along the trench & found that a man had been injured in a "dug out" behind No 11 traverse (I 10 b 9½-7). I also found that my telephone wire was cut just over this dug out.

There were shrapnel bullets from the shell in the trench & the nose & fuze were recovered in one piece in the dug out. I was not

4) has taken the rifling.
In any case the deformation of the body & setting up of the head would probably seriously reduce the range of the shell.

I am
Sir
Yr obedient servant
T.H.S. Johnston
Mjr.

9.30 p.m.
30. 7. 15.

P.S. The central tube of the shell is not made in accordance with the drawing in the handbook
T.H.J.

P.T.O.

To C.R.A. 55th Division
From O.C. 1st North'n H.B. R.G.A.

I have the honour to forward
report from O.C. 3rd North'n Bty
regarding the shell which fell in
trench 73 today. I have ordered
search to be made for body of this
shell. In my opinion the
accident was due to a defective
shell. Major Johnston will
report personally at 9 a.m.
tomorrow. I also enclose
Lieut. Walker's report.
I have the honour to be
    Sir
        Your Obedient servant
30-7-15   H.S. Bell Major

Fire trench   "Dug out"   Timber Support

Dug out.

Loose Earth held by wire netting.

Lovell Lt   30/7/15

Headquarters,
    2nd Corps.

Herewith report from C.R.A. 50th Division.

It appears that the accident may have been caused by a faulty shell. I therefore forward the head of the shell for examination, in case this supposition is considered correct.

Headquarters,
50th Division.
1st August 1915.

Major General.
Commanding 50th (Northumbrian) Division.

Headquarters,
    50th Division.

I beg to enclose herewith a letter from the O.C., 1st Northumbrian Brigade R.F.A., forwarding reports from the O.C., 3rd Northumberland Battery R.F.A., and the Officer who was acting as the latter's Forward Observing Officer on the 30th instant, in regard to a shell fired by the Battery referred to above falling into our Trench No 73.

I sincerely regret that the accident should have been attended with fatal results. I am of opinion that the accident was caused by a faulty shell, that the head of the shell for some reason set back into the body, that the head became twisted and consequently the range of the shell was decreased.

I forward the head of the shell, from which it will be seen that it has been cut away on one side. The body of the shell has not yet been recovered; if found, it will be forwarded.

                        (Signed) C.G. Henshaw. Brig. Genl.,
H.Q. 50th D.A.   C.R.A., 50th Division.
31/7/15.

B.M/344

Headquarters,
    50th Division.

I beg to enclose herewith a letter from the O.C., 1st Northumbrian Brigade R.F.A., forwarding reports from the O.C., 3rd Northumberland Battery R.F.A., and the Officer who was acting as the latter's Forward Observing Officer on the 30th instant, in regard to a shell fired by the Battery referred to above falling into our Trench No. 73.

I sincerely regret that the accident should have been attended with fatal results. I am of opinion that the accident was caused by a faulty shell, that the head of the shell for some reason set back into the body, that the head became twisted and consequently the range of the shell was decreased.

I forward the head of the shell, from which it will be seen that it has been cut away on one side. The body of the shell has not yet been recovered; if found, it will be forwarded.

Brig. Genl.,
C.R.A., 50th Division.

Hq. 50th D.A.
31. 7. 15.

To O.C., 1st Northumbrian Brigade R.F.A.

Sir,
    I regret to report that during firing (to register) this afternoon at about 4-15 p.m. one shell fell short, and the head, with the fuze, grazed the parades of the shelter trench (behind the firing trench) and, entering a dug-out, wounded an Infantry man, who I regret to learn has since died.

    The rounds fired were as under:-

Rd.1.   3000 - Cor. 160
        observed 40 yards left, Graze plus.

Rd.2.   Cor. 156 - 2950.
        Observed 40 yards left, Air. 10' high. Range.

Rd.3.   Repeat.

This was the round which caused the accident.

    The map range had been worked out by me some days ago as 2950. Before firing I again verified this on the 1/10,000 map since supplied to me.

    As our trenches are shewn 250 yards short, I considered I was safe in firing at 3000 seeing that the 50% zone for the 15 pdr. B.L.C. gun is 80 yards and the 100% consequently 320 yards. Seeing also that in all previous shooting (during which no such accident has occurred) the gun had been found to shoot pretty closely to map range.   Mr Walker has now returned and brought with him the head of the shell with fuze attached.

    From the marks on the part it is evident that the fuze and head were not supported by the central tube as they should have been, with the consequent result that the head has set back into the body of the shell. This has expanded the mouth of the body to such an extent that at one place the body has been expanded so as to nearly clear one of the rotating (or twisting) pins. When the shell burst this pin was consequently left in the head intact and unsheared.   I think from the marks that the shell body (were expanded) has taken the rifling.   In any case the deformation of the body and setting up of the head would probably seriously reduce the range of the shell.

        I am, Sir,
9-30 p.m.   Your obedient Servant,
30/7/15.   (Signed) F.G.D. JOhnson. Major.

P.S.   The central tube of the shell is not made in accordance with the drawing in the handbook.   F.G.D.J.

Friday, 30.7.15.
8-30 p.m.

To, O.C. 1st Northumbrian Brigade
R.F.A. T.

Sir,

In accordance with your orders just received by telephone, I have to report as follows on the accident which took place in 73 trench this afternoon.

I was acting as F.O.O. in 73 trench during registering. Firing began about 5-45 p.m. to register the enemy's trench near the point I.11.a.4.2½ at which it crosses the ARMENTIERES - PERENCHIES Railway.

I observed from No.4 Traverse (I.10.b.9½.6.). The distance between the trenches at this point is given by the Infantry as 260 yards. (Taken with Machine gun range-finder, Barr and Stroud type). I judged that my shell would fall on the Northern curve of the small salient in the enemy's trench near the point I.11.a.4.2½. My observations for line refer to the fall of the shell right or left of this point.

I observed Round No 1 as "40 yds. Left.Graze. Over. and Round No.2 as "40 yards left. Air 10' High.Range." Round No.3 I did not observe. I did hear it burst, apparently behind me and to my left.

One of my telephone operators immediately informed me that it had burst behind 73 trench. I went along the trench and found that a man had been injured in a "dug out" behind No.11 traverse (I.10.b.9½.7.). I also found that my telephone wire was cut just over this dug-out.

There were shrapnel bullets from the shell in the trench and the nose and fuze were recovered in one piece in the dug-out. I was not able to recover any other parts this morning, which could be of value in trying to account for the accident.

I examined the dug-out of which I attach a cross-section. Nothing appeared to have entered the dug-out except the nose and fuze.

The dotted line shows the line of flight as judged from the marks.

I have the honour to be, Sir,
Your obedient servant,
(sgd). W.E. WALKER, Lieut.

To C.R.A., 50th Division.

From O.C., 1st Northumbrian Brigade R.F.A.

I have the honour to forward report from O.C., 3rd Northumberland Battery regarding the shell which fell in Trench 73 today. I have ordered search to be made for the body of the shell. In my opinion the accident was due to a defective shell. Major Johnson will report personally at 9-0 a.m. tomorrow.

I enclose also Lieut. Walker's report.

                    I have the honour to be,

                        Sir,

                        Your obedient servant,

30/7/15.   (sgd) H.S. Bell, Major.

www.ingramcontent.com/pod-product-compliance
Lightning Source LLC
Chambersburg PA
CBHW080803010526
44113CB00013B/2315